Secrets of Antarctica

The Untold History of the Ice Continent

by BRAD OLSEN

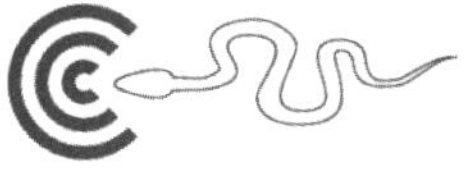

CONSORTIUM OF COLLECTIVE CONSCIOUSNESS PUBLISHING

www.CCCPublishing.com • www.BradOlsen.com • www.EsotericSeries.com

Secrets of Antarctica: The Untold History of the Ice Continent

1st edition
Esoteric Series :: Volume IV

Published by the Consortium of Collective Consciousness Publishing™

As is common in a historic and reference book such as this, much of the information included on these pages has been collected from diverse sources. When possible, the information has been checked and double-checked. Almost every topic has at least three data points, that is, three different sources that report the same information. Even with special effort to be accurate and thorough, the author and publisher cannot vouch for each and every reference. The author and publisher assume no responsibility or liability for any outcome, loss, arrest, or injury that occurs as a result of information or advice contained in this book. As with the purchase of goods or services, *caveat emptor* is the prevailing responsibility of the purchaser, and the same is true for the student of the esoteric.

Library of Congress Cataloging-in-Publication Data:

Olsen, Bradford C.
Secrets of Antarctica: The Untold History of the Ice Continent / Brad Olsen
p. cm.
Includes index
ISBN 13: 9781888729986 (Pbk.)
ISBN 13: 9781888729993 (Ebk.) (all formats)

1.. Antarctica—Guidebooks. 2. Metaphysics—Esoteric. I. Title

Library of Congress Catalog Card Number: 2025924275

Printed in the United States of America.

10 9 8 7 6 5 4 3 2

A NOTE ON THE IMAGES: Almost all of the images used in the Esoteric Series of books are public domain pictures, and a few of the images were submitted anonymously. Most of the images did not have an attributed artist or photographer's name, largely because a name could not be found. Although we try to verify every image submitted image by our sources, some could very well have been faked or artificially enhanced. Consider the photo images as illustrations if you dispute their authenticity. They are used to graphically illustrate the text. No part of the text of this book was created by AI.
To assist in universal understanding, all measurements of length, distance, area, weight, size, and volume are listed in both standard and the metric system.

Endorsements for *Secrets of Antarctica*

"*Antarctica is a riddle wrapped in a mystery inside an enigma to paraphrase Winston Churchill. The truth of what's under Antarctica's massive ice sheets has long been kept from humanity at large by the secrecy keepers who don't want humanity to learn the truth about its ancient history and the incredible technologies found beneath the ice sheets. Enter Brad Olsen, a modern-day Indiana Jones, who has visited the frozen continent to learn about its mysteries and to get answers to what lays hidden beneath it. His latest book,* Secrets of Antarctica: The Untold History of the Ice Continent, *presents new documents revealing the path taken by Nazi U-boats to explore the icy interior and to establish secret bases that were expanded over the subsequent decades and continue to operate today. Olsen's exposé reveals the latest information what's really happening in Antarctica and is essential for solving the Antarctica riddle.*"

–Michael Salla, Ph.D., author of *Antarctica's Hidden History: Corporate Foundations of Secret Space Programs*

"*Imagine a world where ancient maps reveal ice-free coasts, traced by sea kings lost to time, while Patagonia giants loom as shadowy legends. In 1938-39, Nazis carved out Base 211 in* Neuschwabenland, *smuggling* Die Glocke *wonders via U-boats. Admiral Byrd's 1929 South Pole flight—his seized journals hint at vast holes leading to Agartha, a hollow realm with a central sun. Operation Highjump's 1947 retreat faced advanced crafts from subglacial Lake Vostok, where geothermal caves hide unknown life. UFOs flicker over Antarctica's pyramids, Atlantean ruins buried deep, and the Black Goo—a sentient oil from South Thule's ET bases—silenced Marconi scientists during the Falklands' Operation Keyhole. Olsen, who sailed there in 2019, uncovers suppressed truths: preglacial shifts, no-fly zones, and UFO sightings at Belgrano II. Are you ready to pierce the veil? This tome unlocks the ice continent's darkest enigmas—dive in, and let the revelations ignite your quest for truth.*"

–Richard Syrett, Guest-Host *Coast to Coast AM,* author of *Tales from the Rock & Roll Twilight Zone* (TrineDay July, 2026)

"Secrets of Antarctica *is a bold exploration of the southernmost continent as a repository of hidden history and occult technology. Drawing on ancient maps, explorers' journals, 20th century military missions, and modern UFO lore, the author invites readers to see Antarctica not as barren ice but as a palimpsest of lost civilizations and covert experiments. Structured like a guided expedition, the book moves from a reflective "Author's Karma Statement" and natural history of the Ice Continent into a series of provocative chapters where science meets mysticism, politics, and prophecy. Documented expeditions mingle with oral traditions, remote-viewing claims, and speculative physics to form a mosaic that is part history, part visionary cosmology from a brilliant mind such as Brad Olsen to connect so many dots and expand the mind. This book offers a sweeping, imaginative journey, an invitation to wonder and an opportunity to question what we think we know about the most remote place on Earth.*"

–Laura Eisenhower, author of *Awakening the Truth Frequency*

Endorsements for *Secrets of Antarctica*

"This gripping book takes readers on a chilling journey through secret wartime experiments, the shadowy remnants of ancient lost civilizations, and whispers of alien underground bases buried beneath the ice. Brad Olsen's exceptionally bold research unveils the controversial legends of German-engineered UFOs during the Second World War, challenging what we think we know about history. A must-read for truth-seekers and adventurers alike, it blends fact, speculation, and the unknown into a thrilling expedition to the edge of human understanding."
–Steve Mera, CEO of *Phenomena Magazine* and *Awakening Events,* Executive Producer of the *Erich von Daniken Legacy Night,* Bafta 2016

"For years, researchers have tried to uncover the mysteries of the Lost Continent of Antarctica. All of us have failed to do little more than scratch the surface. In Secrets of Antarctica, *author and explorer Brad Olsen cracks the secret code, puts the pieces together and finally shines the light of Truth on the secret history of the land at the bottom of the world. Brad finds connections that no one else saw, connects timelines that had been shrouded in mystery, and shows us that our future may depend on exposing the past of this mysterious land."*
–Mike Bara, author of *Ancient Aliens on Mars*

"Brad Olsen published a book fueled with fascinating and controversial subjects about Antarctica ranging from ancient maps suggesting pre-Ice Age civilizations to Nazi expeditions, Admiral Byrd's alleged encounters with advanced beings, and modern UFO sightings over research stations. Secrets of Antarctica: The Untold History of the Ice Continent *is a captivating dive into the enigmatic world of the southernmost continent, that blends historical accounts, conspiracy theories, and esoteric speculation in with the excellent research of anthropologist Robert Sepehr in a magnificent way. Olsen's enthusiasm and firsthand anecdotes from his personal 2019 expedition to Antarctica, also add a personal touch and is a thought-provoking read. Recommended for all those open-minded explorers willing to venture that little bit further down the rabbit hole ready to enjoy even the most controversial claims that challenge the mainstream narratives."* **–Leo Lyon Zagami, Author of the *Confessions of an Illuminati* series and *Rise and Fall of a Frankist Monster***

"This book is fascinating from start to finish. We truly have a lost, alien world at the bottom of our planet. Brad ventures into more esoteric territory, examining ancient maps and documents recovered from Germany after the war. Forget the old saying, "They can't get there from here." What if a hidden settlement of cryptoterrestrials has been living in a hollow Earth adjacent to us all along? Could a contingent of Germans have fled to Antarctica at the end of the war to live beneath the ice sheet, in caverns and volcanic tubes? Might they have engineered advanced technology—flying saucers and other innovations—on their own? If even part of this proves true, then everything we think we know about humanity and its history would be turned on its head." **–Ron Janix, Executive Producer of *ContactInTheDesert.com* and host of *BeyondContactPodcast.com***

also by Brad Olsen

2025

Beyond Esoteric:
Escaping Prison Planet

2018

Modern Esoteric:
Beyond our Senses

2016

Future Esoteric:
The Unseen Realms

2008

Sacred Places North America:
108 Destinations

2007

Sacred Places Europe:
108 Destinations

2004

Sacred Places Around the World:
108 Destinations

2001

World Stompers:
A Global Travel Manifesto

1999

In Search of Adventure:
A Wild Travel Anthology

1997

Extreme Adventures: Northern California

1997

Extreme Adventures: Hawaii

Secrets of Antarctica

The Untold History of the Ice Continent

by BRAD OLSEN

CONSORTIUM OF COLLECTIVE CONSCIOUSNESS PUBLISHING

www.CCCPublishing.com • www.BradOlsen.com • www.EsotericSeries.com

TABLE OF CONTENTS:

Author's Karma Statement 9

Introduction to Esoteric Antarctica . . . 17

Ice Continent 35

Lost Lands and the Patagonia Giants . . 63

Maps of Ancient Sea Kings 81

Nazis in Antarctica 100

Admiral Richard E. Byrd 149

Operation Highjump 169

Hollow Earth Entrance at the South Pole . . 195

Antarctica ETs 221

The Black Goo 249

Conclusion 277

AUTHOR'S KARMA STATEMENT

"For nothing is hidden that will not be disclosed, nor is anything secret that will not become known and come to light."

–LUKE 8:17

IN January and February of 2019 I had the great honor of traveling to the mysterious land called Antarctica on a sailboat. I wanted to explore the evidence indicating a preglacial period and potential pole shift trigger that thrust the ice continent into a deep freeze. There is still the continued speculation on the existence of portions of Atlantis on the Palmer Peninsula, as well as rumored massive UFO crafts under the ice. I feel strongly there is a suppression of information by powerful interests down there covering up many secrets of Antarctica. This book was written because of the importance of transparency. The people of the world deserve to know the truth.

I may be the only researcher in this field to self-finance a trip to Antarctica in search of the multitude of mysteries said to exist down there. In my personal encounters with other sea captains and personnel working at the research stations, I was able to confirm a massive no-fly zone is strictly enforced near the South Pole. In addition, the staff at one Argentinian research station have been witnessing UFOs overflying their base, which they were told not to discuss, but one worker broke his silence to reveal a UFO encounter over the Argentinian Belgrano II research station. Could it be that they witnessed the *Flügelrads* described in Admiral Byrd's diary? In an upcoming chapter we'll learn about those German UFOs and their bases in Antarctica. I was also interested in taking a close look at: (1) different locations and coordinates of pyramids in Antarctica; (2) a three-mile-wide disc buried under the Antarctic ice; (3) an explanation of why the world's elite have been visiting the mysterious continent; and (4) the potential of antediluvian civilizations.

I specifically went there to investigate UFOs, massive holes in the ice, Inner Earth, pyramids, or evidence of an antediluvian civilization (including megafauna, megaliths and giants). What I discovered will

Clues to an advanced civilization can be found in a recently discovered Google Earth satellite image taken in Antarctica. It appears to be step pyramids, or the plan to a square city plan. At hundreds of feet across, it has too many perfect geometric shapes to be random natural formations. Mother Nature does not create in perfect right angles.

astound you. For example, one of the greatest mysteries under the water is a very mysterious antenna at the bottom of the deep Drake Passage. The perfectly-symmetrical Eltanin Antenna was discovered in deep water between South America and Antarctica. What could it possibly be used for?

THE UNTOLD HISTORY

One of the biggest cover-ups and subjects of mainstream media and educational bias is the true account of who we are as a people and our untold history on Earth. A good amount of our edited history can still be found around the world "hidden in plain sight" at archaeological sites and mystical landforms. You need to know where to look, and how to look, then they become plain as day. It is as if nodes on the planet are screaming for their story to be told.

I will explore the historical mysteries and rumors of a Nazi secret base in Antarctica; the 1947 flying saucer attack on Admiral Byrd's ill-fated "Operation Highjump" expedition; the occult origins of Third Reich anti-gravity engines, flying discs and ancient Atlantean technologies; viewed through the lens of perhaps the three most mysterious twentieth century German organizations of all: the Thule Society, the Vril Society and the Ahnenerbe.

Rumors persist about extraterrestrial life's existence in this frozen land, with UFO sightings reported year after year. There are also

There is clearly the masking of certain "sensitive" sites on Google Earth. There are established no-fly zones over Antarctica, the largest being near the South Pole. There are other reported huge holes in the ice that are also classified as no-fly zones, according to recent Naval officer whistleblowers, and structures that appear to have been designed by a higher intelligence.

Deep ice crevasses have always posed a danger to any Antarctic over-the-ice expedition.

There are SCUBA diving expeditions for advanced divers to explore sunken wrecks, under the ice sheet dives, and marvel at the colorful wildlife on the ocean floor. The rusted, ghostly wreck of the *Guvernøren* stands out like a broken time capsule against the blue-white dazzlement of the Antarctic surroundings. It is one of the best wreck dives in the world.

suggestions of a lost city of Atlantis concealed beneath the frozen surface. Some people even believe that ancient civilizations might have thrived in Antarctica, later buried by the encroaching ice.

Admiral Byrd was the commanding officer in "Operation Highjump." He was part of one of the most mysterious military expeditions in modern history—an operation that officially went to Antarctica to "train" but ended in chaos, with Admiral Byrd himself dropping cryptic warnings about an enemy with advanced technology. Read his diary. The Admiral was dead a year after he wrote it.

The Nazi connection? 100% real. The German Antarctic base in *Neuschwabenland*, the disappearance of top Nazi scientists, and Project Paperclip—where the U.S. absorbed Nazi intelligence, scientists, and occultists into its own government—tie it all together.

Brad Olsen sets his sight on Antarctica's Palmer Peninsula aboard the *Chief One* sailboat. Over 90% of cruise ships and private sailboats leave from Ushuaia, Argentina to visit the northern Antarctic Peninsula, which stretches north toward South America. It's known for the Lemaire Channel and Paradise Harbor, which are striking, iceberg-flanked passageways. Also popular to visit is Port Lockroy—a former British research station turned museum. The peninsula's isolated terrain also shelters rich marine wildlife, including five species of penguins.

Some Paperclip Nazis who spoke German after World War II participated in Operation Deep Freeze, acting as a translator for Byrd and our Generals. You see, the Nazis who didn't "lose" World War II were just relocated.

A VOYAGE TO THE WHITE CONTINENT

As a life-long traveler I have had the privilege of visiting all seven continents, including Antarctica. There are so many mysteries and myths of what might be down there, I took it upon myself to self-finance an expedition by sailboat to investigate the claims of what is reportedly within the Frozen Continent. I wanted to see with my own eyes if there was an impenetrable ice wall as Flat Earthers maintain (there is not). I also wanted to inquire if any of the stories are true of massive mothership UFOs becoming visible from the rapidly melting ice; the massive hole in the two-mile deep polar plateau that gives entrance to Inner Earth; the Great Pyramid-sized monuments poking through the ice; or evidence of an antediluvian civilization including megafauna, megaliths and giants!

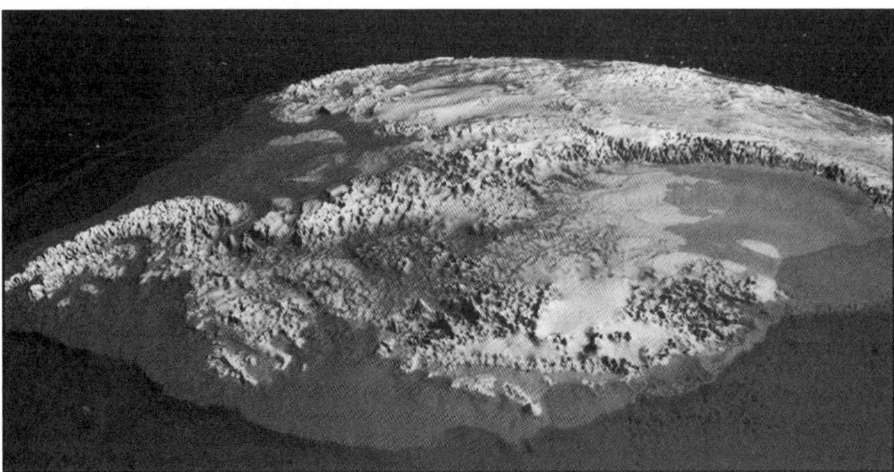

The underlying geography of Antarctica has garnered scientific interest, particularly regarding its historical climate and environment. Approximately 3 million years ago, the region exhibited a temperate and verdant landscape, contrasting sharply with its current glaciated condition. The Bedmap2 project has produced a comprehensive topographic map of the topography concealed beneath the ice, utilizing over 25 million measurements. This initiative has illuminated the ancient terrain, providing insights into the continent's pre-glacial state. The mapping reveals a complex landscape characterized by expansive mountain ranges and profound valleys, offering a narrative of Antarctica's climatic evolution prior to its transformation into the ice-covered expanse observed in contemporary times.

Author's Karma Statement

In the early months of 2019, I embarked on a 26-day expedition to Antarctica on a 72-foot Polish sailing vessel named the Chief One. There were 11 Poles and three Americans on the voyage. It was one of the most challenging and difficult trips I have even undertaken. I became violently seasick on the crossing of the Drake Passage between southern Argentina and the Palmer Peninsula. The Southern Ocean surrounding Antarctica is largely regarded as the stormiest seas in the world. After a rough 92-hour passage, we finally made it to our first anchorage, offshore of King George Island and the Polish Arctowski base. The trip of a lifetime started here. This book and subsequent research is all about what I discovered on the trip, and the best evidence for the enduring mysteries and unknown unknowns.

Every year, thousands of scientists, researchers, station staff, and even artists descend on Antarctica's 45 research bases to live and work at the end of the world, of which just a persistent several hundred stay during the six nearly sunless winter months. So, the "winter-overs" come prepared ... some with heaps of alcohol. At the South Pole is the Club 90 South.

The Amundsen-Scott South Pole Research Station is located at the Geographic (Geodetic) and the Ceremonial Pole at 90 degrees south location, at the southern end of the Earth's rotational axis where all the lines of longitude meet. The elevation is 9,301 feet above sea level resting on a solid sheet of ice.

HOLLOW EARTH?

I had a personal encounter in the vicinity of a massive under-ice cave system when I visited the Vernansky research station. The year 'round staffed Ukrainian base was donated by the United Kingdom in 1996, and another outstation a few miles away became an abandoned museum of sorts. We hiked over the snow to visit the abandoned base that was left "as-is" from the time it was decommissioned after Operation Tabarin. It was like taking a trip back in time. All the while, a massive cave system was located under the ice that made world headlines when it was discovered a year later.

In the hidden pages of Admiral Byrd's diary is a jaw-dropping expedition that takes the reader beyond known history! The legendary explorer claimed to have discovered vast inner-earth landscapes beneath both the North and South Poles. These secretive missions, including an early flight during Operation Highjump, reportedly revealed breathtaking worlds—complete with advanced technology, lush landscapes, and mysterious civilizations. As Byrd and his radioman ventured into these forbidden territories, they witnessed incredible marvels: advanced flying craft, towering cities unlike anything on the surface, and interactions with beings that seemed to defy our understanding of humanity's history. This account was kept secret for decades, its revelations echoing in whispers among historians, conspiracy researchers, and truth-seekers alike. Are these hidden realms the key to untapped potential and ancient wisdom? We shall find out!

Yours in extreme travel,

Brad Olsen

Yerington, NV

August 2, 2025

INTRODUCTION TO ESOTERIC ANTARCTICA

"We must torture nature until she reveals her secrets."

–Sir Francis Bacon

THERE'S no question that Antarctica remains one of the last great frontiers on Earth. Its vast icy landscapes, hidden lakes, mysterious mountains, and the potential secrets they hold continue to draw the attention of scientists, explorers, and the curious alike. As we delve deeper into its mysteries, we are continually reminded of the wonders and enigmas our planet holds.

The secrets of Antarctica abound in so many different ways. Beneath the ice there are more than 400 subglacial lakes, such as Lake Vostok, which could be home to life forms never seen before, and isolated for millions of years. Antarctica is a key place to find meteorites, as its ice preserves these space fragments, providing clues about the origin of the solar system. Also fascinating are the ancient maps, such as the Piri Re'is map, suggesting that Antarctica was inhabited or explored before it froze over, possibly by an advanced civilization. There are theories about hidden military and scientific facilities in Antarctica, including alleged Nazi bases started to be built before World War II and still in operation. Despite being a continent dedicated to peace and science, access to many areas is strictly controlled, fueling theories about discoveries hidden by governments and organizations. Indeed, some restricted areas are impossible or very difficult to access.

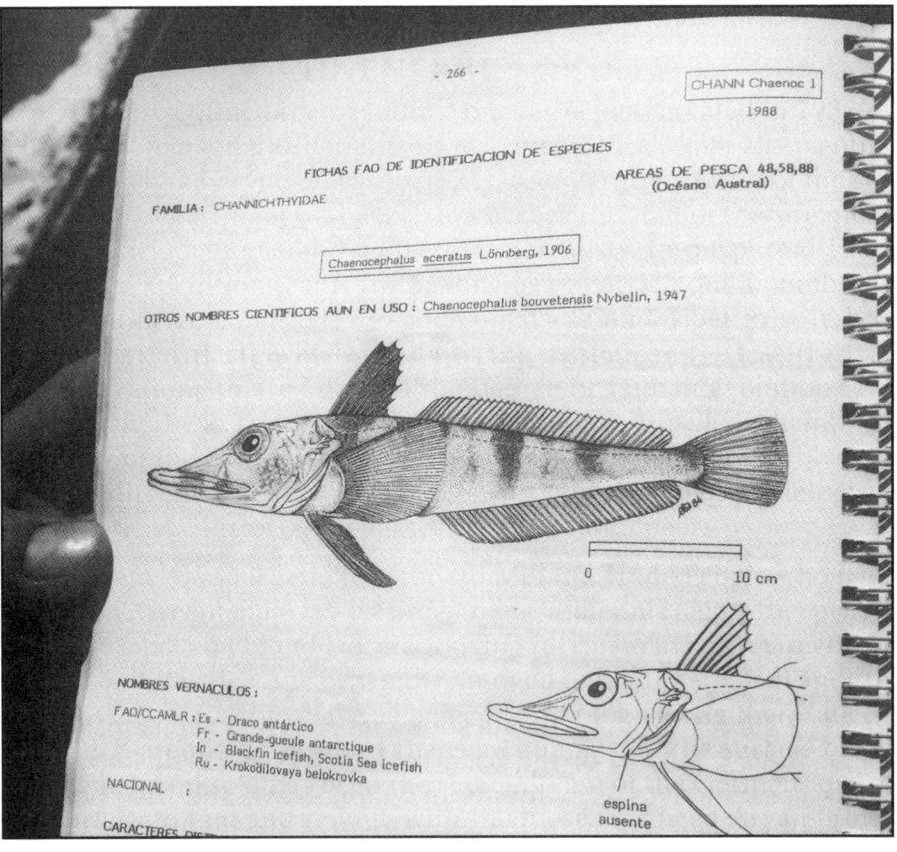

Beneath Antarctica's Weddell Sea, scientists have uncovered the world's largest known fish breeding site, spanning 240 square kilometers. Home to 60 million nests of Jonah's icefish, this discovery highlights the species' ecological importance and underscores the urgent need for marine protection in the region.

Introduction

There are stories from the research stations of people going crazy because of the long winters and solitude down there. When informed he would be staying over, one Chilean doctor burned down the old Gonzalez base as the ship was leaving for the winter. The fire forced the ship to return to pick up the crew and the doctor, as they would all surely perish from the harsh elements and from running out of supplies.

Antarctica is the only sizable landmass on our planet that is not owned by any country. Ninety percent of the world's freshwater ice covers this single continent. This ice also represents over seventy

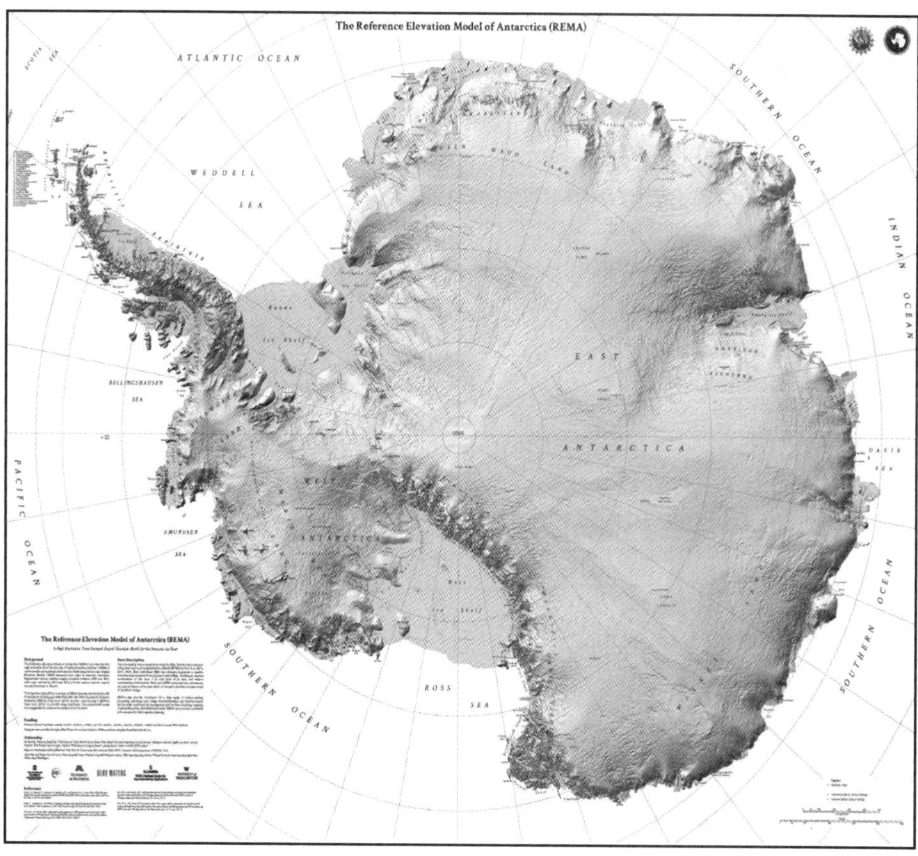

This is the recently completed Reference Elevation Model of Antarctica (REMA). Antarctica is an extremely cold continent at the south pole almost entirely below the Antarctic Circle. It is the highest elevation continent in the world, and is covered by an ice cap up to 4776m thick (over 13,000 feet deep). Antarctica is twice the size of Australia, and almost twice the size of the contiguous Lower 48 states.

percent of all the fresh water in the world. As strange as it sounds, however, Antarctica is essentially a desert; the average yearly total precipitation is about two inches. Although covered with ice (all but 0.4% of it is ice), Antarctica is the driest place on the planet, with an absolute humidity lower than the Gobi Desert. In fact, the driest place on Earth are the "Dry Valleys" of the Antarctic near Ross Island. There has been no rainfall there for two million years.

Antarctica was only first discovered in 1820 by Russian navigators Bellingshausen and Lazarev. The following year merchant marines hunting whales and seals stepped ashore the continental land mass. Since then, this mysterious continent, which has an area larger than Europe, attracts researchers and explorers like a magnet. However, the craggy shorelines and the steep ice shelf walls hundreds of feet high made the interior of the continent impregnable for another century. Until the last few decades almost nothing was known about the great expanses across Antarctica. Only coastal maps were plotted.

Though no country holds indisputable title over any part of Antarctica, eight nations have territorial claims. This sovereignty is not internationally recognized, but the eight nations (Argentina, Chile, the UK, Norway, New Zealand, USA, Australia and France) continue to strengthen their own claims of control. From 2007 to 2009, for example, the UK, Chile and Argentina all filed for rights to mine Antarctica's sea floor. All agree on reserving Antarctica for peace, prohibiting nuclear explosions and guaranteeing the freedom of science.

The time of strict military expeditions to Antarctica is long past. This all happened during World War II. Other military activities during the 1950s and early 60s led to the ground breaking Antarctic Treaty. Since that was fully ratified in 1961, there has only been military support of Antarctic expeditions, but direct military expeditions are prohibited: "Antarctica shall continue forever to be used exclusively for peaceful purposes and shall not become the scene or object of international discord."

ANTARCTIC TREATY

The Antarctic Treaty was signed by 12 countries in 1959, prohibiting all nations from testing weapons or constructing military bases on the south polar continent. The treaty entered into force in 1961, and has since been acceded to by many other nations. The total number of parties to the treaty is now 56—agreeing that only scientific investigations can be conducted, with results shared and made freely available. The USA and Russia maintain several bases and claims, but no new claim or enlargement of an existing claim to territorial sovereignty in Antarctica is permitted while the present treaty is in force.

Guidelines in the Antarctic Treaty which are designed to limit the cumulative impact of tourism have even been adopted. Treaty countries agree that Antarctica is a peaceful, free and demilitarized place of international cooperation and scientific research, open to all, and with minimum human impact.

That is the public version of the Antarctic Treaty, but there are actually two components of the Antarctic Treaty. Regarding the treaty itself, there is a public version and there is a classified version. Admiral Richard Byrd's final mission to Antarctica called Operation Deep Freeze, was to enable the corporate cabal globalists to build and establish their bases in Antarctica. It also allowed them to go through the negotiations with the Antarctic Germans,

The Antarctic Treaty was originally signed in 1959 by the 12 nations operating there at the time. With now 56 nations signed on, the Antarctic Treaty ensures that countries active on the continent and surrounding islands south of 60 degrees consult on the uses of resources where there are no wars, where the environment is fully protected, and where research is the priority.

who were already firmly established. At this time the Antarctic Germans continued their political espionage as the "Third Force," fanning the flames of discontent between the NATO countries and the Soviet Bloc during the Cold War. They wanted to infiltrate every country, major corporation, and major organization on the planet. That was how the Antarctic Germans were going to run the world with their new fascist globalist allies—and that is how they were able to gain control over technology. [1]

In 1959, the year that the Antarctic Treaty was enacted, what did the Antarctic Treaty do well? It granted the Antarctic Germans about 150,000 personnel from the rest of the world. Now what does that mean? They were going to pick them up from a place and time of their choosing. They had assured the rest of the leaders of the world that they would pay them and take care of them. They would feed and house them, give them fair medical treatment and anything that they needed. They would give them the opportunity to become German citizens if they chose to at the end of five years. If they didn't want to become citizens then they would send them back home. But because everyone was groomed and had a role to play, no one chose to leave. Also a part of the Antarctic Treaty is that they had at least one Paperclip/ Antarctic German on the governing board of directors of all major corporations. Not only do they have senior executive positions, but at least one larger corporation had 5 to 10 former Nazi Germans. They eventually got their own people on the board of directors—filling thousands of worldwide positions at corporations, universities, medical research facilities, banks, financial institutions, and senior government positions. This became the Fourth Reich in America.

CORPORATE TAKEOVER

The other portion of their plan was to have at least one executive of their citizens on the executive branch of every government on the planet. The United States government had multiple civilians from the Antarctic Germans within the multiple branches. There is a German Antarctic embassy in an unmarked building in downtown New York City, on an unmarked floor, that takes a special key to access the elevator.

For decades, their society was to remain classified and hidden from the general public. They didn't want the information coming out and they didn't want the world ganging up on them. The cabal

1. Olsen, Brad. *Future Esoteric: the Unseen Realms,* 2018, CCC Publishing.

would lose their power and control if that happened. So it was a "win-win" for both of them to keep the whole operation quiet.

Concluding their show of force, the Antarctic Germans stopped their overflights of Washington D.C. They began to work with the U.S. secret government in "shadowing" of both civilian and military aircraft throughout the 1960s. The cabal and the Antarctic Germans continued their cat and mouse game for decades.

The United States' effort to put a man on the moon was an opportunity for siphoning off millions of dollars to invest into Black Projects. The Antarctic Germans used their embedded citizens to great effect because if they had a technology that turned out well and that had a lot of promise they would have first dibs. This was something that would actually work in a military or civilian field. They used their citizens both in government and in the military or civilian field/ corporations to either close the project down publicly, take it back, or transfer it completely. That is precisely why certain technologies just go missing while looking through the records in a Google search. They started disappearing during the 1950s, beginning with anti-gravity.

This is why the Antarctic Germans and the cabal both continued to work on their mind-control programs, and this includes technology as well as pharmaceuticals during the 1960s. They used the MK-Ultra programming exported from Nazi Germany. Both the cabal and Fourth Reich Germans developed their own secret space programs.

The World War II German psychiatrists and the Third Reich had pioneered a lot of new technology and included among them were "mind-control," spelled *kontrolle* in German. The scientists, engineers, doctors and technicians that became part of the Antarctic Society continued their mind control programs on the rest of the world.

WHY SUCH AN INTEREST?

The biggest discoveries in the last few decades are three massive craft under the ice, and some are connected to megalithic buildings, along with giant bodies uncovered in the structures. These crafts were named Nina, Pinta, and Santa Maria by the NSA. Advances in technology have allowed ice-penetrating radar to reveal the coordinates of these large craft and monolithic structures below the Antarctic ice, and these are now being excavated in the "Illuminati Disneyland" of Antarctica.

There is new evidence emerging of an ancient civilization that once existed in Antarctica when it had a much different climate. These remnants could be from Atlantis, or an even earlier planetary civilization. They could also be the surviving colony of a semi-functional crashed mothership UFO. There are leaked images of different "mother ships" buried over a mile deep under the Antarctica ice, showing the top portion being slowly exposed even more each summer as the ice shelf retreats. Also poking out from the ice fields are several four-sided pyramids in several different areas. Mother Nature does not create in perfect right angle symmetry on a megalithic scale.

Among a dozen royal family members, politicians, and celebrities going down to Antarctica in 2016-2017, was former Apollo 11 astronaut Buzz Aldrin. Before he was emergency evacuated out of there, he cryptically tweeted "We are all in danger. It is evil itself." He needed emergency care for health reasons.

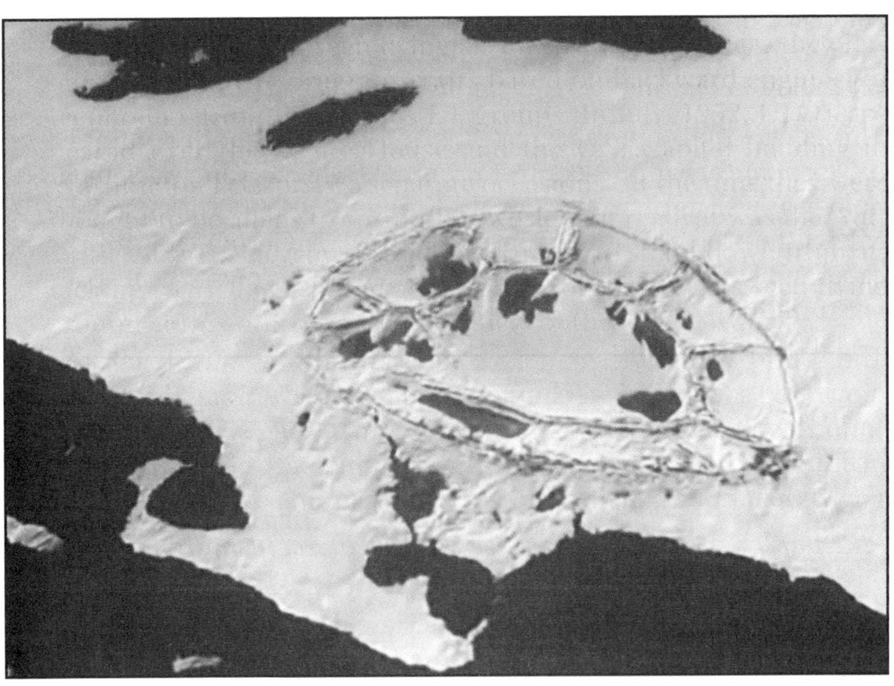

In 2012, a satellite image captured this mysterious oval shape in one of the most remote regions of Antarctica. Measuring over 400 feet across, it seems to show an ancient fort from a lost civilization that once inhabited this desolate region. The photo shows what looks like the top of a large building protruding from under the ice.

An in-depth understanding of different Secret Space Programs has revealed several locations of operations in Antarctica, replete with visible entrances to underground bases, and above ice runways and snowmobile roads. Even remote viewers have targeted an "Interplanetary Corporate Conglomerate" series of under ice bases, heated and fueled by geothermal energy.

Could the elite be gaining access inside a massive three-mile wide mother ship? This is the likely nicknamed "Illuminati Disneyland," where they're all going down for a "look-see" visit.

IRAN INTENDS TO BUILD A SOUTH POLE BASE

The Republic of Iran has rejected the Antarctic Treaty and recently announced in early 2024 its own claim to Antarctic territory—insisting that it will build a military base on the South Pole.

In a February, 2024 interview, Navy Chief Rear Commander Admiral Shaham Irani said, "Tehran has property rights in the South Pole where it is planning to build a naval base"—declaring that the Aryan nation owns Antarctica and will flex its property to not only carry out scientific work, but to raise its flag over a new military installation. "Many of our people are wondering if the army will be able to raise the flag of the Islamic Republic in the South Pole?"

The Interviewer asked: *"As a commander of the strategic navy forces—can you make this promise to our people—that we will have a base there?"*

Sharam Irani replied: *"With regard to the South Pole, as you know—the beautiful beaches of Makran connect us to the South Pole. We have property rights there, and they belong to the public. Our plan is to raise the flag there, inshallah."*

The Interviewer inquired: *"It is not only military work—but also scientific work that needs to be carried out?"*

Sharam Irani said: *"Yes, right, our scientists are getting ready for a joint operation encompassing the efforts of all our people—in keeping with the guidelines of our leader, inshallah."*

The Interviewer confirms: *"so we can declare that Admiral Irani promises that we will build a permanent base in the South Pole?"*

Sharam Irani: *"inshallah, inshallah!"*

Even if Iran still allegedly has a polar presence, a more likely scenario may be in regards to its close ally Russia which also maintains military bases near both poles, with six scientific research stations in Antarctica alone. That said, in December 2023, the Islamic Republic claimed it was building "smart cruise missiles" for its navy arsenal, which has some Western and military intelligence analysts concerned, given that Russia publicly claims to have the most advanced hypersonic missiles systems in the world. While Russia signed the Antarctic Treaty which became effective in 1961, barring it from expanding the military bases at the South Pole, Iran is not a signatory of the treaty.

NAZI GERMANY TERRITORIAL CLAIM

Ever since the early 20th century, Antarctica has been a point of interest for several world governments and secret societies—including the German National Socialists that sent several expeditions to the South Pole with its third "*Deutsche Antarktische Expedition*" conducted in 1938 and 1939—resulting in Germany annexing a portion of eastern Antarctica.

In 1939, the Germans acquired what was formerly claimed as Norwegian territory known as Queen Maud Land, and renamed it as *Neuschwabenland.* Most of the territory is covered by the east Antarctic ice sheet and a tall ice shelf stretching along its coast. But below the surface there are not only massive caverns melted away from the subterranean volcanic vents, but a thriving ecosystem where the Germans established a U-boat port called Base 211. While the details surrounding this German base remain shrouded in mystery, New Swabia emerged as the only successful colony of the German Empire. Another location called New Berlin was also established. After World War II the United States and its allies mounted a military invasion of Antarctica in 1946 called Operation Highjump, which still remains a classified operation. [2]

There are reports from *Nexus* magazine of massive men in stature who were impervious to the cold conditions that would kill ordi-

2. https://althistory.fandom.com/wiki/New_Swabia_(Great_White_South)

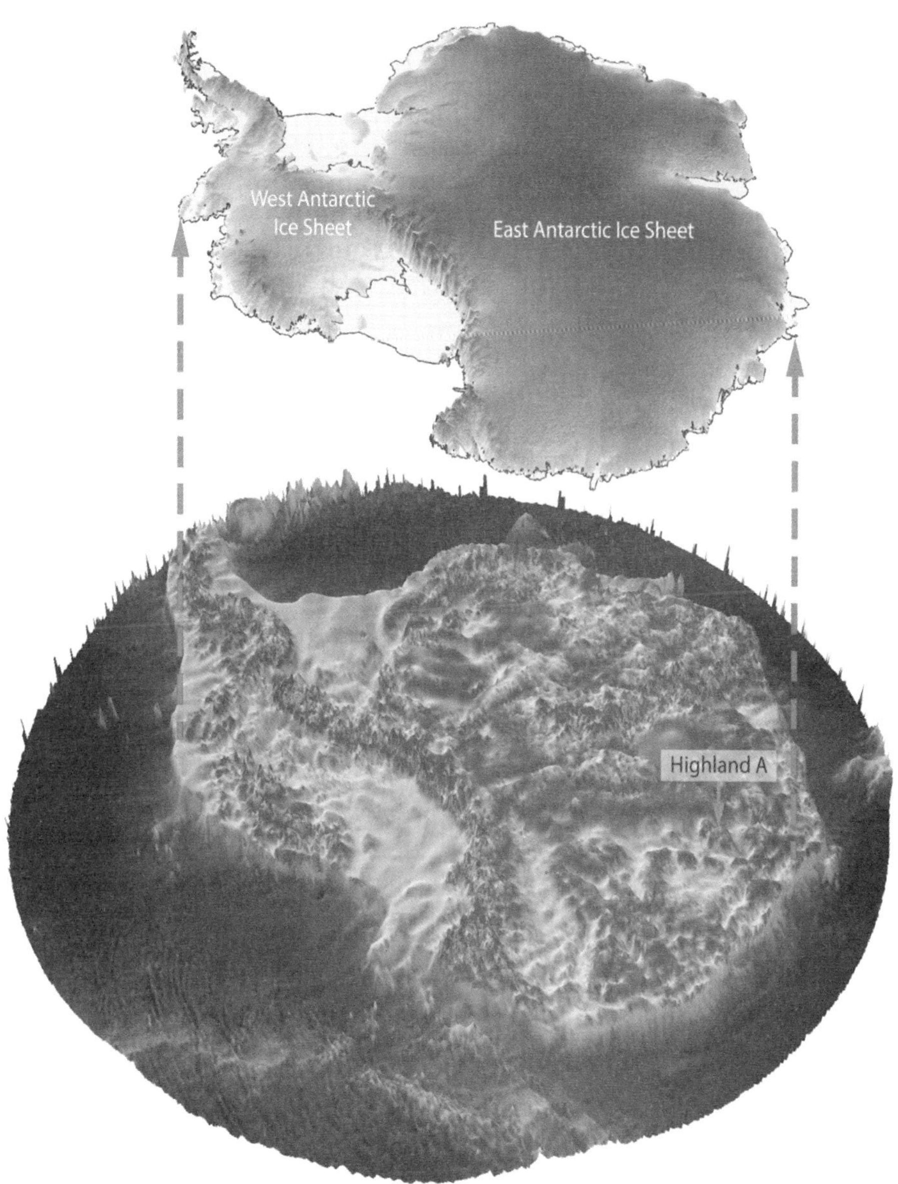

What if all of Antarctica's ice vanished? This image reveals the buried landscape beneath—and with it, a shocking discovery. "Highland A" is a lost world, a remnant of an ancient landscape of valleys and ridges carved by rivers at least 14 million years ago.

Before Antarctica froze over, mountain rivers shaped this land. Now, against all odds, part of that prehistoric world still exists, untouched beneath miles of ice. Scientists expected it to be ground away by the crushing weight of the ice sheet. But instead, it's been perfectly preserved like a time capsule. Credit: Stewart Jamieson/Durham University nary men. They reportedly chased down and killed some British soldiers who were able to breech the security going into the Nazi bases. The Nazis set up at least one base in *Neuschwabenland* before World War II, and presumably secretly kept them going. During the Cold War the Neumayer and Kohnen bases were established by West Germany, and they both remain there today under the unified Germany flag. The Germans never left their claim to *Neuschwabenland.*

There is emerging satellite images of what appear to be pre-ice civilizations in several locations, including symmetrical formations under the water. Interestingly, most are clustered around the Nazi-claimed *Neuschwabenland* region of Antarctica. Personnel on the bases near New Swabia have reported seeing unidentified flying objects, underwater submersible objects, and flying orbs.

HIGHJUMP AND SOUTH POLE COVER-UPS

The American intelligence services were always fascinated with the Inter-magical heritage of Germany, and especially the "Techno Magical" advancements in exotic flying technology. Immediately following World War II suddenly something inexplicable happened in Antarctica. A U.S. Navy expedition designed for six months, hastily folded and left the shores of *Neuschwabenland* after two months. In early 1947, the next expedition of the legendary American polar explorer Richard Byrd approached the shores of Antarctica in a very strange expedition, the largest military operation ever going down to Antarctica. Unlike the first three, it was fully funded by the U.S. Navy and had the military name Operation Highjump.

Admiral Byrd, a 33 degree Freemason, led the expedition of 30 ships and 4700 militarized soldiers. The mission had three task forces that were sent out in different directions and was to last 6-8 months, but the fleet started back in just eight weeks.

The expedition was filmed by the Navy and brought to Hollywood to be made into a commercial film called *The Secret Land.* It was narrated by Hollywood actor Robert Montgomery, father of *Bewitched* star, Elizabeth Montgomery, who was, himself, an officer in the Naval Reserve.

It seems incredible that so shortly after a war that had decimated most of Europe and crippled global economies, an expedition to Antarctica was undertaken with so much haste (it took advantage of the first available Antarctic summer after the war), at such cost, and with so much military hardware—unless the operation was absolutely essential to the security of the United States.

The 1st rank doctor of history Dimitry Filipovich said in a conference presentation:

> *It seems that other nations—such as Russia are more forthcoming concerning the details of the alleged SS military colony that refused to surrender. At the beginning of 1947, yet another expedition by the American explorer Richard Byrd arrived on Antarctica shores. It was a very strange expedition—unlike the previous three. This one was completely financed by the U.S. Navy. Operation Highjump was its one name under the command of the admiral Richard Byrd—there was a military squadron, an aircraft carrier, 12 surface ships, one submarine, more than 20 airplanes and helicopters and about 5,000 people on staff. You will agree a strange team for a scientific expedition on 12/2/1946.*

Before the start of this expedition, Admiral Byrd at a press conference said, "my expedition is military in nature" and gave no further details. Shortly after Operation Highjump, Admiral Byrd said the following to a reporter: "in the event of another war, America can be attacked by an enemy that has the ability to fly from pole to pole with incredible speed." Secretly, Admiral Byrd was tasked to capture or retrieve a Nazi flying disc.

By the end of January 1947, full scale aerial reconnaissance began surveying the Antarctic region of Queen Maud Land. It all went according to plan in the first weeks—tens of thousands of photos were taken. Then suddenly the inexplicable happened—a third of the way into the six-month expedition Operation Highjump was terminated, after only two months. They had to flee the Antarctic coast post haste. The armada lost the destroyer USS Maddox, almost half their carrier-based aircraft, and dozens of sailors and officers. Afterwards there was a secret investigation by members of the U.S. Congress.

Indeed, there is an ongoing cover-up about the 1946-1947 mission called Operation Highjump. This is because the Allies suffered a resounding defeat in the single day Battle of Highjump. It

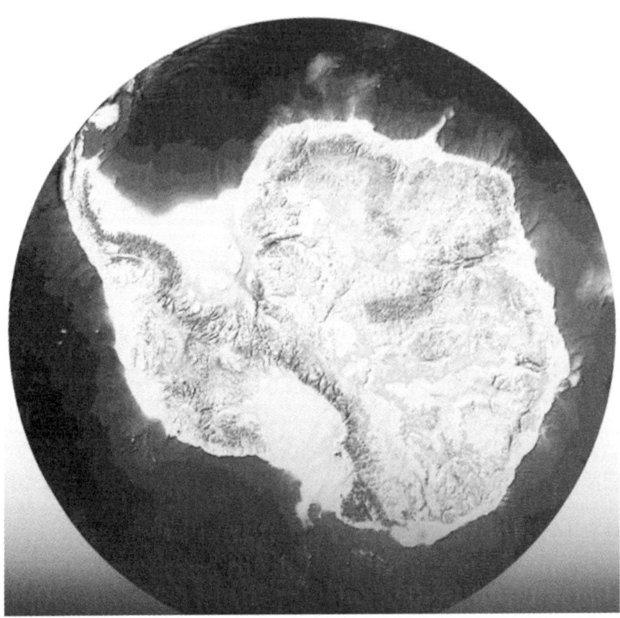

The British Antarctic Survey (BAS) has unveiled the most detailed map yet of Antarctica's landmass—without its ice. Compiled from six decades of data, the Bedmap3 project reveals the hidden bedrock beneath the continent's massive ice sheet, which holds over 70% of the world's fresh water. The new map offers unprecedented detail, uncovering Antarctica's highest mountains, deepest canyons, and areas where ice reaches depths of nearly 4,800 meters.

is still classified by the U.S. as top secret. There are also cover-ups to hide the mysterious entrances and massive holes in the ice leading to underground bases of Inner Earth, including a massive no-fly zone with a circumference hundreds of miles across near the South Pole. [3]

UNDERGROUND BASES

One of the core themes of this book is the alleged existence of Base 211 and the New Berlin colony—the legendary underground Nazi bases in Antarctica—and the actual geo-physical possibilities of other underground bases or "domains" located under the ice.

Drawing upon the pre-war Nazi interest in Antarctica and the creation of New Swabia, the testimony of German U-boat submarine commanders and the alleged disappearance of thousands of Nazi scientists and engineers at the end of the war, personnel that can-

3. Antarctica Disclosure - ROBERT SEPEHR
https://www.youtube.com/watch?v=hIjxbV7pDlc&t=3s&ab_channel=RobertSepehr

not be accounted for by the Vatican and ODESSA "rat lines" or American "Project Paperclip" activities.

Another core theme is the alleged existence of a Nazi flying saucer program and the many evidential strands that this area generates. From the supposed channelling of extraterrestrial engineering schematics by members of the German occult group Vril Society and the Thule Society in the early part of the 20th century, to the implosion engine of Victor Schauberger and its possible appropriation by the Third Reich.

In the latter part of the twentieth century there have been many sightings of unknown crafts around the Antarctic region and the theoretical basis for polar wormholes as entrance and exit points for visiting extraterrestrial spaceships, the possible involvement of HAARP, as well as asking why nearly all American Antarctic bases seem to be populated by agents of the National Security Agency and the CIA. Just as the study of any phenomena and/or events that exist at the edges of consensus reality, occupy imaginal realms and are subject to historical revisionism; the interface of myth and reality is a shifting mosaic of fact, speculation, disinformation; and fantasy, or to use the phrase of head CIA counter-intelligence spook, James Jesus Angleton, we have entered a "wilderness of mirrors."

Likewise, there is the scant information on the existence of the U.S. Navy destroyer USS Maddox, sometimes spelled Murdoch, in the testimony recounted by pilot John Sireson in his description of the flying saucer attack on Admiral Byrd's fleet (testimony taken from an interview by the late pioneering American researcher Leonard Stringfield). Equally, the testimony of Admiral Byrd that flying saucers attacked the "Operation Highjump" fleet is of historical record as is his testimony to Congress of enemies that have the ability to fly "pole to pole at incredible speeds." [4]

PROJECT PAPERCLIP

Operation Paperclip was the code name for the 1945 Office of Strategic Services, Joint Intelligence Objectives Agency recruitment of German scientists from Nazi Germany to the U.S. after VE Day. President Truman authorized Operation Paperclip in August, 1945. What nobody realized at the time was that a Fourth Reich was forming as a covert operation in America and the West. These active Nazi scientists, bureaucrats and businessmen man-

4. "Third Reich - Operation UFO (Nazi Base In Antarctica) Complete Documentary" https://www.youtube.com/watch?v=MwUpPwyyvLw&ab_channel=ElfWave

At the conclusion of World War II in 1945, Operation Paperclip was tasked with secretly bringing in hundreds of Nazi scientists into America, where many were hired into the Military Industrial Complex. Operation Paperclip was the code name for the 1945 Office of Strategic Services, Joint Intelligence Objectives Agency recruitment of German scientists from Nazi Germany to the U.S. after VE Day. President Truman authorized Operation Paperclip in August, 1945. Eventually, these active Nazi scientists managed to infiltrate and take over every institution in the USA, Canada and South American countries, from businesses, academia, politics, and medical fields.

aged to infiltrate and take over every institution of importance in the USA, Canada and South American countries in the fields of banking, academia, politics, medical, and senior government positions. The Nazis didn't lose World War II, they just moved to the Americas. The famous Wernher von Braun, who was an SS officer, helped form NASA along with fellow Paperclip Nazis turned NASA rocket scientists Arthur Rudolph and Hermann Oberth.

"We are still in the middle of a war waged in the corridors of power, in boardrooms, in the dark recesses of the internet. Our enemies aren't just armed with weapons; our enemies wield disinformation, propaganda, and economic influence," said Joseph P. Farrell, in an interview entitled "The Nazis Never Lost." The real war is between Satanists and humanity. The CIA and the Freemasons organize our elections and wars so nations remain divided and are destroyed. [5]

There are elements of the advanced Third Reich technology that give cause for concern, such as the alleged "Special Bureau 13," the Nazi secret flying saucer research group and its similarity to the top-secret government agency in the early 1980s role-playing

5. The Nazis Never Lost – Joseph P. Farrell – Solari Report with Catherine Austin Fitts – May 8, 2024 https://roserambles.org/2024/05/08/the-nazis-never-lost-joseph-p-farrell-solari-report-with-catherine-austin-fitts-may-8-2024/

game "Bureau 13: Stalking the Night Fantastic." American scientists were playing catch-up in understanding and backward engineering flying disc technology in the decades after the war. Meanwhile, the secret Nazi international organization clandestinely extended its tentacles across dozens of nations, in Antarctica, and even into outer space.

SOUTH POLE RESEARCH STATION

On June 12th, 2023, Dr. Steven Greer held a press conference at the National Press Club that contained all-new military and government whistleblower testimony on the advanced technology/UAP phenomenon. A so-called insider gave his testimony as a Raytheon Contractor based out of the United States built Amundsen–Scott South Pole station. During his testimony, the whistleblower discussed an advanced technology called the IceCube Neutrino Observatory. It was built to explore and understand more about neutrinos, the most abundant particles that have mass in the universe. In simple terms, it looks at spectrums of light we cannot detect optically to understand more about the nature of our reality. Research at the facility also includes glaciology, geophysics, meteorology, upper atmosphere physics, astronomy, astrophysics, and biomedical research. However, this whistleblower claims there is more going on.

Eric Hecker claims the IceCube indeed does what its primary purposes are, but additionally claims the technology can also be

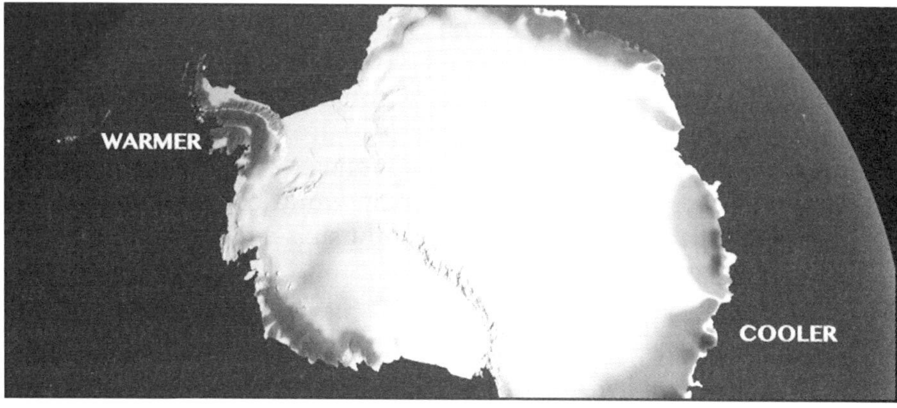

This map is the mass or accumulated Antarctica change in the 20th century, as depicted by NASA's Scientific Visualization Studio. Ninety percent of the world's ice covers Antarctica, but the ice is melting at an alarming rate in certain areas (dark grey), but it also paradoxically has areas that are accumulating ice and are colder than average. This ice shield of Antarctica represents seventy percent of all the fresh water in the world.

used as a directed energy weapon. This is because the 5160 Digital Optical Modules (DOMs) embedded into the ice can transmit at 2047 volts of power each. Hecker claims the technology can also provide faster-than-light communication, and is essentially an air traffic controlling system from highly advanced spacecraft (perhaps some human, but mostly non-human) not disclosed to the public. With such huge power output, he questions what the sources of power may be. Perhaps it is a non-sanctioned Nuclear Station that's being kept under wraps. But he claims it's likely an exotic and highly advanced power generation unit. If this is true, it would mean that for the last 15 years as this technology has been fully operational, the U.S. government may have been using a highly advanced energy technology at this facility and is in violation of the Antarctic Treaty.

This would be problematic given the U.S. government claims the only way forward in solving our energy and climate woes is to tax citizens via a carbon tax while we move to wind and solar. Worse, Hecker claims the use of this technology could have been linked to earthquakes, and the technology may have been used for nefarious purposes, such as triggering the Christchurch, New Zealand earthquake a decade ago.

The original idea of Project Blue Beam was to use the Antarctic blue beam direct energy weapon to create earthquakes and use the advanced weapon to create chaos using Electro-magnetic frequencies. These are neutrino weapons that can create thoughts and install ideas in people on a mass scale. Smart phones, smart TV and smart radio can activate voices, false illusions, and feelings in humans. This is the same reason McDonalds wanted to use technology to advertise to people who are sleeping and infiltrate dreams with electro-magnetic frequencies using smart technology. However, the deep state military mind control operation is decades ahead of McDonald's idea of using neutrinos to manipulate people. [6]

6. 5/31/2024 -- *RESTORED REPUBLIC* https://operationdisclosureofficial.com/2024/05/31/restored-republic-via-a-gcr-as-of-may-31-2024/

ICE CONTINENT

"The ANTARCTIC — A country doomed by nature,
Never once to feel warmth of the sun's rays,
But to lie buried in everlasting snow and ice."

-Captain James Cook

ANTARCTICA is an extremely cold continent centered around the South Pole, and located almost entirely below the Antarctic Circle. It is the highest elevation continent in the world, because it is almost entirely covered by an ice cap up to three miles thick. Antarctica is twice the size of Australia, and almost twice the size of the contiguous Lower 48 states. Ninety percent of the world's solid ice blankets Antarctica, yet in certain regions the ice is melting at an alarming pace (according to Bernie Sanders, 3x faster than just 10 years ago). This ice also represents seventy percent of all the fresh water in the world. If the ice were ever to completely melt, or slide off the continent, there would be catastrophic flooding of coastal communities worldwide.

For all its remoteness, Antarctica was once verdant jungle at a different latitude millions of years ago. Fossil remnants of a 280-million-year-old forest were found by Dr. Erik Gulbranson and Dr. John Isbell of the University of Wisconsin and their international team of researchers when they trekked across Antarctica in late 2017. The researchers determined that the ancient forest of Antarctica existed before the dinosaurs, which lived on Earth between 252 and 66 million years ago.

Antarctica, now covered by an ice sheet that reaches over 13,000 feet deep (5,000 meters thick), once had a mild climate and was covered with vegetation. Temperatures reached 10 degrees Celsius above zero, and the ground was covered by coniferous forests and tundra. This was the discovery made by researchers at Rice University in Houston and reported by ANSA.

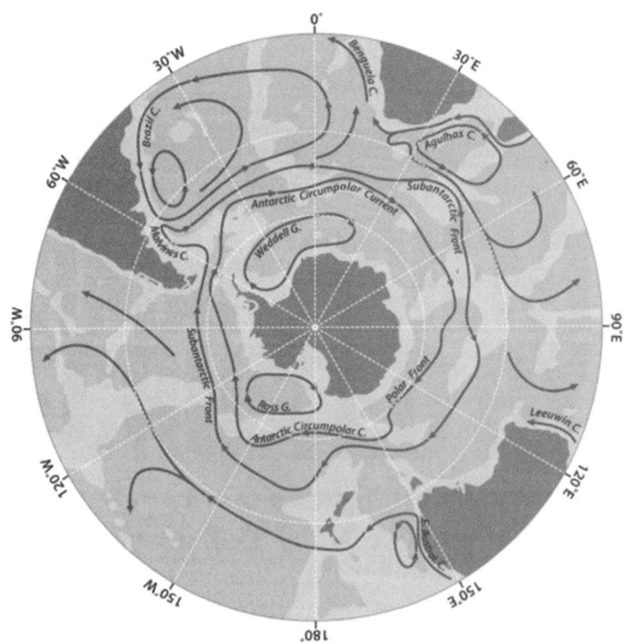

Comprehensive studies of the complex circulation and ecosystems of the Southern Ocean will be of increasing global importance. According to NASA: "The United States must enhance its polar fleet to maintain scientific leadership in the Southern Ocean and support its national interests under the Antarctic Treaty."

According to marine geologist John Anderson, lead author of the study, the climate history of Antarctica can be "read" in the pollens that have been deposited on the bottoms of the continental shelves surrounding the continent. It was not easy to take pollen from the sedimentary rock layers of the seafloor, but in 2003, with an ice-breaker ship equipped for drilling, rock cores a hundred meters long were extracted. Pollen of many plant species were detected, some found in New Zealand today. The presence of pollen is evidence that a very long time ago, perhaps even many millions of years ago, lush vegetation existed in Antarctica.

STORMY SEAS

The Southern Ocean is the most influential and consequential of the Earth's five oceans. Its major eastward flow, the Antarctic Circumpolar Current (ACC), connects with the waters of the

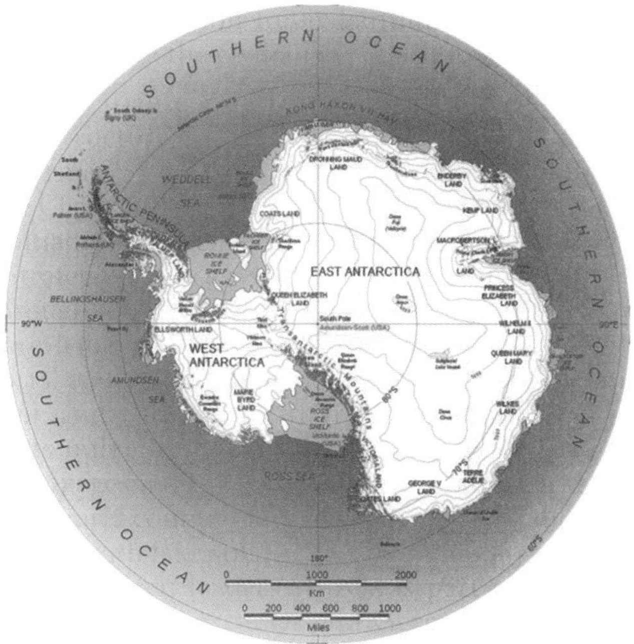

The southernmost continent and site of the South Pole, Antarctica is a virtually uninhabited, ice-covered landmass. Before it became frozen solid, the ancient supercontinent Gondwanaland once contained Antarctica and other continents with the same tropical flora and fauna. The enormous amount of ice has formed through the accumulation of snow over millions of years, and exists in a state of dynamic equilibrium. The amount of snow deposited in any one year is relatively very low—Antarctica is classified as a desert and is the driest continent on Earth. The Antarctic Circumpolar Current (ACC), which travels from west to east, defines the boundaries of the Southern Ocean.

Indian, Pacific, and Atlantic Oceans. Only the Arctic Ocean is not directly linked to this complex fusion of waters with the world's largest ocean current. The Southern Ocean has been rightfully called the "hub" of the global ocean. The Southern Ocean is defined as the waters that encircle the Antarctic continent below 60 degrees South latitude. This marine expanse is estimated to be 1/16 of the total global oceans area. Notably, in June 2021, the U.S. National Geographic Society designated the Southern Ocean as the planet's fifth ocean, taking a cue from a 2000 report by the International Hydrographic Organization. However, the research community decades earlier recognized these waters as a distinct marine environment with global implications for climate and oceanic ecosystems.

Strong westerly winds push the ACC on an uninterrupted, clockwise flow around Antarctica. The only restriction to this unimpeded flow is the 522 nautical mile-wide Drake Passage between Cape Horn and the Shetland Islands off the Antarctic Peninsula. The average depth of the Southern Ocean is 10,722 feet, and within these depths a critical process takes place: the upwelling and mixing of deep waters that come to the surface and interact with the atmosphere, exchanging heat and carbon dioxide. Recent climate change research indicates the Southern Ocean plays a critical role in storing excess heat and anthropogenic carbon (one study estimates 40 percent heat and 44 percent carbon). Understanding the outsized role the Southern Ocean plays in sequestering heat and carbon is a global research imperative. In addition, more fully understanding the physical oceanography of the Southern Ocean—both the large scale, horizontal circulation and vertical circulation—will provide clues to its links in the surrounding oceans. [1]

The point where the Pacific and Atlantic Oceans meet is a fascinating natural phenomenon, often characterized by a visible line where the two bodies of water appear to clash but do not fully mix. This unique phenomenon occurs primarily due to differences in the salinity, temperature, and density of each ocean's water. While these differences do not create a solid barrier, they create a gradient that makes it difficult for the waters to fully blend, resulting in a striking contrast that can be seen on the surface.

One of the most notable places where this phenomenon occurs is at Cape Horn, the southernmost tip of South America, where the Pacific Ocean meets the Atlantic. Here, the waters of the Pacific, typically cooler and less salty, encounter the warmer, saltier waters of the

1. "Southern Ocean: Hub of the Global Ecosystem." By Captain Lawson W. Brigham: https://www.usni.org/magazines/proceedings/2025/january/southern-ocean-hub-global-ecosystem

Atlantic. These differences cause each ocean to retain its unique characteristics for a while, before they gradually blend through diffusion and currents. This phenomenon is further influenced by powerful ocean currents, like the Antarctic Circumpolar Current, which flows around Antarctica and affects the waters where these oceans converge.

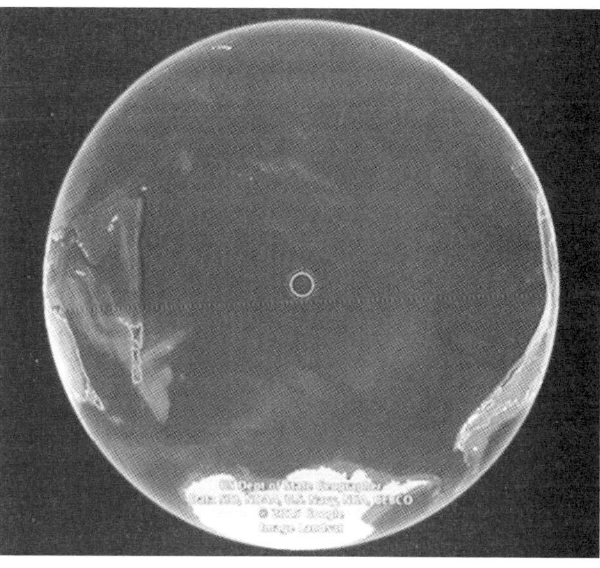

Most people don't realize we really live on a water planet, because 29% of the surface is land mass, and 71% of the surface is water. Point Nemo is a tiny island located further from any landmass than any other spot in the seas. It's located so far out into the Pacific Ocean, that it's known as the "Oceanic Point of Inaccessibility."

Such currents contribute to the distinct separation line that travelers often observe in photos and videos. Beyond the physical aspects, the meeting of the Pacific and Atlantic Oceans has long held symbolic and cultural significance. It represents a natural boundary between two vast and diverse ecosystems, each home to unique marine life adapted to its environment. This convergence zone also poses challenges for marine navigation, as the differing currents, temperatures, and wave patterns can create unpredictable conditions, making it a notorious area for sailors. Needless to say, there are dozens of shipwrecks around Cape Horn. Scientists study these oceanic differences to understand more about climate patterns, marine biodiversity, and the ways in which these two major bodies of water influence global systems.

A CHANGING LANDSCAPE

Beneath the icy exterior of Antarctica is a dynamic continental geologic plate. Tectonic plates are at work, and in places the continent is slowly being torn apart by rifting, similar to that in East Africa. Active volcanoes are found today in three primary areas of Antarctica: the western Ross Sea, including the stratovolcano Mount Erebus, which contains a permanent convect-

The Atlantic and Pacific meet at Cape Horn, at the southernmost tip of Chile, South America. In this region, a strong current carries water from west to east, sweeping water from the Pacific into the Atlantic. Antarctica has the most active volcano system in the world. It is also the home of the Jonah's icefish, which are the only vertebrate fish that do not have hemoglobin in their blood.

ing lake of molten magma (at 1000 degrees C); West Antarctica, where most volcanism occurs along the front of the Transantarctic Mountains; and in the Antarctica Peninsula, including Deception Island, which lies at the southern end of the Bransfield Strait.

Accelerated climate change is especially pronounced in certain regions of Antarctica. The Western Antarctic Peninsula is one of the most rapidly warming places on the planet. The average wintertime temperature in the Palmer area has risen more than six degrees Centigrade in the last 50 years. This has resulted in a decrease in winter sea-ice extent and has caused the glaciers to recede. Bob Farrell is the Station Chief of Palmer Base, and he pointed out a painting in the Palmer galley of "Pie Island" as it appeared in 1999 while still connected to Anvers Island by glacier. 15 years later the glacier connecting the two islands broke off on "Pie Day" March 14th and have not reconnected. The site of "Old Palmer" was revealed in 2004 to be a separate island (now named Amsler Island), and also not part of Anvers Island. In Arthur Harbor near the base, the Marr Ice Piedmont has receded, and two distinct islands have emerged. Bob Farrell has said in his 20 years at the base he has noticed the volume of the Anvers glacier reduce in size considerably, so much that you can see the high mountains behind the base that were not visible when he first arrived.

Effects of climate change have already been observed in many natural systems, on all continents and in most oceans. Glaciers are melting; frozen ground is thawing; and damage associated with coastal flooding is increasing. Recent changes in climate have already had significant impacts on biodiversity and ecosystems, including changes in species distributions, populations sizes, the timing of reproduction or migration, and higher frequency of pest and disease outbreaks.

Among the many changes as the local weather warms, chinstrap and gentoo penguins from the pari-Antarctic islands are moving southward and increasing in numbers, while the more cold-loving Adelies are decreasing (85% since 1974). By 2060, 30% of Adelie colonies are expected to be in decline with continued warming, and by 2099, that number is predicted to be 60% lower still. Yet, paradoxically, there are regions of Antarctica that are cooler and receive more snowfall on average. This may be why there has not been a drastic sea level rise in coastal areas.

The south geomagnetic pole focuses auroral and cosmic ray activity in the Southern Hemisphere. The Southern Lights of the polar region are called *aurora australis*. Scientists travel specifically to Antarctica to study auroras (named after the Roman goddess of the dawn). Millions of miles away, the sun produces electrically charged particles that are blown outwards across the solar system in a continuous "solar wind." As the solar wind passes the Earth, the charged particles are attracted by the planet's magnetic field and are drawn to its two geomagnetic poles. As the particles pass through the atmosphere, they interact with atoms, molecules and ions in the upper atmosphere, causing them to release as light.

The Southern Lights are very rarely seen by humans because of their extreme proximity. The Northern and Southern Lights occur almost simultaneously, but the *aurora australis* holds a particular mystique because so few people have been lucky enough to observe it in real time. This is because the majority of people visit Antarctica in the astral summer, when daylight hides aurora activity. It's only visible in Antarctica from April to October in the darkest months and best seen near the south geomagnetic pole, close to where the Russian Vostok Station is located.

ICE DOME DOMAINS

An entire previously unknown ecosystem has been discovered under the polar plateau on the covered landmasses of West and East Antarctica. Because of its volcanic activity, and the abundance of warm water and geothermal heat vents, the "Land of the Lost" is confirmed to have dozens, if not hundreds, of massive under-ice domes. There is a propensity for flora and fauna to exist in these realms of as-yet-discovered species. Scans under the ice sheet have confirmed over 150 subglacial lakes discovered in Antarctica, and many interconnect via under-ice rivers that eventually flow out to the sea.

Subglacial lakes empty into rivers at the base of large ice sheets and remain liquid, as opposed to Antarctica's seasonal frozen lakes on the surface. The under-ice lakes flow year 'round due to geothermal heating from the Earth, the insulating effect of the overriding ice, and the enormous pressure of the ice overburden. Meltwater collects in hollows, forming the lakes in bedrock indentures, and are connected to other lakes by under-ice rivers.

The first of the subglacial lakes were discovered in the late 1960s by British glaciologists using ice-penetrating radar. Over 150 subglacial lakes have been identified, most of which are about 3 to 6 kilometers (2 to 4 miles) in length. At Dome C, so many subglacial lakes have been discovered that it has been called the Antarctic "Lake District."

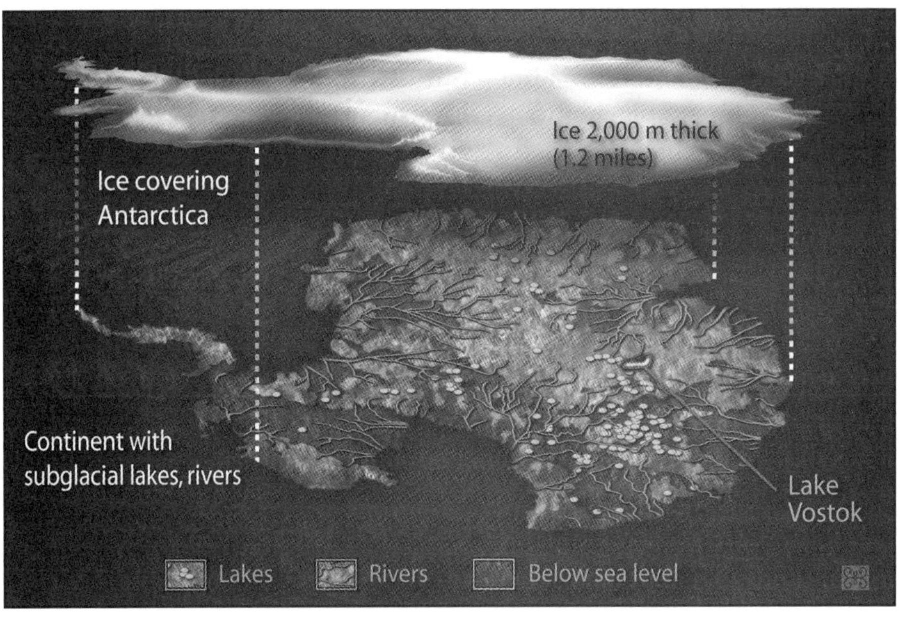

Much of the cutting edge scientific research is coming out of the South Pole Station. A previously unknown ecosystem has been discovered under the polar plateau, revealing over 150 subglacial interconnected lakes in East Antarctica alone. These subglacial lakes empty into rivers that flow year 'round due to geothermal heating to the sea, and has confirmed dozens of under-ice domes. There is a very strong probability that new lifeforms will be discovered in these ecosystems. The recent project WISSARD probing under the ice has determined there is more than meets the eye to a lost world never before seen by humans. Could subglacial Lake Vostok be a possible home to "alien" life?

Massive subglacial Lake Vostok is one of the largest freshwater lakes in the world that nobody has ever heard of. Lake Vostok is about the size of Lake Ontario and is much larger than any other subglacial lake. Lake Vostok is in the Top 10 List of the largest freshwater lakes in the world. It is 50 kilometers (31 miles) wide and extends in a crescent shape more than 240 kilometers (150 miles). It is located a few kilometers under the ice north from the Russian Vostok Station. Lake Vostok has very deep depths, approximately 510 meters (1680 feet) deep at its southern end, and is very old—possibly as old as 20 million years. Its trough formed well before the ice sheets covered Antarctica. No one expects marine mammals or other large sea creatures to exist in Lake Vostok, but biologists think there are unique microbes that use chemicals to power biological processes, leading researchers to postulate that Lake Vostok is a possible home to "alien life." The Vostok scientists also detected a certain bacteria that only grows on fish. These organisms would have developed in complete isolation from the outside world for as long as one million years. There are leaked reports that the Russians were able to lower SCUBA diver down to the lake, and they encountered a deadly squid-like creature called Organism 46-B that tore the limbs off the divers.

Lake Vostok was the first subglacial lake to be tapped, in 2011-2012, but samples were contaminated because of the kerosene used to keep the drill holes from freezing shut. A successful sample of Lake Vostok water was taken in 2016. By testing equipment in Antarctica, NASA seeks to solve different problems because it wants to use similar technology to explore Europa, one of the moons of Jupiter, which also contains kilometers-thick ice crusts covering a liquid ocean that some scientists suspect might harbor life, even alien life never before discovered.

Vostok Station rests on ice that is 3.7 kilometers (2.3 miles) thick, and because of the fierce winds and its elevation, it holds the record as the site of the lowest temperature measured on Earth: -89.2 degrees Celsius (-128.56 Fahrenheit), recorded on July 21st, 1983. The highest temperature ever recorded is a mere -12.3 Celsius (9.86 Fahrenheit), giving the station its enduring nickname "the Pole of Cold."

A WORLD UNDER THE ICE

One of the most captivating mysteries of Antarctica is its under-ice lakes and flowing rivers. Discovered in the 1970s through radar scans, there are around 400 of these lakes lying under a few kilometers of ice. These subglacial lakes, such as Lake Vostok, the largest among them, don't freeze due to the immense pressure exerted by the ice sheet above. Despite being sealed beneath the ice for over 20 million years, Lake Vostok's water temperature is approximately -3° C. In 2014, scientists made a groundbreaking discovery at Lake Whillans, where they found a thriving ecosystem of microorganisms using methane and ammonium as energy sources, even though they hadn't seen sunlight for millions of years.

A big discovery was made in the 2022-2023 season by the WISSARD project, which showed massive wetlands underneath the ice in Western Antarctica that likely contains life unseen anywhere else on this planet. The Whillans Ice Subglacial Access Research Drilling project was officially commissioned by the National Science Foundation to formally scan underneath Antarctica's ice. The discovery was made around 820 meters (2,700 feet) below the ice as WISSARD reported that they followed the Lake Whillans outflow to see where it emptied into the sea, only to find out that a massive cavity almost a kilometer below the ice exists.

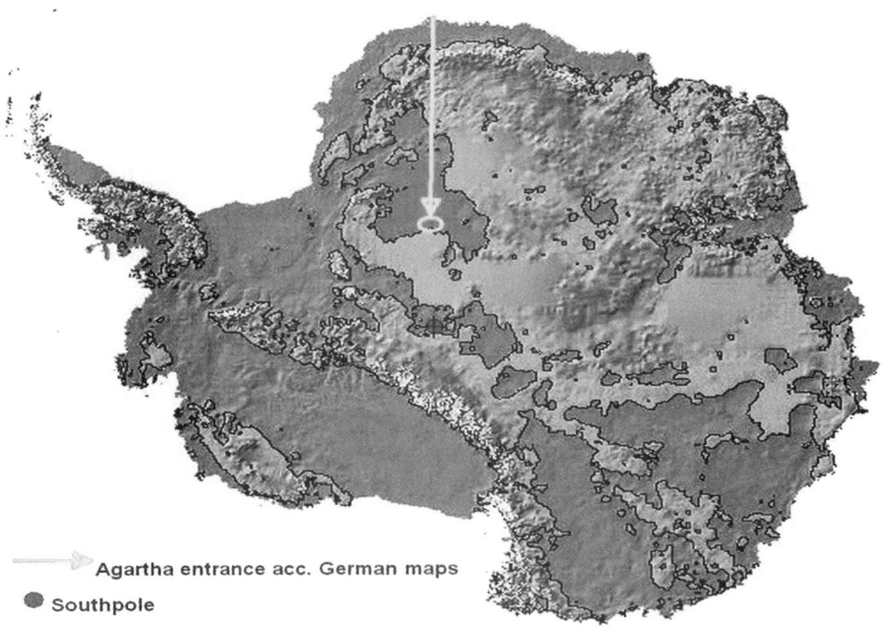

This entrance of the tunnel leading to the interior of Antarctica is about 50 kilometers off the coast, at a depth of 500 meters. In the time of U-boat production in World War II, this was as deep as a sub could reach at a very high risk, but the Germans had reportedly received secret techniques from the Aryans in Agartha how to overcome the huge pressure by using a double hull, with a fluid substance like liquid hydrogen in-between, and designing the "Walter" (Sterling) engine.

The largest subglacial lake is called Lake Vostok, one of the largest freshwater lakes in the world, and is filled with mysteries. The Russians were the first to drill through the Polar Plateau to take water samples, discovering a new form of bacteria. There are theories this bacteria comes from an unknown species of fish, and an entire freshwater ecosystem ready to be discovered. There are even leaked reports by Russian SCUBA divers in the lake being confronted by squid-like creatures that killed a few divers. It is also speculated there could be military or extraterrestrial bases at Lake Vostok and at other subglacial lakes in Antarctica.

Buried beneath the expansive ice sheets of Antarctica is one of the oldest mountain ranges on the planet. The majestic peaks of the Gamburtsev Mountains stretch across 1,200 kilometers (800 miles) and tower 3,000 meters (10,000 feet) high. They were discovered in 1958 by Russian scientists. Despite their age, which spans approximately a billion years, these mountains remain standing tall, mostly cloaked on all sides by ice. The mystery surrounding their origin and enduring existence continues to captivate researchers.

Another fascinating phenomenon is the "singing" of the Ross Ice Shelf. This immense ice sheet, several hundred meters thick, produces an eerie, haunting melody due to relentless winds sweeping across its snow dunes. These winds create surface vibrations, generating near-constant seismic tones. Although these vibrations are beyond the range of human hearing, scientists have captured and analyzed this icy symphony, which changes in response to environmental shifts.

Beyond mapping, the research of the moving glaciers helps scientists understand how ice flows over the terrain and how hidden warm water rivers beneath the ice influence glacial movement. These insights are crucial for predicting future ice loss and sea level rise. If all Antarctic ice were to melt, global sea levels could rise by 58 meters (190 feet), significantly reshaping coastlines and submerging coastal communities. Virtually all of Florida would be under water.

Interestingly, removing the 26.5 million cubic kilometer ice sheet would also cause the continent to rebound upwards, much like landmasses in the Northern Hemisphere have been rising since the last Ice Age. This study highlights the complex and dynamic nature of Antarctica's massive polar plateau, shaping both the continent and the world's oceans.

LAKE ENIGMA

Scientists peered into a secret Antarctic lake hidden beneath the ice for a closer look and uncovered a never-before-seen ecosystem teeming with strange microbial communities. The study was undertaken over the course of several seasons.

Antarctica's Lake Enigma certainly lives up to its name. The permanently ice-covered lake, named for the peculiar cone of frozen debris at its center, was until recently thought to be one solid chunk. But scientists have discovered a layer of fresh water hidden beneath the ice-covered surface—and it is populated by a diverse range of microorganisms.

During an expedition to Antarctica from November 2019 to January 2020, researchers surveyed the lake with ground-penetrating radar and detected at least 12 meters (40 feet) of liquid water under the ice. The researchers then drilled into the ice and sent a camera to explore the lake's depths.

The team first tested the water to determine where it originated. This was important to establish because the area has extremely low precipitation, high winds and intense solar evaporation, so any water in Lake Enigma should have dried up long ago. Based on the chemical composition of salts in the water, the researchers hypothesized that the lake's water is consistently replenished by the nearby Amorphous Glacier through an unknown underground pathway.

The scientists found that, despite being isolated from the atmosphere, the waters of Lake Enigma are home to several kinds of microbial life, which cover the bottom of the lake in blobs known as "microbial mats." Many of these organisms are photosynthetic, giving the lake a high concentration of dissolved oxygen.

Some of the mats formed thin, spiky coatings upon the lakebed. Others resembled "a crumpled thick carpet, sometimes forming large amorphous tree-like structures up to 40 centimeters (16 inches) high, and up to 50 to 60 centimeters (20 to 24 inches) in diameter," the researchers wrote in the study, published in the journal *Communications Earth and Environment.* [2]

The microbial residents included several species of Patescibacteria — tiny, single-celled organisms that attach themselves to larger host cells to form either mutually beneficial or predatory relationships. These organisms had never before been found in ice-cov-

2. https://www.livescience.com/planet-earth/antarctica/scientists-peered-beneath-a-frozen-antarctic-lake-and-uncovered-a-never-before-seen-ecosystem

ered lakes and don't normally thrive in high-oxygen conditions, suggesting that these Patescibacteria may have developed unique metabolic evolutionary traits to survive.

VOLCANIC TERRAIN

Over a billion years ago, Pangea or Gondwanaland once contained Antarctica and other continents as one super continent. This connection is known because of the same tropical flora and fauna species that are found in the fossil record within several continents which are now separated by vast oceans.

Plate tectonics suggest the continents can rise and fall abruptly during a pole shift event, colliding newer land masses with older remnants of the continent of Gondwanaland. Currently there are two landmasses: the newer West Antarctica joined by a grounded ice sheet to the very old landmass of East Antarctica. Radar penetrating under the ice has revealed the possibility of a water channel between the two landmasses. The rocky coastline of West Peninsula and the much older plate of East Antarctica meet each other along the TransAntarctic Mountains near the South Pole.

The grid plan for an ancient metropolis deep within a crack in Antarctica's ice can be found at the location coordinates: 76°08'10"S 162°28'39"E

Looking more thoroughly around the crack in the ice, there are what appear to be remnants of an ancient metropolis spread out organically just like cities do today. This Google Earth image is evidence of right-angle roads and walls that cannot be dismissed as a creation of Mother Nature.

The fifth largest continent Antarctica contains the most active volcano system in the world—with 93 geothermal locations and 14 known active volcanoes. There must be dozens more uncharted volcanoes and geothermal vents under the ice. Plate tectonics suggest the continents move abruptly during a pole shift event, thrusting portions of Antarctica in different directions. Through plate displacement the geologically younger West Peninsula and much older East Antarctica later joined near the South Pole. Both Ernest Shackleton and Captain Robert Scott found coal beds and plant fossils on their early explorations of the TransAntarctic Mountains—clearly indicating that the Antarctic was not always covered in ice. Since then much more fossil evidence of pre-glacial periods have been uncovered, including petrified wood sometimes in pieces as long as 20 meters (66 feet) and fossil pollen, but fossils of animals are much less common. These fossils provide evidence of the connections between the parts of the ancient continent Gondwanaland, give indirect information about the changes in the Antarctic climate over millions of years, volcanic activity, and offer an insight into the evolution of present Antarctic species.

MELTING ICE AND MOVING CONTINENTS

Might a pole shift be precipitated by the movement or melting of the Antarctic ice? Charles Hapgood, along with Albert Einstein, who wrote the preface to Hapgood's 1958 book, believed that the accumulation of ice at the north and south poles would be the trigger for a crustal displacement (geophysical pole shift). Einstein explained the triggering mechanism as follows:

> *In a polar region there is continual deposition of ice, which is not symmetrically distributed about the pole. The Earth's rotation acts on these unsymmetrically deposited masses, and produces centrifugal momentum that is transmitted to the rigid crust of the Earth. The constantly increasing centrifugal momentum produced in this way will, when it has reached a certain point, produce a movement of the Earth's crust over the rest of the Earth's body, and this will displace the polar regions toward the equator.*

This gives rise to the notion that portions of Atlantis might have existed on the Palmer Peninsula, and had drifted to their current location during the last pole shift. With all of the new findings coming out, and many of the discoveries that have been made which mainstream media completely ignores, we are clearly not being told about the true origins of humanity and ancient alien visitors. The idea that a powerful group of people protecting their interests by suppressing information in multiple fields is unsettling. For a planet and its people to thrive, it must live in complete transparency.

The National Geographic Society first began making maps in 1915, but the society had only formally recognized just four oceans, which they defined by the continents that bordered them in the Arctic, Pacific, Atlantic and Indian Oceans. In contrast, the newly appointed Southern Ocean is defined not by the continents that surround it, but by the Antarctic Circumpolar Current (ACC) that flows from west to east. Scientists think the ACC was created 34 million years ago when the Western continent of Antarctica separated from South America, allowing water to flow unimpeded around the "bottom" of the world.

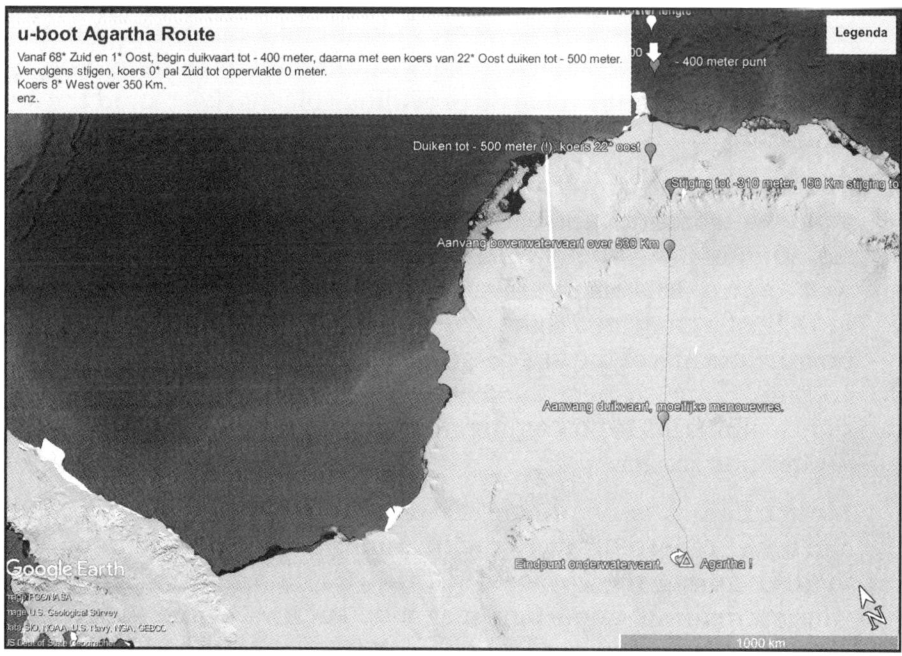

At the end of the trip, the German Navy map says to continue due south at full speed with a Zero degree heading south. After two days they will see a lighthouse from the port of Agartha, and continue for the light. The map even instructs the captain to then open another numbered set of instructions on the appropriate protocol interacting with the people in Agartha!

This Google map created by Dutch researcher Frank van dem Kommer shows the approximate route, and location of Agartha. He plotted along the "one degree longitude," and the distances. That's how he came to the exact location of Agartha under the ice.

In addition to the Geographic (Geodetic) and the Ceremonial Pole at 90 degrees south location at the southern end of the Earth's rotational axis, where all the lines of longitude meet, there are three other poles. Although the South Magnetic Pole drifts northwest by about 5 to 10 kilometers per year (currently off the coast near Commonwealth Bay), this is where a magnetic needle will try to point straight down. The South Geomagnetic Pole also moves, and this is where the Earth's electromagnetic field would manifest if it were the extension of a dipole magnet placed at the Earth's center. Russia's Vostok Station is nearby, and the Pole of Maximum Inaccessibility, which is the point furthest away, in all directions, from any Antarctic coastlines.

"MONATOMIC GOLD" COMING OUT OF MOUNT EREBUS

The most active volcano in Antarctica spews tiny crystals of gold worth thousands of dollars per day. It sounds like a dream, but it's true in Antarctica, where gold literally rains from the sky. Tucked in among the glaciers, fiery Mount Erebus is the southernmost active volcano on Earth, providing volcanic heat amid the icy landscape.

The frozen continent features 138 volcanoes, according to a 2017 study, with around nine of them reported as active. With a summit elevation of 3,794 meters (12,448 feet), Mount Erebus is the most well-known. It is also the location of the Air New Zealand crash in 1979 of a chartered sightseeing trip that killed all 257 people on board. Remains of the wreckage are still visible on the slopes of the volcano. Some suspect the plane was shot down to prevent more sightseeing trips from coming. None ever have returned, since the mysterious crash.

Mount Erebus is one of three volcanoes that form Ross Island, and it was reportedly in a state of erupting when it was discovered in 1841 during the voyage of British Captain James Clark Ross, who carried out important magnetic surveys in the Arctic and Antarctic and discovered and named the Ross Sea and the Victoria Land region of Antarctica. "HMS Erebus" was the name of one of his ships.

Because the landscape of fire and ice is so extreme, scientists observe the volcano through the Mount Erebus Volcano Observatory and conduct field campaigns to look for exotic life forms that can exist in such harsh conditions. The largest Antarctic settlement called McMurdo Station, operated by the United States, is located about 42 kilometers (25 miles) south of Mount Erebus, and is within sight of the volcano.

Satellite images of the volcano reveal a lava lake that has been bubbling since at least 1972, according to *IFL Science*. It is one of only a few volcanoes in the world with a constant lake of lava. In its excited state of eruption, the volcano regularly pumps out plumes of gas and steam and has been known to eject boulders of partially molten rock known as "volcanic bombs."

While volcanic bombs are interesting to observe, it's the bursts of gas spraying tiny crystals of metallic gold that has surprised scientists, who estimate the volcano spews around 80 grams of gold a day, that can be worth around $8,000.

What's more, the gold has been found hundreds of miles away from Mount Erebus, depending on the direction the wind is blowing. Antarctic researchers have detected traces of the gold dust in ambient air up to 621 miles away from the volcano. [3]

THE "BLOOD" FALLS

There is a very alien ecosystem that is very slowly pouring out of the Taylor Glacier in one of the McMurdo Dry Valleys. When geologists first discovered the frozen waterfall in 1911, they thought the red color came from algae, but its true nature turned out to be something much more spectacular.

Roughly two million years ago, the Taylor Glacier sealed beneath it a small body of water which contained an ancient community of microbes. Trapped below a thick layer of ice, they have remained there ever since, isolated inside a natural time capsule. Evolving independently of the rest of the living world, these microbes exist in a place with no light or free oxygen and little heat, and are essentially the definition of a "primordial ooze." The trapped lake has very high salinity and is rich in iron, which gives the waterfall its red color. A fissure in the glacier allows the subglacial lake to flow out, forming the falls without contaminating the closed ecosystem within.

The existence of the Blood Falls ecosystem shows that life can exist in the most extreme conditions on Earth. Though tempting to make the connection, it does not prove, however, that life could exist on other planets with similar environments and similar bodies of frozen water—notably Mars and Jupiter's moon Europa—as such life would have to arise from a completely different chain of events.

3. Monica Danielle https://www.upi.com/amp/Odd_News/2024/04/25/Mount-Erebus-volcano-gold/3971714052176/

Even if it doesn't confirm the existence of extraterrestrial life, Antarctica's Blood Falls is a wonder to behold both visually and scientifically. The Dry Valleys are only accessible by helicopter from McMurdo Station (USA), Scott Base (New Zealand), or a cruise ship in the Ross Sea and trekking several miles overland. [4]

STRANGE ANIMALS

It is clear that there have been world-shifting changes in Earth's ancient past. The skeletons of monster-size dinosaurs being uncovered in Antarctica is definitive proof, including a *Cryolophosaurus ellioti* land animal which lived during the early Jurassic period in Antarctica. This dinosaur weighed at least 1,000 pounds, stood 8.2 feet at the hips, and was more than 20 feet in length. Scientists say the reptile was only a sub-adult, which begs the question on how big his parents became. According to the Geological Society of America, *Cryolophosaurus ellioti* is the most complete dinosaur skeleton ever found in Antarctica. It was discovered in 188 to 196-million-year-old sediment. At that time, Antarctica was covered in dense jungles and had a tropical climate.

Furthermore, some dinosaur bones uncovered, such as *Kryostega collinsoni,* are unique to Antarctica. Two large capitosaurids, *Paratosuchus* and *Kryostega collinsoni,* with skulls nearly a meter long, lived during the Middle Triassic. *Kryostega collinsoni* is a new genus and species found only in Antarctica.

Ribs of a prosauropod were found in the mouth of a cryolophosaur when it died, leading to the assumption that the carnivore may have choked to death on its last meal. Prosauropods were smaller (7.5 m-long) predecessors to the well-known large sauropods (*Apatosaurus, Brachiosaurus*) of the later Jurassic. A new taxon was named (*Glacialisaurus hammeri*), the second dinosaur known to be unique to Antarctica. [5]

Marine biologists at the Argentinian Brown Research Station located on the Palmer Peninsula study the *Chaenocephalus aceratus,* or the commonly named Ice Fish, which are endemic only to the ocean waters surrounding Antarctica. They use the underside of the ice shelves to lay their eggs, usually around 10-20,000 eggs per laying. Penguins feed on the juvenile Ice Fish, while several species of seals rely on the adult Jonah's Icefish to survive. These keystone species of fish can grow to about two feet long (70 cm).

---

4. https://www.atlasobscura.com/places/blood-falls

5. Aver buck, Alexis, *Antarctica,* Lonely Planet Publications, 2017.

Members of the Ice Fish family unique to the Southern Ocean have no hemoglobin. Instead of having red blood like most other fish, it is "white" or translucent. Other traits that make these fish unique are the bones are reduced in weight with less calcium, and the glyco-proteins in their bodies contain "anti-freeze" proteins in their blood. Oxygen is carried in their blood plasma, but this has only 10% of the oxygen-carrying capacity of fish blood containing hemoglobin. To make up for this, Ice Fish have more blood, a larger heart, larger blood vessels and more gill surface area, and can even exchange oxygen through their tails. There are multiple sub-species of the mackerel Ice Fish which only exist in the Southern Ocean in subzero waters without freezing to death.

WHO CLAIMS IT?

Though no country holds indisputable title over any part of Antarctica, eight nations have territorial claims. This sovereignty is not internationally recognized, but the eight nations

In addition to other terrestrial animal fossils found, large extinct marine plesiosaurs have been found on the islands near the Antarctic Peninsula. These long-necked animals with paddle-shaped fins (made famous by the Loch Ness Monster) are not dinosaurs but lived concurrently. One of the more spectacular plesiosaur specimens was discovered on Vega Island in 2005. It is a nearly complete, well-preserved juvenile plesiosaur that was apparently killed suddenly by a volcanic eruption.

(Argentina, Chile, the UK, Norway, New Zealand, USA, Australia and France) continue to strengthen their own claims of control. From 2007 to 2009, for example, the UK, Chile and Argentina all filed for rights to mine on Antarctica's sea floor. All agree on reserving Antarctica for peace, prohibiting nuclear explosions and guaranteeing the freedom of science.

Signed in 1959 by the 12 nations operating bases in Antarctica at the time, and now by 56 nations, the Antarctic Treaty ensures that countries active on the continent and surrounding islands south of 60 degrees consult on the uses of resources. It is also where there are no wars, where the environment is fully protected, and where research is the priority. Even guidelines designed to limit the cumulative impact of tourism have been adopted. Treaty countries agree that Antarctica remains peaceful, and a demilitarized place of international cooperation and scientific research, open to all, but with a minimum of human impact.

The time of strict military expeditions to Antarctica is long past. This all happened during World War II. Other military activities during the 1950s and early 60s led to the ground breaking Antarctic Treaty. Since that was signed in 1959, there has only been military support of Antarctic expeditions and base support, but direct military expeditions or testing of weapons is prohibited. The Treaty states: "Antarctica shall continue forever to be used exclusively for peaceful purposes, and shall not become the scene or object of international discord."

There are no permanent human residents in Antarctica, although there are always some people there. 60 scientific stations operate year 'round by the Antarctic programs of 23 nations. The winter population at the bases is about 1,000; and this number increases to around 3,750 in the summer. Roughly one third of these are scientists, while the others are support staff. Tourism season begins in November until March. For every 100 people in Antarctica, 56 would be tourists; 38 would be staff and crew; and only six would be scientists.

Some travel is restricted south of the 60th parallel. Only non-military scientific research stations are allowed to erect permanent structures under the ratification of the 1959 Antarctic Treaty. Independent sea travelers must register in the Ushuaia, Argentina Naval Base and Customs Office. All ships must submit an itinerary and submit passports for all persons on board. It is the one place in the world where you will get stamped out, but not stamped back in until you return to the country of departure.

PRE-WAR GERMANY'S KEEN INTEREST IN THE ICE CONTINENT

The actual beginnings of German interest in both polar regions may date back before the earliest U.S. Navy polar expeditions. For instance, one segment of the PBS show *NOVA* related that the remains of Captain Charles Hall of the ill-fated Polaris expedition, one of the first American ventures to the North Pole, were discovered in an ice grave by a subsequent polar expedition. It seemed that when the body was examined it was found to contain poison. It was also found by searching the records that the cook (who

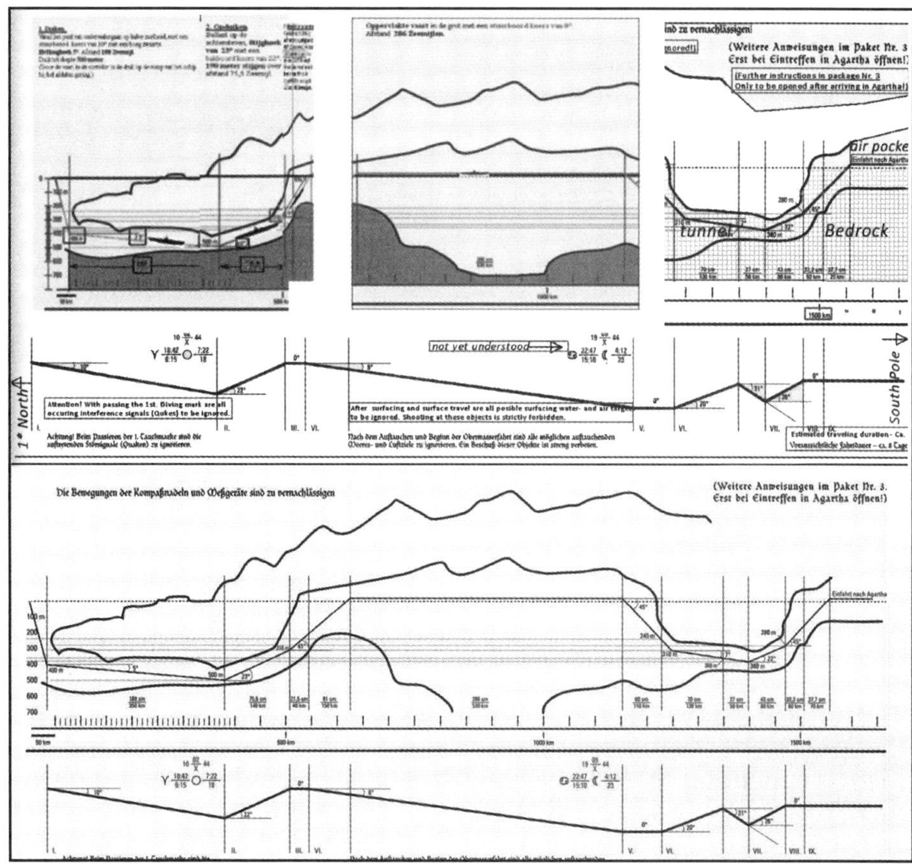

This German Navy map was acquired by Russian Journalist Nikolay Subbotin who bought it along with other old KGB / World War II Nazi files at a "flea market" in Moscow. It contains many exact diving instructions with courses, depths, angles of decent and trim, sea-miles to travel and days to travel. All written in Gothic characters. It is even known that this map was made in a sub camp of the "Buchenwald" concentration camp by specialized design and graphically educated printers and editors. English captions added by Dutch researcher Frank van dem Kommer.

would be in the perfect position to administer poison) and the first mate on the Polaris expedition were both German occultist spies!

Take note that the German secret societies of Bavaria, which had helped to precipitate the First and Second World Wars date back to ancient times when—following the occupation of Egypt—the Holy Roman Empire military forces based in Germany, and the seat of government for the Holy Roman Empire, brought back from Egypt the black Gnostic "Serpent Cults" which later gave rise

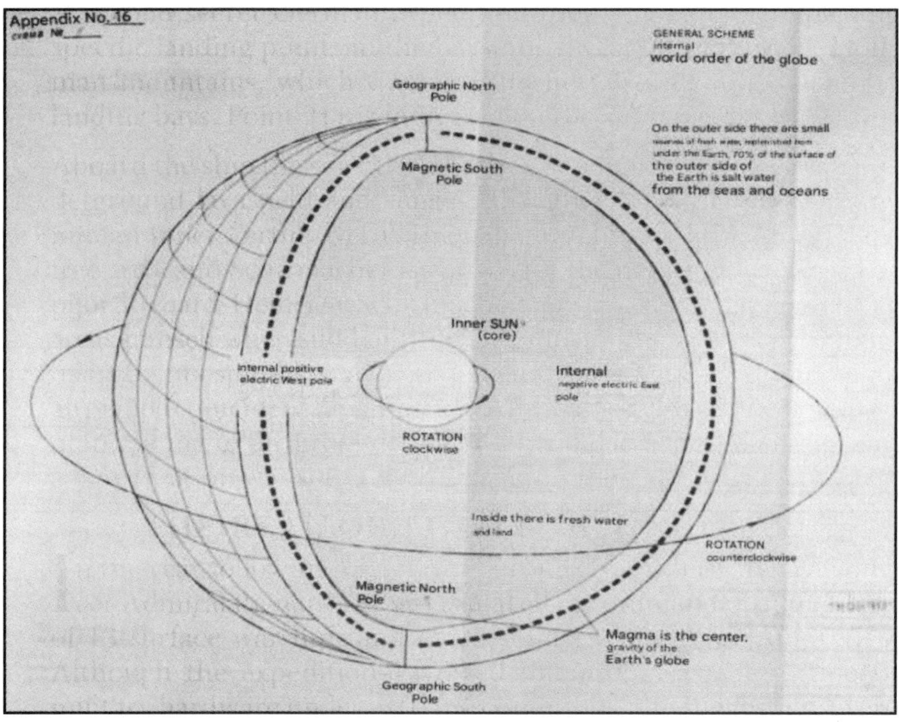

The Russian study called the "Orion File" is a multi-file report based on the Ahnenerbe documents captured at the end of World War II. Indeed, there is a mention of "Agartha" based on the Ahnenerbe conclusion that there really is an Inner Earth! And the Soviets were very anxious to find an entrance to it. Based on all the very detailed conclusions the Germans made, researcher Frank van den Kommer can only conclude "their detailed scientific data have their origin *from the Arianni!* They refer to and cite facts that we today can only start to grasp with or computers and satellites. The Germans wrote about it in the early 1940s. They describe planetary revolutions, distances, mass and elementary compositions, etc. They knew about it! The Soviets, in 1982 and 1983 with the first computers, were able to confirm these findings."

to the Bavarian Illuminati, the Bavarian Thule Society, and a host of other Satanic racist cults which gravitated around these other two. Could the occultist spies who sabotaged the Polaris expedition have been attempting to protect a secret hidden deep within the polar regions? Could this secret have had something to do with an ancient collaboration between Bavarian Satanic cults and reptilian-based aliens in Antarctica?

The Germans had long held an interest in the South Polar region of Antarctica, with the first Germanic research of that area being undertaken in 1873 when Sir Eduard Dallman (1830-1896) discovered new Antarctic routes with his ship the *Gronland* during his expedition for the German Polar Navigation Company of Hamburg.

Early on, the Germans considered the idea of "taking" the land mass of Antarctica in the name of Germany. While most other nations were content in just exploring and going home, the Germans were already considering what might be gained if they established a lasting colony on the Ice Continent, and how this might well offer Germany the land that it so badly needed to grow. At the time, the conditions there were so harsh that the equipment of the era would not allow men to survive through the brutal winters on the surface, so it had to be put off. But the idea was never forgotten in Berlin.

Over the next 75 years at least three further missions took place, and two complete expeditions were fulfilled, namely in 1910 under Wilhem Filchner with his ship *Deutschland*, and in 1925 under the command of Albert Merz on the polar expedition ship the *Meteor*. The top-secret *Atlantis* research vessel launched right after the "Richter Expedition" returned on the *Schwabenland*. The *Atlantis* was under the commission of Captain Bernard Rogge and set sail on December 19th, 1939. Besides hoisting weapons, Rogge was a master of disguises for his ship, and would at different times pose as a British, Japanese, Russian, Norwegian or Dutch ship flying a "false flag." In the early years of World War II, the *Atlantis* created havoc with Allied shipping lanes by approaching enemy ships under the guise of being a friend, then suddenly revealing the guns and forcing the other ship to surrender. The German U-boats followed the same practice all across the North and South Atlantic, but would more commonly torpedo and sink enemy ships. The U-boats also discovered nautical routes under the ice and deep into the interior of Antarctica.

THE ELITE IN SEARCH OF THE "ILLUMINATI DISNEYLAND"?

Fast forward to the middle teens of the new century, and a very curious assortment of visitors to Antarctica arrived. The most unusual was U.S. Secretary of State John Kerry during the lead-up to one of America's most contested presidential elections. Rather than campaigning for his party in a pivotal election, active Secretary of State John Kerry flew down there on Election Day, 2016, as a "climate champion." Adding to the mystery were all the high profile celebrities, politicians, and royal family members making a journey to the White Continent. There seemed to be a window of opportunity in 2016-2017 when dozens of the elite were going down there. And what might they be going to see? The most notable of other visitors were: Former House Speaker Newt Gingrich and his wife Calesta Gingrich, who also served as the U.S. ambassador to the Vatican; Actor Tom Hanks (recently accused of sexual harassment); several heads of the defense force and senior cabinet ministers from New Zealand; the Governor-General, His Excellency General the Honorable Sir Peter Cosgrove AK MC (retired from Australia), and Lady Cosgrove; and possibly Barack Obama, who wanted to extend his trip after his Argentina Patagonia visit to San Carlos de Bariloche. Obama had been vocal about wanting to limit tourism to Antarctica.

Secretary of State John "ketchup" Kerry, who took time during a diplomatic junket in 2016, to divert to the polar continent, ostensibly to get a first-hand look at "global warming." The fact that this occurred during a diplomatic junket led many to speculate that perhaps the real purpose of the diversion was to conduct high-level secret diplomacy, perhaps with a world leader, or perhaps with "someone else," away from prying public eyes. Or was Secretary Kerry summoned there?

Another curious arrival was the Russian Orthodox Patriarch of Moscow, Kiril III, who went down there to bless a tiny Orthodox chapel in 2017. When Kiril III came back, he warned Vladimir Putin and the rest of the world that the Apocalypse is upon them. Russian Orthodox Patriarch of Moscow Kirill III, who, fresh from a meeting with "*Novis Ordo* Roman Catholic" Pope Francis in Havana, Cuba travelled directly to Antarctica after the papal meeting. Again, there was a "story" that was put out that the Patriarch of Moscow went there to bless the Orthodox chapel that had been built. Indeed, the Russians did build a chapel there, but basically any hierarch could have blessed it. But the *Patri-*

DIVE AT THE POINT WITH THE COORDINATES: EXACT JUNCTION: 68° SOUTHERN LATITUDE AND 1° EASTERN LONGITUDE, TO A DEPTH OF 400 METERS.

THESE INSTRUCTION MUST BE STRICTLY FOLLOWED !

1. Diveing. From the point of descent at full speed, a starboard slope of 10° with a permissible angle, angle inclination of 5°. Distance 188 nautical miles. Predetermined depth-500 meters. (Driving in a corridor reduces the pressure on the hull during maneuvering.)

2. Surfacing. Ballast with a stern trim, area angle 23° with a port slope of 22°. Distance 75.5 nm. (Nautical mile)

3. Difficult maneuver ! Emerge. Ballast with a Heck covering, surface angle 410. 110 meters up, distance 21.5 Nautical miles. Then starboard slope of 80 to the surface in the cave. Distance 81 nm.

4. Sailing on the surface of the cave with a starboard slope of 80. Distance 286 nm.

5th, 6th difficult maneuver ! Immerse. With a pulling weight pressure of 450 to a depth of 240 meters, distance 60 nautical miles. Then with a ramping of 20°, with the descent continuing to 310 metres to the entrance of the corridor. After the 310-metre marking, the permissible descent must be continued. Diving angle 7° to 360 meters. Distance 70 Nautical miles. Further starboard slope from 31° to a depth of 380 meters.

7. Diving. Tolerance, surface angle 22°. 100 meters up with a rampin of 26°. Distance 43 Nautical miles.

8. Surface. Rear upholstery. Dive angle 45°, continuously straight ahead, until you see Agartha on the surface.

9. Heading for Agartha. Full speed. Head straight until the lighthouse light goes out. Changes to the magnetic poles take place. The movements of the compass needles and measuring instruments are negligible!
(Further instructions in package No. 3. Only open when you arrive in Agarha!).

Diving instructions translated in English

Karte für das Passieren der Meerestiefen

Nur beim Manövrieren verwenden !

Anweisung zum Passieren von Räumen und Koordinaten zur Fahrt nach Agartha.

ABTAUCHEN AM PUNKT MIT DEN KOORDINATEN: EXAKTER SCHNITTPUNKT: 68° SÜDLICHER BREITE UND 1° ÖSTLICHER LÄNGE, AUF EINE TIEFE VON 400 METERN.

Der Anweisung ist strikt zu folgen !

1. Abtauchen. Vom Punkt des Abtauchens mit halber Fahrt, einer Steuerbord-Schräglage von 10° mit einer Buglastigkeit. Neigungswinkel 5°. Entfernung 188 sm. Vorgegebene Tiefe – 500 Meter. (Aufgrund des Fahrens im Korridor ist der Druck auf den Schiffskörper beim Manövrieren ein unwesentlicher.)

2. Auftauchen. Ballast mit einer Hecktrimmung, Auftauchwinkel 23° mit einer Backbord-Schräglage von 22°. 190 Meter nach oben. Entfernung 75,5 sm.

3. Schwieriges Manöver ! Auftauchen. Ballast mit einer Hecktrimmung. Auftauchwinkel 41°. Fahrt – geradeaus. 110 Meter nach oben. Entfernung 21,5 sm. Danach Steuerbord-Schräglage von 8° bis zum Auftauchen an die Oberfläche in der Grotte. Entfernung 81 sm.

4. Fahrt an der Oberfläche innerhalb der Grotte mit einer Steuerbord-Schräglage von 8°. Entfernung 286 sm.

5., 6. Schwieriges Manöver! Abtauchen. Mit einer Buglastigkeit, Neigungswinkel 45°. Bis auf eine Tiefe von 240 Metern. Entfernung 60 sm. Danach mit einer Backbord-Schräglage von 20°, wobei das Abtauchen bis auf 310 Meter bis zur Einfahrt in den Korridor fortgesetzt wird. Nach der Marke 310 Meter ist das Abtauchen mit einer Buglastigkeit fortzusetzen. Abtauchwinkel 7° bis auf 360 Meter. Entfernung 70 sm. Weiter Steuerbord-Schräglage von 31° bis auf eine Tiefe von 380 Metern.

7. Abtauchen. Buglastigkeit. Auftauchwinkel 22°. 100 Meter nach oben mit einer Backbord-Schräglage von 26°. Entfernung 43 sm.

8. Auftauchen. Hecktrimmung. Auftauchwinkel 45°, immer geradeaus, bis zu Auftauchen an die Oberfläche von Agartha. Entfernung 70 sm.

9. Fahrt nach Agartha. Volle Fahrt. Fahrt geradeaus, bis das neue Licht ausgemacht wird. Änderungen der Magnetpole. Die Bewegungen der Kompaßnadeln und Meßgeräte sind zu vernachlässigen!

(Weitere Anweisungen im Paket Nr. 3.
Erst bei Eintreffen in Agartha öffnen!)

The orders for this "Map for Passing of the Ocean Depths" instructs the crew to sail straight "to the lighthouse of Agartha," without naming the U-boat base or the City of the Ases. The detailed diving instructions are on the map. A verified German U-boat seaman's letter back home that read: "The Earth is hollow! The whole crew is well but they cannot come back. We are not prisoners."

arch? At his elderly age? At approximately the same time, Turkey announced that it wanted a "share" in Antarctica and would be starting its own outposts there, and there was a strange story from Saudi Arabia that they had found "something" while excavating parts of Mecca, and that the "something" was so dangerous they contacted the infidel Patriarch of Moscow to take it and deal with it. It is said the deadly stampede in Mecca in September, 2015 was a cover story for the 2236 people who died from an energy blast emanating from the Ark of Gabriel when it was first uncovered. Months later an armada of Russian warships arrived in Jeddah, Saudi Arabia to supposedly transport the Ark of Gabriel and repatriate the relic to Antarctica. But the media portrayed the blessing and consecration of the chapel, then the Patriarch posed for some photo-ops with the penguins, and returned to his daily routine in Moscow.

Pope Francis made mention in October, 2023 that he would be the first Roman Catholic pope to visit Antarctica. Just before Patriarch Kirill visited a Russian Antarctic research station as part of a trip to Latin America, his trip included a historic meeting with Pope Francis in Cuba. Seemingly, if the Patriarch can do it, the Papacy should not be "one-upped" by the Orthodox, and assert its own presence there. Several articles suggested a pope visit goes on to mention that there have been Catholic chapels on the continent under the jurisdiction of Argentina's military bishopric. But Pope Francis never went. It is not clear if the new Pope Leo XIV will visit instead.

All sorts of European royals had made trips down there, beginning with Prince Philipp of Britain. Other notables among the world's royal elitists who have made recent visits to feed the penguins include Prince Harry of Great Britain and King Juan Carlos of Spain.

Great Britain's Prince Harry went in November 2013, on a visit that was a "charity function" for wounded soldiers. Prince Harry joined one of three teams of wounded servicemen and women to ski or trek to the geographic South Pole for "Walking With the Wounded South Pole Allied Challenge." But why cross-country ski one degree away from the South Pole when there is absolutely nothing to see on the Polar Plateau for hundreds of miles in all directions? Unless they gained permission to see the giant hole in the ice about 50 kilometers (35 miles) from the South Pole.

King Juan Carlos of Spain and his Queen made a little trek through the Straits of Magellan on a Chilean navy vessel, before the King "fulfilled an ambition" by visiting Antarctica in 2004.

And what else might these elite be allowed to see in the "Illuminati Disneyland?" The biggest prize would be being able to go inside one of the three massive multi-mile-wide discs. Leaked images of one of the three "mother ships" buried over a mile deep under the Antarctic ice, showing the top portion being slowly exposed even more each summer as the ice shelf retreats. First discovered in 1975, one massive craft continues to reveal itself more and more each Antarctic summer with the receding ice field, and reportedly can be entered at a location called "the door," possibly at the German Kohnen base. Is this what all the elite are flocking down to the Southern Continent to see? Or is there even more than this?

Let's not forget the story about Buzz Aldrin visiting Antarctica in December, 2016. The Apollo 11 "Moon astronaut," another penguin lover, supposedly tweeted: "We are all in danger! It is evil itself!" alongside an image of the Antarctica Great Pyramid. Aldrin was then evacuated from the Antarctic with a medical emergency and put in quarantine.

In 2016, legendary astronaut Buzz Aldrin (the second man to walk on the moon) visited Antarctica on what was described as a "scientific expedition." What happened next is still unexplained.
Shortly after arriving, Aldrin tweeted a cryptic warning:
"We are all in danger. It is evil itself."
Then, just as quickly as it appeared, the tweet was deleted.
Aldrin was rushed out of Antarctica after reportedly falling ill. Official reports claim it was due to altitude sickness, but sources and friends like David Adair say he was shaken, terrified, and unwilling to discuss what he had seen.

Several decades earlier, Colonel Fletcher Prouty, one time Pentagon-CIA-White House liaison officer loyal to President John F. Kennedy, was dispatched by his boss, none other than General Ed Lansdale of Yamashita's gold-Three-Tramps-in-Dallas-on-the-day-of-the-assassination fame, to accompany some dignitaries to and from Antarctica during the exact time period of the JFK assassination. L. Fletcher Prouty wrote about how the CIA controls the USA and world governments in his book *The Secret Team.* He was played by actor Donald Sutherland in Oliver Stone's movie *JFK.* Another interesting coincidence that Prouty would be sent to Antarctica at the same time the president would be killed.

LOST LANDS AND PATAGONIA GIANTS

"There were giants in the Earth in those days; and also after that, when the sons of God came in unto the daughters of men, and they bear *children* to them, the same *became* mighty men which were of old, men of renown." —*Genesis*, 6:4

COULD the land of Antarctica actually be considered a "lost continent?" Researchers from Kiel University in Germany and the British Antarctic Survey think so. Underneath Antarctica's millions of square miles of ice, lies a bedrock foundation similar to every other continent. There are flat plains, inlets to the sea and towering mountain ranges, but almost entirely covered over by an ice sheet. These scientists now say they've discovered a collection of hidden continents under Antarctica left over from millions of years ago. The researchers were relying on data from the European Space Agency's GOCE satellite. GOCE was a simple satellite that measured the pull of Earth's gravity as it orbited the planet. Using data from that satellite, the researchers took a look at Antarctica under the ice. They discovered geologic structures called cratons, which are the core regions of most tectonic plates. They also found orogens, which are folded-up regions of plates that are the precursors to mountain ranges. By studying the amount of cratons and orogens, researchers can compare the continental plates beneath Antarctica to other regions around the world.

The closest continental land mass to Antarctica is South America. Patagonia is a geographic region that covers the southern tip of South America with a shared border by Argentina and Chile. It is famous for its remarkable and varied landscapes, including

A pyramid-shaped structure in Antarctica can be seen on Google Earth at coordinates 79°58'39.25"S 81°57'32.2"W, located in the Ellsworth Mountain range. It has been given the nickname the Great Pyramid of Antarctica.

arid plains, rugged mountains, glaciers, dense forests and crystal-clear glacial lakes. At its southern end is the archipelago of *Tierra del Fuego*, the "Land of Fire." It is one of the few regions in the world where virgin forests and unspoiled nature still exists. During the Age of Discovery, European explorers witnessed and interacted with a very tall tribe of white-skinned natives. They were renowned for wearing next to nothing in one of the most inhospitable climates in the world.

PYRAMIDS ON THE ICE CONTINENT

Ancient astronaut theorists say that below the ice there are remnants of an antediluvian civilization that once existed in Antarctica when it had a much different climate. These remnants could be from Atlantis, or an even earlier civilization. Poking out from the ice fields are several distinct four-sided pyramids. There is a 300 million-year-old pyramid-like structure in Antarctica, located in the southern part of the Ellsworth Mountains, in an area called the Heritage Range. Indeed, there's a mountain that looks like a giant pyramid. It's about two square kilometers on all four sides, and 1,260 meters (4,150 feet) tall. The shape is so perfect that it almost seems unnatural, or crafted by the hand of a higher intelligence. Glaciologist Eric Rignot from the University of

This peak, first noted during Lincoln Ellsworth's 1935 flight, gained attention online around 2016 due to its striking four-sided shape, resembling a pyramid. It stands about 4,150 feet tall, and measures approximately two kilometers on each side.

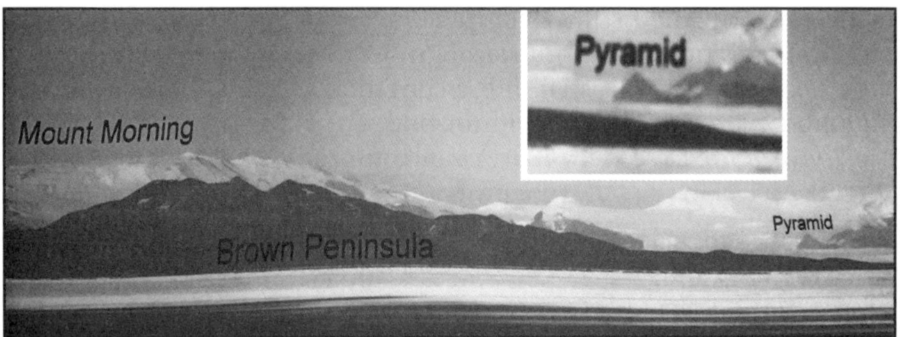

The McMurdo Sound is an open-water sea in Antarctica, known as the southernmost passable body of water in the world, located approximately 1,300 kilometers from the South Pole. Captain James Clark Ross discovered the sound in February of 1841 and named it after Lieutenant Archibald McMurdo of the *HMS Terror*. On official maps of the McMurdo Sound is a curious landform indicated as "Pyramid."

California-Irvine explains, "This is just a mountain that looks like a pyramid." Still, its sharp, pyramid-like shape makes it feel like a mystery hidden in the ice.

"Pyramid shapes are not impossible—many peaks partially look like pyramids, but they only have one to two faces like that, rarely four," he explained.

He went on to explain that the huge points emerging from the land are known as "pyramidal peaked mountains," or nunataks that are formed from the convergence of glaciers on the sides of an existing landmass. [1]

There are four known pyramids (or pyramidal-shaped mountains) that exist in Antarctica. A curious pyramid in Antarctica is located directly south of the German Neumayer Station in the Shackleton Range of mountains, offshore from the Filchner Ice Shelf. There are different coordinates offered for multiple locations of pyramids, and even others are reported to remain completely covered under the ice. Another one poking through the ice is off the McMurdo Sound, simply identified on official maps as "pyramid." It is located near Mount Mourning and the Brown Peninsula across the wide bay from McMurdo Station. Another pyramid appears to be directly south of New Zealand in Oates Land.

The many pyramid-shaped mini-mountains in Antarctica could harken back to the times when Antarctica was the fabled conti-

1. https://www.ladbible.com/news/science/pyramid-mountain-antarctica-explained-874461-20240203

nent of Atlantis, with a good-sized population that needed the convenience of advanced flying crafts to get around their then-tropical paradise. Some researchers contend that the Great Pyramid of Antarctica in the Ellsworth Heritage Range is the smoking gun for an antediluvian civilization. Others dismiss such claims and call these "nunataks," or simply attractive pyramidal-shaped mountains poking up through the ice.

In 2012, a satellite image took a picture of a mysterious oval with a very symmetrical shape in one of the most remote regions of Antarctica. At over 120 meters (400 feet) across, it appears with too many perfect geometric lines within it to be a random natural formation, but appears to have been crafted by an intelligent race. Another image from Google Earth looks to be a pair of step pyramids, within the design of a very precisely angular city grid plan. However the skeptics care to explain away these monuments, it should be remembered that Mother Nature does not create perfect right angle symmetry in building form.

Several of these pyramids can still be viewed on Google Earth today, though some claim visibility has changed over time due to snow cover or updates. This pyramid near Oates Land is located at 73°3'33.80"S 167°56'52.15"E

IN SEARCH OF ATLANTIS?

Of all the strange goings on down in Antarctica, there seems to be some kind of intersection. The locations are related, or tied together somehow, by the list of people visiting the continent. It is evident that there is a lot of uninhabited land down there, and that the moment it became clear that the Piri Re'is map showed the coastline of the continent, a small group of people realized its significance. Just imagine the implications: an entire continent under ice, that is to say, under water. It is suggestive of Atlantis. It is suspected that the moment this was realized, that the hunt was on for its lost technology, archives, and corroborating evidence. But most importantly, perhaps the hunt was on for ancestors. At the core of the Antarctic high strangeness is not a "what," but a "who" ... And whoever *It* is, it is an important who, important enough to attract the attention of Nazi *Reichmarschalls*, American Fleet Admirals and Secretaries of Defense and State, billionaires, kings, princes, patriarchs, and popes.

The legend of Atlantis being located in Antarctica can be indirectly placed on the Egyptian priesthood of Sais and the ancient Greeks. The renowned Athenian statesman Solon was given a story by the "mysterious Egyptian priests" of Sais, according to Plato in the *Timaeus* conversation and the incomplete *Critias* dialogue (638 BCE, and 558 BCE). About 200 years after it was told, Plato (428–348 BCE) indirectly acquired this tale and used it as one of the sources for his account. In this story, Plato accounts a lot of details. He mentions a "Big Island" that is located close to the "Pillars of Hercules," which he refers to as "Atlantis" or "Atlas Land." The Greeks of Plato's era were aware that the present-day Moroccan mountain range was referred to as "Atlas" in the "Stories" of the renowned historian Herodotus (484 - 430 BCE) more than 40 years before Plato. By the way, the Atlas Mountains go by that name still to this day. The term "Atlantis" or "Atlas Land" denoted a land that was obviously situated at the base of the Atlas Mountains to Greek speakers of the time. However, everyone was aware that the "Big Island" at the base of the Atlas Mountains did not exist, but was a subcontinent out in the Atlantic Ocean somewhere.

Other proposed locations for Atlantis include the Mediterranean Sea around Malta, the Aegean Sea near Crete, or just off the coast of present-day Portugal and Morocco. Further afield are various locations around the Caribbean Sea, off the North Sea from England, Antarctica, the Mexican Yucatán, and deep off the coast of Cuba or the Bahamas. Other writers have proposed that ascended masters of esoteric wisdom inhabit subterranean caverns, or a "hollow Earth." Antarctica, the North Pole, the Yukon Territory, Tibet, Peru, and Mount Shasta in California, have all had their advocates as the locations of entrances to a subterranean realm referred to as Agartha, with some even advancing the hypothesis that certain UFOs have their homeland in these places.

Several whistleblowers describe Antarctica as containing an antediluvian civilization with frozen Ice Age mammals and even a race of human-like giants, both long-dead frozen, and others in stasis chambers only now coming out of a state of hibernation. The bodies of giants found in Antarctica show unique body shapes and elongated heads. The "Pre-Adamite" giants of Antarctica are described as having a distinct Egyptian flair in their dress. These were discovered as part of the Antarctic ancient alien ET saucer relics, which include the 12-foot tall, 12-fingered and 12-toed, dual sets of teeth, red-haired Nephilim frozen in the ice shelf.

ELTANIN ANTENNA

A possible underwater base connection can be made with the Eltanin Antenna, discovered in deep water between South America and Antarctica. This ocean floor object was photographed

Lost Cities **author David Hatcher Childress stated on** ***Ancient Aliens*** **that there is a distinct possibility the Shackleton Pyramid (seen above) is the oldest of its kind on Earth.**

He said: "If this gigantic pyramid in Antarctica is an artificial structure, it would probably be the oldest pyramid on the planet and in fact it might be the master pyramid that all the other pyramids on planet Earth were designed to look like."

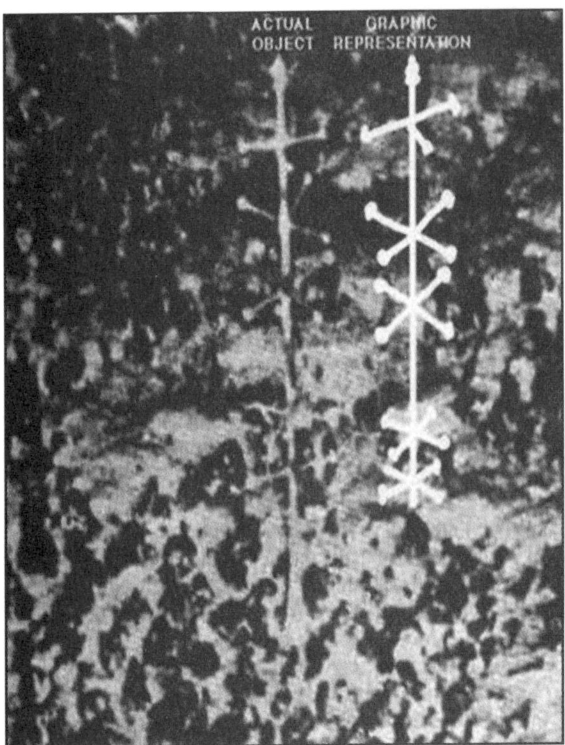

One of the greatest mysteries under the water is a very mysterious antenna at the bottom of the deep Drake Passage. The perfectly-symmetrical Eltanin Antenna was discovered in deep water between South America and Antarctica. What could it possibly be used for?

by the Antarctic oceanographic research ship USNS Eltanin in 1964, while they were surveying and photographing the sea bottom west of Cape Horn in the Drake Passage. On the 29th of August 1964, while taking sample cores and photographing the sea floor west of Tierra del Fuego, Chile, the Eltanin took the famous photograph at position 59°07'S 105°03'W, at the remarkable depth of 3,904 meters (12,808 feet). Because of its regular antenna-like structure and upright position on the sea floor at such a great depth, many have speculated it must be an artifact from an advanced civilization beyond any known human means.

The upright Eltanin Antenna at such an amazing depth have given rise to the theories that it is an inner-terrestrial artifact, a guide for a sea-faring underwater UFO system, some kind of ancient relic, an advanced Nazi submarine radar system guiding U-boats to underwater bases near Antarctica, or even a connection with the mysterious Black Knight satellite.

Is it possible to identify high-tech artifacts from an advanced civilization, including the deepwater Eltanin Antenna? Or could this be an advanced Nazi submarine relay station connecting to the land bases, or built inside the Earth by inner-terrestrials? Speculation exists that it could have been placed by extraterrestrials, and is used by the Black Knight satellite monitoring the entire planet on a very rare pole to pole orbit trajectory. The Black Knight satellite was observed by the Soviets when they sent cosmonaut Yuri Gagarin as the first man in outer space on April 12, 1961.

LOST PEOPLE OF MU

A vast continent known as Lemuria existed long ago in the Pacific Ocean. Parts of the land survived a cataclysmic flood. Easter Island, Hawaii and portions of Melanesia/Polynesia and the Marquesa Islands are the main outward remnants of a continent that vanished, or was largely wiped-out in a cataclysm. The remaining survivors made their way to Antarctica, South America, and the American Southwest.

Interestingly, all shared a common hieroglyphic language called the lost kingdom of Mu. James Churchward was a military man who, in 1926, claimed that while he was a soldier in India, he befriended a high-ranking “Sadhu” priest who showed him a set of ancient clay tablets. The tablets contained symbols which would later enchant Churchward, who dedicated many years of his life to deciphering them.

The curious Monte Urbano Map was made in 1587. Not only does this map show Antarctica 300 hundred years before its discovery, but it also shows much of animals and the giant inhabitants that once shared this realm with us.

On this close-up of the Monte Urbano Map it shows the "Region of Giants" living down in southern Patagonia in South America, the closest continental land mass to Antarctica.

The clay tablets were written in a "Naga-Maya language" (Serpent-Maya) which only two other people in India could read. Having mastered the language himself, Churchward found out that they originated from "the place where (man) first appeared—the lost world of Mu." All the Pacific peoples were at one time united with a hieroglyphic language and a set of similar protector spirits called Moai and Tiki. Interestingly, although officially said not to exist, there was a language based on hieroglyphics which was widely understood amongst ancient people in the Pacific. The mysterious Rongo Rongo script of Rapa Nui (Easter Island) has never been deciphered. It most closely resembles the script from the ancient Indus culture in present-day Pakistan.

The Moai statures of Easter Island each had a set of eyes made from white coral—for some unknown reason, the eyes were removed when the statues were toppled. It is suggested that both the Moai of Rapa Nui and the Māori people of New Zealand, as well as the aboriginals of Australia, are also remnants of the Lemurian race or culture, and that this advanced empire existed several precessional cycles ago, more in the range of 30-60,000 years before the present. The Polynesians are among the tallest races of people on Earth. There might be relics of the Lemurian culture in Antarctica.

In *Bringers of the Dawn, Teachings from the Pleadians* author Barbara Marciniak writes:

> *There were species of humans on Earth perhaps 500,000 years ago who developed very highly evolved civilizations. We are not speaking of the civilizations that you call*

Lemuria or Atlantis; to us, those civilizations are modern. We are talking about civilizations that are ancient, civilizations that are buried under some of the ice caps of the far southern continent of Antarctica. [2]

PATAGONIAN GIANTS

In 1520, the famous explorer Ferdinand Magellan reached San Julian Bay in Patagonia. Aboard the ship was Antonio Pigafetta—a Venetian nobleman—who joined the expedition of Magellan as the official chronicler of the voyage. Pigafetta kept a richly detailed diary of the expedition in which he made entries every day of the entire odyssey. Unlike most of the crew, Pigafetta was a close friend with Magellan and almost died defending him at the Battle of Mactan in the Philippines, where Magellan was killed. Pigafetta was one of only 17 survivors whose ship, the *Nao Victoria*, arrived back safely in Spain on September 8, 1522. While wintering over in southern Patagonia the Magellan crew made first contact with a tribe of giants. Diary entry of Pigafetta, page 51:

Leaving that place, we finally reached 49 and one-half degrees toward the Antarctic Pole. As it was winter, the ships entered a safe port to winter. We passed two months in that place without seeing anyone. One day we suddenly saw a naked man of giant stature on the shore of the port, dancing, singing, and throwing dust on his head. The captain-general sent one of our men to the giant so that he might perform the same actions as a sign of peace. Having done that, the man led the giant to an islet into the presence of the captain-general. When the giant was in the captain-general's and our presence, he marveled greatly, and made signs with one finger raised upward, believing that we had come from the sky.

Diary of Pigafetta, page 52:

He was so tall that we reached only to his waist, and he was well-proportioned. His face was large and painted red all over, while about his eyes he was painted yellow; and he had two hearts painted on the middle of his cheeks. His scanty hair was painted white. He was dressed in the skins

2. Marciniak, Barbara. *Bringers of the Dawn: Teachings from the Pleadians,* Bear & Company, 1992.

"He was so tall that we reached only to his waist," was the report by Magellan's historian Pigafetta, who described in detail the Patagonia giant physique. This lifesize replica of Magellan's ship *Nao Victoria* is a tourist attraction in San Julian, Argentina located in southern Patagonia.

of animals skillfully sewn together. That animal has a head and ears as large as those of a mule, a neck and body like those of a camel, the legs of a deer, and the tail of a horse, like which it neighs, and that land has very many of them. His feet were shod with the same kind of skins which covered his feet in the manner of shoes. In his hand he carried a short, heavy bow, with a cord somewhat thicker than those of the lute, and made from the intestines of the same animal, and a bundle of rather short cane arrows feathered like ours, and with points of white and black flint stones in the manner of Turkish arrows, instead of iron. Those points were fashioned by means of another stone.

The name *Tierra del Fuego* or "Land of Fire" refers to the fact that the Fuegian native people had big bonfires burning in front of their huts every night. In Magellan's time the giant Fuegian Indians were more numerous, and the light and smoke of their fires presented an impressive sight as seen from a ship or another island.

The Fuegians were the indigenous inhabitants of Patagonia and Tierra del Fuego, at the far southern tip of South America. The name has been credited to Captain James Weddell, who supposedly created the term in 1822. When Chileans and Argentinians of European descent invaded and settled on the islands in the mid-19th century, they brought with them diseases such as measles and smallpox for which the Fuegians had no immunity. The Fuegian population was devastated by the diseases, and their numbers were reduced from several thousand in the 19th century to a few hundred in the early 20th century. In the late 19th century some *estancieros* and gold prospectors launched a campaign of extermination against the indigenous peoples of Tierra del Fuego. Today, there are no pure-blood Fuegian people left. Similarly, the language spoken by the Fuegians is also extinct. [3]

GIANTS FROM INNER EARTH

A book called *The Smoky God: A Voyage to the Inner World* by Willis George Emerson was written in 1908. It presented a nonfiction account of a Norwegian sailor who sailed with his father through an entrance to the Earth's Interior in a location around near the North Pole. The story opens with Olaf Janson reminiscing about his childhood in a coastal village in Norway.

3. https://en.wikipedia.org/wiki/Fuegians

Later in life, on a sailing expedition, Olaf and his father discovered a habitat called "Eden." He observed in the book that the inhabitants were very tall with a blue-eyed Aryan phenotype, and benevolent beings who possess ancient technology and wisdom. Eden had towering spires and gleaming domes. People there had been living in harmony with nature for centuries. They used their knowledge to maintain a perfect balance between the elements through their interactions with the "unseen." As they spend more time with the

Ferdinand Magellan personally met with the Patagonian giants while wintering his ships at San Julian Bay in 1520, and his historian recorded the encounter. The large island *Tierra del Fuego* is named the "Land of Fire" not because of active volcanoes, but because of the large bonfires made by the Patagonian giants every night and seen by the mariners passing through the Strait of Magellan. Many other explorers encountered the Patagonian giants and depicted them on their maps.

Inner Earth people they gain insights into the mysteries of the universe and the "Interconnectedness of All Living Beings."

On another voyage on the surface of the Earth, Emerson writes in the book: "as we approach the Equator, the stature of the human race grows less. But the Patagonians of South America are probably the only aborigines from the Inner part of the Earth. Those who came out through the aperture usually designated at the South Pole, and they are called 'the giant race.'" Emerson described the Patagonia giants in his book *The Smoky God*:

> *There was not a single man aboard who would not have measured fully 12-feet in height. They all wore beards, not particularly long, but seemingly short-cropped. They had mild and beautiful faces, exceedingly fair, with ruddy complexion. The hair and beard of some were black—others sandy and still others, yellow.*
>
> *The captain, as we designated the dignitary in command of the great vessel—was fully a head taller than any of his companions. The women averaged ten-eleven feet in height. Their features were especially regular and were refined—while their complexion was of a most delicate tint heightened by a healthful glow.*
>
> *They are richly attired in a costume peculiar to themselves and very attractive. The men were clothed in handsomely embroidered tunics of silk and satin and belted at the waist. They wore knee-breeches and stockings of a fine texture—while their feet were encased in sandals adorned with gold buckles. We have discovered that gold was one of the most common metals known, and that was used extensively in decoration.*
>
> *I never saw such a display of gold. It was everywhere. The door-casings were inlaid and the tables were veneered with sheetings of gold. Domes of the public buildings were of gold. Gold was used most generously in the finishing of the Great Temple of Music.*

The story concludes around the surface of Antarctica when the father and son emerge from Inner Earth. The father died in a storm trying to navigate his ship away from the lost continent. The son, though rescued, was thrown into an "insane asylum" for "daring to tell the world where he and his father had been." [4]

INNER EARTH RACES

According to researcher Elena Danaan, there are certain races that compose the majority of the Inner Earth populations. Indeed, they are third density humans like us who migrated underground after dramatic global catastrophes or the threat of extinction. Among them are Atlantian descendants, the Hyperboreans, and diverse indigenous surface populations who have made it down. Included are a variety of extraterrestrial colonies such as the Alpha Centaurians, and the Telosians who built the renowned Telos civilization. The Telos civilization was extended in a big part of the Earth underground, especially below Mount Shasta, California and in the Yukon Territory of Canada. These were places like the central city of Telos, which was located deep down under the middle of western North America and extended out for hundreds of miles.

They were a pacifist race living harmoniously in their colony until the Ciakahrr reptilians from Alpha Draconis came back. In recent history they coerced the Telosians to give them their web of underground networks, as well as the Nagas. The Ciakahrr had forcibly taken hold of Telos until it was liberated in 2021. Not all Telosians complied by fear and threat—many of them formed a Maki resistance and held their ground against the Ciakahrrs. The Naga also did the same. Not all the Naga reptilian race joined the forces with the dark side of the Ciakahrrs. Many of them also rebelled and stood their ground like the Sasquatch or Bigfoot, who live half underground and half in remote, densely forested areas.

The people of Telos decided to open some of the entrances to Inner Earth to the surface humans and allow a vetted number of them physical access to some of the Halls of Records, but the knowledge that would be shared could not be turned into weapons such as in the fields of medical science and spiritual development. Since that meeting, some entrances to Inner Earth have been reopened in certain locations under the military protection of the Earth Alliance to prevent any unwanted intrusion by undesirable forces working against the good of this planet. In addition to the military

4. Emerson, Willis George. *The Smoky God: A Voyage to the Inner World*, Lamp of Trismegistus, 1908.

presence, elected civilians were a welcome presence. Elected civilians were welcome to visit Inner Earth facilities and meet with the local populations. The kingdoms of Inner Earth are spread throughout the various layers of the planet's mantle—shifting to higher densities as they go deeper into the Inner Earth—where there are indigenous people of various origins. [5]

AGARTHA INNER EARTH CIVILIZATION

For a few million years the Inner Earth has been home to a very highly advanced civilization, called Agartha. According to Inner Earth researchers, this world inside the globe consists of a large continent and more than 120 underground cities. Its citizenry is a gathering of different heritages, cultures and races.

The vast majority had originally lived on the surface, but have eventually relocated to the Inner Earth. These include the ancestors of Hyperborea, Atlantis, and Lemuria. All live peacefully and in total harmony with nature. As inner-terrestrials themselves, they are in regular contact with extraterrestrial civilizations.

Many animal species already extinct on the surface, like mammoths, giant sloths and saber tooth tigers, continue to live in the Inner Earth. Everything is better, cleaner and especially bigger! There are "*Avatar*" like trees, hundreds of meters tall. Grapes grow as big as plums and are more flavorful than we know them on the surface, as is the hydroponic tomato—which is reportedly a sensation to the taste buds.

In some cities the people are much bigger than our types. A few reach over four meters (12 feet) tall. These were the people who first greeted the Norse fisherman, Olaf Jansen, during his unbelievable sea journey in the 19th century. One can only imagine how he must have felt when these giants invited him and his father onto their boat.

Agarthans live much longer than we do. Some of their "pensioners" live to be 30,000 years old. Because aging is not a factor in their lives, most of them choose to look around 30 or 40 years old, while in reality they could be much older. When an Agarthan feels a certain incarnation has been completed, they can leave their body at will.

There is no use for money in Agartha. People use the barter system and there is plenty of everything for everyone. Energy is free. The cities are accommodated with moving sidewalks and for shorter

5. Danaan, Elena. STAR NATION NEWS #28~ April 29 2024 https://www.youtube.com/watch?v=PidZ9ozv0Hc

distances a sort of scooter is used. An electromagnetic system called “the tube” is used for travel from one city to another. It can reach speeds up to four thousand miles per hour.

The Agarthans are fully integrated into the galactic way of interaction and are part of the Confederation of Planets. They make spaceflights in ships that are capable of changing dimensions, which makes it impossible for us to see them when they wish to remain invisible.

It is crowded at places such as Mount Shasta and Mount Adams, where spaceships come and go all the time. Contactee James Gilliland built his ECETI Ranch at the foot of Mount Adams, to search the night skies with visitors from all over the world. With binoculars they watch the lightships move in and out of the mountain. The outside of the mountain is no obstacle for their ships since they can dematerialize without any problems. [6]

6. Teachings from the Hollow Earth: https://operationdisclosureofficial.com/2024/05/17/the-1st-galacticjack-hollow-earth-agartha-underground-civilizations-giants/

Maps of the Ancient Sea Kings

"Most of these maps were of the Mediterranean and the Black Sea. But maps of other areas survived. These included maps of the Americas and maps of the Arctic and Antarctic seas. It becomes clear that the ancient voyagers traveled from pole to pole. Unbelievable as it may appear, the evidence nevertheless indicates that some ancient people explored the coasts of Antarctica when its coasts were free of ice. It is clear, too, that they had an instrument of navigation for accurately finding the longitudes of places that was far superior to anything possessed by the peoples of ancient, medieval, or modern times until the second half of the 18th century."

–Charles H. Hapgood, *Maps of the Ancient Sea Kings: Evidence of Advanced Civilization in the Ice Age*

ANTARCTICA is a vast frozen desert in the far south of the planet. It is the most inhospitable and least explored continent on Earth. Beneath its thick layer of ice, which can exceed four kilometers in thickness, lie secrets that could change our understanding of the world. From secret bases to ancient maps and clues of lost civilizations, Antarctica is a place where mystery and science intertwine, sparking fascinating new research about the geographical and geophysical nature of the landmass. Yet its remoteness also fuels fringe theories like the Flat Earth, where Antarctica does not exist as a continent, but is replaced by an ice wall surrounding the Southern Ocean.

Indeed, Antarctica is a real place and the southernmost continent on Earth. Because so little is known it has long been a subject of intrigue and speculation. This vast icy expanse, larger than Europe and almost twice the size of Australia, is a land of extremes. It's the coldest, driest, windiest and the least explored continent, and yet, it holds secrets that continue to baffle and fascinate us.

The Ptolemy map from 150 CE shows a large continent linking Africa and Asia. Claudius Ptolemy lived in Alexandria, Egypt during the period of the fabled Library of Alexandria which is mentioned as a source map in the liner notes of the Piri Re'is map.

Maps of the Ancient Sea Kings

Antarctica wasn't always the icy desert it is today. Fossilized wood, tropical tree remnants, and leaf impressions have unveiled the existence of ancient rainforests in this once warm land. Beyond that, the treasure trove of fossils found in Antarctica extends to marine creatures, birds, and even dinosaurs from the Cretaceous Period. Some of these creatures are seen alive on the oldest existing maps of Antarctica. The fossil evidence suggests that before becoming the icy desert we know of today, Antarctica was a warm tropical region, possibly even hosting civilizations and seafarers from long ago.

Antarctica, unlike any other continent, was believed to exist long before it was actually set foot upon in 1821, by the crew of a seal hunting vessel. From the ancient Greeks until the Age of Discovery, a Southern Continent was postulated as having to exist, in order to offset the heavy continental mass of the Northern Hemisphere. The ancient Greeks, beginning with Pythagoras, proposed the Earth to be round. Aristotle refined the idea, suggesting that the symmetry of a sphere demanded that the Earth's northern region should be balanced by a southern region—without it, the top-heavy globe might tumble over. The idea of earthly balance gave rise to the name we give the Southern Continent today; *Antarctos*, or "opposite Arctos," the constellation seen in the northern sky. In Egypt, Ptolemy agreed that geographical equilibrium required an unknown Southern Continent—a map he drew in 150 CE showed a large continent connected to Africa and Asia. And this was long before Antarctica was ever set foot upon. Or was it?

KNOWLEDGE OF A SOUTHERN CONTINENT

There is a large body of early maps depicting the coastlines of the Americas which cannot be explained by known Age of Discovery explorations. Those maps are: (1) Mercator's 1569 World Map, which shows all of Greenland without ice at its coasts; and (2) the Finaeus' 1531 World Map, which shows Antarctica without coastal ice, all of Greenland without coastal ice, and an ancient shoreline of Hudson Bay. No 16th century explorer could have reached Antarctica and northern Greenland during this time period, much less have seen them ice-free at their coasts. Based on an analysis of historic rates of isostatic rebound in lower James Bay, it appears that the ancient surveys for these maps of Antarctica and northern Greenland were made in approximately 1675 BCE. Following a major global warming period after the last Ice Age called the Younger Dryas starting 12,900 years ago, another minor warming period around 3,700 years ago was sufficient to result in the coasts of Antarctica and Greenland being ice free.

The continental landmass of Antarctica was only landed upon rather accidentally in 1821, by the crew of a seal hunting ship. But there is ample evidence that the continent was previously known many millennia ago. The ancient Greeks proposed the Earth to be round, or more precisely, spherical. They named a land they never saw *Antarctos*, or "opposite Arctos," to the constellation seen 180 degrees around the globe in the northern sky. This was known over 23 centuries before the continent was discovered.

The Antarctic Peninsula is part of the larger peninsula of West Antarctica, protruding 1,300 kilometers (810 miles) from a line between Cape Adams at the Weddell Sea, and a point on the mainland south of the Eklund Islands. The Antarctic Peninsula is the closest landmass to any other continent. Beneath the ice sheet that covers it, the Antarctic Peninsula consists of a string of bedrock islands; these are separated by deep channels whose bottoms lie at depths considerably below the current sea level. They are joined by a grounded ice sheet. Tierra del Fuego is the southernmost tip of South America which is the closest continental landmass, about 1,000 kilometers (620 miles) away across the Drake Passage.

Because of its close proximity to South America, the Antarctic Peninsula is currently dotted with numerous research stations, and eight nations have made multiple claims of sovereignty. Also known as the Palmer Peninsula, it is part of disputed and overlapping claims by Argentina, Chile, and the United Kingdom. None of

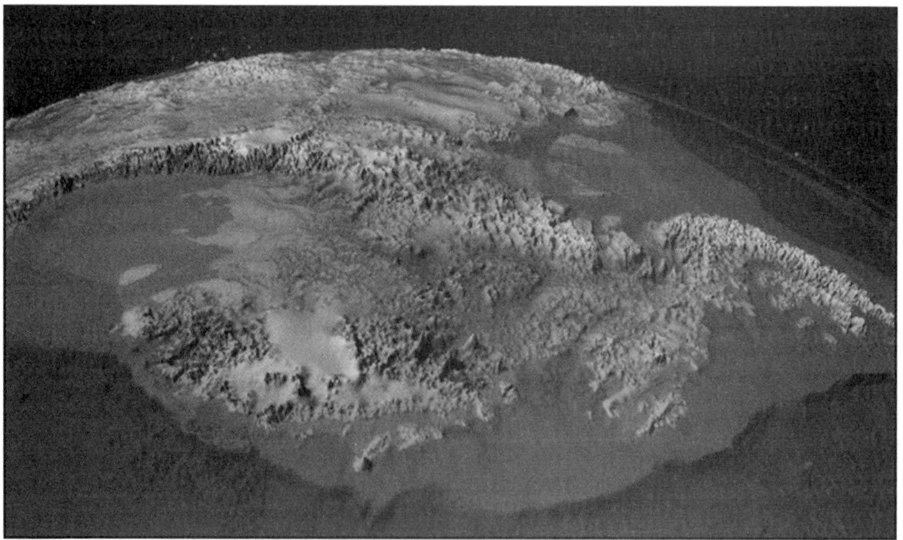

If all the ice was removed from Antarctica and the sea levels didn't rise, this map depicts the continental landmass before the ice accumulation.

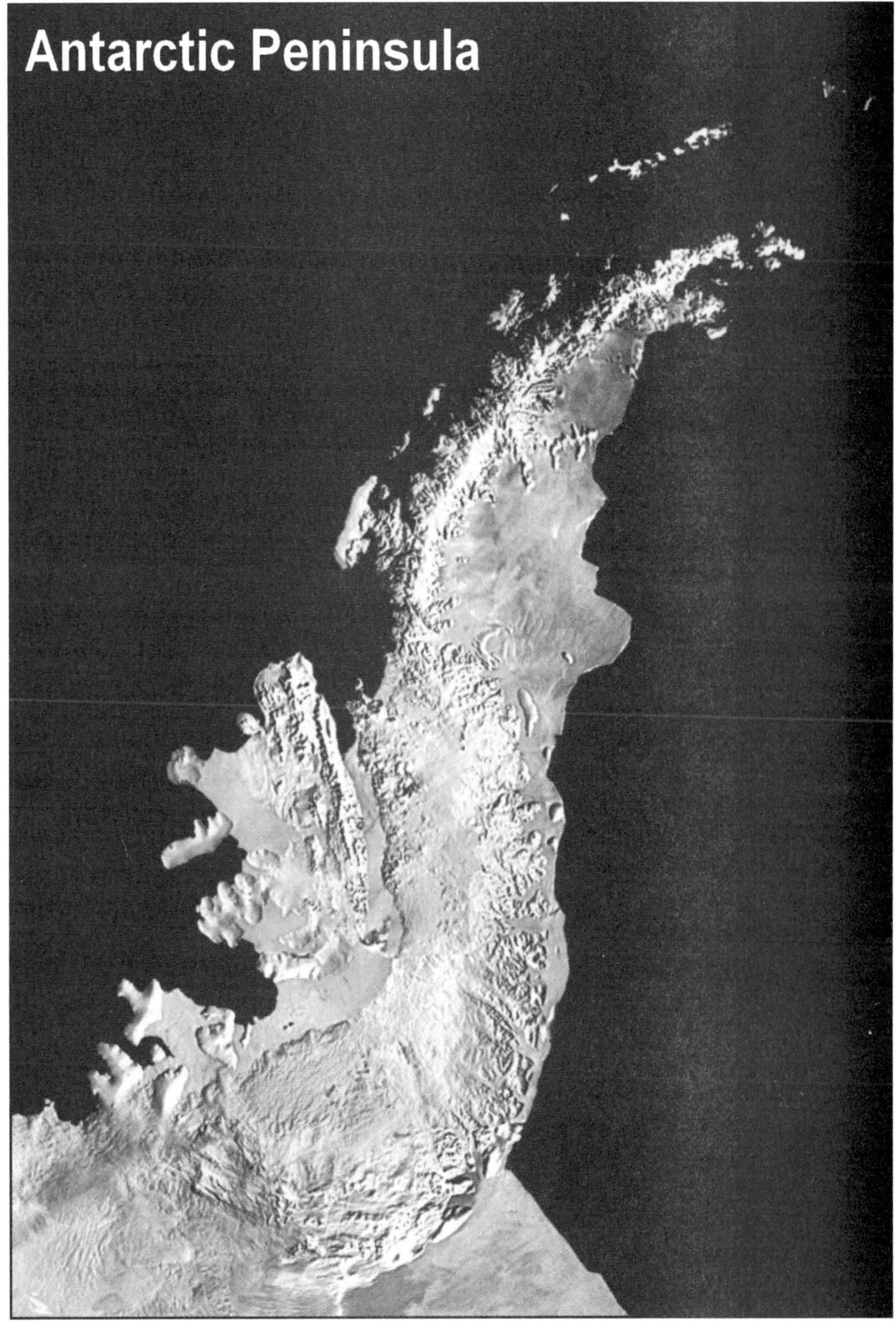

This Antarctic Peninsula satellite image shows the entirety of the Palmer Peninsula, plus the pan-Antarctic island chains of the South Shetlands and the Elephant Island group. The mariners during the Age of Discovery first set sight and landed on the continent of Antarctica in locations around here.

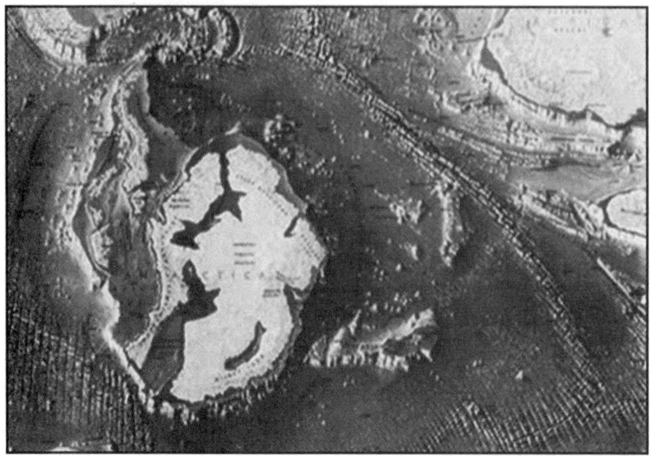

If all the ice melted from Antarctica and raised the sea levels by 30 meters (100 feet), this map represents the continent where the flooded new coastlines would extend. Notice the deep fjords that extend deep into East Antarctica from several directions, and the open ocean connection through West Antarctica.

these claims have international recognition and, under the Antarctic Treaty System, the respective countries do not attempt to enforce their claims. The British claim, however, is recognized by Australia, France, New Zealand, and Norway. Argentina has the most bases and personnel stationed on the peninsula than any other nation. Like the Falklands and South Sandwich Islands, Argentina still makes claim to these far-flung territories, although most are now controlled by the United Kingdom.

MAPS OF THE ANCIENT SEA KINGS

According to author Charles H. Hapgood, the maps he discusses in his book contain precise representations of Antarctica as it was before the last Ice Age—during a pre-diluvian age. *The Maps of the Ancient Sea Kings* including the 1519 Piri Re'is map, the 1531 Finaeus map, and the Buache map from the 18th century, and all depicting versions of Antarctica when it was free from ice. How could this be known many hundreds of years before the continent's discovery?

In Hapgood's book there are 20 maps and charts referenced in the notation: eight maps were Ptolemaic of the known world according to Hellenistic or Greek Society in the 4th century. Some scholars have long claimed that a super-civilization existed over 4,000 years ago at a period congruent with ancient Egypt.

Some of the mysteries under the water are the old maps showing as-yet discovered islands, a vastly different known coastline, and a water passage between East and West Antarctica continental plates. Charles H. Hapgood writes:

Maps of the Ancient Sea Kings

The evidence presented by the ancient maps appears to suggest the existence in remote times, before the rise of any of the known cultures, of a true civilization, of a comparatively advanced sort, which either was localized in one area but had worldwide commerce, or was, in a real sense, a worldwide culture. This culture, at least in some respects, may well have been more advanced than the civilizations of Egypt, Babylonia, Greece, and Rome. In astronomy, nautical science, mapmaking and possibly ship-building, it was perhaps more advanced than any state of culture before the 18th century of the Christian Era. It was in the 18th century that we first developed a practical means of finding longitude. It was in the 18th century that we first accurately measured the circumference of the Earth. Not until the 19th century did we begin to send out ships for purposes of whaling or exploration into the Arctic or Antarctic Seas. The maps indicate that some ancient people may have done all these things.

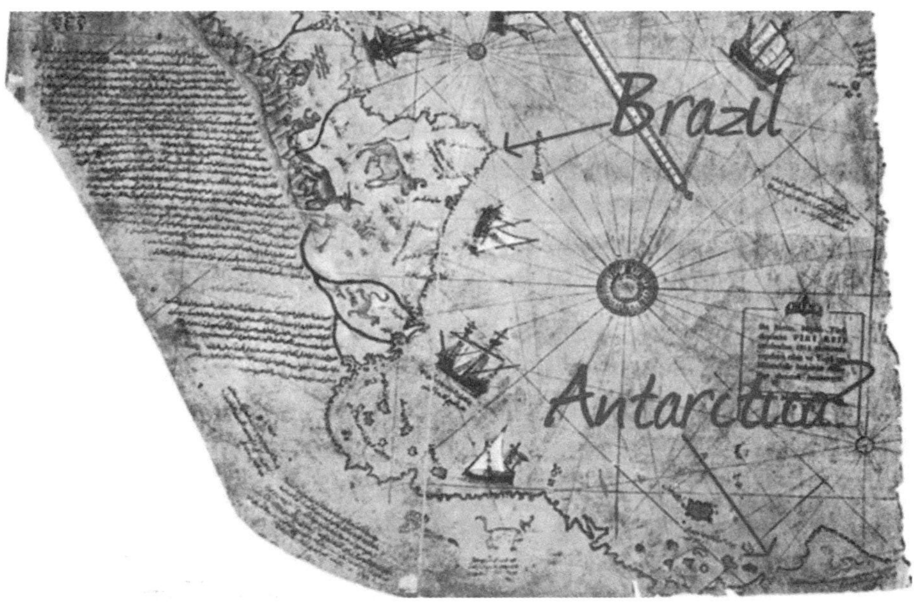

The Piri Re'is map, drawn by Ottoman cartographer Piri Re'is in 1513, depicts the coastlines of Europe, Africa, and Brazil with remarkable accuracy. However, the map's depiction of the Antarctic coast free of ice has sparked controversy, considering Antarctica wasn't officially discovered until 1821. Some theorists claim it as evidence of prehistoric exploration or ancient advanced civilizations, while others argue it's a result of misinterpretation or exaggeration.

The most important evidence for the age of the maps ... is to be found in those showing the Antarctic, especially in the maps of Mercator, Piri Re'is, and Oronteus Finaeus. All of these maps appear to show the continent at a time when there was a temperate climate there. Some geological evidence, in the form of three sedimentary cores from the bottom of the Ross Sea, has been presented to suggest that such a warm period may indeed have existed there down to about 6,000 years ago.

How is it that the Piri Re'is map depicts Antarctica of having no ice or snow? Maybe a very large comet hit Antarctica and basically put the ice and snow right on top of that landmass. That would explain how it got covered so quickly with ice and snow. Or could there have been a pole shift, which is what Hapgood seems to believe. [1]

The fossil record shows Antarctica once supported megaflora and megafauna. It had very large animals, a tropical rainforest replete with fern meadows. Perhaps the Atlantean civilization was caught in the nuclear wars—affecting Atlantis and Lemuria, and causing them to sink in a great deluge about 12,000 years ago.

Cited in Hapgood's notes is a map which is a known copy of a much older original dating from the Library of Alexandria, implying that North and South America were mapped over a thousand years before Columbus. When viewed on its side to account for the global projection on a 2D surface, the islands in the Caribbean and the islands off South America were also accurately mapped and charted. Ancient maps of Antarctica uncover what may contain lost civilizations now trapped below the ice.

PIRI RE'IS MAP

The Turkish admiral Piri Re'is commissioned a map in 1513, depicting the known-world using older source maps as described in the side notes. The map accurately corresponds to the European and African coastlines, but it also shows the Caribbean, South America and possibly Antarctica when it was free from ice. How was this information known shortly after Columbus made his first voyage to the New World? To his dying day, Christopher Columbus believed he had discovered an island off India, not two massive continents. Even today, the Antarctic coastline is still far from being perfectly charted with most of it covered. Almost all

1. Hapgood, Charles H. *Maps of the Ancient Sea Kings: Evidence of Advanced Civilization in the Ice Age.* Illustrated, paperback. Adventures Unlimited, 1997.

of the continental coastline remains buried under a thick layer of ice. Considering Magellan did not discover the water route through Patagonia and Tierra del Fuego until 1520, how did Piri Re'is chart the southern portion of South America so accurately in 1513?

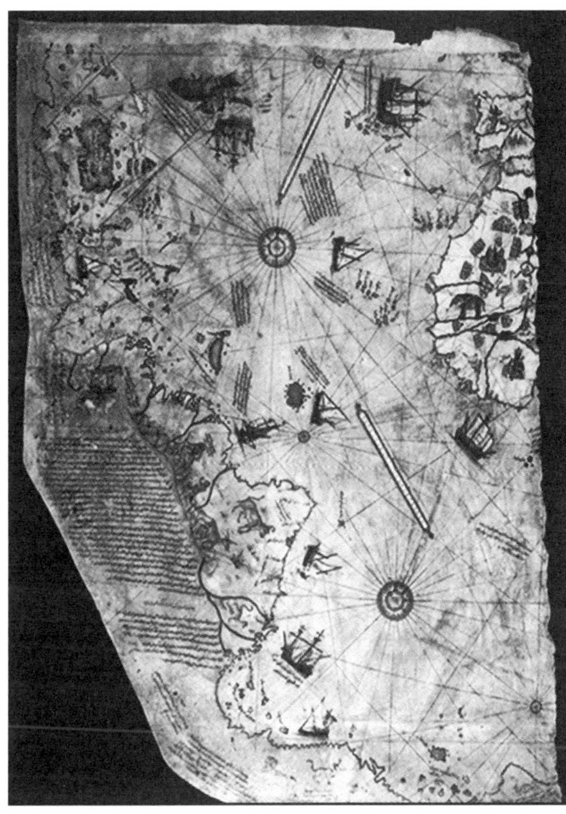

The Piri Re'is map was drawn by a Turkish admiral for navigational purposes. It accurately depicts the southern Atlantic Ocean, which was scantly explored in 1513. Researchers believe it likely derived from a combination of sources, including early Portuguese maps and possibly African and Arab navigational charts. The debate surrounding the map remains contentious, with no consensus on its true origins or significance.

A mutated giant is depicted in South America on the Piri Re'is map. Magellan mentioned that his sailors were only half the size of the Patagonian giants. When subsequent seafarers were sailing around *Tierra del Fuego* they saw enormous bonfires with enormous giants dancing around them in the "Land of Fire." In the notes on the map, Admiral Piri Re'is reports that he compiled it from numerous source maps, some of whom were at least a few hundred years old. Not only maps from Ptolemaic times but source maps that came from the Library of Alexandria in Egypt.

Before World War II, without a doubt, the German Ahnenerbe Society were aware of the amazing discoveries of archaeologists at the beginning of the 19th century, and the famous Turkish admiral Piri Re'is map. German cartographers must have been struck by the fact that the northern coast of Antarctica was depicted on this map, and this is 300 years before the official discovery of this continent. The far eastern portion of the map is the area of Antarctica later claimed as a colony of the Third Reich.

After multiple fly-overs the verdict of the German Air Force specialists was that the coastline was mapped before it was covered in ice. On this territory it has a thickness of about a mile. However, nobody knows how this data could have been obtained in 1513. International expeditions that checked the voyage map came to the conclusion that it was more accurate than maps compiled in the mid-20th century, and seismic exploration has confirmed what has not been reported until recently. They guessed that some mountains that were considered part of a single massif turned out to be in fact islands, and this is what is indicated on the old map. The Piri Re'is map made a strong impression on the adherents of the Aryan theory.

The remarkable Piri Re'is map also accurately depicts the Iberian peninsula and West African coast lines. It includes exotic animals and the sultanates that were once in power. In West Africa there are ostriches, elephants and other exotic animals. In the same year Columbus first ventured west in 1492, the Muslims were ejected out of the Iberian Peninsula. The Muslims' city of Granada is depicted at the bottom of the map in Spain. The liner notes on the map reference other source documents and maps—mostly in Portuguese and one in Arabic—depicting the southern land mass of Antarctica.

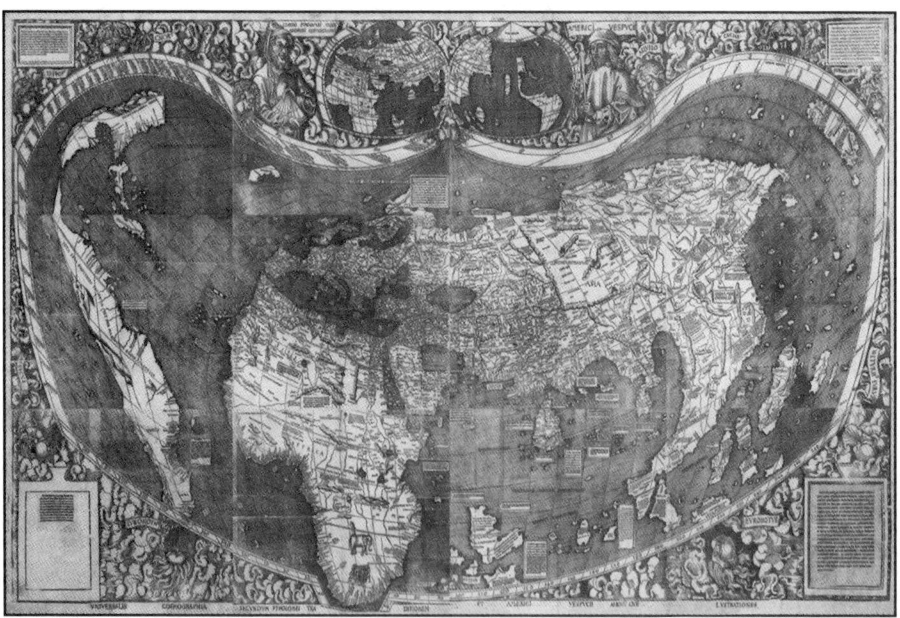

Martin Waldseemüller's world map is the first map to depict the Western Hemisphere as a distinct continental landmass, surrounded by water and not connected to Asia.

WALDSEEMÜLLER'S WORLD MAP

Martin Waldseemüller's World Map was first published in 1507, and is remarkably older than the Piri Re'is map by six years. The Turks and the Europeans were at odds with each other in the early 16th century, but Turkish spies or pirates could have acquired this map and submitted it to Piri Re'is. Waldseemüller's is the first map to depict the Western Hemisphere as a distinct continent—surrounded by water and not connected to Asia. It also marks the first time "AMERICA" was used on a map. The map is drafted on a modification of Ptolemy's second projection, expanded to accommodate the Americas and the high latitudes. On the left side of the Waldseemüller map the discoveries of Christopher Columbus, Amerigo Vespucci and others are represented as a long strip of land extending from about latitude 50 degrees North to latitude 40 degrees South. The western coasts of these trans-Atlantic lands discovered under the Spanish crown are simply described by Waldseemüller as *Terra Incognita* (Unknown Land) or *Terra Ulterius Incognita* (Unknown Land Further beyond).

Amerigo Vespucci was a Florentine navigator who explored the New World four times and gave his name to the Americas. His discoveries, his letters, and his role in navigation cemented his name in history for being one of the first to understand the American

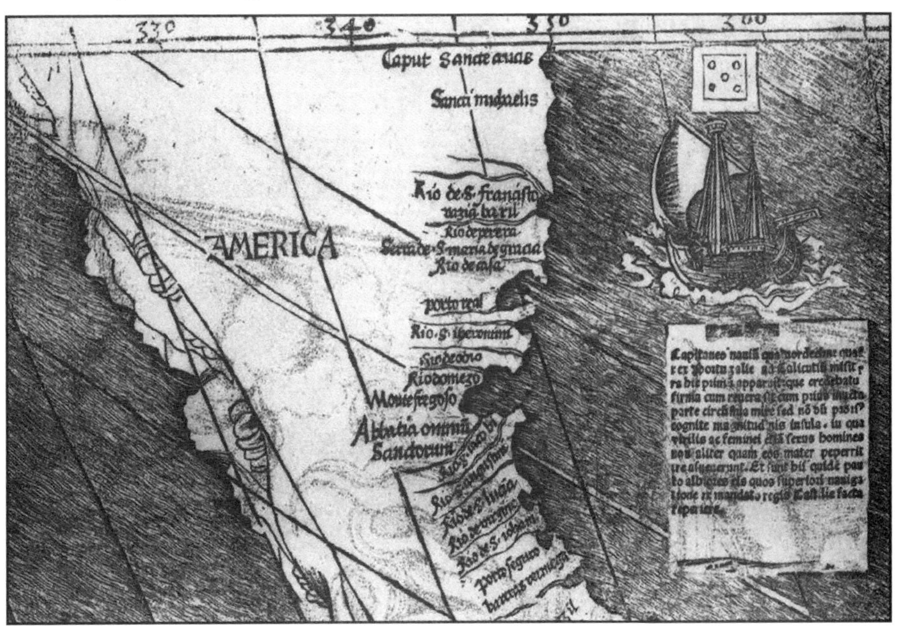

Waldseemüller's world map published in 1507 also marks the first time "AMERICA" was used on a map.

continent as a separate land mass. At the very bottom of South America inside Patagonia, located at the lower right is the name of "AMERICA" appearing for the very first time on any map. Amerigo Vespucci put his signature at the bottom of this map because he was the very first map dealer of Martin Waldseemüller—and so his name became very familiar with these maps depicting North America, Middle America and South America as the New World. But most mysterious is the southern tip of South America coastline depicted without any ice cover.

FINAEUS MAP

Another map depicting Antarctica from the very early period of world exploration is the 1531 Finaeus map. The geography of the continent was well-known centuries before its exploration and had already been measured precisely, as is evident in the map by Italian cartographer Oronce Finé (called *Orontius Finaeus* in

The Oronce Finé Map of 1531 shows Antarctica as though it was covered in ice, including the northernly most extent of the sea ice.

Latin). Finé was an important mathematician who also designed geographical maps based on geometric studies of different types of spherical projection, or cordiform. His map shows an area around the South Pole of a continent called *Terra Australis.*

The 1531 Finaeus map of *Terra Australis Incognita* depicts Australia and Antarctica as one supercontinent. The Finaeus map is an accurate depiction of what the continent looks like completely covered with ice and the extent of the sea ice. There can be little doubt that the Oronce Finé map was also made using earlier source maps as a reference. We can see by comparison with the recent NASA image revealing Antarctic mountains under the ice that there is an uncanny resemblance between the two. There is clearly an aerial perspective to these ancient maps of the Sea Kings.

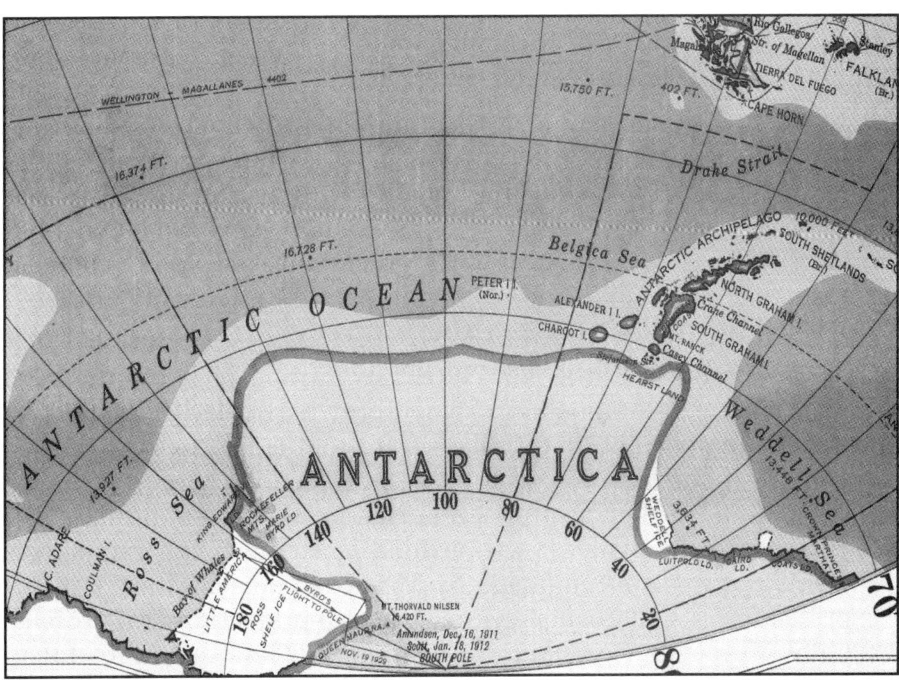

This Ranally school map of Antarctica in 1940, shows how little was known about the coastline less than a century ago. During the 1946-47 Operation Highjump, the flight crew mapped hundred of miles of mountain ranges and coastline. Admiral Byrd claimed that one of the pilots discovered a 300 square mile "warm oasis" where it was too warm for there to be any snow, and there was a chain of freshwater lakes free of ice. They named this area Bunger Hills after the pilot who discovered it, and landed his plane on one of the lakes to record film footage of the area. This discovery was not denied by the U.S. government, and in fact, the film footage can be seen in a U.S. government made film about the expedition called *The Secret Land.*

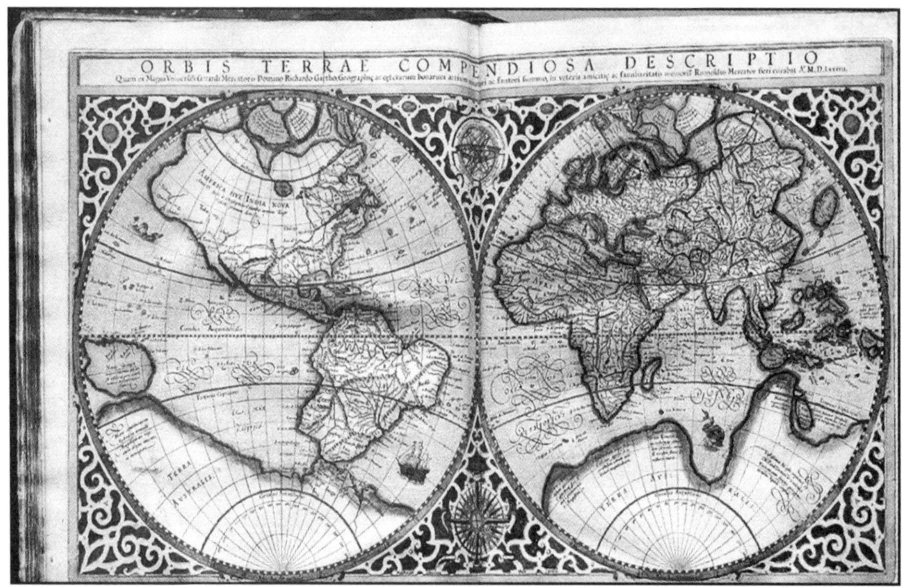

The Mercator World Map of 1569 begins showing the world three dimensionally. It also depicts fairly accurately the Americas and Tierra del Fuego, but it is connected to Antarctica. Gerardus Mercator is named the "inventor of the world map" because he accurately "projected" a 2-D map from a 3-D globe.

MERCATOR'S PROJECTION

The discovery of the New World by Europeans led to the need for new techniques in cartography, particularly for the systematic representation on a flat surface of the features of a curved surface—generally referred to as a projection. Mercator's 1569 map was a large planisphere, that is, a projection of the spherical Earth onto the plane. It was printed in eighteen separate sheets from copper plates engraved by Mercator himself. The Mercator projection is a conformal cylindrical map projection first presented by Flemish geographer and mapmaker Gerardus Mercator in 1569. In the 18th century, it became the standard map projection for navigation due to its property of representing rhumb lines as straight lines. Rhumb are any of the 32 points on a compass. When applied to world maps, the Mercator projection inflates the size of lands the further they are from the equator. Therefore, landmasses such as Greenland and Antarctica appear far larger than they actually are relative to landmasses near the equator. This map excited the imagination of early explorers who could then understand the planet as a sphere.

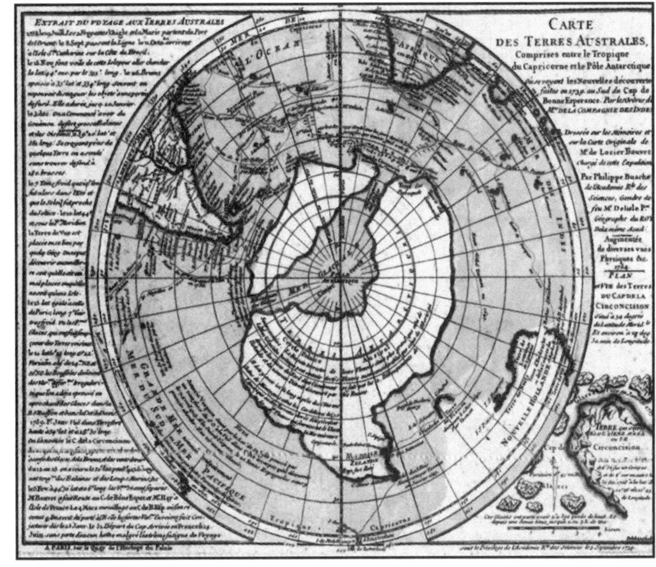

The Buache Map of 1737 depicts a water passage through Antarctica.

A comparison with world maps before 1569 shows how closely Mercator drew on the work of other cartographers and his own previous works, but he clearly stated that he was also greatly indebted to many new charts prepared by Portuguese and Spanish sailors in the portolan tradition. Earlier cartographers of world maps had largely ignored the more accurate practical charts of sailors, and vice versa, but the Age of Discovery, from the closing decade of the 15th century, stimulated the integration of these two mapping traditions. Mercator's World Map is one of the earliest fruits of this merger. [2]

BUACHE MAP

Age of Discovery maps such as the Buache Map from the 18th century depict Antarctica with a water channel right through the middle of the ice-covered continent. The Buache Map is commonly described as accurately depicting the continent of Antarctica before it was buried by ice. It has been claimed that this map is evidence that an ancient civilization had mapped Antarctica when it was free from ice, and that it was this now-lost source map that the Buache Map was based upon. The Buache Map was drawn by a French geographer by the name of Philippe Buache de la Neuville, hence its name. The full title is "Map of the Southern Lands contained between the Tropic of Capricorn and the Antarctic Pole, where the new discoveries made in 1739 to the south of the Cape of Good Hope may be seen." The Buache Map draws a stark similarity to modern radar systems mapping below the ice. Indeed, there is a high-water connection between West and East Antarctica!

2. https://en.wikipedia.org/wiki/Mercator_1569_world_map

Amazingly, there are two main water corridors under the ice in Antarctica that nearly connect. Mainstream history teaches the first recorded landing on the Antarctic continent took place on February 7, 1821. Men from the American sealer Cecilia, under Captain John Davis, landed at Hughes Bay (64°01'S) looking for seals. Though they were on shore for less than an hour, these men were unwittingly the first modern humans to set foot on this newly re-discovered southern continent.

MAPS WERE THE REAL TREASURE

In the notations alongside the Piri Re'is map is the disclaimer that it was based on much older source maps. Accurate maps were

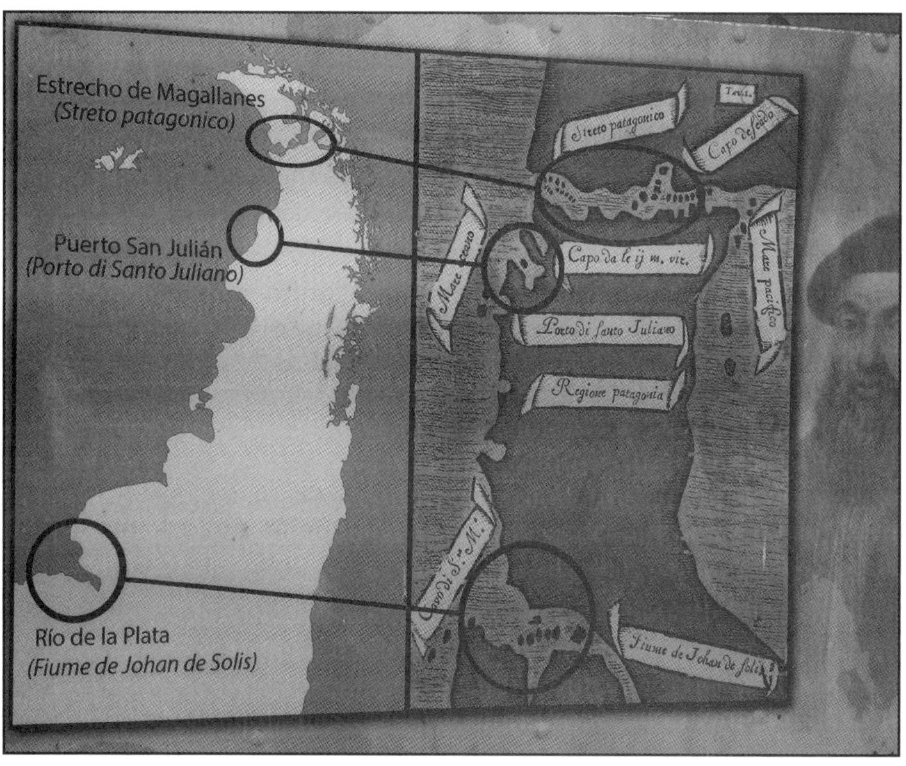

Only a few years after the Piri Re'is map was made, Ferdinand Magellan with five ships attempted to "sail around the world" in 1520. Magellan got through the Straits of Magellan, which became very important to the world of exploration. He got through to the Pacific with three of his ships. One ship sank off the coast of Patagonia before they went through. Another ship mutinied and went back to Spain because they did not believe in the success of the mission. When Magellan got through the Strait of Magellan, he named the new ocean "Pacific" because it was so "peaceful" at that time.

the most valuable commodity in the Age of Discovery. Every time a pirate ship would overtake another vessel by using a "false flag" of an allied nation (this is where the term false flag comes from), they would try to get close enough for cannon shots or to overtake by force. The pirates would put up the flag matching the vessel on the sea that they wanted to capture and lure them closer. Then when the pirates went aboard the captured ship, the first thing they would do is break into the captain's quarters and steal the maps which were always secured in the captain's lockbox. Maps were more valuable to pirates than any pieces of gold that they could capture. It was a common practice to copy the maps and keep that information in protective hands. The pirates did not want their enemies to get the maps.

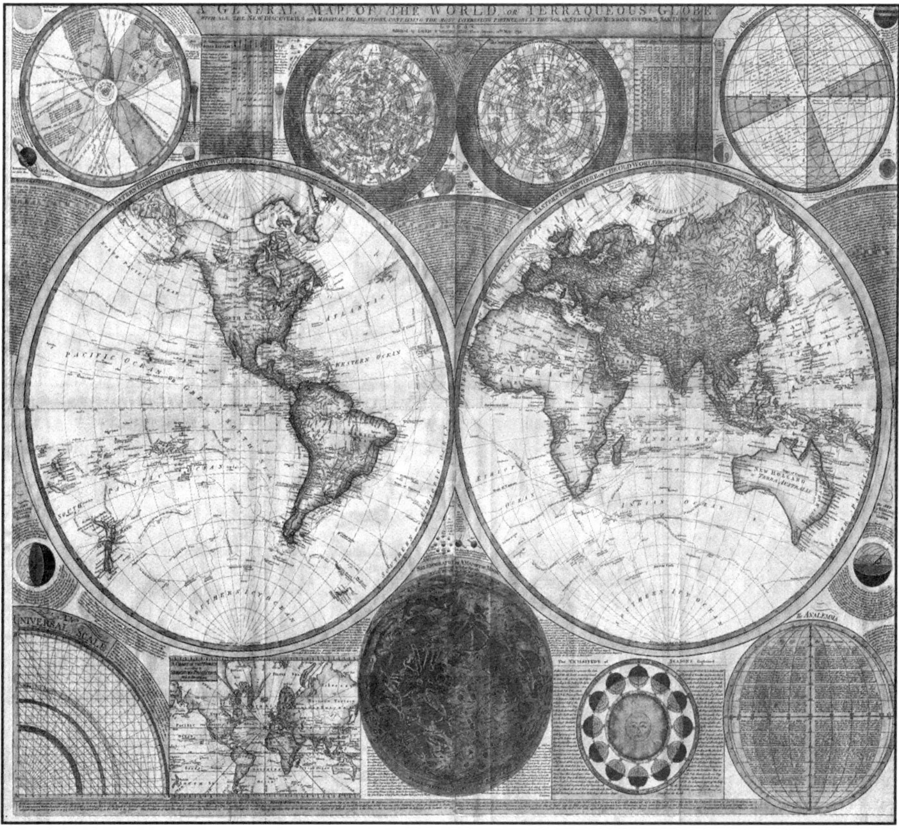

The Samuel Dunn "Wall Map of the World in Hemispheres" published in 1794, shows the route of Captain Cook's circumnavigation of Antarctica from 1768 to 1771 in the *Resolution*, but does not represent Antarctica in any way because Cook never sighted the continental landmass.

Even the continents got their names from copied maps. Before the continent was discovered they called the unknown southern landmasses *Terra Incognita de Australia.* When Australia was discovered it got the name. The Greeks knew of the northern "Arctos" constellation, and presupposed there must be a southern continent in the opposite region, and so named it "Antarctica." The 1570 map by Abraham Ortelius depicted *Terra Australis Nondum Cognita* "The Southern Land Yet Not Known" as a large continental blob on the bottom of the map. Even Ranally High School pull-down maps in 1940 showed there was still much uncharted land less than 100 years ago.

The early maps inexorably changed the European and Turkish knowledge of the known world. Suddenly it was a navigable globe. The remarkable 1794 Samuel Dunn map of the world depicts both hemispheres, and shows the route of Captain Cook's circumnavigation around Antarctica in the Southern Ocean from 1768 to 1771 aboard the *Resolution,* but he never set sight on the continental landmass. Captain Cook observed a "southern icy ocean" but no significant land sighting, just some pan-Antarctic islands. Antarctica now disappears on the latest world map supported by the Royal Society. Cook's journals were published upon his return, and he became something of a hero among the scientific community. His journal entries of abundant whales and seals in the South-

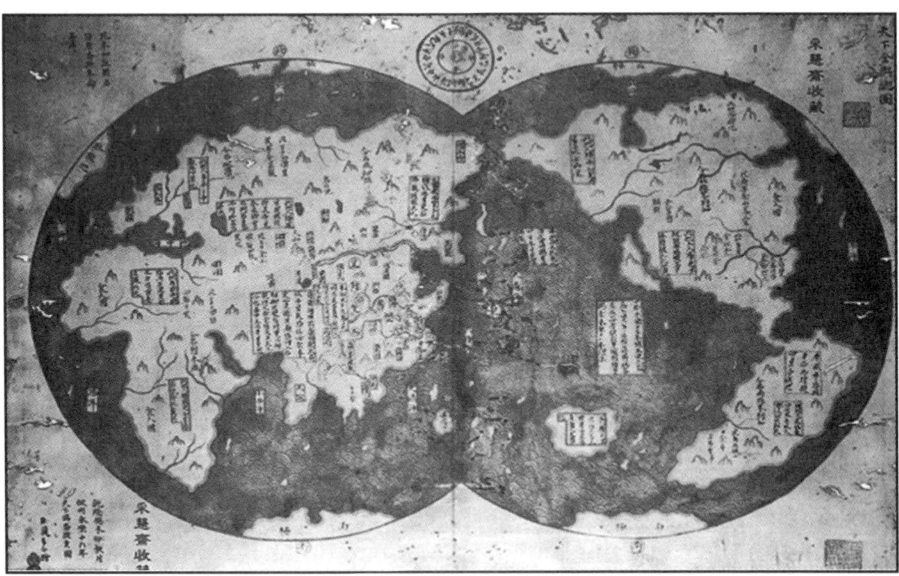

The Chinese World Map drawn in 1421 depicts the Americas over 70 years before the first Columbus voyage.

ern Ocean inspired the whale blubber and seal hunters to venture down there and eventually discover the continent.

On January 28, 1820, a Russian expedition led by Fabian von Bellingshausen and Mikhail Lazarev ventured far below the Antarctic Circle. They were the first to theorize a large landmass must be near, on account of the numbers of birds. Ten months later an American sealer, Nathaniel Palmer, became the first to sight Antarctica on November 17, 1820. The first landing was most likely just over a year later when English-born American Captain John Davis, a sealer, set foot on the continent.

Also of note are the first world maps produced in the Far East. Did Chinese navigators discover the Americas over 70 years before Columbus? According to Gavin Menzies in his bestselling book entitled *1421—The Year That China Discovered America* they did just that. Menzies was a royal Navy submariner, and the chart he studied had all the hallmarks of the original mapping of the Americas on both coastlines. Interesting that up until 1855, California was depicted as an island, as it is on the Chinese World Map several centuries prior. And there's Antarctica drawn on the map too, which was not officially discovered until 400 years later.

NAZIS IN ANTARCTICA

"We cannot take credit for our record advancement in certain scientific fields alone. We have been helped, and we have been helped by the people of other worlds."

–Nazi Paperclip scientist Herman Oberth

ANTARCTICA has been home to a lot of mysteries since it was first landed upon in 1821. Because of its extreme remoteness, it remains little studied and understood in barely a century of exploration and mapping. The Nazis surveyed hundreds of miles of mountain ranges during the *Neuschwabenland* expedition of 1938-39. The British, for their part, mapped and set up spying stations of the Nazis along the Palmer Peninsula during the World War

II in Operation Tabarin. Largely under the leadership of Richard E. Byrd, the Americans charted the regions of land near Little America, the South Pole and around the American McMurdo base in Eastern Antarctica. Since it is such a massive continent with no land resources to aid in supplying an expedition, large portions of Antarctica have remained free of human contact. There are still mountains that have yet to be climbed or even named.

The Imperial German Antarctic Expedition under Captain Alfred Ritscher 1938/1939 did not map and measure just one significant part of Antarctica, the so-called area of *Neuschwabenland,* but created the conditions at the same time for the permanent occupation of this area. During the war, the Antarctic base was expanded further and served as a refuge for those after the fighting ended, and the high technology transferred in the final months of Nazi Germany.

The transport of this technology and the one to operate it required a crew that was made by a fleet of ultramodern submarines with partly revolutionary properties. The submarines left the uncaptured ports of Hamburg, Germany and the Norwegian port of Kristiansand in early May, 1945 and headed for the North Atlantic.

The last naval battle of the war took place near Iceland and resulted in the complete annihilation of an allied warship formation. The news about it in Europe was hushed up, but found its way into in the South American press *Precipitation*, and in the Chilean daily newspaper *El Mercurio.*

After this successful battle, the Imperial German base located in the Arctic with the designation Point 103 is described by the German historian Wilhelm Landig in the first part of his trilogy. Landig was a former SS member who revived the Aryan mythology of Thule. He was born on December 20, 1909, served in World War II, and wrote the Thule trilogy *Götzen gegen Thule* (1971), *Wolfszeit um Thule* (1980) and *Rebellen für Thule–Das Erbe von Atlantis* (1991). As the Landig account of history goes, the main submarine fleet then headed south with the aim of *Neuschwabenland.* Two of the U-boats from the Führer's Convoy dropped out mid-way on a return voyage because of technical difficulties. Several months after the war ended they had to port in Argentina, to where the U-boats were confiscated and the crew was interrogated by the Americans. The remaining U-boats cleared any opposition in the final push to the Antarctic base. The other part secretly dispatched into the mainland of South America.

LAND CLAIMED BY THE THIRD REICH

A secret Nazi expedition undertaken in 1938-1939 was led by Captain Alfred Ritscher, who was dispatched to Antarctica by Field Marshal Hermann Göring, the head of the *Luftwaffe*. Göring was interested in both claiming territory and protecting Germany's growing whaling fleet in the Southern Ocean. The military rank of *Reichmarschall* was created specifically for Göring, who founded both the *Gestapo* and the *Luftwaffe*, and co-sponsored the 1938-1939 Nazi expedition to establish a Third Reich colony, along with *Stellvertreter* Rudolf Hess, "Deputy" Führer of Nazi Germany. Some of the highest ranking Nazi officers were overseeing the expedition.

The expedition used seaplanes to overfly vast stretches of the ice sheet, dropping 1.5-meter long darts inscribed with swastikas to establish sovereignty—claims that were never recognized by the international community. Perhaps the Nazis discovered an anomaly under the ice, and the Kohnen Station is a summer German research station which exists to this day. In 2013 there was a major excavation, and it is presumed people continued to work there in an area below the ice.

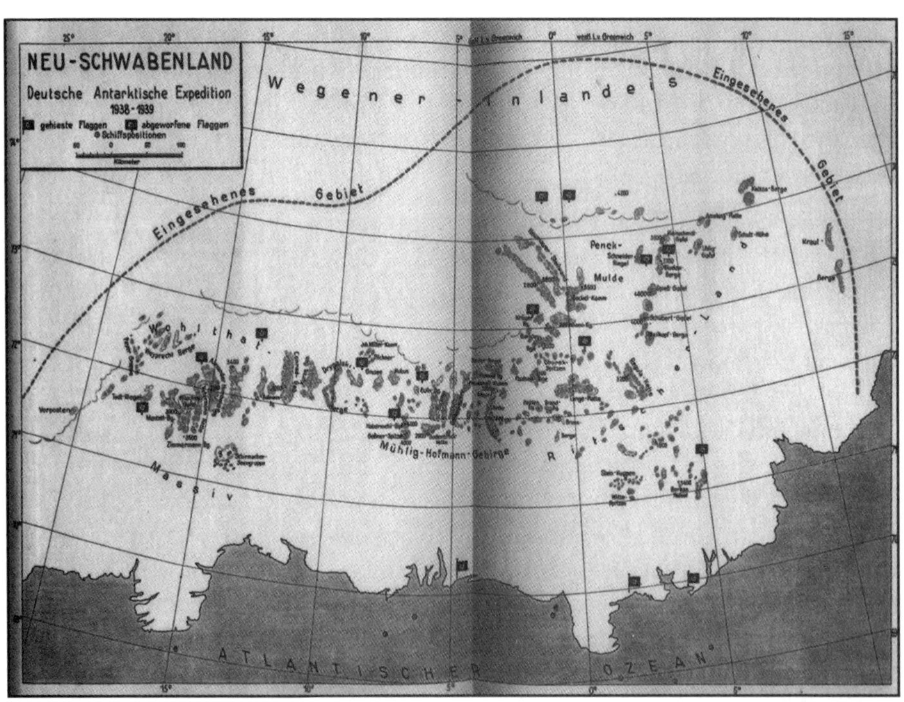

The pre-World War II Nazi Base "Point 211" as indicated on military charts in "Neu-Schwabenland" was founded within the Schirmacher Hills.

Nazis in Antarctica

After the Tibet excursions in the mid-1930s, the distant and uselessly icy continent manifests an incomprehensible interest to the government in Germany, which allocated huge funds for the study of Antarctica in the late 1930s. At least two research expeditions were organized, and this was before the outbreak of World War II. The expedition was ready to be born with day after day operations by January, 1939. Two Passat and Barey aircraft, which with the help of catapults, the *Luftwaffe* pilots begin to explore the vast areas of Queen Maud Land. In three weeks after arriving the name *Neuschwabenland* was declared in April, 1938. The Expedition Commander, the experienced polar Captain Alfred Ritscher reports:

> *I have fulfilled the mission assigned to me. Marshal Göring for the first time flew German planes over the Antarctic continent every 25 kilometers. With our planes 350,000 pictures were photographed by Göring's air wasps.*

Upon arrival back in Germany, the mysterious baton is taken over by the Sea Wolves of the Führer's fleet of U-boats, under the leadership of Admiral Karl Dönitz. Throughout the war years, German submarines secretly headed for the shores of icy Antarctica, and after a while Dönitz dropped a strange phrase that his submariners had discovered a real earthly paradise. In 1943, in the midst of the brutal war with Russia, Grand Admiral Dönitz delivers another

The Nazis claimed a large area of Antarctica, during the *Neuschwabenland* expedition of 1938-39 and began construction of Base 211.

no less mysterious quote that "the German submarine fleet can be proud of what's on the other side of the world. We created an impregnable fortress for the Führer," who was then Commander-in-Chief. Today we can assume that meant Admiral Dönitz not so long ago in Antarctica, under a mile of ice, discovered huge lakes with warm temperatures.

The first Nazi "Base 211" occupied an area known as the Schirmacher Hills, an ice-free year-round "oasis" dotted around 180 geothermal lakes and ponds. Below the surface the Germans followed caves to domed vaults under the ice formed by the warm water. These lakes were constantly heated from below, and flowed out into rivers of warm water for thousands of years. In this area the Nazi colony could have inhabited the massive under the ice domes, and burrowed under the ground digging huge tunnels, quite suitable for the construction of secret U-boat bases entering from the ocean side. The submarines could transverse under the coastal ice and safely enter the under-ice ports. Here was a ready-made base without storms and polar cold, and absolutely hidden from prying eyes out of reach for anyone if the Germans decided to place some secret bases, or create secret zones that seem to have extraterritorial status. The fact that the Nazis would occupy the polar zones, including Antarctica, was completely natural when the tide of the war turned in 1943. Judging by the discovered documents and the memories of the participants, an undersea U-boat base and permanent colony were actually created by the Nazis in Antarctica.

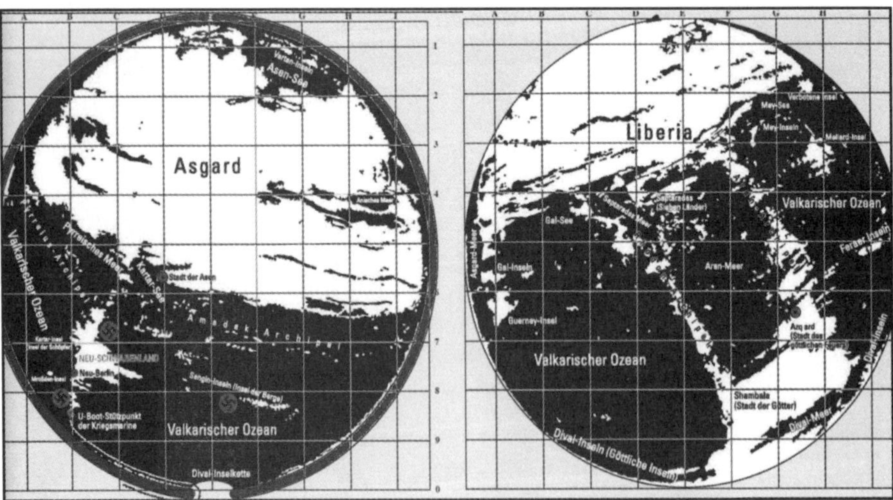

At the bottom left of the globe, we can see an opening with a grey dotted line going from the surface, through an opening, to the inside, showing us the entrance to this supposed inner world.

The *Die Glocke* or "The Bell" mysteriously vanished at the end of World War II. A remote region of Poland was the *Die Glocke* testing area. Some ruins are still there.

IN SEARCH OF FLYING SAUCERS

After the war, a huge stash of intriguing photos and drawings were discovered in Nazi secret archives. They proved that German scientists were actually engaged in the development of disc-shaped aircraft. At the time, nothing like this existed. How did Nazi scientists manage to make such a massive technological leap forward?

Ralph Ettl was an Austrian living in London when he received a packet of documents in 1989 from an anonymous source. The documents showed the schematics and drawings of several different flying saucers series, with innovative electromagnetic gravity engines, and vehicle names that had been floated around for years. Ralph Ettl shared the material with researchers in the 1990s. The story goes that production locations were scouted in 1935 by the Thule Society who were looking for a location to test a new powerful armament. The Hauneburg testing ground in Northwest Germany was well-suited for this top secret test. The project was referred to as the "Hauneburg Device," and later, for security, its name was shortened to "Haunebu." The early Haunebu craft was 25 meters (82 feet) in diameter, held a team of eight people, could reach a speed of 4,800 km/h (3,000 mph), with an operation time of 18 hours. According to the archive documents, a few prototypes were constructed but later disappeared under mysterious circumstances. Witnesses said that members of the Thule Society left Germany in March, 1945 using "flying saucers." During World War II, another one of the Nazi's most classified project was known as *Die Glocke* "The Bell" that incorporated time travel properties, and other top secret backward engineered flying disc and energy technologies. Several of the Vril women and Hans Kammler were said to have escaped at the end of the war in The Bell time travel craft. They were never seen or heard from again. [1]

To explain the rapid technological developments, it would appear that the Germans had established a connection with extraterrestrial beings early in their saucer development history. There are videos showing UFOs hovering and in flight from 1939, precisely at the dawn of World War II. There were years of development before the first prototype crafts took flight. The early timing might shed light on Germany's early military technology superiority over other nations. No other country at the time was even close to Germany's technological development.

---

1. Childress, David Hatcher. *Vril: Secrets of the Black Sun*, Adventures Unlimited Press, Kempton, IL 2024.

It cannot be overstated that, throughout the war, German inventors and engineers developed several glide bombs, marking the first "smart" weapons. These include the V-1 "flying bomb," recognized as the first cruise missile, and the infamous V-2 rocket that rained down on London, acknowledged as the first ballistic missile. American pilots were the first to encounter the German manned jet in 1944, significantly way ahead in technology. The initial encounter captures the pilot's astonishment: "What the hell was that? It went by like we were standing still!" Could it be the Germans achieved their rapid development with "otherworldly" assistance as Nazi Paperclip scientist Herman Oberth suggested?

In the decades before the War, the Americans had an engineer who was also working on disc craft technology. The TT Brown Electrokinetic Apparatus (U.S. Patent 2,949,550, August 16th, 1960) demonstrates the link between electro-magnetics and gravity. Originally published in 1929, this link was shown mathematically with Einstein's Unified Field Theory. TT Brown had been experimenting with the link between electrostatics and gravity since 1923. By the late 1940s, Brown experimented with disc-shaped airfoils, which mimicked flying saucers. In 2000, Independent scientists have demonstrated the patent with multi-meter diameter prototype flying saucers. The TT Brown EK apparatus is not only

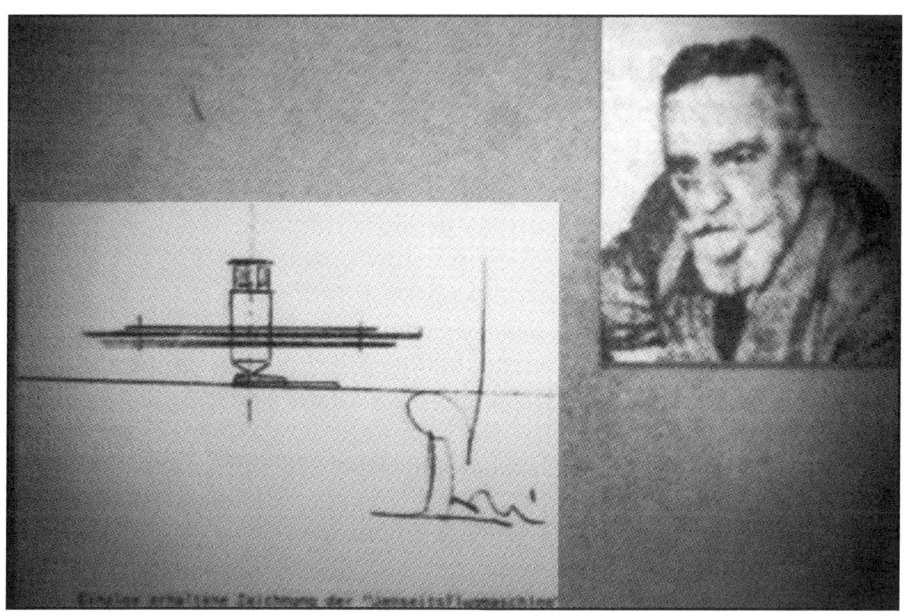

Maria Orsic channeled Nordic ET designs for a space craft which Viktor Schauberger had found viable physics for development in 1922.

a simple gravitational drive, but it fulfills all the requirements of the Alcubierre warp-bubble "wave-rider" theory that allows faster than light travel, within the framework of General Relativity. Recently, scientists have created warp bubbles in the lab capable of at least ten times the speed of light. We have opened the door to a new age, where science fiction has become reality, and physics has finally advanced past the 20th century model. [2]

TO FLY A DISC

In July 1934, Hitler's scientists of the Thule and Vril secret societies were able to heat and drive machinery using only air and water. After this breakthrough, the inventor needed only to create an engine specifically for flying discs. Consent was obtained and five years later, in 1939, an experienced sample of a Vril disc with a Schauberger engine was created. A rare photograph of the test pilot of this device has been preserved. It was covered in camouflage, and with all flying disc craft it advanced slowly, mainly because there were no experienced specialists in this field. They had to make these extraordinary decisions on the spot. The development of "super disks" was connected to the probe called Bureau 13. This special SS research unit was engaged in the rather unique topic of studying unidentified flying objects, or magic discs. Either the mysterious circumstances, or the involvement of the best scientists and test pilots, the German Armed Forces reluctantly moved forward with extreme caution, but perhaps too slowly because none of the prototypes were ever engaged in combat activity. Plus, the *Luftwaffe* had lost most of its best pilots in combat by the end of the war.

At the end of 1942, German engineers developed an air-lifted and lightly armed flying disc into production, with a diameter of 11 meters. It is claimed that by the end of the war, 17 such devices were made. There were single prototype copies of such devices, apparently they would only be used as an observer craft because they were too valuable to risk being shot down and falling into the hands of the enemies. Because of its shape when looked at from the side, it was difficult to discern the thin craft. Generals who participated in the world's largest tank Battle of Kursk, and Soviet pilots said that something like that was seen, some kind of disk that hung in the sky observing the Battle of Kursk. At the time no one knew if they were the Germans, ETs, or Soviet secret technology.

In the history of aviation, among the discovered drawings and photographs of flying discs, the Haunebu series stands out. The in-

2. http://discaircraft.greyfalcon.us/HAUNEBU.htm

formation about the ships looks like classic science fiction technology, judging by the description. They were clearly using an alternative energy source. The so-called Hans Kohler converter, which did not require the usual fuel, including the Haunebu 3 with the objective of being launched into space. If not outer space, then at least high in the stratosphere.

Aus reichsdeutschen SS-Geheimarchiven (Planskizzen, Beschriftung aus Fragmenten rekonstruiert).

Blueprints for the Andromeda cigar-shaped mothership sent to Ralph Ettl indicates it could transport and dispatch four smaller Vril craft and one Haunebu flying disc.

Another mysterious document found in the Trophy Archives is a diagram of the huge 139-meter long cigar-shaped ship called the Andromeda. The hangar could contain four or five type 2 Vril flying discs, and one mid-sized Haunebu. Why was such a development needed? Some believe that it was used for long-term space flights. A simpler explanation is the design of an underwater container that could be used for the transportation of cargo, equipment, and personnel to the secret bases of the Third Reich, including in the Antarctic. According to American intelligence, by the end of World War II, the Germans had a researcher Willow Flying Discs investigation revealed that of these enterprises, together with UMI and key figures were successfully evacuated from Germany. The ninth structure was blown up, recalls Lieutenant Colonel of American intelligence Wendell Stevens, that we had classified information that some of these research enterprises were transported to Antarctica instead of under the name of *Neuschwabenland.* A mini drive enterprise was developed in the Amazon area, and a third on the northern coast of Norway. All of these enterprises allowed the recently evacuated to relocate to secret underground bases.

The Third Reich did not have enough time to implement their grandiose plans. Apparently, until the end of the war, the "techno-magical" discs would not reach the stage of industrial production. Several projects of such models were created, and some of them showed themselves quite well. No doubt, it was a colossal breakthrough. In technology, Germany's opponents did not have a trace of such discs, but even these discs were far from the same. They could only operate in the air, or at least fly on solid or water surface, just like now on a hovercraft, they oscillate, as well as they fly in the air. This is with the fact that all of them were the so-called "fan-type." The advantage over conventional aircraft is that they do not fall into a tailspin in any way, these are the disks that are very easy to use. Here they are not designed for high speeds, because their early developmental quality was very low.

Prototype One of the most advanced models, the so-called Belon disc passed the first and last test on February 19, 1945 at the Skoda Works testing facility near Prague. The main lifting force was created by the silent and flameless Schauberger engine, according to some sources at that time. In its day, the unmanned version of this prototype reached an altitude of 15 kilometers in three minutes and developed a horizontal speed of 2,200 kilometers per hour. It could hover in the air without turning, and it could fly forward and backward with success. [3]

By early 1945, with the war already raging in the territory of Germany, and without waiting for a complete occupation, the Nazis destroyed not only the exported production facilities and prototypes of unusual aircraft, but also humiliated the developer of its main engine, Victor Schauberger. Victor later recalled the model, tested in February 1945, was built in collaboration with first-class engineers and explosion specialists from among the prisoners of the Mauthausen concentration camp. For those who worked on the discs it was the end of the war, but they could not go home. Those who refused to leave for Antarctica were found with a bullet in the back of their heads.

When the Nazi's developed the Haunebu and other anti-gravity craft, they essentially became a breakaway civilization with bases off-planet. There is a swastika-shaped base on the dark side of the Moon. If the history books were accurate, they would reflect the

---

3. Childress, David Hatcher. *Haunebu: The Secret Files: The Greatest UFO Secret of All Time,* Adventures Unlimited Press, Kempton, IL 2021.

Nazi astronauts being the first humans to the Moon, as well as other planets including Mars.

In the years following World War I, the women of the Vril Society were able to telepathically download complex blueprints of advanced energy and flying craft designs from beings of the Andromedan star system. The Andromedans recognized the Germans as the best engineers on Earth to use this technology for peaceful purposes. When the Thule Society usurped the Vril Society for use in the war machine, the transmissions ended.

In the years during and after World War II, the Nazi's created an interaction and alliance with the Antarctic inner-terrestrial Nordics of the highly advanced Arianni civilization. They were also aligned with the Draco reptilians who helped the German engineers develop their highly advanced weaponry and flying craft.

TECHNO-MAGICAL HERITAGE

In the post World War II years, intriguing photographs were discovered in the secret Nazi archives, and drawings of them unequivocally indicate that German scientists were really engaged in the development of disk-shaped flying devices. There was nothing like them in the world at that time, and Nazi scientists and engineers were making amazing technological breakthroughs. Its secrets are still hunted by the special services of the leading superpower nations today, so it is no wonder that this is the only known period of development in history.

The early technological engagement which morphed into the study of magic and mysticism had official support and funding from the government. Occultist of Knowledge of Paranormal Phenomena of the GNR went even farther, and with the blessing of the SS resources.

At the expense of a massive army, the Germans knew they could not win future wars unless they had a technological advantage. Therefore, the concept of so-called qualitative superiority was used, which implied that it would be possible to win future wars with fewer forces in quantity, and with better trained troops in quality. It was to ensure the so-called qualitative superiority that attracted specialists in occult knowledge and in non-traditional paranormal research in order to achieve a breakthrough in those areas where their opponents were incompetent.

The ideology of Nazism was based on the fact that once there was a powerful civilization on Earth, which did not have access to all the secrets of the universe and somewhere encrypted and scattered this higher knowledge has been preserved should contribute to the revival of the superman in Germany, the descendant of the ancients. The Aryans were particularly interested in Atlantis, which Nazi scholars believed was the original homeland of the Aryan race. It is to Germany that the technological Atlanteans, who, according to legend, were able to look for knowledge on the history of civilization, the origins of civilization, both Germanic, and any civilization in general.

Throughout the war, the Germans were hoping for a breakthrough in search of the techno-magical heritage of the Atlanteans, because according to one of the hypotheses, Antarctica is the former Atlantis, which was under the ice as a result of displacement of the poles. Since supporting documents such as the Piri Re'is map exist, then somewhere other secret documents could be found.

Throughout the 1930s, the German government commissioned secret expeditions in search of ancient manuscripts all over the world. They funded special explorations from Tibet to South America, and especially hunted for the archives of the Knights Templars, who, according to a number of indications, visited America long before Christopher Columbus. Apparently the Templars possessed secret manuscripts similar to the Piri Re'is map, and therefore could know something important about Antarctica in the occupied territories.

One of the main goals of the Nazi leadership, by and large, the SS was looking for special knowledge of a very sacred chalice called the Holy Grail, which, together with the sacred spear, opens the way to the world domination of this legend. Hitler knew full well about these objects. In 1938, after the annexation of Austria, he did not have the Holy Grail, but it was enough to possess the legendary Spear of Destiny on display in an Austrian museum.

The Nazis set to reign supreme over the world, to subordinate it to a chosen race, including with the help of magical knowledge and technologies for scientific research in the Ahnenerbe Society. The best personnel were involved, often those who were world-renowned scientists, and hundreds of employees who were engaged in mathematics and astronomy, genetics and medicine, and magic. They also sought to develop non-traditional types of weapons, methods of psychological and psychotropic influence on the masses, and to delve into the occult sciences by religious-mystical mediums and scientists. This is quite seriously evidenced by the fact that, on the instructions of the Ahnenerbe leadership and on the instructions of Himmler, before the war started in 1939, research was carried out into the paranormal abilities of the employees of Ahnenerbe and it was noted, so to speak, in the personnel files of who possessed some certain paranormal abilities. And already during the war, these employees who had paranormal abilities, were reduced to one of the departments of the People's Republic of Bulgaria. Unfortunately, no data exists on what this department was engaged in and, most importantly, what results it achieved.

There was an opinion at the time that they were channeled techno-magic devices that became the prototype of future flying disks on non-classical principles of flight by developing these super discs of Nazi Germany first. There is also the idea of creating a superman, a hybrid warrior capable of withstanding the elements of a "super soldier," who could withstand the harsh conditions of outer space and Antarctica.

The second very important aspect of mastering the techno-magical technology was to win the war. This should include not only the possibility of mastering nuclear energy but, of course, by using disc-shaped devices, flying machines, that is, the creation of a fundamentally new type of flying technology. Indeed, the search

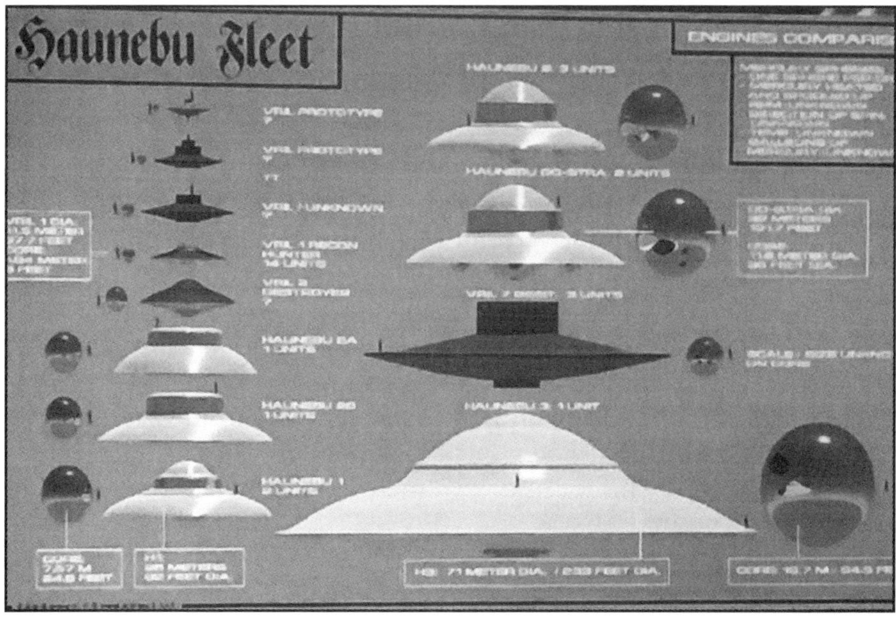

The evolution of the German Vril and the Haunebu flying saucer programs are seen in this chart, from prototypes to fully functioning aerospace combat craft.

for ideas was going on in all directions. They involved not only mediums and engineers, but also historians even before the war, from the expedition of Germans to Tibet that delivered hundreds of ancient parchments, ancient Chinese, other oriental languages, and were all subjected to close scrutiny by the Ahnenerbe Society.

Esoteric researchers would say the collapse that the Nazis suffered was not by chance, because the Grail cup is a symbol not only of ancient knowledge, but also of centuries of moral experience. This experience was deliberately rejected by the Nazis. There are a lot of legends and rumors associated with the flying disks of the Third Reich. Apparently stories about German discs can also be attributed to this category as it emerges. The flights of unidentified flying submersible objects emerging from the seas, oceans, lakes, and wide rivers of the world have been recorded worldwide. [4]

AHNENERBE SOCIETY

The scientific organization "Ahnenerbe" was created in 1935 on the personal orders of Adolf Hitler. Since 1938, all scientific research in Germany was carried out under the control of the scientific department of the SS Ahnenerbe. The staff of this organization included outstanding German scientists. In the period 1937-1938, expedition teams from Ahnenerbe carried out a number of scientific research trips to the Himalayas and Tibet in search of ancient artifacts which testify to the existence of extraterrestrial civilizations that controlled the course of human evolution. The Ahnenerbe carried out the search for the so-called Shambhala (City of the Gods). About seven thousand people were involved in this direction, famous archaeologists, anthropologists, biologists, geneticists, historians, engineers and mountaineers.

Ancient Aryan legend tells the story of the Thule People who lived when Greenland was ice-free many millennia ago. The people were a tall and blond Nordic-looking race who lived on Greenland until the last Ice Age, when they moved to the Inner Earth and still remain there. They have advanced technology flying their saucers which are more advanced than the humans on the surface of the planet. And so it has been the secret dream of the Germans on the surface to find and reunite with the more advanced Aryan brothers from the Inner Earth.

Indiana Jones' race to find the Ark of the Covenant and the Holy Grail before the Nazis may be the realm of fiction, but in reality, there was a Nazi organization tasked with finding relics. However, this lead organization called Ahnenerbe, went far beyond just

---

4. Sepehr, Robert. *Occult Secrets of Vril: Goddess Energy and the Human Potential*: Atlantean Gardens, 2015.

finding religious artifacts. The Ahnenerbe Society was one of the most mysterious organizations in the Third Reich. Even now the secret services of leading powers continue to hunt for its secrets. But the question must be asked why? In modern history this was the only known historical structure engaged in the study of the occult and mysticism to have state financing and support. No organization in the world had at its disposal such a volume of data, or had such influence on the development of culture and technology as the Ahnenerbe Society. Research on occult knowledge and paranormal phenomena by the Ahnenerbe received blessings from the highest echelon of the SS Reich. Heinrich Himmler head of the SS not only acted on his own initiative, but also with direct instructions from Adolf Hitler.

Officially, the society was founded in 1935, and was intended to explore historical roots of the German nation. *Ahnenerbe* when translated means "legacy of ancestors," however, the society's scope of interest was broader than ancient German history study. Third Reich leaders understood an army size could not necessarily win future wars. Therefore, they adopted the so-called concept of qualitative superiority. Thus, one can win a war with relative low quantitative troops, while utilizing high qualitative armaments and the best-trained forces. To provide them with qualitative superiority, the Ahnenerbe brought in specialists in the occult, including non-traditional and paranormal knowledge in order to achieve any kind of qualitative or quantitative advantage.

Nazi ideology was based on the theory that in the past there was a powerful Earth civilization with access to secrets of the universe somewhere encrypted and scattered. This knowledge was preserved, specifically they were tasked with reviving the superhuman in Germany in their role as an ancient Aryan descendant. They were very interested in Atlantis. Their scientists believed it was the Aryan race's native home.

According to this logic, the German people were the “rightful heir” to Atlantean knowledge. In March, 1945, word got out that the Soviet troops were approaching on German territory, and so the Ahnenerbens began frantically trying to evacuate all the occult books from the Postonski library. It is quite possible the Ahnenerbe historians learned something incredible about Antarctica. They made the study of the continent one of the main Nazi leadership goals. Actually the SS were after very specific knowledge, that is, ways to better the German people and win the war. The Ahnenerbe collected a huge library, according to the librarian from one of the

Postonski libraries, and in the end tried to carry away 140,000 volumes. Most of these books were never recovered.

Studies were carried out concerning paranormal abilities for the employment into the Ahnenerbe society. The results were recorded on personnel files. When the war started, officers with any kind of paranormal abilities, along with others who could display paranormal skills, were merged into a single Ahnenerbe department. Unfortunately, there are no records on what this department was working on, or more importantly, what results were achieved.

One of the main objectives pursued by the Ahnenerbe experts was the use of paranormal abilities to contact unknown beings, or "outsiders" as they called them. The aim was to obtain, from highly developed extraterrestrial, and ancient terrestrial civilizations, superior technological knowledge to give the Germans that almost mythical qualitative advantage coming into the war.

VRIL AND THULE SOCIETY

The Ahnenerbe predecessor was the secret Thule Society and Vril Society. Their members were researchers, scientists and those who had psychic abilities. Among them selected were two experienced mediums or contactees. One of them is shrouded under the mysterious name of Sigrun. The other is Maria Orsic of the Vril Society. All the women wore their hair long to aid in telepathic transmissions. In a trance state, Maria Orsic began to speak of blueprints and outlines for spaceships from an advanced extraterrestrial civilization. She received incredible technical information on exotic propulsion, energy and antigravitic devices. This knowledge shocked no one in the Thule or Vril Societies. On the contrary, it attracted huge interest as these devices concerned eventually led to the construction of unusual flying vehicles which could alter the flow of time around it, while traveling through space. This was *Die Glocke* or "The Bell" time machine which was said to penetrate way back into history in order to obtain knowledge of ancient high civilizations.

From her youth, Maria Orsic always spoke about "a voice" calling her name. Around age 19, living in Vienna, she and the Baron from Sebottendorf founded the Vril Society and she was able to contact this voice, and the voice introduced itself as "Ashtar" or "Isias" from the star system Aldebaran. Eventually the spirit of Ashtar instructed the other civilian Vril members to gather in an effort to build a space ship and travel to Aldebaran. There were many attempts to build a first one, and subsequent better ones. But the SS and

Abwehr (counter intelligence) got hold of their activities and at first had them arrested. Within a few days they were released because Himmler ordered them to do so. Himmler, together with Albert Speer, Hermann Göring and Adolf Hitler himself were members of the Thule Society. They visited the Vril meetings and proposed to move the technological developments to the SS and the Thule Society. Adolf Hitler was often seen sitting with Karl Haushofer, who was a geologist and scientist and developed great skills in Eastern languages and culture. Haushofer and the Baron from Sebottendorf were also connected with the development of the Ahnenerbe organization.

Just after World War I, Maria Orsic with the Vril Society were working with beings from Aldebaran, the Andromedans and the Nordics from Inner Earth. Another Nazi-sponsored occult group was a *Schutzstaffel* (SS) think tank called the Ahnenerbe, or "Ancestral Heritage." This secret society was tasked with investigating the Aryan and Nordic roots of the German people.

The Vril soon became, with the help of the SS and material supplies, able to construct "Vril" fighter disks and a larger "Haunebu" craft that would eventually rocket into space on several occasions. The Vril Society had telepathic contact with the Aryrans on Aldebaran through Maria Orsic. She herself did not understand the information that was passed through her. She could not even remember most times. Vril members took the notes when she spoke. On occasions Maria did some auto-handwriting and this was, as experts confirmed, in the old Sumerian (pre-Cuneiform) Semitic language. In the final days of the war, at the end of April 1945, Maria Orsic was then the head of the Vril Society. She decided that their entire group would board a Haunebu craft and leave Germany for Aldebaran. Sure enough, right after the war neither Maria Orsic, nor her fellow Vril members were ever to be seen from again! Not a dead body or a letter back home was to be found. They all just vanished. Only one friend who refused to follow them

The specially-designed badge or emblem of the *Deutsche Antarktische Expedition 1938-1939* has occult origins. The swastika and oak leaves clearly reveal Thule Society paternity.

and saw them depart, related the departure and how this story is known. She got married and settled in Norway after the war.

In the late 1930s, the Germans started building out and stocking their base in *Neuschwabenland* so that they would be able to contain, feed and house upwards of 300,000 people. The Ritscher Expedition badge of 1938-1939 displayed two oak leaves indicating Thule Society paternity. There were thousands involved in building Base 211. Most of them were native Germans, and this information was kept compartmentalized to keep the secrets contained. They were able to use the geothermal properties underneath the mountains for their power source initially. Later on, they developed alternative advanced technology so they wouldn't have to rely solely on geothermal. But it was there around 1941 when the base went operational, which was also the same year the Germans made their first trip to the Moon in the Haunebu I. The same time period back on Earth was the period when the German navy had commissioned a pair of auxiliary cruisers which basically are converted civilian ships to do supply runs from allied South Africa to Antarctica. One of them was named *Pinguin* and the other was called *Atlantis.* All escorts across the South Atlantic were protected by killer U-boats. Any foreign ship was sunk sight unseen to protect the Antarctica base secret. After 1941, the Allies were able to sink some of the German auxiliary cruisers, stalling some of their progress on Base 211. They moved from using surface ships to using subsurface ships for transportation to and from their Antarctic base. From their base they had advanced technologies on their U-boats, so that they didn't have to surface and risk being sighted and sunk. Their new submarines were also some of the first stealth technology that had even been released (1945-1948).

When it was clear the war was lost, the Germans started their infiltration into South American governments. Their purpose was to undermine the Allies and get their own people in place for what would become a "Third Force" countering the NATO and the Soviet block of countries. They got their people into the military ranks, including getting younger men enlisted, and getting businessmen involved in politics so that they could get them deeply embedded into Western governments, especially the United States as part of Project Paperclip. Sometimes members of the Thule Society were the top scientists and military officers who were brought over and assigned top positions. After all, the war was over and the Germans were very adaptable as U.S. citizens. There is a saying that Germans make the best Americans, but the worst Germans. Indeed, Germans are the largest ethnic group in the United States.

NAZI OCCULTISTS MOVE TO ANTARCTICA

The *SchutzStaffel* (SS) was a major paramilitary organization under Adolf Hitler and the Nazi Party, and later throughout German-occupied Europe during World War II. It began with a small guard unit known as the *Saal-Schutz* made up of party volunteers to provide security for party meetings in Munich. In 1925, Heinrich Himmler joined the unit, which had by then been reformed and given its final name. Under his direction it grew from a small paramilitary formation during the Weimar Republic to one of the most powerful organizations in Nazi Germany. From the time of the Nazi Party's rise to power until the regime's collapse in 1945, the SS was the foremost agency of security, mass surveillance, and state terrorism within Germany and German-occupied Europe.

Towards the end of World War II, it is believed that about 250,000 senior officers belonging to the Nazi Party managed to escape in U-boats from Germany to locations in South America and Antarctica. There is strong evidence that Adolf Hitler staged his own suicide in the Berlin bunker and was also one of the escapees.

For over a century before the war the German people were interested in esoteric mysticism, as well as a wide range of alternative views on life, synchronistic connections and different energies. They scoured the entire planet looking for clues and more information. The Germans decided to open their investigation into the far reaches of the globe, searching for lost technology or advanced races. Their search took them down to Antarctica. It would appear they found something very important, because by the late 1930s the decision was made to go there multiple times and establish a series of colonies. Towards the end of World War II when the Germans realized that they were losing, the SS and Thule Society transferred all their manpower, knowledge and technology to the South American and Antarctic bases. It should be noted that the Third Reich and the SS never surrendered after World War II. Only the fighting forces *Wehrmacht* (army), *Kriegsmarine* (navy) and *Luftwaffe* (air force) surrendered. The craft seen flying during Highjump and over the U.S. Capital in 1952 were the early renditions of the German Secret Space Program called *Nacht Waffen* or the "Dark Fleet."

Early on, the Thule Society split into two separate groups. One faction of the Thule Society was working with reptilians based in our Solar System, and Maria Orsic who was communicating with benevolent extraterrestrials and Nordics from Inner Earth. Many of the UFO's originally seen flying around at this time were the German Secret Space program crafts based on backward engineered technology from the various ET groups. In July, 1952, UFO's appeared over the White House and the U.S. Capital building in Washington D.C. on two separate occasions. At the time they were thought to be aliens from another world, but really it was the Antarctic Germans forcing President Truman to stand down from attacking *Neuschwabenland* again. Many of these crafts seen flying around at this time were the products of the *Nacht Waffen.*

The new colony land claim was named after the original expedition ship "Schwabenland."

Once the United States entered World War II in December, 1941, it became obvious to anybody who had a geo-political education in Germany that the country was doomed to lose the war. The numbers just didn't add up. By the end of 1944, for every German plane that was produced and sent into battle, there were six allied planes in production also being launched. The Germans had less than one in five of the planes to fight the war. It is logical to assume the ratios of artillery or tanks and other armaments were not much different. Then the tide of the war turned after the tank Battle of Kursk in the summer of 1943, when it became clear that Germany would lose the war. They simply didn't have the industrial capacity to match the Americans, the British, and the Russians coming in from both sides. By the end of 1943 the decision was made to lose the European war in order to win the South Pole war. They had almost two years to evacuate the highest technology, priceless art pieces including perhaps the Spear of Destiny, and key personnel. They financed the operation with an intaglio press smuggled out of Germany that could forge "virtually undetectable" paper currency U.S. Dollars and Pounds Sterling. They were further supplemented by the many metric tons of gold that were looted from countries captured by Germany during the war. [5]

NEUSCHWABENLAND

In 1938, the Nazis sent a large team of explorers—including scientists, military units and building crews on war ships and submarines—to the Queen Maud Land region of Antarctica. Over 230,000 square miles of the frozen continent were mapped from the air. While surveying the area, they discovered a vast network of underground hot springs flowing out to rivers, and forming massive caves under the ice. One of these caverns extended 30 miles down to a large hot-water geothermal lake deep below. The cave was explored, and construction teams were sent in to build a city-sized base, named Point 211 or Base 211. Another larger location was dubbed New Berlin, which may have merged with the "Domain of the Arianni," near the South Pole on the continental surface of East Antarctica. Various scientific teams were moved into the area, including hunters, trappers, plant specialists, mycologists, parasitologists, marine biologists, ornithologists, and many others. The new colonies also hosted SS officers, anti-gravity scientists, the Thule Society, "serpent cults" of various Nazi occultists, the Illuminati, and other shadowy groups who fled on U-boats just before Germany surrendered in World War II.

5. Earth Defense Headquarters, *Operation Highjump 1947 and After*. An EDH Technical Brief, Winter 2002.

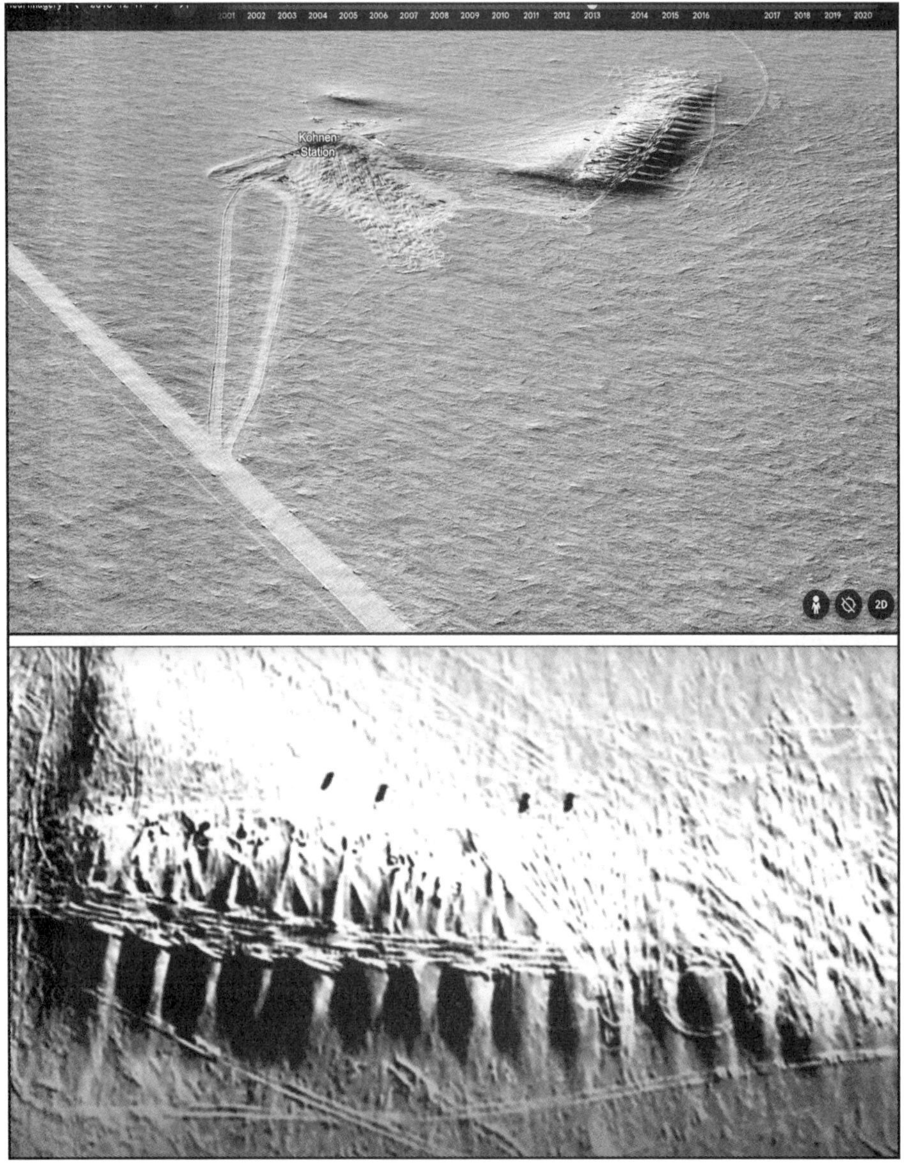

The Nazi overflights of ***Neuschwabenland*** discovered a massive anomaly poking out from under the ice—years later the gigantic craft is classified as one of the three motherships nicknamed by the NSA as the Nina, Pinta and Santa Maria.

Because the Polar Plateau and much of the continent remain unexplored, Google Earth has been invaluable in looking deep into the fabric of Antarctica to spot anomalies, including what could be disc-shaped crafts. Under the ice "craft" in ***Neuschwabenland,*** is the exact location of the West German Kohnen base: (75°00'47.0"S 0°04'52.7"E)

By the end of the expedition in 1939, the Nazis set up the foundations of secret Base 211, in a region of Antarctica they claimed known as *Neuschwabenland.* A suitable location was found outside the Schirmacher Hills at the Muhlig-Hoffman massif, which was hollowed out into a military base. The secret Nazi expedition in 1938-1939 led by Alfred Ritscher, was dispatched to Antarctica by Field Marshal Hermann Göring, who was interested in both claiming territory and protecting Germany's growing whaling fleet. At least this was the propaganda cover story. Similar to Operation Highjump, the Nazi expedition to *Neuschwabenland* was a covert military operation. The expedition used Dornier Wal flying boats from the *MS Schwabenland* to overfly vast stretches of the Polar Plateau ice sheet, dropping 1.5-meter (5-foot) darts inscribed with swastikas to establish sovereignty—claims that were never recognized.

While surveying the Dronning Maud Land previously claimed by Norway, it is likely the Nazi seaplanes discovered a massive anomaly poking out from under the ice, and is the reason the Nazis chose this particular region of Antarctica to claim for Germany. The gigantic craft, one of the three motherships nicknamed by American three-letter-agencies the Nina, Pinta and Santa Maria, is still there in *Neuschwabenland.* There is a seasonal research station there named Kohnen Station. This summer German base exists to this day to continue excavation work and take ice-core samples. The Germans never gave up their claims to *Neuschwabenland.*

The mysteries of *Neuschwabenland* continue to this day. Much of the narrow strip around the Schirmacher Hills, 17 kilometers (12 miles) long and 3 kilometers (2 miles) wide, is ice-free year-round, making it an "oasis." Dotted with as many as 180 geothermal lakes and ponds, the terrain is hilly, and were originally discovered by a pilot named Richard-Heinrich Schirmacher who flew the exploratory seaplane during the secret Nazi Antarctic expedition, and was dispatched to claim territory for Germany in the late 1930s. Schirmacher stayed behind with the plane and took water samples in the ponds determining they were warmed by geothermal vents. His crew went overland for several days to determine the best location for a base. It is speculated that the Nazis set up either Point 211, or the U-boat entry for the New Berlin base, near the Schirmacher Ponds and the Muhlig-Hoffman massif. This was geothermal land with an extensive cave system at the surface and well below the ice.

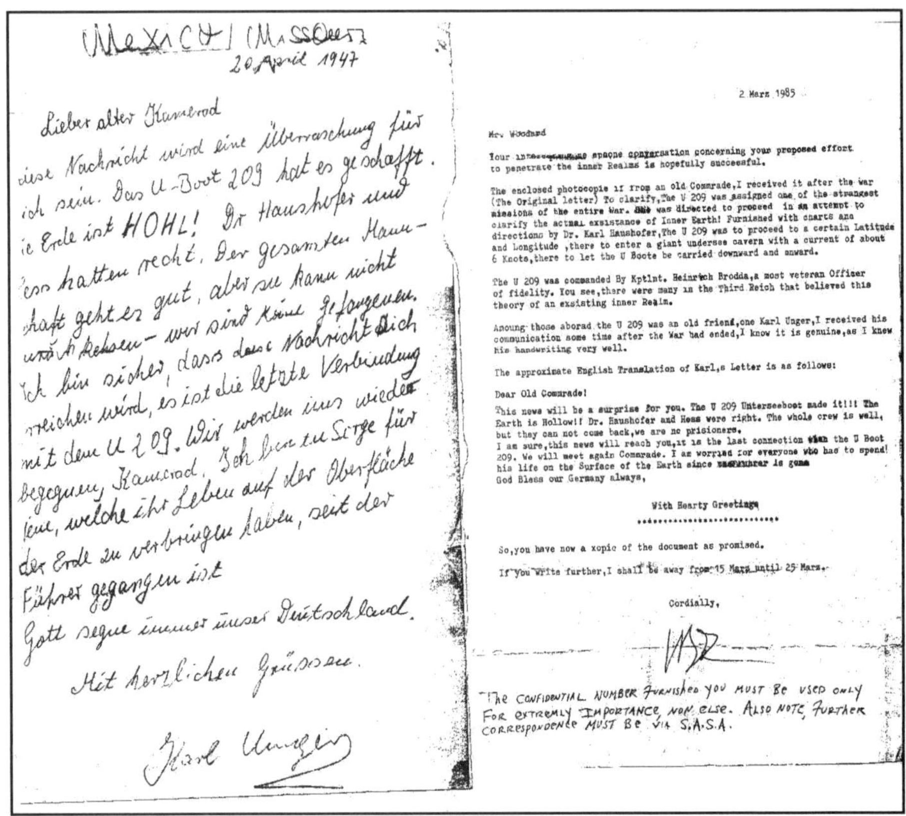

Mexico / Missouri
20 April 1947

Lieber alter Kamerad
iese Nachricht wird eine Überraschung für
ich sein. Das U-Boot 209 hat es geschafft.
ie Erde ist HOHL! Dr Haushofer und
ess hatten recht. Der gesamten Mann-
haft geht es gut, aber sie kann nicht
urückkehren – wir sind keine Gefangenen.
Ich bin sicher, dass diese Nachricht dich
rreichen wird, es ist die letzte Verbindung
mit dem U 209. Wir werden uns wieder
begegnen, Kamerad. Ich bin in Sorge für
jene, welche ihr Leben auf der Oberfläche
der Erde zu verbringen haben, seit der
Führer gegangen ist
Gott segne immer unser Deutschland.
Mit herzlichen Grüssen.
Karl Unger

2 Marz 1985

Mr. Woodard

Your interesting telephone conversation concerning your proposed effort to penetrate the inner Realms is hopefully successful.

The enclosed photocopie is from an old Commrade, I received it after the war (The Original letter) To clarify, The U 209 was assigned one of the strangest missions of the entire War. She was directed to proceed in an attempt to clarify the actual exsistance of Inner Earth! Furnished with charts and directions by Dr. Karl Haushofer, The U 209 was to proceed to a certain Latitude and Longitude, there to enter a giant undersee cavern with a current of about 6 Knots, there to let the U Boote be carried downward and onward.

The U 209 was commanded By Kptlnt. Heinrich Brodda, a most veteran Officer of fidelity. You see, there were many in the Third Reich that believed this theory of an exsisting inner Realm.

Amoung those aborad the U 209 was an old friend, one Karl Unger, I received his communication some time after the War had ended, I know it is genuine, as I knew his handwriting very well.

The approximate English Translation of Karl,s Letter is as follows:

Dear Old Commrade!

This news will be a surprise for you. The U 209 Unterseeboot made it!!! The Earth is Hollow!! Dr. Haushofer and Hess were right. The whole crew is well, but they can not come back, we are no prisioners.
I am sure, this news will reach you, it is the last connection with the U Boot 209. We will meet again Commrade. I am worried for everyone who has to spend his life on the Surface of the Earth since the Führer is gone
God Bless our Germany always,

With Hearty Greetings
****

So, you have now a xopie of the document as promised.

If you write further, I shall be away from 15 Marz until 25 Marz.

Cordially,

The CONFIDENTIAL NUMBER FURNISHED YOU MUST BE USED ONLY FOR EXTREMLY IMPORTANCE, NON ELSE. ALSO NOTE, FURTHER CORRESPONDENCE MUST BE VIA S.A.S.A.

A notebook was acquired by Russian journalist Nikolay Subbotin along with the under ice maps. It describes the recommendations (for New Berlin) and the Führer's orders. Order #8 of January 10, 1940 outlines how to choose personnel and staff to work on the Antarctic under-ice base: "Using the experience of the past selection of the personnel, people with families must be excluded, and personnel must be prepared and aware that most likely they will be going there for good (forever) in the name of The Reich and for the sake of building a new state." Interestingly, a 1947 letter from U-boat seaman Karl Unger explains how he too will not be returning.

A ONE-WAY MISSION

Formed in Missouri in 1977, the ISCE (International Society for a Complete Earth) is in possession of a letter written by a former Nazi U-boat crewman to his comrade back in Germany. The curious aspect of the letter is that it was written after U-boat 209 disappeared in Antarctica while searching for the entrance to Inner Earth, using charts drafted by German General Karl Haushofer. The letter arrived in Germany in 1947, and the handwriting was confirmed by the man's family. Translated from German the letter states:

04/20/1947

Dear Old Comrade!

This news will be a surprise for you. The U-209 submarine made it!!! The Earth is Hollow!! Dr. Haushofer and Hess were right. The whole crew is well, but they cannot come back. We are not prisoners.

I am sure this news will reach you. This is your last connection with Submarine 209. We will meet again Comrade. I am worried for everyone who has to spend his life on the Surface of the Earth since the Führer is gone. God Bless our Germany always,

With Hearty Greetings,

your friend, Hans

The larger Type XX had a range capable of diving to the depths indicated on the U-boat captain maps. These U-boats were kept top secret. If these submarines were available much earlier, that is, before 1945, this might explain the use of the under ice Antarctica maps. The details of the colossal U-boats in Bremen harbor was only fully released in the 1990s. These U-boats were even used in German navy service up until the 1980s, into the age of nuclear submarines.

For undersea transportation, there were German cargo submarines that could hold 5,000 tons, which is about 2 1/2 times as much as the standard allied liberty class transport ships. The Germans had 2 1/2 times bigger submarines than the allies, who were primarily building surface ships. The German submarines were so huge they could carry bulk cargo, they could carry personnel, they could carry armaments—really anything. They were building them in sections on assembly lines on several dry docks at incredible speed. From 1942 until the end of the war, about 100 submarines were allocated for service in the South Atlantic and Indian Ocean—basically for use in the southern polar regions.

In the final years of World War II when the Germans realized that they were losing, the SS (*Schutzstaffel*) and the Thule Society began the transfer of their manpower, knowledge and technology to the Antarctic. It is reported that the reptilians donated an abandoned underground base in *Neuschwabenland* to the Nazis. The Schirmacher landing party was tasked with finding the unused base, which they did. They also discovered under the ice passages that allowed the U-boat fleet to supply the newly-refurbished Base 211. It would be completed in 1945.

Today the *Neuschwabenland* region is the reported headquarters of an elite alliance that is the global NWO-Illuminati of the Fourth Reich. The group, also known to be involved with secretive space exploitation, are said to be present (even in South America) thanks to its links with the CIA who for decades deposed democratically elected governments in favor of fascist dictators who gave cover to Fourth Reich Nazis. The CIA was created just after the war by covert Bavarian Illuminists as a fifth-column operation to serve and protect the Fourth Reich. The partnership has been going on since Project Paperclip when many top German scientists went to work for the U.S. after Germany's loss in World War II. The political party of the Third Reich and the SS never surrendered after the war. They went underground, infiltrated, and started taking over. [6]

WHERE DID THE PEOPLE AND TECHNOLOGY GO?

When the estimated war victims were subtracted from the pre-war German population, the number cannot account for many thousands that went missing, even figuring in MIA (Missing In Action) and otherwise. Numbers vary from 250,000 adults to even half a million. True or not, a great number of Germans went missing after the war without a trace. In addition, there were about 200 U-boats in total unaccounted for at

6. The Russian documents from the Merkulov folder: https://plati.market/itm/merkulov-s-folder/

the end of the war. Some of course were found to be sunk. But 100 or more were not reported as being sunk, not even as "target unknown." They were being mass produced in 1945, and never tracked back after the war. Especially the huge common supply vessels "Type XIV," and the "Milk Cows" which are suspected to have carried large numbers of men and women to the Antarctic colony, since they were equipped to carry large number of rescued sailors, and had also a doctor on board as well as ample food and water. There were also thousands of young Ukrainian women who disappeared at the end of the war, presumably taken to Antarctica to become the wives of the men shipped down there. Even 40,000 Croatians sympathetic to the Nazi cause volunteered to relocate in *Newschwabenland.* [7]

It is little secret the Germans were exploring many unusual aspects of science, from new physics models, nuclear power, different medicines, para-psychology, the occult, ancient religions, untold history, molecular biology and so on. This automatically led to the installation of top-secret departments in the advanced research branches of the Third Reich. Germany was way ahead of its Anglo-Saxon opponents when it came to nuclear physics and engineering. The V-1 and the V-2 rockets are good examples, but also the advanced submarine development. The German navy perfected the capabilities of their U-boats by introducing the "snorkel," which was a Dutch invention that they stole, and the "*Elektroboot*," which was a complete nuclear submarine, but supposedly not usable because of the lack of a proper reactor. They also developed the radio directed gyro compasses for the V-2 rocket in its second stage long range missiles, and much more. The German navy was also responsible for the introduction of a silent non-fuel consuming "Walter Motor." They mastered the construction of "segmented" U-boats, where parts were not just built in the northern ports, but even in the Bohemian region around Prague called the Skoda Works. In some of these underground "Richard" factories the Tiger-I tanks were being built. The sub-sections of U-boats were transported by train to the northern docks for assembly. Even in 1945, Germany was still able to raise the production of U-boats to the highest level since the entire world war. One has to wonder why such an urgency to construct so many U-boats when the war was all but lost by 1945? Unless it was for shepherding out personnel and technology to South America and Antarctica.

7. Childress, David Hatcher. *Antarctica and the Secret Space Program: From WWII to the Current Space Race*, Adventures Unlimited Press, Kempton, IL 2020.

Back in the USA there has long since been a narrative like "the Hun in the Sun" and all kinds of silly generalizations and disparaging narratives to belittle the Germans' giant leap in technology. The truth is the Allies were terrified that the Germans might unleash their "Wonder Weapons" at the end of the war, especially regarding the development of the atomic bomb. Many of the German scientists working on atomic bomb research were recruited in Project Paperclip to work on the Manhattan Project developing the atomic bomb in the USA.

FÜHRER'S CONVOY

A year and a half before the expedition of Admiral Byrd, in the summer of 1945, at the Argentine port of Mar del Plata entered and surrendered to the authorities two German submarines, months after the conclusion of World War II. These were very unusual U-boats, submarines from the so-called Führer's Convoy, which was a top-secret submarine fleet that carried out the most sensitive tasks. The details of which still remain in deep secrecy. Eventually the crews of the submarines were interrogated and reluctantly testified.

The American interrogators managed to find out that the U-boats had just returned from Antarctica with empty cargo holds. The German commander of U-boat 530 spoke about his participation in Operation Valkyrie 2 for three weeks before the end of the war. The submarine 530 left its keel in Germany and headed for Antarctica. On board the submarine were soldiers whose faces were covered with bandages, as well as relics of the Third Reich. The commander of another submarine U-977, Hans Schaefer, testified that also in the closing days of the war, his sub like U-530, left Germany and repeated the same route. It also turned out that there were other German submarines repeatedly coming and going to Antarctica. But why exactly?

The two captured U-boats were state of the art design, operating on the advanced Walter engine. The most advanced ran a "cold fusion" system of 2000* C steam and could travel at an astonishing 25 knots speed underwater. It also utilized a new technique of not emitting bubbles which could be detected by aircraft. Because of its nuclear engine design it could travel unseen underwater all the way to Antarctica, and transport heavy equipment and dozens of personnel. Some of the Paperclip Nazis were submarine engineers who brought their know-how to the USA military contractors.

Today's nuclear submarines require only four kilograms of uranium to power the vessel for 30 years without refueling. The reactors used in modern nuclear submarines are based on highly enriched uranium (HEU), which contains 90% or more uranium-235. This enriched uranium can produce a large amount of energy in small quantities. Only four or five kilograms of enriched uranium can power a nuclear submarine for several decades, as nuclear fission reactions generate a tremendous amount of energy. The energy produced by the fission of one kilogram of uranium-235 is equivalent to approximately 24,000,000 kilowatt-hours. The efficient use of fuel in nuclear reactors and the design of the reactor itself eliminate the need for frequent fuel replacements. Nuclear submarines do not require fuel replacements for 20-30 years, which is a significant technological advantage for their long-term missions. This is why nuclear submarines have greater autonomy than conventional diesel-electric submarines. [8]

In one of Adolf Hitler's final speeches in 1945, he referred to the "Last Battalion" as a force that would fight

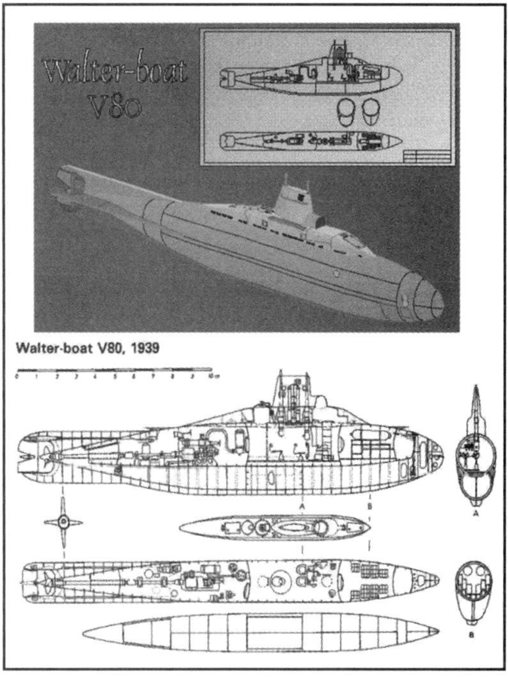

Walter-boat V80, 1939

By 1945, the Nazis had developed two new secret type of U-boats that would allow the craft to go unseen underwater all the way to Antarctica and transport heavy equipment, supplies, and personnel. It was operating on the advanced Walter engine, which ran a "cold fusion" system of 600* C steam (vapor) and a percentage of hydrogen peroxide. It could make up to 18 knots speed underwater. The later-version Walter engine ran on the same idea but with steam of 2000* C. It incorporated special piping and pressure vessels for greater efficiency. The Germans also managed to change from hydrogen peroxide to another substance (not Ethanol but another type of alcohol), that was capable of mixing with water, by which the propellers (combined with the exhaust gasses) didn't produce the known "bubble trails" that submarines used to produce. They were experimenting with these new kinds of propulsions at the wars end. A special boat was constructed to do just that. It was a "Type V80" of the secret Type XXVI and it reached a record speed of 25 knots underwater in 1945!

8. https://uboat.net/types/projects.htm

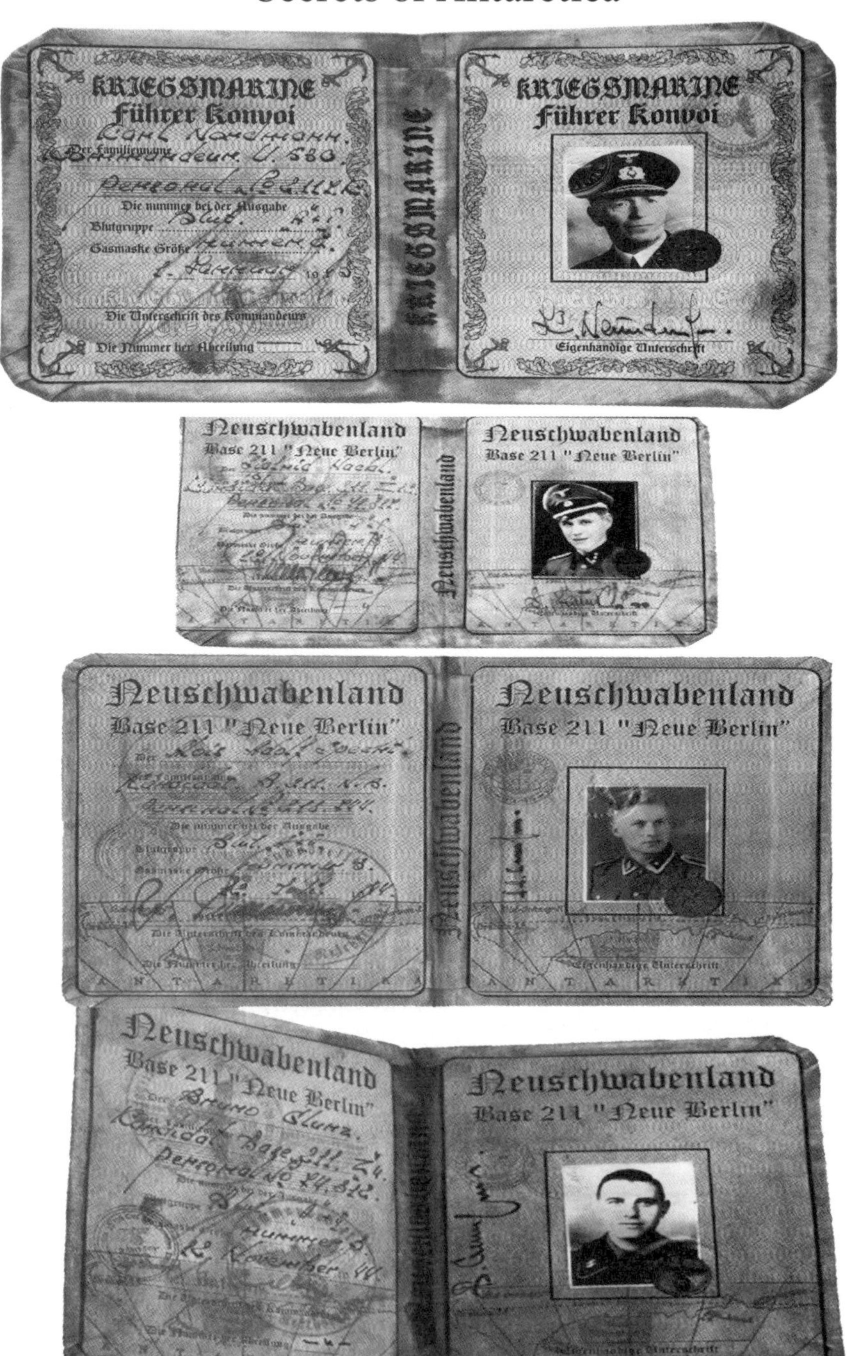

Passports to *Neuschwabenland* were issued for officers and servicemen, including the "Führer Konvoi Navy Captains ID" and regular enlisted men. Many of these passports were military-issued passports for selected young men who were hand picked to be sent overseas. Orphans and young men without a family were preferred.

"from the outside" after the war. On February 24th, 1945 Hitler made a prophetic speech at the end of which he said these words: "In this war there will be no victors and no vanquished either, but only the dead and the survivors. The Last Battalion however, will be a German one." In the final months of the war *Kriegsmarine* Admiral Karl Dönitz was tasked with a secret mission to move the Last Battalion out of Germany, presumably to Antarctica. At the end of the war there were over 100 U-boats that were unaccounted for and disappeared. In Hitler's absence, Admiral Dönitz signed the surrender documents for all the German armed forces in early May, 1945, but not for the Third Reich or the SS. They went underground.

Knowing where to go and how to go, the Germans just needed the equipment. Transport U-boats like the "Milk Cows" (of which only 10 were built) made single trips and returned after which they joined the battle, and were all destroyed by 1943. But then the Top Secret newer boats appeared with a "Snorkel" and better batteries. Later the first Walter engines (Sterling) were in the type XVII, which gave them tremendous speed and without the need for refueling. The XVII's that were built without Walter engines were overhauled and refitted (just like today).

Since Type XX or XXI the boats were even equipped with oxygen and fresh water distiller installations, so they could travel all the way under water to Antarctica like speedboats.

And the greatest U-boat invention the Germans made at the end of the war was to enable a craft to dive to 400 meters in depth. That is twice as deep as a regular sub could go in those days. Perhaps a double hull would do the trick? And it was just exactly that which the Germans came up with. All a captain would need to do is dive into an under-ice tunnel, navigate on a gyro compass and coordinate "tables" with currents and tides, allowing them to travel anywhere they wanted to go. [9]

PROJECT PAPERCLIP

On May, 8th 1945, the armed forces of Germany unconditionally surrendered to the Allies in what's known as Victory in Europe (V-E) Day. However, the Third Reich political party and the SS never surrendered—eventually leading to the formation of a Fourth Reich outside of Germany. Quite a few very prominent SS Nazis escaped justice by taking on new identities in sympathetic South American countries, where most of them lived out

9. van den Kommer, Frank. *Map Details Redacted*, Lightning Press, 2024.

their natural lives. One of them was Martin Bormann, who rose to the rank of Hitler's top deputy, and started 750 companies after the war, bolstering the power of the Fourth Reich. Bormann had escaped like other Nazis along the Rat Lines to Switzerland, then to Rome via South America. He was rumored to have settled in Argentina, where he was living secretly as a millionaire, allegedly spotted in Brazil and also in Chile all throughout the 1950s.

In the post-war division of assets, the Americans and Soviets gained access to elements of German disk technology and the remaining scientists who managed to stay alive. In the final days of the war, the German Nazi elite had neglected to completely eliminate all the engineers before their hasty departure. The British and Canadians also had access to some of the records that the United States had acquired, as well as some data directly from the German efforts. On September 20th, 1945 Wernher von Braun and several other V-2 colleagues arrived in Boston, MA and were transported to White Sands, NM to work in the U.S. missile program. It should be noted that Wernher von Braun, along with other "Paperclip" former-Nazi SS personnel were at the "treaty signing" event at Muroc-Edwards AFB in 1954, according to Dr. Hank Krastman. It was at this Greada Treaty signing that the NSA officially entered into a pact with the malevolent Reptilians and Grays. Previous to this, and before the Nazi Party took power in 1933, the Bavarian

THE NATION'S NEWS SOURCE

GERMAN SCIENTISTS RECRUITED BY U.S.

The Third Reich did not lose World War II ... they just moved to the Americas. From 1945 to 1955, Operation Paperclip granted over 1,600 German scientists and Nazi officers American citizenship. Many had been longtime members of the Nazi party and *Gestapo*, and had conducted experiments on humans at concentration camps and committed other war crimes. The scientists ended up in the U.S. military industrial complex, worked with the CIA, NASA and more. One of the Nazi experiments that continued in the USA was mind control, known as the CIA's Project MK-Ultra.

Thule Society and Scottish Rite Masons (Bavarian Illuminati) had established their own "treaties" with subterranean-based Grays and Reptoid species, that were in contact with others of their kind beyond the confines of planet Earth.

Project Paperclip recruited over 1,500 Nazi scientists and engineers who were transported to the United States by Bavarian cult members operating in high-level economic and political positions in America. Combined, they became the "Corporate-Fascist" government and were given false papers in order to work for the "U.S. Government." These Nazi SS infiltrators are multi-generational and continue to infiltrate the electorate government of the United States of America via their fascist "parasitic" fifth-column government centered around Project AQUARIUS, the CIA, NSA, and other three-letter agencies. Some of the German scientists told American military intelligence officers of the South Pole base, and of the Bavarian connection to civilian intelligence operations in the United States and the civilian power elite.

In 1946, the Bavarian-connected agents within the United States eco-political structure, such as the Dulles brothers, specifically repatriated German SS intelligence officers in an effort to form what became the Central Intelligence Agency in the following year. This Agency, initially an "intelligence gathering" operation called the Office of Strategic Services, soon commenced to spreading its influence throughout the entire U.S. intelligence community to the point where it became the controlling influence over all intelligence efforts. Indeed, the CIA became a "secret government" in and of itself, and went rogue from presidential or congressional oversight. Its influence spreads beyond the borders of the USA, as the CIA engages in a "covert war" against the world superpowers and third world counties, assassinating undesirable leaders and replacing them with fascist CIA-backed military juntas, including democratically elected leaders. This was part of a plan that was first formulated by Allen Dulles and German intelligence officer Reinhard Gehlen in 1943, when a deal was cut with the German spy operation to provide the United States government with a viable intelligence operation as well as provide German spy operatives with "a place to go after the war." A good enticement, indeed. Remember that the Nazis were backed by American bankers who were, and still are, members of the Bavarian secret society lodges, as were the Nazis themselves. Did millions of Allies shed their blood during World War II, only to be betrayed by traitors in our midst?

In twin Secret Space Program developments, half the German advancements and Project Paperclip scientists ended up in the United States. The other half escaped to Antarctica and South America with the most advanced technology. The Americans were forced to come into an agreement with the Dark Fleet and the Draco aliens after the July, 1952 flyover of Washington D.C. by craft flying to and from Antarctica. After this, the secret bases of the fascists in *Neuschwabenland* came to dominate the United States government.

On July 29th, 1958, NASA was created and run by former Nazi SS scientists, whose task it was to keep Americans believing we needed primitive rocket propulsion to venture into outer space. Project Paperclip offered a safe haven for Nazi scientists to relocate in the USA. The famous rocket scientist Wernher von Braun was one of them, who arrived with ready-made rockets which were tested and re-engineered at the White Sands proving grounds in New Mexico. Von Braun and his Nazi team were then allocated millions of taxpayers' money to develop a whole new Space Program.

One of those Paperclip scientists to come to the United States was Victor Schauberger, the developer of the implosion engine capable of producing light, heat, and mechanical motion, with only air and water. While in Germany, he developed an aircraft with three parallel discs. When brought in motion, the upper and lower discs rotate in opposite directions, creating a very strong magnetic field and anti-gravity effect. This aircraft design not only floats in the air, but wraps the structure of time around it. It is believed this was the prototype of future "techno-magical" flying saucers, based on non-classical flight principles. These super-discs were developed by a special technological unit of the SS, connected to the Ahnenerbe Society. It is vital to credit the German scientists and engineers, who achieved huge successes, possibly even landing the first man on the Moon decades before the Americans in 1969. The Third Reich's leap in science and technology wasn't accidental. Combining scientific research, with an analysis of ancient knowledge, brought incredible results. [10]

RAPID TECHNOLOGICAL DEVELOPMENT

Fresh out of service as a decorated and wounded soldier in World War I, Adolf Hitler joined the occulted Thule Society in 1919. In the cosmology of the German Thule Society the "Black Sun" played a prominent role as a "sacred" symbol of the Aryans. Some researchers argue one faction of the inner core within the

10. Olsen, Brad. *Beyond Esoteric: Escaping Prison Planet,* CCC Publishing, Yerington, NV, 2025.

Thule Society were Satanists. They were able to "make a deal with the devil" so to speak. In this case, they communicated and conspired with the Draco Reptilian ETs, who already occupied Inner Earth bases in Antarctica and elsewhere.

In 1922, Maria Orsic of the Vril Society channeled Nordic ET designs for a spacecraft which Dr. Schumann discovered had viable physics for development. In 1934, the Nazi SS developed operational anti-gravity craft 20 years ahead of the U.S., with the assistance of the Draco ETs of the Ciakahrr Empire. Elena Danaan reports: "Creation of the Dark Fleet after the end of World War II when a breakaway branch of the Nazis moved to Antarctica, as they allied with Reptilian ETs who offered them to share underground facilities with them, there."

By 1932, Adolf Hitler had gained enough control of German society to force scientists to work in laboratories on advanced aircraft design. Aided by the implosion vortex technology of Victor Schauberger, and the technical expertise of scientists like Schriever, Habermohl, Ballenzo and Miethe, the Germans made extraordinary progress. There is evidence that they were aided by contact with Reptilian and Gray entities from inside the Earth, and an "Ashtar" group connected with humanoid aliens from Aldebaran.

The Jet Propulsion Labs was founded on Halloween October 31, 1936 by a man who baptized himself as the Satanic Antichrist. As a boy, Jack Parsons exchanged letters with his idol, Wernher von Braun, who became an SS officer and built rockets which would blitz working class people of Britain. Jack Parsons also financially supported "The Wickedest Man in the World" Aleister Crowley in the final years of his life.

From 1941 to 1944, the advanced V-1 and V-2 rockets were used to bomb the cities of Great Britain, but remarkably, the British people had a "war spirit," and the Royal network of aristocrats who had funded the Third Reich became concerned that the general public would discover that they had a role in fomenting the war. If history were to tell the truth, on August 23rd, 1942 the first German astronaut walked on the moon. The Vril Society / Nazi SS would later establish a swastika-shaped moon base on the "dark side" with their anti-gravity craft.

In 1944, a Nazi plan of infiltration was hatched in the U.S. to create a matrix of perception using "world view warfare" called the *Weltanschauungskrieg* plan. Also in 1944, the Nazis began to escape en masse to Antarctica and South America with over 100 U-boats,

250,000 Germans and Reich's top scientists vanishing and being unaccounted for. From that moment on, the Vatican sponsored "Rat Lines" were established to evacuate war criminals, dressing them as priests and nuns, and then shipping them off to mainly sympathetic South American countries. [11]

In 1945, the British discovered German plans for advanced craft and joined the efforts of the United States to subvert the German program. Obviously those agents who would later become the core of the "CIA" were not involved in this attempt to subvert the secret German projects. In that, the CIA was originally established as a fifth-column for Bavarian intelligence operations in America. On February 16, despite allied efforts, the Germans successfully flew a crew-carrying version of the "fireball" from the underground facilities in Thuringia. The craft had a top speed of over 12,500 mph. The craft was called the *Kugelblitz.*

The Germans in the scientific community knew the war was lost as early as 1942, due to signs of an imminent alliance between the superpowers USA, Great Britain and Russia. They decided to establish a plan for continuing the dream of the Third Reich in spite of the war. They decided that the establishment of a separate society founded on Nazi principles of genetic purity was the answer. The development of gravitational technology aided that plan. On February 23, the newest engines of the *Kugelblitz* were tested and then extracted from the craft. The "shell" or "casing" of the *Kugelblitz,* minus the engines, was blown up by SS personnel and the scientists, plans and engines were shipped out of Germany to the South Polar regions, where the Germans had maintained underground construction activity since 1941. Two days later, on February 25, the underground plant at Khala was closed and all the workers sent to Buchenwald and gassed. The Germans also sent their "Aryan elite" children and other elements of their society to the underground bases. General Hans Kammler, who disappeared in April 1945, was instrumental in the evacuation operation, as was General Nebe. There, the Germans developed a eugenic society that apparently is limited to a specific number of people. What's more, they're still there. Apparently they also maintain underground technical colonies in various South American countries. On April 12, President Roosevelt died and Harry Truman, a high Mason (as was Franklin D. Roosevelt), became President of the United States. On May 8, 1945, the military fighting forces of Germany surrendered. Both the Americans and the Soviets gained access to

11. https://chriseverard.gumroad.com/l/zzBZy

1897 42 Años de Tradición y de Exito 1939
"EDEN HOTEL"
LA FALDA

EL GRAN HOTEL DE LAS SIERRAS DE CORDOBA
COCINA DE PRIMER ORDEN, CONFORT MODER NO, CANCHAS DE GOLF Y DE TENNIS, PILETA DE NATACION, EQUITA CION

After the war, prominent Nazis were hired by the CIA and NASA—while Hitler retired in the comfort of the Eden Hotel in the Argentinian mountain town of La Falda. The political turmoil of Latin American governments is due to the fact that Nazis fled Europe and bred their own colonies, and these colonies earned vast amounts of money.

elements of German disk technology and scientists, of which the German Nazi elite had neglected to completely eliminate before their hasty departure at the close of the war. The British and Canadians also had access to some of the data that the United States had acquired, as well as some data directly from the German efforts. [12]

By 1947, the Germans, having had two years to reformulate after the war, started making flyovers of the United States in their discs, which had by then achieved a remarkable degree of development. This prompted the United States to undertake plans to ascertain both the exact location of the German bases in Antarctica and

12. The OMEGA File NAZI HISTORY PART II http://pages.suddenlink.net/anomalousimages/images/text/omega4.htm

their technical capabilities. On January 17th, 1947, Admiral Byrd's Operation Highjump was totally defeated by disc-shaped craft emerging from the depths of the Southern Ocean near the Antarctic coast. Also in 1947, the construction of a network of Deep Underground Military Bases (DUMBs) in USA commenced with Hitler's mastermind Xaver Dorsch under Project Paperclip.

World War II was a war engineered for the creation of a new European Reich. After the war a clandestine Fourth Reich was formed with a more global perspective. On May 29th, 1954, former Nazi SS Prince Bernhard of the Netherlands started the first of the yearly ongoing Bilderberg secret meetings, which coordinates the agenda for Western governments and the mainstream media today. The meetings were organized under the Nazi leadership, and with King Edward leading it. The post-war Nazi network controlled the Deep State from the highest levels. Lest we forget the ardent Nazi Kurt Waldheim, who became the Secretary General of the United Nations, and his counterpart, Walter Hallstein, who was Hitler's former lawyer, became president of the new undemocratic European SuperState government the E.U.

THE THIRD FORCE

The history we've been taught is an accumulation of lessons, laced with lies by omission. One glaring omission is what takes place literally and figuratively underground. That is, advanced technology beyond our wildest dreams being developed in underground bases, and the ongoing operations of a Fourth Reich or "Third Force" intelligence operation that has existed since the end of World War II. The Rothschild/Rockefeller controlled mass media has promoted a false narrative concerning the events of World War II for the past 80 years. To be sure, the difference between state media and Western media is that in state media the government controls what information the public is given about what's going on in the world in order to prevent political dissent, whereas in Western media, this control is maintained instead by billionaires. Meanwhile, the United States government continues to suppress the knowledge of German "Vril" free-energy technology, in order to maintain the status quo of our oil-based globalist slave economy. The breakaway Aryans (German free-energy scientists) have expanded an enormous secret space program, which does not use or need "fossil fuel" oil.

While it is widely accepted that the Nazis were defeated with the German government's formal surrender in 1945, this is only partly true. The Third Reich political movement never surrendered, and why would they? Continuing what they started in the Skoda Works before and during the war, the Antarctic Nazis were able to further develop their "Vril" spacecraft far in advance of anything possessed by the USA. They swiftly defeated the massive "post-World War II" Antarctica military attack by Allied forces led by Admiral Byrd, who retreated in fear and disgrace after suffering substantial damage and heavy casualties.

German Navy Grand Admiral Karl Dönitz stated in 1943: "The German submarine fleet is proud of having built for the Führer in another part of the world a Shangri-La on land, an impregnable fortress." Yes, there were large numbers of people and materials sent to Antarctica, and Admiral Dönitz returned to Germany and seemed to be bragging about building a "Shangri-La" on a distant continent. Not that "we're going to do it," or "planning to do it," but that is was already done.

It is important to note that NATO is essentially a Third Force organization, and is the home of Operation Gladio which remains functional. The false flag Gladio attacks on European train stations are still used to blow up and mass-murder innocents all over the world in order to create synthetic terror and chaos. This is done to justify the taking of more and more taxpayer money, freedom and rights, all done in order to facilitate the attainment of the globalist hierarchy's New World Order evil agenda. Problem-Reaction-Solution is the manufactured pattern. Yet more and more people all around the world are learning about Operation Gladio, also known as the left-behind Fourth Reich army that runs NATO. The CIA is also a Third Force construct, at the behest the globalists. The "enforcement arm" of the CIA uses false flag events to start wars and cause conflicts with other countries. In America, the CIA stages false flag events like Sandy Hook as legal propaganda to create narratives that control American perception, such as the need to disarm U.S. citizens. Can we make the case that this "trauma based mind control" management, laced with subliminal media messaging, is tantamount to mass brainwashing?

FOURTH REICH IN SOUTH AMERICA

Escaped Nazi officers strapped gold bars to their legs and then wore Catholic priest robes to hide the gold, boarded German U-boats and sailed to Brazil, Chile and Argentina. These ardent Nazi war criminals were greeted with open arms by thousands of German migrant families who had formed Nazi cults in the Andes mountains and Amazonian jungle long before World War II ended. Some of these cults operated as if they were "micronations" and flying Nazi and German flags proudly on their properties in various countries of South America. Once in South America, the escaped Nazis were provided with blank identity documents that allowed them to assume new lives, often in barbed-wire ringed micronation settlements away from prying eyes.

The film series by Chris Everard called the "Fourth Reich of the Rich" begins at the end of World War II, and traces the journey Adolf Hitler made after the war. It starts with a body-double left in a fire pit in Berlin, while Hitler escaped and spent his first eight months having a holiday in sunny Spain. He then flew to Argentina, and the SS moved him to various safe houses all across South America. Hitler did not die until the early 1960s. During that time, a new post-war Fourth Reich network was formed, which still to this day secretly controls many governments from behind the scenes.

San Carlos de Bariloche on the shores of Lake Nahuel Huapi in Argentina appears much like a Bavarian-styled city. It should be little wonder that many fugitive Nazis after World War II were seen at or around the city of Bariloche, feeling especially safe in the late 1940s under the quasi-protection of the fascist leader Juan Perón. The Lake Nahuel Huapi is much like the Koingsee of southern Bavaria in Germany, close to Bertchesgarten where Hitler had his Eagle's Nest retreat home, and where the Vril women were telepathically communicating with ETs in a Bavarian hunting lodge.

Hitler had several hideout homes in South America, most replete with an airstrip or a seaplane in a boathouse for a quick getaway. Hitler first arrived via U-boat in late 1945, and settled for about a year at the infamous Inalco House, on the Estancia San Ramon Bay near San Carlos de Bariloche in the central Andes range of Argentina. It was a protected estate, and had the means to allow Hitler a quick escape by various ways if the authorities were drawing near.

Hitler's residences in South America changed depending on the dictator in power, and where the SS felt he would be safe. His first long-term house was the Inalco House from May, 1946 until mid-June 1947. He then spent a one year vacation in Casino, Brazil. He eventually moved back to Argentina after spending nine years in Colombia. Declassified documents reveal that the CIA was told about a man claiming to be Adolf Hitler who lived in Colombia among a community of ex-Nazis during the 1950s. At that point, Hitler could have been arrested for war crimes, but instead lived in luxury homes in the Andes mountains. CIA agents recorded a testimony from a former SS soldier informing the station chief in Caracas, Venezuela to send a report to Langley CIA headquarters, complete with a photo of the aged Hitler.

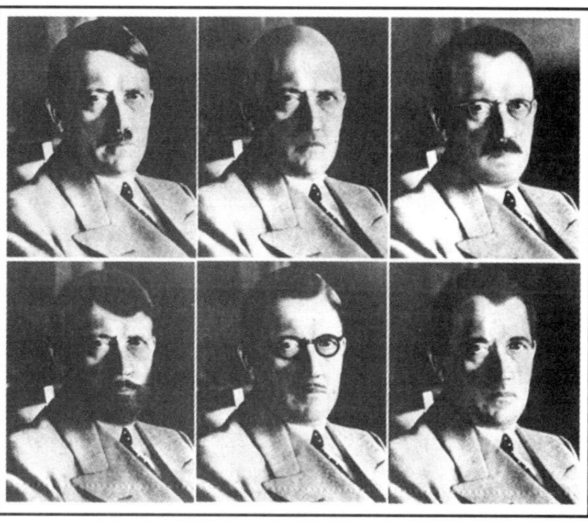

The U.S. Government produced these visual mockups of how Adolph Hitler could have disguised himself after surviving World War II. The FBI was keenly aware that Adolph Hitler would fake his own death and escape to a country sympathetic to the Third Reich. He did exactly that, and fled initially to Argentina. The FBI Vault has now declassified over two hundred documents pertaining to Hitler and other prominent Nazis escaping to South America and Antarctica.

CIA files claim that Monsieur Phillip Citroen approached agents in 1954 to say that he had met a man claiming to be Hitler who was living in the town of Tunja, north of Bogota, Colombia.

He used the name Adolf Schuttlemayer, which is similar to his real family name of Schicklegruber, which is recorded as Hitler's mother's maiden family name. Returning to the house at Inalco towards the end of his life, Patagonia is almost certainly Hitler's last refuge. The Inalco House is located about 60 miles north of Bariloche, and could be considered as his permanent residence. He most likely died in Asuncion, Paraguay, and is buried in a hidden chamber below a prominent hotel in the capital.

Some works, such as the 2011 book *Grey Wolf: The Escape of Adolf Hitler* by British authors Simon Dunstan and Gerrard Williams, and the 2014 docudrama film by Gerrard Williams based on the book, suggest that Hitler and his wife Eva Braun did not commit suicide, but actually escaped to South America. The scenario proposed by these two authors is as follows: a number of U-boats took certain fugitive Nazis and war loot to Argentina, where the Nazis were supported by future president Juan Perón, who, along with his wife Evita, had been receiving money from the Nazis for some time. Hitler allegedly arrived in Argentina, first staying at Hacienda San Ramón, east of San Carlos de Bariloche. Hitler then moved to a Bavarian-styled mansion at Inalco, a remote and barely accessible spot at the northwest end of Lake Nahuel Huapi, close to the Chilean border. Around 1954, Eva Braun left Hitler and moved to Neuquén with their daughter, Ursula. The authors maintain that "Uschi" is Barry Obama-Hitler's real mother, and Hitler died in February, 1962.

On the History Channel series *Hunting Hitler* (2015–2018), investigators (including Gerrard Williams) cite declassified documents of interviews with witnesses, which allegedly indicate that Hitler escaped from Germany and travelled to South America by U-boat. He and other Nazis then allegedly plotted a "Fourth Reich." According to *Wikipedia*, such conspiracy theories of survival and escape have been widely dismissed. Contradictorily, in 2017 the series was praised by the tabloid-style *National Police Gazette,* which historically was a supporter of the Hitler-escaped theory. The History Channel series *Hunting Hitler* also called upon the Russians to allow Hitler's jawbone remains to be DNA-tested, which turned out to be a woman. [13]

The Eden Hotel in La Falda, Argentina was a location where Adolf Hitler was seen alive on several occasions after World War II. Located in the Cordoba Sierras, the Bavarian-like town of La Falda and several other surrounding communities have long supported a large German immigrant population. There was a close relationship between Hitler and the wealthy hotel owners the Eichhorns. The Eichhorns owned the Eden Hotel, and who a FBI document described as "enthusiastic supporters of Hitler since the Nazi Party was founded." This FBI document dated Sept. 17, 1945, specifically mentions a "Hitler hideout in Argentina." Other remnants of Nazis are found all over South America, including in the Amazon.

> *If the Führer should at any time get into difficulties, he could always find a safe retreat at LA FALDA where they have already made the necessary preparations. ... Even before the Nazis came into power (Ida Eichhorn) placed immediately by cable her entire bank account, amounting to 80,000 Marks at GOEBBEL'S disposal. This was in response to the letter's request to her for 3-4,000 Marks for propaganda purposes. HITLER never forgot this act and during the years he came into power they would (reside at) the same hotel on the occasion of their annual stay in*

13. https://en.wikipedia.org/wiki/Conspiracy_theories_about_Adolf_Hitler%27s_death#cite_note-grey-42

> *Germany on the PARTEITAG. They were then permitted to enter the private rooms of the Führer at anytime without being previously announced.*

Also in the Cordoba Sierras near La Falda is the UFO hotspot around Cerro Uritorco mountain. There are alien-motif billboards in the town Capilla del Monte referring to the many UFO sightings around a famous local mountain. Burn spots on the grass where crafts were reported near the ground, human abductions, and numerous sightings of craft above and around the Cerro Uritorco mountain have been reported for decades. But these were not alien craft from a distant planet. They were German backward engineered discs that were being test flown near a Deep Under-

Adolf Hitler dining with Ida and Walter Eichhorn, the owners of The Eden Hotel in La Falda (Cordoba), Argentina, where he stayed after the war.

Located in the Cordoba Sierras, the Bavarian-like town of La Falda, Argentina and several other surrounding communities have historically housed a large German ex-pat population. One of those families was the Eichhorns who owned the Eden Hotel, and who a FBI document described as "enthusiastic supporters of HITLER since the Nazi Party was founded." In addition to the fugitive Adolph Hitler after the war, the Eden Hotel hosted many other luminaries of the era. Guest include members of European royal families including Edward Prince of Wales, music and film stars, Albert Einstein, and even the Latin American revolutionary Che Guevara. The close relationship with the Jesuits, the Vatican and fascist dictator Juan Perón would have made it easy for the Eichhorns to host virtually anyone after World War II.

ground Military Base (DUMB) from inside the Cerro Uritorco mountain. [14]

SOUTH AMERICAN MICRONATIONS

Once in South America, former Nazis were provided with blank identity documents that allowed them to assume new lives, often in barbed-wire ringed settlements with armed guards. There are massive land holdings in Brazil, Argentina and Chile owned by the Germans.

A "micronation" is an entity that claims sovereignty, while being surrounded by another nation. A micronation is not formally recognized as an independent country, regardless of its claims. However, even though micronations (like the Swedish-adjacent Ladonia), aren't recognized by other countries or international bodies like the United Nations, that hasn't stopped some of these unofficial territories from acting as independent lands. Some micronations have even adopted their own currencies, postage stamps, passports, Army, Navy, Air Force, Space Command and other common affiliations associated with real countries.

When compared to "real" countries and territories in the world, the concept of a micronation is a fairly new concept. The oldest record of a person declaring their own sovereignty on land already claimed by a country dates back to the early 20th century. Martin Coles Harman claimed the British Isle of Lundy as his own nation because he also owned the land. Then in 1945 during World War II, the Principality of Outer Baldonia was formed when Russell Arundel, the chairman of Pepsi-Cola Company, declared sovereignty over a rocky island off the coast of Nova Scotia. It's usually very wealthy people who wish to create their own micronations.

Over the years, micronations have been created by eccentric people like Ernest Hemingway's brother, as well as government idealists, separatists, and people or groups focused on making political statements. Most notably, during the 1980's, several Japanese villages in the northern part of the country declared their independence from Japan as a show of protest against Japan's strong embrace of modernization. There can be other such dissenters from the MIC or the Deep State. Famed CIA pilot turned whistleblower John Lear wrote:

> *Everybody who is cleared to work inside the Nevada National Security Site signs a form, probably in such*

14. Childress, David Hatcher. *Andromeda: The Secret Files: The Flying Submarines of the SS*, Adventures Unlimited Press, Kempton, IL 2022.

complex wording they don't even know what they are signing, that they agree to be a citizen of the (Kingdom) of the Nevada National Security Site. And they are informed of the penalties if they try to breach their allegiance. Not in those terms but in terms they would agree to, without hesitation, to get access to what they think are the secrets held within. Of course, most of them don't get to find out anything other than the mundane tasks assigned to them. And when they find out what is really going on, it's too late to back out. And if their objections are more than just words, they are placed in the Nevada National Security Site Super Max, one of the most formidable prisons on the face of planet Earth.

So this micronation has an Army: the 750 armed combat soldiers living and training in the five underground installations built adjacent to the secret base inside Paiute Mesa. They have their own Navy: The U.S. Navy Secret Space Command with 13 orbiting Direct Energy Weapons; their own Air Force: all the highly advanced combat fighters at the Tonopah Test Range, Gold Flats and Groom Lake. And all of the advanced back engineering of the ET saucers and equipment given to us before and after Roswell. And an agenda: the Nazi/Zionist Alliance which the Dulles brothers allowed to get into our country after World War II, which has subverted our nation in its entirety.

Impossible? Improbable? You wish. [15]

NACHT WAFFEN

Alternative historians claim the Nazis landed on the Moon over 27 years before NASA's 1969 Apollo 11 Moon landing. By the late 1960s the Antarctic Germans had already built their new Moon base called New Warburg, which was their second post-war city to New Berlin. They were also building out their first space carrier task group. The Antarctic Germans also expanded further into the solar system to exploit the many resources on Mars and Ceres. The *Nacht Waffen* "Dark Fleet" were the first humans to set up a Moon base for operations, and then went further afield to ex-

15. Olsen, Brad. *Future Esoteric: The Unseen Realms*, CCC Publishing, Yerington, NV, 2018.

ploit resources. This was also the timeframe in which the Western Cabal had learned more about some of the threats to Earth from certain alien sectors. Any advancements in dimensional, scalar or advanced physics were black projects that were buried out of the purview of Congress or the American people. By the 1970s, the Cabal were continuing to buy as much time as they could because still, they know that number one they were infiltrated by the Paperclip Nazis, and there was little they could do about it. The Antarctica Germans allied with the malevolent aliens would always have the upper hand.

The truth embargo as it relates to UFOs has been going on for at least a century. Any researcher of "deep" esoteric subjects knows the rabbit hole has to include extraterrestrials. As the late William Cooper emphatically stated, "you put the aliens into the middle of this stuff and you've got all the answers." But what is the human involvement? In this Modern Age at least, backward-engineered space travel started with the Germans, who were the first to master development of flying saucer technology in the middle part of the 20th century. In the years just after World War I, psychic me-

The Revell plastic model kit is based on a combat-ready Haunebu flying disc. The outside and inside of the Revell model of a Haunebu craft are based on the blueprints of the actual craft. This model kit is forbidden to be sold in Germany today.

diums were used to channel advanced technology blueprints with remote extraterrestrial civilizations. The Vril Society was established after medium Maria Orsic received a communication from extraterrestrials who had once lived in Sumeria, what is now Iran and Iraq. She discovered that these human-like beings eventually departed Earth for the Aldebaran solar system. With the data collected, and the recovery of downed UFOs such as the craft recovered from the Black Forest in the 1930s, the Germans were ready to build. For the next decade, they called their spaceships the RFZ-1, Haunebu, Vril and the Bell craft. Kronos was a secret name for the Nazi space project. They were the first modern humans to fly out into space, and that's where they made many incredible discoveries. There were various civilizations that have colonized our solar system long before us. Some are still there. They left behind many artifacts, including some old bases that could be sealed up, pressurized, and made habitable.

That's what the Germans did on the Moon and on Mars, as well as in Antarctica. In order to accurately discuss the history of the secret space program, facts to be acknowledged are that the Nazis not only arrived in outer space first, but they were the first humans to colonize the Moon and Mars. They lost World War II on the battlefield, but they came back and basically took over the U.S. Military Industrial Complex through trickery—and through having better technology. They blackmailed the U.S. after Admiral Byrd led a failed expedition to confront them in Antarctica, and also because the U.S. did not want to reveal the secrets gained from the Roswell crash. Top U.S. officials knew the Fourth Reich Nazis had the upper hand.

The Nazis started overflying the U.S. capitol in 1952 with their craft from Antarctica, and essentially forced the U.S. to join them in a partnership. This is the origin of the militarization of outer space and our solar system. *Nacht Waffen* or "Dark Fleet" is the name of the German military in space. Their culture is called *Das Bundes,* which translates to "The Federation." Solar Warden had become the main component of the American secret space program, and other countries also have their own covert space programs, most of whom are allied with Solar Warden. What was once used for the benefit of the elite to escape off-planet, has turned around. Now benevolent ETs have given the Solar Warden human groups advanced technology that is allowing them to defeat the Cabal and malevolent ETs. Since at least June, 2015, Solar Warden is now enforcing a no-fly zone around the Earth. Nobody can fly in or out of the Earth anymore unless they have permission. Something has been put around our solar system (that they) call the Barrier. This means that nobody can get in or out. And communications cannot get in and out either. Timing is everything because when the Barrier was put up, the vast majority of all the reptilians in their so-called Dark Fleet were outside the solar system. And now they cannot get back in because Earth is quarantined. Earth humans are now for the first time in our history unobstructed by a malevolent alien influence. How will we conduct ourselves?

Admiral Richard E. Byrd

"It is a system which has conscripted vast human and material resources into the building of a tightly knit, highly efficient machine that combines military, diplomatic, intelligence, economic, scientific, and political operations."

–John F. Kennedy, describing the Deep State

RICHARD Evelyn Byrd Jr. (October 25, 1888 – March 11, 1957), was a decorated American naval officer, a pioneering arctic aviator, an Antarctic explorer, and organizer of polar logistics. He was awarded the Medal of Honor, Navy Cross, two-time Navy Distinguished Service Medal, two-time Legion of Merit medal, and a Distinguished Flying Cross Congressional Gold Medal. The aircraft flights in which he served as a navigator and expedition leader crossed the Atlantic Ocean, a segment of the Arctic Ocean, and a segment of the Antarctic Plateau. He is also known for discovering Mount Sidley, the largest dormant volcano in Antarctica.

Byrd said that his expeditions had been the first to reach both the North Pole and the South Pole by air. His belief that he reached the North Pole in 1926 is disputed, based on the airplane's speed and time recorded in the air. Nevertheless, on November 28, 1929, the first flight to the South Pole and back was launched from Little America base. Byrd, along with pilot Bernt Balchen, co-pilot/radioman Harold June, and photographer Ashley McKinley, flew the Floyd Bennett to the South Pole and back in 18 hours, 41 minutes. They had difficulty gaining enough altitude, and they had to dump empty gas tanks, as well as their emergency supplies, to achieve the necessary altitude to the Polar Plateau, and they were ultimately successful.

For his bravery, he was a recipient of the Medal of Honor, the United States Armed Forces' highest military decoration, and the Navy Cross, the second highest honor for valor given by the U.S. Navy.

Before the war, Richard E. Byrd helped brief the Nazi expedition in the late 1930s on what conditions they would encounter. He was later chosen to lead the post-war Operation Highjump expedition to the continent in 1946-1947 to ostensibly confront the Nazi bases in operation there. The people of the world were told that the operation was necessary because the Arctic might become a theater of war, and that it was necessary to test their equipment and tactics in Arctic conditions. Of course, there was Alaska and Canada available for that, and these frozen lands were much easier to reach. At the time, the Alcan Road was just completed during World War II and could transport supplies by road through Canada to Alaska. It was not necessary to send an entire flotilla to Antarctica. But there was another reason for the Americans' (and the Nazis') interest in the continent. The planning committee for Admiral Byrd's expedition involved Fleet Admiral Chester Nimitz, and more importantly, Secretary of Defense James Forrestal.

BYRD VISITS PRE-WAR GERMANY

In 1938, Admiral Byrd was asked by the German High Command to give a lecture about his three previous Antarctica expeditions. Upon arrival, he was received by a sergeant on behalf of Captain Alfred Ritscher at a ship in Hamburg by a committee of 82 high ranking officials, among them Himmler and Göring. Byrd felt intimidated by the reception. A small group claims that Byrd staged his travels to Germany, but Ritscher stood up for Byrd. When Byrd asked when the Nazi expedition would start, he was told that it would commence on the 17th of December, 1938 and will go ashore on the 18th or 19th. He learned there were two previous

German Antarctic explorations before the 1938-39 MS Schwabenland expedition.

Karl Dönitz introduces Byrd to the Expedition Leader Alfred Ritscher and Captain Kotters and also to a flight Captain, who was introduced as leader of a group called the *Boreas* or "the inhabitants of Hyperborea." Later a question was raised whether Byrd "swallowed the story." Byrd was asked to join the expedition to map Queen Maud Land, but since it appeared a war was approaching, he declined the offer.

Admiral Byrd did not take seriously the warning about possible encounters with armed UFOs before Highjump. And when mysterious objects appeared out of the water and in the sky, the naval fleet opened fire on them with no success. In a show of force, the squadron lost several airplanes, a submarine and at least one escort ship.

On the day of the departure of the *MS Schwabenland*, a courier arrived with a package from Göring for the *Schwabenland*'s Officers (Ritscher and/or Kotters) with the "message" that it is "artwork" from "Nuremberg" (obviously a coded message, because how would a courier know what the contents were?) There was also a letter from Himmler direct to Ritscher, urging that "the contents are precious and you should defend it with you life" and keep it for the arrival of the Führer! The message was named "Boreas" (obviously a mission or secret order) which had absolute priority!

After arrival in Antarctica, the crew immediately began scouting locations for Base 211. It's possible they were looking for a defunct base in which they could retrofit for themselves, because they were soon tasked to start building an energy plant and a "generator field." Ritscher lets himself slip "that those in Nuremberg are in a great hurry and that no time can be wasted!" Before departure from the *Schwabenland* an officer reports back (by radio transmission?) "that the plant is running and everything is ready for the first 'test.'" They were advancing at breakneck speed.

At a certain moment in 1939 when Ritscher is preparing for the home voyage he gets interrupted. The pilots have discovered an anomaly! Between the mountains and ridges they have found an area without any ice and snow. Films the pilots record leave no doubt about discovering an "Antarctic oasis." Byrd's survey team eight years later would discover another massive Antarctic oasis. A second secret German expedition took place in 1940, picking specific landing points in the bays northwest of the Muhlig-Hoffman mountains, which Captain Ritscher also identified as good landing bays. Point 211 is indicated on the survey maps.

Aboard the ship the scientist and the geo-engineer discover an underground lava field and suggest that they have found their way into an Inner Earth cavern! The name Ritcher is chosen for the ice free area, and Schirmacher is chosen for the name of the lakes. The pilot Richard-Heinrich Schirmacher now makes a flight over the areas himself when suddenly they fly into another anomaly, and the instruments spin like crazy in a gigantic magnetic force field. The airplane (coincidentally also named the "Boreas") is in danger of plummeting to the ground. The pilots avoided a crash landing, and a new location was selected to be surveyed on a subsequent trip. [1]

THE REAL OBJECTIVE OF HIGHJUMP

In the year following Victory in Europe day, American naval officer Admiral Richard E. Byrd is placed in command of a squadron of 13 surface warships and 4,700 soldiers bound for Antarctica. Although the expedition's avowed intention was the testing of military hardware under extreme conditions, the suggestions were that it was a combat operation aimed at dislodging Nazi troops from their last redoubt. Why else would such an ambitious effort be undertaken with so much haste (it took advantage of the first available Antarctic summer after the end of World War II), at such a cost, and with so much military hardware—unless the operation was absolutely essential to the security of the United States.

The urgency for the expedition was a bundle of secret documents found in the archives of the Nazi Navy General Staff by the Americans. The Soviets and British also found unique documents. According to the newly-acquired intel, the Germans settled a new land they called *Neuschwabenland*. A huge transport ship was built to deliver goods there in 1938. Dozens of submarines were involved in

1. https://diezeitistauchderinhalt.com/1938-1939-deutschland-antarktis/

the operation, and highly qualified specialists were sent to the base without the right to return back. They also learned the Germans had engineered some kind of craft that were not just for flight in Earth's atmosphere—but that some were built for near-space flight as well, with the Moon and perhaps farther away not being out of the question. This explains why the British and the Americans reacted the way they did when the hint of another base at the South Pole was discovered. Neither nation would have been willing to take the risks that they did in 1946 and 1947, unless they believed that the very survival of their nations were threatened. Captain Edward J. Ruppelt Chief of the U.S. Air Force Project Bluebook in 1956, said:

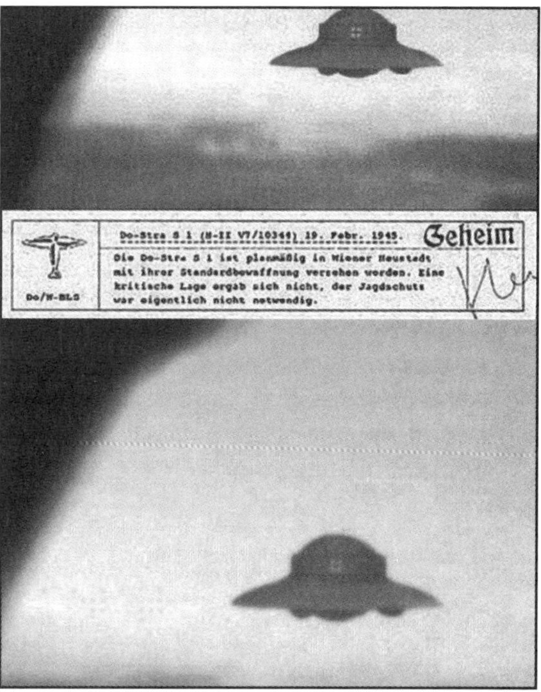

In 1945, after the defeat of the German fighting forces, U.S. intelligence officers discovered a number of top secret documents. They confirmed that the Germans were indeed settling vast areas around *Neuschwabenland*, including the under-ice space of Antarctica. Operation Highjump was tasked with retrieving at least two known UFO flying discs, or Nazi antigravity craft. Highjump was granted unlimited funds and up to eight months to complete the mission.

> *When World War II ended, the Germans had several radical types of aircraft and guided missiles under development. The majority were in the most preliminary stages, but they were the only known craft that could even approach the performance of objects reported to UFO observers.*

The real story of Operation Highjump was a top secret military operation to locate and destroy any Nazi bases in *Neuschwabenland,* and recover any exotic aircraft. Highly trained task forces of several allied nations went to Antarctica in 1946-47 with orders to destroy the remaining bases of the Third Reich and to capture a new unique armament—flying saucers.

The fateful Battle of Highjump commenced on the early morning of February 26th, 1947, when a bombing squadron approaching the Nazi Base 211 and completely disappeared off the radar screen. The planes and crew were never to be seen or heard from again. That same day the Central Group armada of ships offshore the Bay of Whales was attacked by the enemy coming out of the water in flying saucers and were impervious to anti-aircraft fire. In a show of force, one of the flying saucers used a directed energy weapon to slice a destroyer in half with a complete loss of life to the crew, who quickly succumbed to hyperthermia in the frigid waters. The rest of the allied ships in the three battle groups were not sunk, but were forced to flee post-haste, and Operation Highjump ended prematurely. The biggest problem was that it left a functioning German military and science city fully operational in Antarctica.

The resounding defeat at the Battle of Highjump and his prior flight to Inner Earth was not just about Richard E. Byrd. There are several other reports of pilots who saw flat disc-shaped UFOs chasing them, even though they were not fired upon. Other pilots reported how their planes were being followed by balls of light nicknamed "foo fighters." The exotic flying orbs and "*Flügelrads*" witnessed by Admiral Byrd before the Battle of Highjump was the inspiration quoted in the Chilean newspaper *El Mercurio* warning how the Allied nations were confronted by a new enemy that "could fly from pole to pole at incredible speeds." This could only have been created, or at least inspired by, some kind of backward-engineered alien technology. As in that time, and even now, it is basically impossible to travel at such speeds. On July 19th, 1952, a dozen UFOs appeared over the White House and Capitol Building. At first, they were thought to be aliens from another planet, but really it was the Antarctica Germans showing off their hardware, and forcing President Truman to agree to terms of surrender. [2]

When Operation Highjump commenced, there was a very real chance that the U.S. would invade any place or nation on Earth if they had to, in the name of removing any Nazi threat. If an Antarctic base was being supported with material from South Africa, Argentina or Chile, any of these nations were in threat of being attacked. Operation Highjump was but the first front, if it proved out that there really was a German base in the Antarctic. They would not hesitate to return with atomic weapons, which may have been the atomic nuclear tests in the Southern Ocean of the still-classified Operation Argus in 1958.

2. Mera, Steve, *Alien Chronicles: Antarctic Worlds Below*. https://www.youtube.com/watch?v=OIT5JbgYlCU

Flying Objects Near Washington Spotted by Both Pilots and Radar

Air Force Reveals Reports of Something, Perhaps 'Saucers,' Traveling Slowly But Jumping Up and Down

The Cedar Rapids Gazette — CITY FINAL — 5 CENTS — KCRG NEWS

ASSOCIATED PRESS, UNITED PRESS, INTERNATIONAL NEWS

SAUCERS SWARM OVER CAPITAL

MONDAY EVENING, JULY 28, 1952 — 30 PAGES — 5 CENTS

HUNDREDS IN STATE SEE 'FLYING SAUCERS'

Franklin 'Dogfight' Alerts State Troopers

Three "flying saucers" were spotted by hundreds of Hoosiers, including police and military personnel, over South Central Indiana early today.

The objects appeared to have a "dogfight" over Franklin and disappeared as dawn approached.

Troopers from three state police posts—Indianapolis, Seimour and Connersville—kept a running check on the saucers for more than 4 hours.

... tion and called attention to the bounding object in the sky.

Franklin police alerted Wolfe.

"I went out in the country with the police to a place where ...

Flying Saucers Seen Over Washington For 2nd Time In 4 Days

Washington, D. C., saw flying saucers again for six hours early today.

Eight to 12 objects showed on radar screens, flying a 10-mile arc around the capital. Radarmen estimated the objects, or flying saucers, were clipping along at about 120 miles per hour.

The last time the saucers were spotted over Washington, on Saturday, the air force sent jet fighters up to chase them, and when the word of the new appearance was flashed around, it was expected that the jets would be ordered up again, to try to shoot down the objects.

But the jets stayed on the ground. An air defense official explained, "We were too busy with other things, and besides objects aren't hurting anybody."

However, civil aeronautics officials did direct an Eastern air lines pilot to check the objects as he flew over the city. But the pilot didn't see a thing. The officials said the saucers disappeared from the radar screen when the plane reached the area where thy had been tracked.

So it remains a mystery.

The second appearance of the saucers in four days leaves th experts just as stumped as ever. Some think the saucers are space ships from another planet. Some think they're just natural phenomenon we haven't figured out yet.

The air force doesn't know what to think. But it's determined to find out. Top scientists have been called in to launch a major investigation.

Admiral Byrd must have known what type of crafts took flight over D.C. in July, 1952 when the headlines read "Saucers Swarm the Capital." A second sighting happened four days later, but the dispatched fighter jets stayed on the ground this time. An air defense official explained, "We were too busy with other things, and besides the objects aren't hurting anything."

BYRD'S *EL MERCURIO* INTERVIEW

The following is the record of an interview with Rear Admiral Richard E. Byrd which appeared in *El Mercurio*, a Chilean paper, in the Wednesday March 5th, 1947 edition. It was written by an American journalist, the International News Service correspondent Lee Van Atta, but seems never to have been published in English. It is important to interject at this point that Byrd was a highly respected American adventurer and hero, known for his pragmatic and down to earth views, and his extreme courage in the face of adversity was proven. The interview, which took place on board the USS Mount Olympus in 1947, ran while the Highjump armada was resupplying in Chile. The translation with the headline "On Board the Mount Olympus on the High Seas" which follows has been checked in English and Spanish for any double meanings, and there are a few.

As printed in *El Mercurio* in Spanish:

> *El Almirante Richard E. Byrd advirtió hoy que es imperativo para los Estados Unidos de America el iniciar medidas de defensa contra la posibilidad de una invasión del país de parte de aviones hostiles provenientes de las regiones polares. El Almirante explicó que no quiere asustar a nadie, pero es una verdad amarga que, en el caso de una nueva guerra,*

FUNDADO EN VALPARAISO

EL MERCURIO

EDICION DE SANTIAGO

FUNDADO EN SANTIAGO

Año I — Santiago, Viernes 1.° de Junio de 1900 — Núm. 1.

TELEGRAMAS

DEL ESTRANJERO

Enviados por nuestros corresponsales de Europa, Buenos Aires y Lima.

DE CONCEPCION

Ultima hora

"Adm. Byrd declared today that it was imperative for the United States to initiate immediate defence measures against hostile regions. The admiral further stated that he didn't want to frighten anyone unduly but that it was a bitter reality that in case of a new war the continental United States would be attacked by flying objects which could fly from pole to pole at incredible speeds. Admiral Byrd repeated the above points of view, resulting from his personal knowledge gathered both at the north and south poles, before a news conference held for International News Service."

After Operation Highjump, Byrd was quoted in the Chilean newspaper *El Mercurio* warning how the Allied nations were confronted by a new enemy that "could fly from pole to pole at incredible speeds."

los Estados Unidos podrían ser atacados por aviones que pueden volar sobre uno o los dos polos.

Esta declaración se hizo como parte de una recapitulación de su propia experiencia polar, en una entrevista exclusiva con International News Service.

Refiriéndose a la expedición de reciente finalización, Byrd dijo que el resultado más importante de sus observaciones y descubrimientos es el efecto potencial que tienen con respecto a la seguridad de los Estados Unidos. La velocidad fantástica a la que el mundo se está reduciendo —recordó el Almirante—es una de las lecciones más importantes aprendidas en su reciente exploración antártica. Debo advertir a mis compatriotas que terminó aquel tiempo en el que podíamos refugiarnos en nuestro aislamiento y confiar en la certeza de que las distancias, los océanos, y los polos eran una garantía de seguridad.

Wikipedia English translation:

Admiral Richard E. Byrd warned today that the United States should adopt measures of protection against the possibility of an invasion of the country by hostile planes coming from the polar regions.

The Admiral explained that he was not trying to scare anyone, but the cruel reality is that in case of a new war, the United States could be attacked by planes flying over one or both poles. This statement was made as part of a recapitulation of his own polar experience, in an exclusive interview with International News Services.

Talking about the recently completed expedition, Byrd says that the most important result of his observations and discoveries is the potential effect that they have in relation to the security of the United States. The fantastic speed with which the world is shrinking—recalled the Admiral—is one of the most important lessons learned during his recent Antarctic exploration. "I have to warn my compatriots that the time has ended when we were able to take refuge in our isolation and rely on the certainty that distances, the oceans, and the poles were a guarantee of safety.

The general English translation of the first two paragraphs:

> *Admiral Richard E. Byrd declared today that it was imperative for the United States to initiate immediate defense measures against hostile regions. The Admiral further stated that he didn't want to frighten anyone unduly but it was a bitter reality that in case of a new war, the continental United States would be attacked by flying objects which could fly from pole to pole at incredible speeds.*

> *Admiral Byrd repeated the above points of view, resulting from his personal knowledge gathered at both the north and south poles, before a news conference held for International News Services.*

Why would these innocuous paragraphs matter? Much has been made of them, with many versions of translations implying something entirely different. Another version of the quote: "Admiral Byrd spoke of 'flying objects that could fly from pole to pole at incredible speeds.'" This is presumably a more open translation of *los Estados Unidos podrían ser atacados por aviones que pueden volar sobre uno o los dos polos,* more technically "the United States could be attacked by planes flying over one or both poles." But questions remain. Simply, there were no known planes at the time that could even come remotely close to flying nonstop over the South Pole. And why would any enemy attack from there? [3]

So who was the enemy that owned or flew these flying objects? Germany was apparently defeated two years prior, and there was no evidence that the new emerging enemy, the Soviet Union, had any such superior technologies. Certainly there was no other known countries whose activities would be advanced enough to explain the U.S. invasion of Antarctica, nor for the comment of "flying objects that could fly from pole to pole at incredible speeds." Rumors began to circulate that while Germany was supposedly defeated,

3. http://www.strangehistory.net/2012/06/06/admiral-byrd-and-nazi-cobblers/

a selection of military personnel and scientists had fled the Fatherland as Allied troops swept across mainland Europe. These fugitives had established themselves at a base in Antarctica from where they continued to develop advanced anti-gravity aircraft based on extraterrestrial technologies, combined with their own technological advancements.

BYRD'S 1954 TV INTERVIEW ON *LONGINES*

Less than a year before he died, Admiral Richard E. Byrd (recently back from Operation Deep Freeze which took place after Highjump), was the first man to officially fly over and explore both the North Pole and South Pole, gave a 1954 interview on the *Longines* program.

He makes several very interesting revelations and points. The first point he says there's an area the size of the United States "beyond the pole, on the other side of the South Pole" that has never been seen by man. Now this point has been the topic of debate for some time, as to what exactly he meant by that. However notice that he

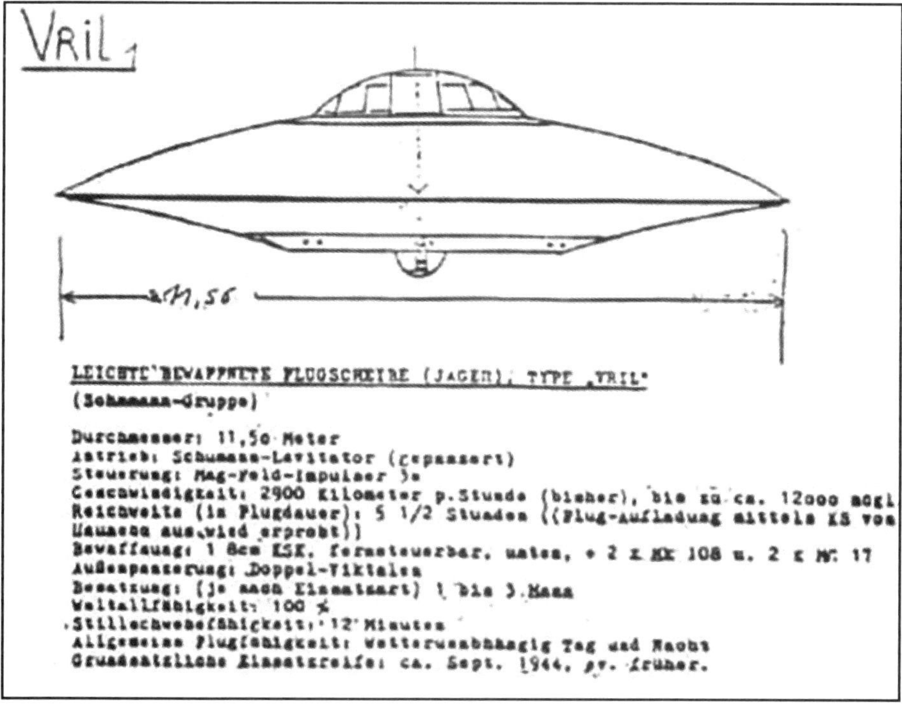

The U.S. Navy Antarctic Development Project, 1946-47, better known as Operation Highjump, had received little attention from historians back in its day. Likely because there was a gag order on reporting about the Battle of Antarctica, still considered classified even to this day. The Antarctic German flying discs could not be revealed to the world.

Byrd's first two Antarctic expeditions prompted the U.S. Postmaster General to honor the event in 1933 on a commemorative stamp. The basic design, featuring a world map, was inspired by President Franklin D. Roosevelt.

didn't say the area where the South Pole is—he's specifically talking about another area beyond that, on the "other side of the South Pole." There is really nothing beyond the South Pole anywhere on the Polar Plateau for hundreds of miles in all directions. Unless he is giving a veiled clue to the massive hole in the ice near the South Pole?

However, as interesting as that is, it's the other point he makes that is even more curious. He says: "the North Pole is really usable; not only to live in, but militarily." He also adds "it's getting crowded up there." But what is up there to "live in" and be "crowded"? On our maps today, there's literally nothing up there; just frigid water and some pack ice. However, on older maps and even ancient maps, for as long as there have been maps of that area, all the way until about 150-200 years ago, there were commonly depicted four mini continents surrounding the North Pole.

Some of these same ancient maps also depicted Antarctica with unbelievable accuracy, half a millennia before it was ever even "discovered" in the 1800s. Since the maps were correct on the shape of Antarctica (even accurately depicting hills, valleys and rivers that, with modern technology, we now know actually were there before it was covered in ice), they clearly knew much more than we previously had thought.

But if they were so astonishingly accurate about Antarctica, then what are those land masses that they also depicted at the North

Pole, that are not present on our maps today? How could they be so wrong about that area, while being so accurate about Antarctica? Admiral Byrd here plainly states not only is there land up there, but that it is "really livable."

Now it would be one thing for him to say that it might be possible to establish some bases up there, with constant maintenance to endure the harsh conditions in northern Greenland or Baffin Island. But the way he's talking about it here is very plainly different; he's suggesting it's just outright "really usable" to "live in."

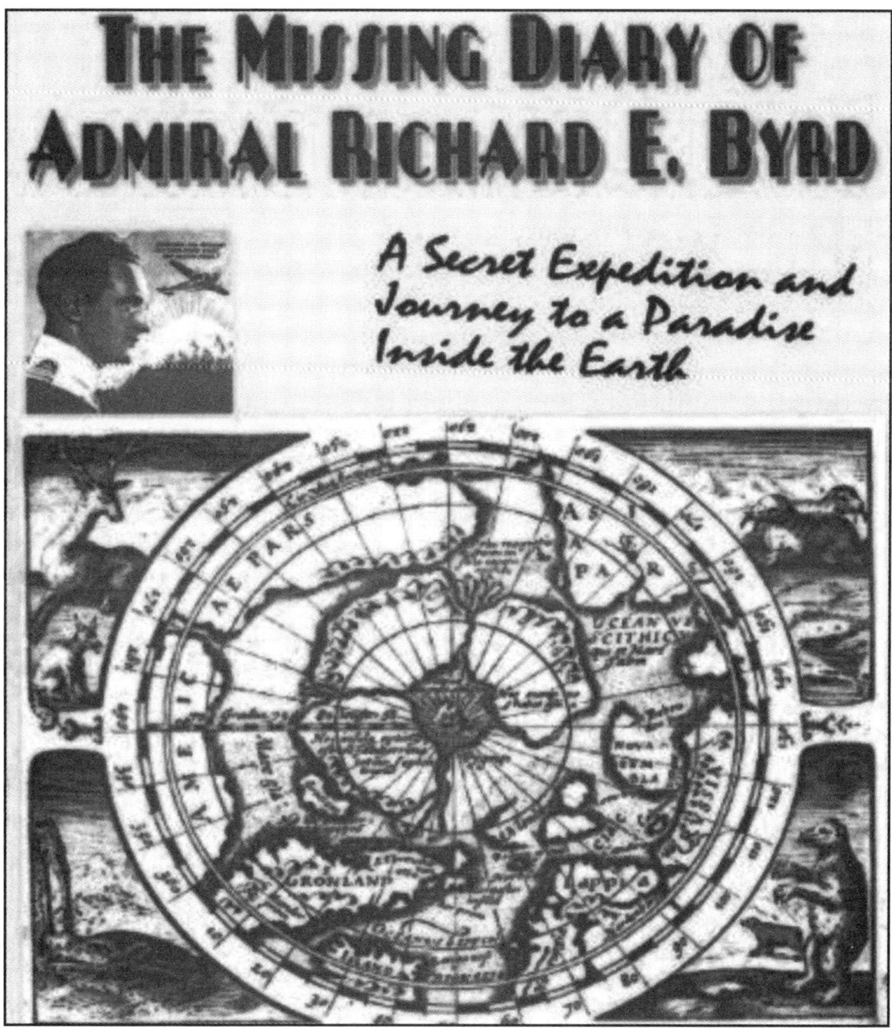

After the untimely passing of Richard E. Byrd, his son found his diary and his nephew eventually published it. The book is entitled, *The Missing Secret Diary of Admiral Byrd*, written by hand and transcribed into the book. It is still available at major book retailers.

For example, nobody describes Antarctica as being "really livable," as that is just not an accurate description. It's more like "it's possible to live there" if you have a scientific research base that's constantly maintained in an extraordinarily expensive and difficult manner, in the harshest of climates. Admiral Byrd knew how hard it would be to live in either polar region.

Not even remotely a convenient place to live, as he's describing the land at the North Pole here in the *Longines* interview. If there's nothing but water and some ice up there at the North Pole, like is shown on our maps today, then what is Byrd talking about? Not to mention, why is no one allowed to fly anywhere near there? "Really livable" and "crowded up there" would definitely describe what is on ancient maps, but is about the furthest thing away from a description of what is seen on Google Earth or modern maps.

BYRD'S DIARY

Richard E. Byrd's diary gives the date of February 19th, 1947, when he allegedly flew a secret mission across the frozen waters of the Arctic Ocean. But on this date, Admiral Byrd was definitely in Antarctica during Operation Highjump. Even the stated plans of Operation Highjump was for Byrd to make another flight over the South Pole. But the flight logs reprinted in his diary call the area the "arctic." Perhaps he changed the location in his diary to make it obscure where it actually took place. What's more, it's pitch black darkness in the Arctic region during February, but these are the best long days of summer for flying in the Antarctic. In the diary he claimed to have seen a previously unknown land with forests and even prehistoric animals. Even more incredible, he encountered flying discs from a technologically advanced civilization hidden deep within the Inner Earth. Operation Highjump uncovered mind-blowing secrets of the mysterious continent of Antarctica, most stunningly a Kingdom beneath the surface inhabited by powerful extraterrestrial beings monitoring humankind's evolution.

On his second expeditionary flight of Highjump, this time to the South Pole, a copy of Byrd's flight diary reveals that Byrd and his radio operator flying a C-47 aircraft was seized down slowly by two disc-shaped crafts flying at the wing tips of his plane. Byrd lost control of the plane and its instruments and its flight controls. The prop-driven C-47 went down much like a helicopter. As the plane landed this way, two tall men, both blond and Nordic looking escorted him and his radio operator to an underground facility, where he was assigned with giving the following message to the so-called surface governments: "Stop exploding nuclear weapons for you will most assuredly experience difficult times ahead." That was all. Byrd and his companion were escorted back to their plane. The strange tall pilots last said over the radio *Auf Weidersehen*, which is German for "Goodbye." They called their craft *Flügelrads*, but this is an unknown word in German.

This incredible adventure is revealed in Byrd's diary which had been missing for many years. Had it been sealed away by the U.S. Government in fear of the haunting message given to Byrd by the inhabitants of the hollow Earth? Did Byrd change the locations in the diary because he was on a lifetime gag order after what he witnessed during Operation Highjump?

We now know that at the time referenced in Byrd's missing diary, he had been leading the Navy invasion mission of Antarctica called Operation Highjump, not in the Arctic Ocean region. This Antarctic mission may have been a massive operation to uncover a secret Nazi stronghold hidden away deep under the ice—a stronghold that allegedly had a connection to Hitler's search for the entrance into the hollow Earth.

What did Richard E. Byrd mean when he said he saw "that land beyond the (South) Pole"? There are only hundreds of miles of flat ice on the Polar Plateau in all directions from the South Pole.

It has long been rumored that the pilot Richard E. Byrd—noted explorer who visited the remotest reaches of Antarctica on behalf of the furtherance of science—actually found much more than he bargained for in the wild climes of the Frozen Continent.

This is the mystery. What is the secret of Admiral Richard E. Byrd's missing diary? Is it government disinformation to hide Byrd's search for the last remnants of the Third Reich? Or is it a warning for the inhabitants of the surface world, such as, "Change your warlike ways before it is too late."

Admiral Richard E. Byrd's missing diary is a shocking revelation of the mystery of the Inner Earth and the possible secret origin of UFOs, which was called "The Greatest Secret Since the Manhattan Project." [4]

FANTASTIC TALES GAG ORDERED

Admiral Byrd was eager to share his story, but was ordered to remain silent. He was put into quarantine, and debriefed for days. When Byrd comes back after his experience he is taken to a government compound, where he is told that he is never to speak of this publicly and that everything he knows is classified. He agreed to not disclose the UFO / Nazi connection to Antarctica. Could Admiral Byrd's story point to a profound connection between the ancient traditions of strange beings living inside the Earth and the modern-day UFO phenomenon?

After the passing of Admiral Byrd in 1957, his son acquired his diary and eventually published the book titled, *The Missing Diary of Admiral Richard E. Byrd: A Secret Expedition and Journey to a Paradise Inside the Earth*, supposedly written in Byrd's handwriting. It is still available at major book retailers. In his diary, Richard Byrd describes his return flight to the polar region on February 19th, 1947. He states how he had flown an airplane with his radioman "Howie" into a verdant green valley and witnessed an ad-

4. Douglas, Geoff, *The Missing Diary of Admiral Richard E. Byrd: A Secret Expedition and Journey to a Paradise Inside the Earth.* Zontar Press, 2017.

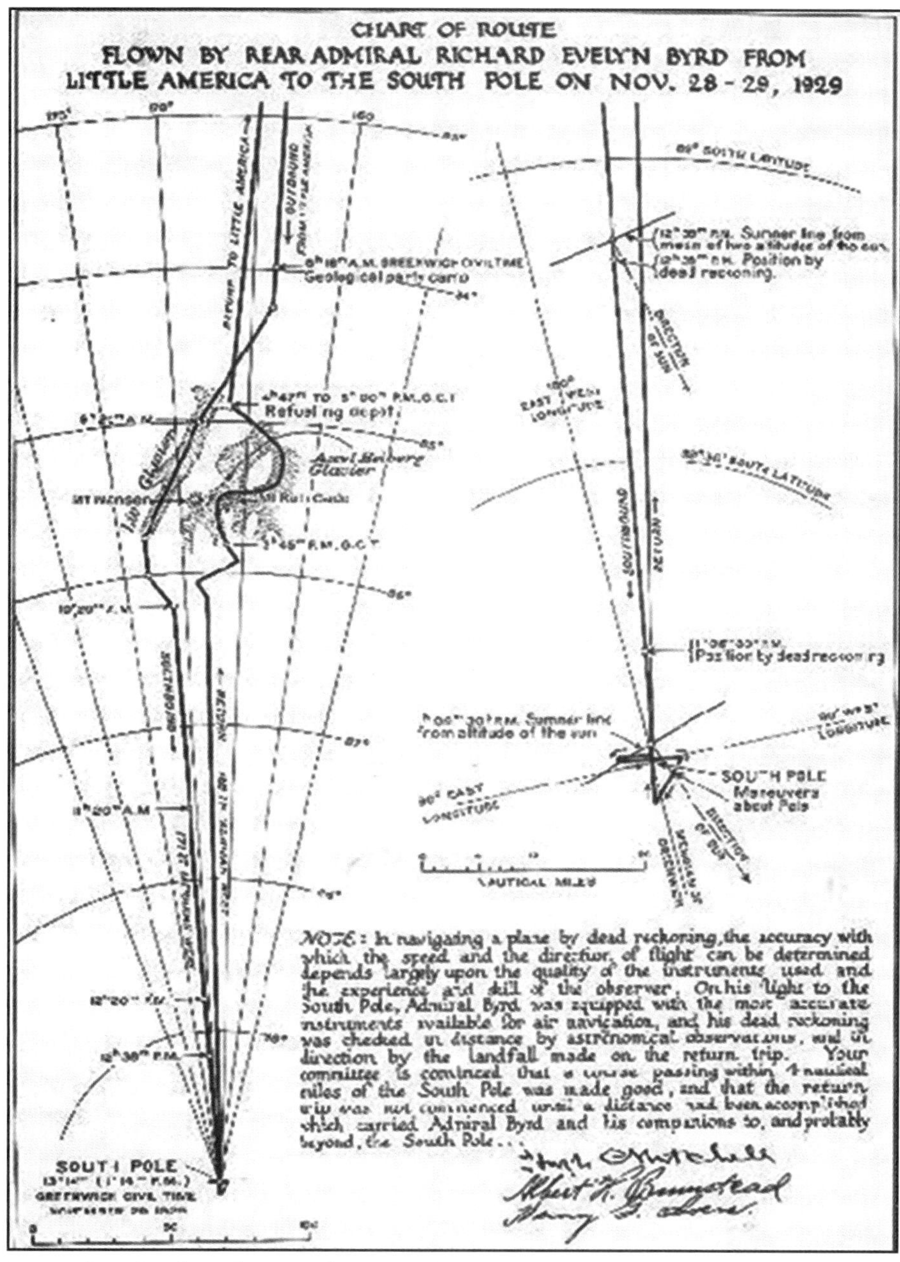

Immediately after the conclusion of World War II, the U.S. military landed in Antarctica and began expanding their airfield at Little America. Admiral Byrd the aviator wrote in his diary that he would follow his previous route to the South Pole. Notice his route after flying over the South Pole the first time in 1929, extended out in a triangular pattern over the area where the presumed hole is located. He would have certainly remembered the giant hole in the ice. After the second flight in 1947, he was given the orders to lead the Allied flotilla to seek and destroy any Nazi bases. Instead of the planned six months, their expedition lasted a mere two months.

vanced civilization. Although the diary starts the chapter with the title "The exploration flight over the North Pole" it would be impossible for Byrd to be there because he was on the opposite side of the planet in this timeframe during Operation Highjump when the dates match up. He also describes multiple mountain ranges which do not exist in the Arctic Ocean. The cover of the book shows a massive hole over the Antarctic continent, not the Arctic. It must be a veiled way of breaking his gag order, by describing his return flight to the massive hole near the South Pole.

The diary describes the story of Admiral Byrd and his radio operator flying a plane to the polar region during Operation Highjump. He gives the account of dipping his plane into an entrance to the underworld, and encountering an advanced Inner Earth civilization. As the most famous arctic explorer to ever live, Richard Byrd making the claim of reportedly discovering an advanced civilization under the ice in Antarctica holds a certain degree of credibility.

On his 1947 flight there are three hours of missing time both on the official flight log and recorded in Byrd's diary when he reported the radio to base channel going quiet. This is the time when he witnessed a verdant green landscape, replete with unusual flora and giant fauna including a woolly mammoth! Both his "Magnetic and Gyro compasses" begin to gyrate wildly, eventually losing use of his navigational instruments and flight controls. Midway into the Inner Earth flight his craft was intercepted by two disc-shaped craft at his wingtips, at which point Byrd lost full control of the plane and it was somehow being flown remotely. A voice with a Nordic or German accent comes over the radio and announces:

> *Welcome, Admiral, to our domain. We shall land you in exactly seven minutes! Relax, Admiral, you are in good hands.*

The three aircraft landed safely outside "a large shimmering city pulsating with rainbow hues of color" clearly of an advanced civilization. He noticed Nazi insignia on the craft and the two tall blond men who were the escorting pilots came out of their cockpits to greet him by name, and both had German accents. After taking a conveyor-belt walkway into the "Buck Rogers" city, the radioman was left behind while Admiral Byrd was summoned to meet "the Master" who seemed telepathic and otherworldly. The two men had a conversation in English, with the Master starting by saying:

I bid you welcome to our domain, Admiral. We have let you enter here because you are of noble character and well-known on the Surface World.

"Surface World?" Byrd half-gasped. "Yes," the Master replies with a smile, and continued:

You are in the domain of the Arianni, the Inner World of the Earth. We shall not long delay your mission, and you will be safely escorted back to the surface and for a distance beyond. ... You see, our Culture and Science is many thousands of years beyond your race.

The Master explains to Admiral Byrd his concerns of the U.S. Military's recent detonations of nuclear explosions at the Trinity site near White Sands, New Mexico, and the bombing of Hiroshima and Nagasaki in Japan. He said their *Flügelrads* flying saucers were sent out to the surface world to witness these events. The Master implored Admiral Byrd to return to the Pentagon to deliver the message not to further advance the nuclear age. Admiral Byrd and his radioman were allowed to leave, and flew out the same way

Admiral Byrd's famous explorations of Antarctica throughout the 20th century yielded him ticker tape parades in New York City. Celebrated for his polar explorations to the general public, there were more extraordinary discoveries that could never be told.

they came. The same two German pilots escorted the men out, bidding farewell in German *Auf Wiedersehen!* over the radio when they allowed Byrd full control of his airplane to fly out of the hole and back to their base at Little America.

Upon arrival back in Washington D.C. on March 11th, 1947 Admiral Byrd is ordered to attend a staff meeting at the Pentagon. He gave his full account of the Inner Earth discovery and the meeting with the Master. "All is duly recorded. The President has been advised," he wrote later in his diary. He is detained for several more hours and interrogated by "Top Security Forces and a medical team." Before leaving, he is placed under strict orders via the national security provisions act to remain silent of what he witnessed "on behalf of humanity." He is reminded that he is a military man and must obey strict orders. His final diary entry states "For I have seen that land beyond the Pole, that center of the great unknown."

He was briefly hospitalized and was not allowed to hold any more press conferences. Still, in March 1955, he was placed in charge of Operation Deep Freeze which was an early part of the Geophysical Year, 1957-58, exploration of the Antarctic. He died shortly thereafter, in 1957 at the age of 68, under questionable circumstances.

Admiral Byrd's eldest son Richard Evelyn Byrd III, was a lieutenant commander in the Naval Reserve, and accompanied his father during Operation Highjump. Sadly, he also died very mysteriously at the age of 68. Admiral Byrd's son, usually referred to as Richard E. Byrd Jr., published his father's infamous diary. He was found dead in October, 1988 in the darkness of an abandoned warehouse in Baltimore, Maryland. In the fall of 1988, Richard Byrd Jr. was traveling by train on his way from Boston to Washington D.C. to give a big speech about his father at a National Geographic Society event honoring Admiral Byrd. He never made it to D.C. and was found dead in an empty warehouse in Baltimore three weeks later wearing different clothing and one shoe. The coroners declared he had died from malnutrition and dehydration. He had already released the diary for publication, and he was likely being monitored as he was preparing to say something exposing the truth of Operation Highjump at the event honoring his father, and there was a botched attempt to silence him before he got to the event in D.C.

OPERATION HIGHJUMP

"The city (of New Berlin) was developed into the Inner Earth and part of the German's South Polar colony, were admitted by the inner earthlings to build a city there. They built most of the buildings that architect Albert Speer was planning to build. ... (they later) established shoulder-to-shoulder cooperation of the Russians and Americans quietly of the Illuminati government."

–Russian researcher Vladimir Terzinski

THE cover story for Operation Highjump is that it was a scientific mission, and the 4,700 men, 13 ships and 33 aircraft were coming along for "training personnel and testing equipment in frigid conditions." In addition to such novelties in Antarctic waters as icebreakers, helicopters, and aircraft combining skis and wheels and equipped with jet-assisted take-off gear, there was also a submarine in attendance, although it proved more of a liability than an asset. Interestingly, the largest Antarctic expedition ever

The ***Schirmacher Seengrouppe*** **are a cluster of fresh water lakes that never freeze. The Schirmacher Ponds and surrounding area are heated by geothermal activity as seen from this satellite image. It is considered an "Antarctic oasis." This is where the German seaplane expedition left from to scout locations for Base 211.**

put into the field was abruptly called-off two months into the six month expedition. There was a confrontation with breakaway Nazis that repelled the Operation Highjump expedition.

Rear Admiral Richard E. Byrd was a strategic choice to lead Operation Highjump. He was a national hero to the American people and had been repeatedly decorated. He had pioneered the technology that would be a foundation for modern polar exploration and investigation. Byrd had already undertaken expeditions to Antarctica, and had flown over both the North and South Poles. The task force itself, however, would remain strictly under the military command of Rear Admiral Richard Cruzen. A central objective of the project was the aerial mapping of as much of Antarctica as possible, particularly the coastline, and also a search for any base locations that might exist.

Following its arrival in Antarctica, the American forces began a reconnaissance of the continent. Byrd himself was onboard the first of the planes to take off on January 29th, 1947 flying towards the unknown, but presumably across the whole territory of *Neuschwabenland*. Over the next four weeks the planes spent 220 hours in the air, flying a total of 22,700 miles and taking some 70,000 aerial photos. The Western Group of ships and planes made a remarkable discovery in January, 1947. A pilot named Bunger discovered an area Admiral Byrd would describe as "a land of blue and green lakes and brown hills in an otherwise limitless expanse of ice." The Bunger Hills oasis covers an area of some 300 square miles with a dozen of lakes that never freeze. When inspected on the ground the geothermal lakes were brackish, and must connect to the surrounding oceans. The team deduced the conditions would be perfect for submarines to hide within. After eight productive weeks of exploration, the mission that had been expected to last for another four months, came to a sudden and early faltering and end. The Chilean press reported that the mission had "run into trouble" and that there had been "many fatalities."

IN SEARCH OF TOP-SECRET BASES

Before the onset of World War II, the Nazis began to set up a pair of secret Antarctic research stations. The first was called Base 211 in a region they named *Neuschwabenland*, and another deep under the ice settlement near the South Pole. This secret research facility near the South Pole was given the name "New Berlin," and was truly a veritable city consisting of technicians, engineers, and scientists who conducted the most advanced Nazi research. When it was certain Germany was going to lose the war, the Nazis started moving their top-secret operations dealing with atomic testing, advanced weapon development, and flying discs to New Berlin via under-ice U-boat transport. Towards the conclusion of the war, the city was fully operational and allegedly continued to operate long after the war was over. These exotic Nazi aircraft and weapons were used in the decisive defeat of Admiral Byrd during his Operation Highjump expedition in early 1947.

The region of Antarctica where Base 211 was established, previously called Queen Maud Land and administered by the Norwegians, contains a rift valley overflowing with geothermal activity, which was discovered by the Nazis in the late 1930s. Warm water ponds that never freeze, named the Schumacher Ponds by the Germans, are teeming with algae, which is also found on surface rocks deep within Antarctica. These ponds never freeze over because of the geothermal activity. Different species of algae reside in different ponds, giving each pond a different color. In the same way that the Icelanders rely on geothermal energy, the Nazis started to con-

After World War II, the largest Antarctic expedition ever put into the field was abruptly called-off two months into the six month operation. Highjump was a top secret military operation to locate and destroy any Nazi bases in *Neuschwabenland* in 1946-47, and they were specifically tasked to capture a new unique armament—flying saucers.

struct a sustainable base deep within an ice crevice near the ponds. Not much more is known about the Nazi Base 211, except that in July and August of 1945, months after the German surrender, two U-boats arrived in Argentina. Had they been to Antarctica to land Nazi treasure or officials? Then in the southern summer of 1946–1947, the U.S. Navy appeared to "invade" Antarctica using a large naval force. The so-called scientific expedition, code-named Operation Highjump, was classified as confidential. In 1958, three nuclear weapons were exploded in the region, as part of another classified U.S. operation, code-named Argus. Was this the final end to the Nazi base in *Neuschwabenland*?

The Russians operate their own top-secret military base at another location closer to the center of Antarctica above Lake Vostok, a vast underground thermal lake covered by a glacial ice dome. It is said during the long days of the Antarctic summer, the ice dome emits enough sunlight to bathe the lake in an endless twilight glow. There is also a strong magnetic anomaly emitting from the area of the lake itself.

The U.S. base at the South Pole is secretly overseen by the National Security Agency (NSA), under the auspices of the National Science Foundation (NSF). This may be because the Nazis and Admiral Byrd found something astonishing near the South Pole during their reconnaissance. First, there is evidence of a large UFO craft discovered in the ice within the *Neuschwabenland* claim, now called the Kohnen seasonal station. There is a huge magnetic anomaly on the southwest shore of Lake Vostok, which may be due to the presence of a vast amount of metal, possibly metal of a buried lost city. Author Henry Stevens in his book *Hitler's Suppressed and Still-Secret Weapons, Science and Technology*, maintains that the evidence points to something artificial, and moreover, something under intelligent control. Could it be something very ancient but working in conjunction with the geophysical anomalous feature? There must be something very important down there for the NSA to be secretly monitoring the situation under the Antarctic Polar Plateau. A few years ago, two Australian women were attempting to cross-country ski over Antarctica when they were captured and detained by American Navy Seal Special Forces. They were released and sent back home but not allowed to complete their excursion, with no explanation given. [1]

According to UFO esoteric researchers, New Berlin was constructed by Nazi ULTRA forces allied to the reptilian Draco em-

1. Stevens, Henry, *Hitler's Suppressed and Still-Secret Weapons, Science and Technology*. Adventures Unlimited Press.

The Catholic elite legitimized Nazism, and after the war helped to set up a network of secret countries in Latin America which became home for Nazi war criminals, including Adolph Hitler.

pire. It was built upon a defunct reptilian base donated to the Nazis, and would have had under-ice connections with Base 211 and the Thule Refuge, an airbase bunker on the outskirts of *Neuschwabenland.* In the early 1930s, the Nazis established treaties with the Draco-Orion forces. The U.S. Government also fell into the alien treaty trap, which continues to this day. If the "Fourth Reich" of the Antarctic Germans were able to win control of the planet with the Dracos, they were promised 25% of the planet for their part in selling out the people of the world with an anti-human depopulation agenda. The New World Order could only be implemented via a human and alien collaboration, named the Fourth Reich of Bavaria. The Nazi ULTRA forces could be the same as the ULTRA Programmable Life Forces in the Dulce, New Mexico facility, which also maintains strong Bavarian connections.

NAZI ESCAPE ROUTES

In 1943, the British Royal Navy launched Operation Tabarin in order to establish permanent meteorological stations at Port Lockroy and Deception Island. This is the cover story. The real reason was to set up bases to spy on the Germans, and to dislodge the Argentinian bases on the Melchior Islands and elsewhere along the Palmer Peninsula. The Argentinians were covertly supporting the German efforts. The British wanted them all out, but *Kriegsmarine* U-boats continued sinking Allied ships in the Atlantic and Southern Oceans.

According to a news release of Admiral Byrd's November 12th 1946 press conference announcing Operation Highjump, "The Navy strongly discounted reports that the voyage will be primarily a lap in the race for uranium. When this expedition was first talked about, uranium wasn't even mentioned. The statement that this is a uranium race for atomic energy is not correct." Admiral Byrd also stated: "However, the basic objectives were not diplomatic, scientific or economic—they were military." Something made the

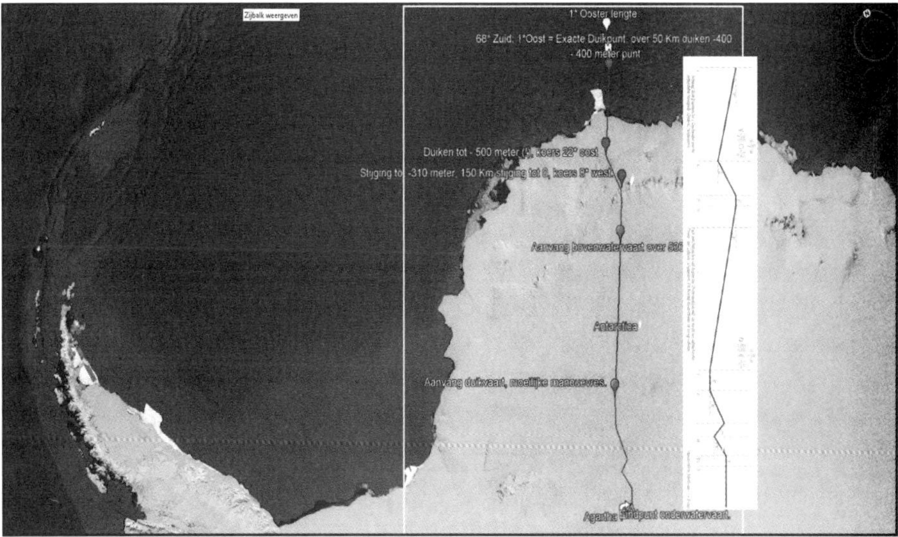

After the Germans returned from Tibet and Ernest Schäfer received the title of SS *Sturmführer* he became one of the heads of the Ahnenerbe in 1937. Right after the Tibetan excursion in 1938-39, the Germans abruptly jumped into Antarctica. It's still unknown what was handed over to them, but they had the maps, and the schematics of the Hollow Earth. And they had all the information about what is inside the Earth in 1941-1942, and the ability to chart a course under the Antarctic ice to some kind of mythical land.

Americans flee their military outposts in 1945, a full 18 months before Admiral Byrd's expedition began. [2]

A few months after the war, two German submarines entered the port at Mar Del Plata in Argentina, surrendering to authorities. But these were no ordinary submarines. They were from the so-called "Führer's convoy." This was the top secret boat fleet fulfilling a top secret mission—"details have remained secret until now," stated Russian researcher Demitry Filipovich.

At first, the submarine crews were reluctant to cooperate. Even so, the American interrogators learned some actionable items. First, the commander of the U-boat 530 spoke of his involvement in an operation code named "Valkyrie 2" two weeks before the war's end. The U-boat 530 left the quay in war-torn Europe heading for the shores of Antarctica. On board of the submarines were passengers with faces covered in bandages as well as a cache of Third Reich relics. The commander of another U-boat 977 named Heinz Schaeffer later testified that he followed the same route. It was found that the German submarines repeatedly followed the Antarctic route—but why go there, the Americans kept asking.

2. http://www.south-pole.com/p0000150.htm (2002)

Recently in Antarctica, huge underground freshwater lakes have been found over a kilometer deep under the ice. The lake's temperature is a constant 18-degrees celsius. Located above the water surface are dome-like vaults filled with warm air. It can be traced from these heated lakes a constant river of warm water flows into the ocean.

For thousands of years, these warm rivers may have formed large underground ice tunnels, which would be perfect for the construction of secret bases a distance from the ocean's edge, which any submarine could easily pass under the coastal ice into these tunnels. It is actually the perfect place for a complete base, one that is immune from storms and polar cold, and totally hidden from satellite scanning and out of the enemy's reach.

Many assume that in case of a German defeat in World War II, Antarctica would be a safe haven for the elite of the Third Reich. It is believed to have been started from an old defunct reptilian base that was donated to the Germans. By 1942, the transfer of inhabitants to *Neuschwabenland* had begun in earnest, including scientists, engineers, members and representatives of the SS and Nazi party, and some civilians of the German state. Only the best top secret industrial technologies were transferred from Germany. Post-war, the Americans recruited German scientists to work in the United States, but were shocked to find thousands of highly qualified Third Reich specialists had simply vanished, never to be found. The Paperclip scientists in the U.S. worked on rocket propulsion, not the imported anti-gravity technology of the South American and Antarctic German scientists. [3]

THE BATTLE OF HIGHJUMP

Shortly after the Allies claimed unconditional victory in World War II, Secretary of Defense James Forrestal sent a naval task force to Antarctica in 1946, including Admiral Nimitz, Admiral Cruzen and Admiral Byrd, and given the operational name "Highjump." Its outward mission was to map the continent and train troops for frigid air fighting. At the end of January 1947, the aviation survey of the Antarctic continent began into the area of Queen Maud Land where it was suspected the Germans had landed. Both the Eastern and Western Groups of Highjump ships were active around the German claim of *Neuschwabenland.* Everything was going according to plan in the first weeks. Tens of thousands of aerial photographs had been taken. [4]

3. https://nexusnewsfeed.com/article/unexplained/why-is-antarctica-a-magnet-for-ufo-stories/
4. *Antarctica.* Reader's Digest, Capricorn Press, London, 1985.

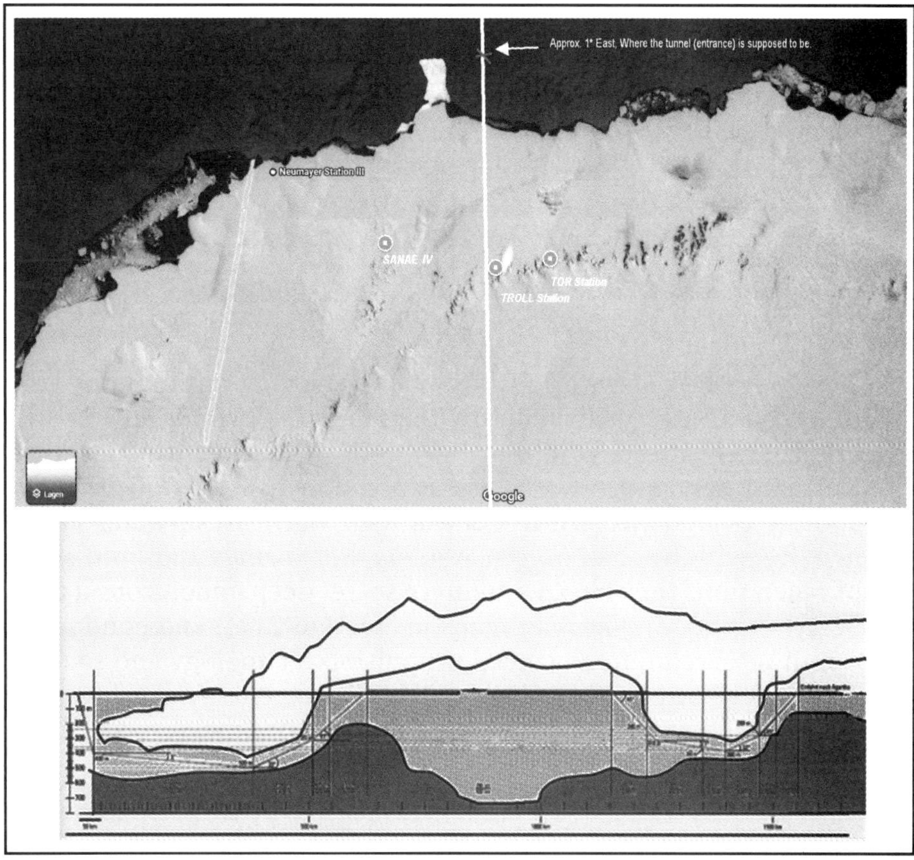

The different toned map gives the impression of an undersea journey on the U-boat map. There were instructions for all the different phases of the journey, including Packet 3 to be opened at the Lighthouse of Agartha with protocol instructions for the officers and servicemen.

The multi-nation armada contained over 4,500 military troops from the U.S., Britain and Australia, consisting of three Naval battle groups, departed Norfolk, VA, on December 2nd, 1946, led by Admiral Byrd's command ship, the ice-breaker "Northwind," USS Mount Olympus and consisted of the catapult ship "Pine Island," the destroyer "Brownson," the aircraft-carrier "Philippine Sea," the U.S. submarine "Sennet," two support vessels "Yancey" and "Merrick," and two tankers "Canisteo" and "Cacapon," the destroyer "Henderson," a floatplane ship "Currituck," and a torpedo boat named "Maddox" (sometimes spelled Murdoch), which was the one ship sunk. According to researcher Frank Joseph, the USS Maddox was "either a torpedo boat, or torpedo-carrying destroyer." He goes on to explain what may have happened to the Maddox mentioned in a declassified Soviet report:

> *A USS Maddox was indeed sunk by enemy action, but five years earlier by a German dive-bomber during the Allied invasion of Sicily. Actually there were at least three American destroyers known by that name (DD-168, DD-622 and DD-731) all of them contemporaneous. The U.S. Navy has long been notorious for falsifying the identity of its ships and re-writing their histories if they embarrass official policy ... So too, the "Maddox" cited by Soviet espionage was similarly consigned to an official memory hole.*

They were tasked with locating and destroying an immense underground base constructed by the Germans before, during and immediately after World War II. American intelligence knew that Germany sent a pre-war naval expedition to *Neuschwabenland* and discovered vast ice-free areas with warm fresh-water lakes, massive subterranean cavern systems, hot springs and even signs of vegetation. They began building a secret deep underground base below the ice (on German maps in "section 211") and conducted occult research into advanced propulsion technology and saucer-shaped Vril aircraft based on universal free energy. An invasion force was organized in the shortest amount of time.

Operation Highjump was basically an invasion of the Antarctic, and consisted of three Naval battle groups, which departed Norfolk, VA on December 2nd, 1946. They were led by Rear Admiral Richard E. Byrd's command ship, the ice-breaker "Northwind."

The U.S. naval task force confronted the flying discs at sea on February 26th, 1947, and the battle was a decisive victory for the Germans. It was over in about 20 minutes. A saucer emerged from the ocean and used a directed energy weapon to slice the Maddox in half. Other saucers appeared to come from holes in the ice. The Allies lost a destroyer and almost half of the carrier-based aircraft, plus dozens of sailors and officers of the Maddox who quickly succumbed to hypothermia. There is still dispute over whether they were German craft, Arianni *Flügelrads* or Draco saucers.

HIGHJUMP AFTERMATH

The main force of Highjump had been divided into three groups of ships and planes. It is established military history that the Central Group was hastily evacuated by the Burton Island icebreaker from the Bay of Whales on February 22nd, 1947. What is still not a matter of public record is the week-long period around the time of land operations being abandoned and the Battle of Highjump out at sea. When the standardized military history narrative picks up again, the Central Group reorganizes itself and begins an official retreat from Antarctica. The Western Group headed home on March 1st, 1947, and the Eastern Group did likewise on March 4th, a mere eight weeks after arrival. When Byrd arrived

Aiding the Allied invasion of Antarctica was a British-Norwegian contingent and a Soviet force, along with some Australian and Canadian troops also involved. Witnesses would state on the record that the Allies suffered "a lot of aircraft and rocket shoot-downs."

back he was immediately summoned to Washington and interrogated by the Security Services. His return on April 14th, 1947 was initially "welcomed back" by Secretary of Defense James Forrestal, who himself would commit "suicide" two years later under highly questionable circumstances.

Because the exiled Nazis won the Battle of Highjump, they could start to dictate terms to the U.S. Government and military. The American people were to be allowed the illusion that they were still a Republic, but were to be ruled through a Liaison. That Liaison is the Director of the Trilateral Commission, founded by Vice President Rockefeller. Thus began the merger of the globalist Cabal with the Antarctic Germans.

On the return from Antarctica, Highjump expedition leader Admiral Richard Byrd emphasized in the *El Mercurio* newspaper that they were preparing to defend the world against "enemy fighters that can fly from pole to pole with tremendous speed." It bears worth repeating Byrd's warning of the need for the United States to adopt protective measures against the possibility of an invasion by hostile aircraft proceeding from the polar regions. He went on

The Battle of Highjump commenced on February 26th, 1947, when a bombing squadron approaching the Nazi Base 211 disappeared off the radar screen. That same day the armada of ships offshore was attacked by an enemy in flying saucers coming out of the ocean and using a directed energy weapon to slice a destroyer in half.

to say "I don't want to scare anybody but the bitter reality is that in the event of a new war the United States will be attacked by aircraft flying in from the poles." In 1958, three nuclear weapons were exploded in the *Neuschwabenland* region, as part of another classified U.S. operation, code-named Argus. These tests led to the Antarctic Treaty the following year, whose first order of business was forbidding nuclear testing. But why would the Treaty mention nuclear testing specifically if it *never* happened? Not even once? Only because it *did* happen.

A TOP-SECRET SURRENDER

By the end of February, 1947, it was all over. The second part of World War II started in November of 1946, when the United States Navy sent a flotilla of ships equipped with airplanes down to Antarctica, ostensibly to test their polar operations. Given the amount of time between the end of World War II and the fact that they had to get close to 5,000 people down there, time was of the essence. Operation Tabarin spies reported the German Antarctic colonies were beginning to take form and posed a threat. By early March of 1947, Operation Highjump ended abruptly and all ships were ordered back to their ports of origin. Most of the Highjump officers returned to Washington D.C. in April. President Truman issued a bizarre executive order in March, in which the loyalty of

In the one-sided Battle of Highjump, half of the planes were shot down, and the other half disappeared on a bombing raid earlier that day. The two flagship aircraft carriers were not destroyed, but forced to immediately turn back.

all federal employees would be evaluated by the FBI. This is when it started for all federal employees having to go through background checks to test their evaluation of national loyalties. This is when McCarthyism was running really hot, so they blamed it on the communists. But what was actually happening is that the Antarctic German infiltrators had escaped with flying discs. That's what they were really after.

The Roswell, NM event happened in July, 1947 when a crashed UFO craft was recovered outside of town. Some find it highly suspect that in the same month Roswell happened the National Security Council and the CIA were also created. Author Joseph Farrell maintains in his book *The Third Way: The Nazi International, European Union, and Corporate Fascism* that the Roswell crash was a German flying disc.

In 1947, the CIA was formulated when it took over the Operation State Security (OSS). The Dulles Brothers made certain the CIA was staffed with Paperclip Germans. During World War II and prior, foreign espionage was handled by the military. When

In 1946, Admiral Richard E. Byrd led a "military in nature" expedition known as Operation Highjump to seek out the Nazi base in *Neuschwabenland* and other Antarctica bases. On his way back to the U.S., Admiral Byrd told a journalist from the *El Mercurio* newspaper that "in the event of a new war, the U.S. would be facing military craft that can fly from one pole to the other at incredible speeds."

President Truman enacted the CIA he put it mostly under civilian hands. This meant that the military was out of the spy business, and only would receive intelligence reports from the CIA. The globalist Cabal now took control of the CIA as their enforcement arm, and hired civilians because they could be better controlled. Later that year, in September 1947, Majestic 12 was created for studying extraterrestrial politics, and collecting any alien recovered craft or technology. This is only months after Admiral Byrd left Antarctica, and took with him alleged reports about a threat to the homeland, and about an enemy capable of incredible feats. The other message that he took from Antarctica was from the Antarctic Germans in which they were requiring a meeting so that they could negotiate a truce, or at least a ceasefire.

A ceasefire was necessary for the Antarctic Germans to buy some time so they could build up their defenses. They had a fleet of antigravitic craft, but it wasn't enough to take on an entire globe of Allies and other world governments that would have been aligned

NAZI BASE IN ANTARCTICA

Latest

MOST OF IRAQ'S AIR FORCE DESTROYED

British Holding Basra

11th DRAFT CALL TO BE ORDERED IN JUNE

Adams Street Slugging Case Baffles Police

Walk-Out at Phyllis Shoe

Former Local Man Killed in New Jersey

Four Nazi Planes Downed Over Crete

Hub Setback May Affect Local Police

Nazi Bases in Antarctic Are Reported

It was first reported on May 5th, 1941 in *The Lowell Sun* newspaper with the headline "Nazi Base in Antarctica" that an emerging threat was detected on the Ice Continent.

against them, so they needed a negotiated truce. They also knew that the Allies had nothing that could compare to their technology, and used it as a bargaining chip. It is believed by some that Byrd's final expedition to Antarctica was to collect a donated German flying saucer, landed in the middle of the night on a special ship and quickly whisked away. Operation Deep Freeze was launched by the U.S. Navy in 1955-1956 with Admiral Byrd at the helm one last time. The goal of Deep Freeze was to establish permanent research stations, extend its logistics support, and assist in scientific research for the upcoming International Geophysical Year (IGY). It would appear the Antarctic Germans won the second part of World War II, this time without a shot being fired after establishing their superior technology during the Battle of Highjump. Richard E. Byrd would die of a heart attack in his sleep the following year.

JAMES FORRESTAL

James Forrestal (1892-1949) was a United States Navy officer and civil servant, and Undersecretary of the Navy. As a Navy man himself, James Forrestal worked closely with debriefing Byrd and the other Highjump officers. In early 1949, he was the acting Secretary of Defense during the Truman administration. In that same year he was sent to stay at the Bethesda Naval Hospital after reportedly walking the halls of the Pentagon warning of a Nazi-UFO threat from Antarctica. After being admitted, he began to discuss Operation Highjump with the hospital staff, including revealing UFOs and a subterranean Nazi city. He was then denied visitors—including his brother, wife and children.

He was admitted to Bethesda under the care of Dr. Raines, who diagnosed Forrestal's illness as *Involutional Melancholia*, a depressive condition sometimes seen in people reaching middle age, often who saw their life as a failure. Upon arrival at Bethesda, Forrestal declared that he did not expect to leave the place alive. In a highly unusual decision for a suicidal patient, Forrestal's doctor was instructed by "the people downtown" (that is, national security) to place him in the VIP Suite on the top floor in solitary confinement.

At around 2 a.m. on the morning of May 22, 1949, America's first Secretary of Defense, James Vincent Forrestal, fell to his death from a small window on the 16th floor of the Bethesda Naval Hospital, with a bedsheet tied around his neck. The mental decline and death of James Forrestal is an unresolved problem of history to this day. There is no question that he suffered from a spectacular mental breakdown during 1948 and 1949. Exactly why he did so is less certain, but the answer may have relevance to American national security, and that pesky topic of extraterrestrials. It is said James Forrestal was the first casualty of the UFO cover-up.

RUSSIANS ON THE TRAIL

At the conclusion of World War II, the Soviet army was the first to capture the German *Ober Kommando des Heeres* (OKH) headquarters in Berlin where they found files of the "Ahnenerbe" organization. This Ahnenerbe is therefore mentioned several times in the KGB-ROMB file, which was put together as a briefing for top Soviet officials. The report also mentions anonymous "German scientists" employed to work on various projects. The Russians were so impressed with the accuracy of the presented facts that they carried out the entire research again in 1983, now with modern insights and techniques. This re-investigation is presented in the KGB-ROMB file. The computer calculations came to the same conclusion as the German files in the 1940s, especially the part about forming an Inner Earth including terraforming techniques. It needs to be remembered that the four Nazi Tibet expeditions in the 1930s, especially the last in 1938 under Ernst Schäfer, contained a great deal of information that they received from the Tibetans

Admiral Byrd presents his friend James Forrestal with a stuffed penguin upon his return from Highjump in 1947. Both men would be dead within a few years, yet both men were in excellent physical condition.

and the Dalai Lama himself! This information goes back to the time when the Tibetans still knew about a "Tibet by the Sea" before the last pole shift that thrust up the Tibetan Plateau.

The Soviets later confirmed the given coordinates of the German U-boat route under the ice from the KGB-ROMB file, from the research of the Ahnenerbe. Besides the precise location, they refer to their own Soviet naval underwater mission to that same place. Amazingly, when Soviet subs reached the under-ice entrance they were met by other menacing submersibles that forced the Soviets to abort their mission and turn back.

The origin of the Russian knowledge and interest stems from their seizure of the Army and Navy archives from Berlin in 1945. These

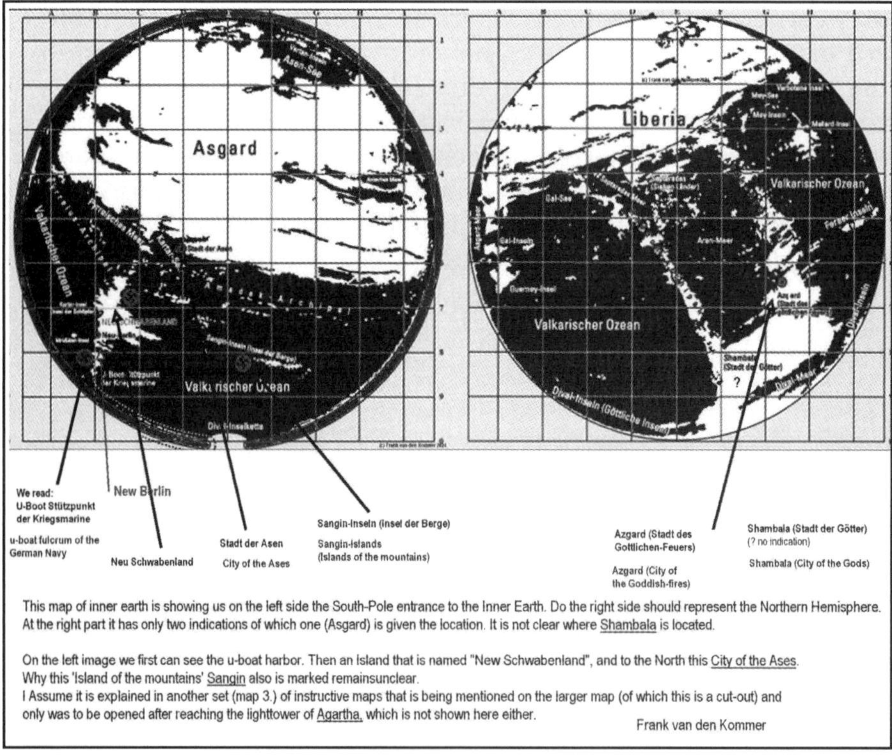

According to the Russian journalist Nikolay Subbotin who acquired the German U-boat directional maps, these two hemispheres depict not some kind of hypothetical imagined Inner Earth, but supposedly this is a direct map of that inner hollow part of the Earth under the ice where the Germans managed to penetrate and chart. Here on one of the halves are drawn those bases that the Germans managed to establish under the ice. This map had 1500 copies produced over the course of the war, as written on the bottom. The 28 copies Subbotin obtained were printed in Dachau camp in 1944. Eventually, everyone who worked on the maps were executed.

offices were closely examined by the KGB and yielded the maps. Later they found a blue notebook of a colonel named "WOLF" inside the headquarters, who wrote about the selection of candidates for the crew at the new base in Antarctica. The KGB archive was closed around 1985 and the results were handed over to the Soviet Party leadership. When the Cold War came to an end, the KGB archives were simply thrown out with the "bulky trash" or sold on the black market. That is how journalist Nikolay Subbotin got his hands on fragments of it. The research results of the Ahnenerbe and their Tibet excursion in 1937-38 form the basis of the entire KGB-ROMB file, recently released on the Internet.

The following is translated from *The 16th Directorate of the KGB of the USSR* (comrade conducted research work study) of the materials found in the scientific department of the SS "Ahnenerbe" (Germany), 1938-1945, concerning the evolution of the Solar System, the Earth (Antarctica) and humanity:

> *As follows from the materials of the KGB organs of the USSR, in 1938, based on the information obtained by the expedition in Tibet into the Trans-Himalayas, the German government equipped an expedition to study the underwater shelf of Antarctica in the region of Queen Maud Land using maps that German researchers had obtained in Tibet. As a result of these studies, Ahnenerbe specialists, together with the German naval forces, penetrated into the cavity of the Earth hidden under the ice of Antarctica, where in the period up to 1944 the German government created naval bases, built a city called "New Berlin" and founded a state called "Neuschwabenland." According to the information that the military counterintelligence organs "SMERSH" had, Adolf Hitler, having replaced himself with a double, left on a submarine for "New Berlin." This is confirmed by the presented materials, collected for a report in 1945 by the People's Commissar of State Security of the USSR, Comrade V.N. Merkulov to the Supreme Commander-in-Chief of the USSR Armed Forces I.V. Stalin.*

> *On June 11, 1945, SMERSH counterintelligence officers of the 70th Rifle Corps discovered 38 "maps of the passage of the sea depths" marked "only for captains of A-class*

submarines of the Führer's Sondereskóhnen" in the building of the headquarters of the German Navy. As follows from the translation of the text of the instructions on the map, it was about the passage of underwater corridors for entering so-called Agartha, hidden under the ice of Antarctica.

For reconnaissance purposes, as follows from the report of the People's Commissar of State Security of the USSR to IV. Stalin dated December 16, 1945, in November-December 1945, by order of the People's Commissar of the USSR Navy, three submarine cruisers of the K type, series XIV Nos. K-56, K-53, K-51 were sent to the area of Queen Maud Land with the purpose of submerging the submarine cruiser K-56 at a point with coordinates of 68 degrees south latitude, 1 degree east longitude. When submerged to 100 meters, the instruments noted the movement of about ten unknown targets around the cruiser, which changed their trajectory at a speed of about 66 knots per hour, which was three times the speed of the cruiser in the surface position. Soviet submariners encountered such a phenomenon for the first time. It did not seem likely to attack these objects due to the sharp change in trajectory underwater. For a repeat operation, it was proposed to involve the corresponding forces of the Soviet naval forces and to resolve the issue of conducting a combat operation in these coordinates with the involvement of the naval forces of the allied powers. (Appendix No. 4 p.d. NeNe).

A year later, in January 1947, American polar explorer Admiral Richard Byrd received an order from the U.S. Government to destroy the suspected German naval bases in Antarctica. The Russians soon discovered a military expedition called "Highjump" was launched, consisting of an aircraft carrier, a submarine, 12 surface ships, more than 20 helicopters and airplanes, and 4,700 military personnel. When approaching the area of the suspected base in the Queen Maud Land region, the expedition was attacked by two dozen flying saucers moving at high speed and striking military equipment with columns of fire. During the twenty-minute battle, the expedition's losses amounted to the destroyed destroyer "Murdock," more than half of the carrier-based aircraft, a submarine, and hundreds of casualties.

As follows from the presented materials on the activities of the Ahnenerbe, it included the so-called "13th Design Bureau" for the design of flying disks, which were successfully tested in the early 1940s. (Appendix No. 5 in the KGB-ROMB file).

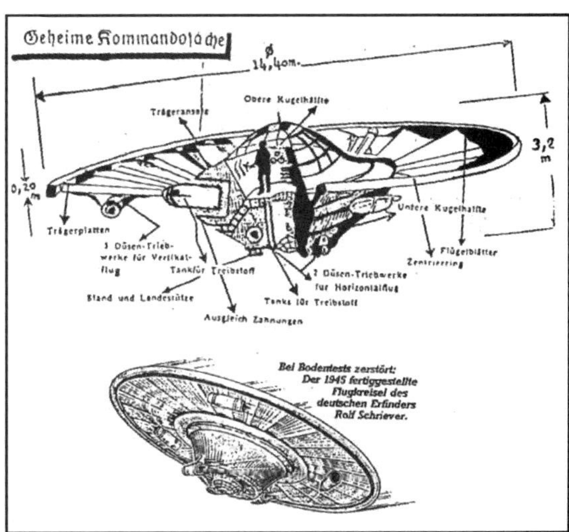

During the Battle of Highjump, an armada of Allied ships was attacked by a legion of flying saucers. But who did the flying saucers belong to? Could they have been the Nazis' backward engineered craft, a malevolent ET force allied with the Germans, or the Arianni *Flügelrads*?

Thc Soviets also discovered by waging war throughout Europe and different places, the Nazis took control of secret societies and used esoteric spiritual resources and hidden underground relics, and some places the hidden technology that needed to be reverse engineered. That's why the Nazis scientists of Operation Paperclip were recruited to come to the USA, and that's why Hitler was obsessed with what was going on in Antarctica. He was obsessed with aliens and that's why he ordered the building of a colony in Antarctica.

What's more, the Ahnenerbe learned through the power of thought control, our DNA, spiritual vibrations and electrical frequencies of the mind, the Nazis were able to set up lines of communication with entities deep underneath the Antarctic ice and other remote regions. They were essentially communicating with the dark extraterrestrial forces. Although the locations were deep underground, they were getting information to create technology to build super weapons and how to control atoms. The Soviet nuclear program began immediately following the war, with their own contingent of captured Nazi scientists. [5]

PROPAGANDA COVER

In December, 1947 a few months after the rout in the Battle of Highjump, Operation Windmill was published. In secret, it was cover for the U.S. to go down again with a military force to establish permanent bases in Antarctica, which were in actuality a part of

5. https://t.me/QTSR2/333

the negotiation between the Antarctic Germans and the Allied nations. Operation Deep Freeze did just that, along with several other Western countries establishing year-round "research stations." All of this would be under the auspices of the future Antarctic Treaty. The world needed to be told something, but not that the USA had capitulated to the Antarctic Germans. Interesting in the next year Operation Mockingbird had its start infiltrating the mass media outlets to control the narrative. 1947 was a very busy year!

Frank Wisner was a member of the newly-created CIA, who was put in charge of propaganda and controlling the media, especially after what happened with Roswell. The "Roswell Incident" cover-up gave the military and government a bad name. So the CIA decided that they would take it on head first. Operation Mockingbird had the CIA cutting checks for a number of "journalists" as employees of the mainstream media to write the narrative they wanted. They dictated the how, why, when and whatever you needed them to say. In 1972, Operation Mockingbird was investigated before Congress with the Church Committee, some 25 years after it was formed. Just because it went public does not mean it stopped.

By February of the next year, Operation Windmill was finished up, in which the Antarctic Germans reached a cease-fire agreement with the Deep State Cabal now running the CIA. What they had expected was a formal treaty to follow, but the Germans wanted to buy some more time so they could fortify their holdings in South America and Antarctica. Frank Wisner said Operation Windmill was really an agreement to a truce with the Cabal and Antarctic Germans to sign a formal treaty to the ceasefire agreement. This established the Antarctic Germans as a sovereign nation in February, 1948, exactly one year after the Battle of Highjump defeat.

The terms dictated their existence was to be kept secret, including their work on antigravitics, which they agreed they would share with the Cabal. The reason for the Antarctic Germans threatening to go public if the treaty was broken was because their hedge was extremely advanced technologies. The D. C. flyover in July, 1952 was a mere taste of what they could do. The secret government did not want that to happen, because they wanted to maintain control and to continue backward engineering their own black projects. Better for both sides to keep everything quiet and top secret.

The Cabal knew that if the Antarctic Germans had gone public, there was a very strong possibility that the rest of the nations would call for an immediate attack, even if it meant nuclear annihilation.

So they decided to keep it all a secret from the people, because the politicians knew that they may not have a choice but to go to war if the public were alerted. They then established their secret embassies, which have at least one senior executive, and thousands of corporations, all under Fourth Reich control.

Meanwhile, the plan to infiltrate and take over Western institutions from the inside was well underway. The kind of a corporations targeted by the Project Paperclip Germans were to infiltrate Ivy League schools, engineering research schools, defense contractors, agriculture, medical research, hospitals, and of course the banks. They strategically placed at least one senior executive into every corporation, mysteriously bought up by funds from a Bormann shell-company in South America. With 300,000 people needing to do something after the war, their plan was to infiltrate the rest of the planet so that they would have their own people in high places. A classic fifth-column maneuver getting your elite operatives in high places within the gates.

From 1948 through 1954, the Cabal was stalling for time, because they knew they could not stand toe-to-toe with the Antarctic Germans. One of the Antarctic German consolidations provided to

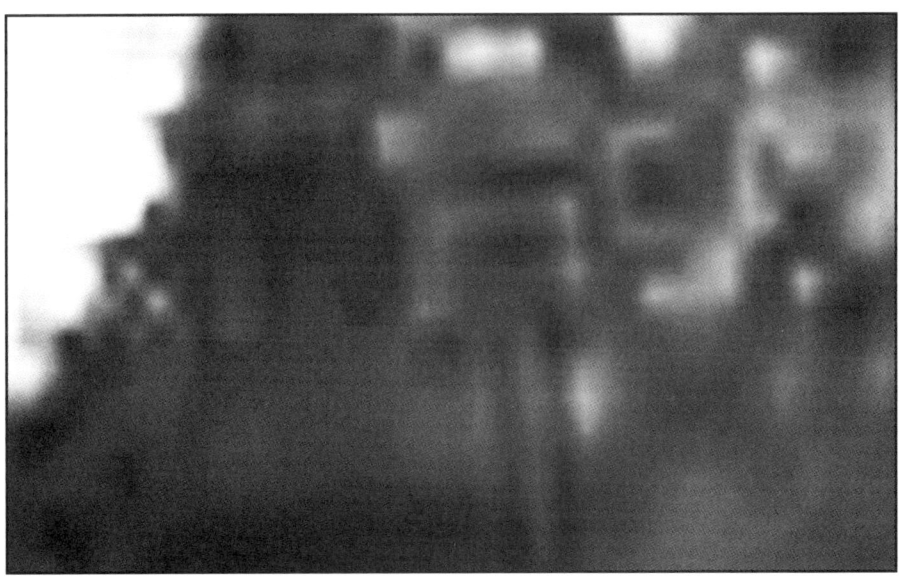

Photographs were taken in the late 1940s of an unidentified German colony in *Neuchwabenland* from an altitude way above the highest stratospheric bombers of the time, which was about 10-12 kilometers, but these were taken 100 kilometers up from basically Earth's orbit. The speculation is that this a photograph of the German *Neuschwabenland* colony was taken from an early prototype saucer at that height.

the Cabal was a delivery of technology. But they only gave them "based theories," rarely the raw technology which they kept for the *Nacht Waffen* "Dark Fleet." They fed the U.S. scientists based theories so they had to do their own homework. Having their own Paperclip people in place meant that they were essentially giving themselves their own advanced theories. Most gained "diplomatic immunity" to travel without search over international borders, and were known to exchange briefcases with others in their network. By getting their own people into corporate executive positions the process of advancement got somebody who has a leg up already. Promotions came quick, especially because they spoke the language of advanced technology, or geographical knowledge for mining sites, for example. These people are suddenly on a fast track to becoming the CEO or a Senior Executive, or any number of senior three-letter agency positions.

OPERATION ARGUS

During the dawn of Ufology in the United States, unidentified flying objects made themselves known to the leaders of the free world, buzzing over the White House, the Capitol building, and the Pentagon on at least two occasions. Seemingly, the unknown objects were defying the very governmental agencies sworn to protect the United States from foreign powers. Washington National Airport and Andrews Air Force Base picked up a number of UFOs on their radar screens on July 19, 1952, over the nation's most sensitive buildings. Most UFO researchers today do not think these craft were extraterrestrial, but back-engineered German craft that remained as a "Third Force" after World War II. The overflight of D.C. was a show of power and forced the U.S. government into a treaty where the German factions were given access to our government and corporate resources to help them build their Antarctica bases and resources to develop their exotic technology, which was to be shared.

A scientific symposium was held in 1957, that was attended by some of the greatest scientific minds of the time, called the JASON Scholars. All three "alternatives" were proposed to combat the decline of living conditions on the surface of Earth. Alternative 1 was to use a series of nuclear devices to attempt to blow a hole in the upper atmosphere as a vent to release pollutants and gases into space. Alternative 2 was the creation of Deep Underground Military Bases (DUMBs) which were completed for the "Continuity of Government." Alternative 3 was creating colonies off-planet, namely on Mars. Completing Alternative 1 may have been the cover story for the 1958 high-altitude nuclear weapons test known as Operation Argus in the Southern Ocean and possibly over Antarctica. The purpose of Operation Argus ostensibly was to test the manipulation of the Earth's radiation belts. Argus was carried out in half the time normally allocated for such a test, and was the only clandestine test series in the 17-year history of atmospheric testing. Additional evidence suggests that the top-secret High-frequency Active Auroral Research Project (HAARP) may also have been tested for such a purpose.

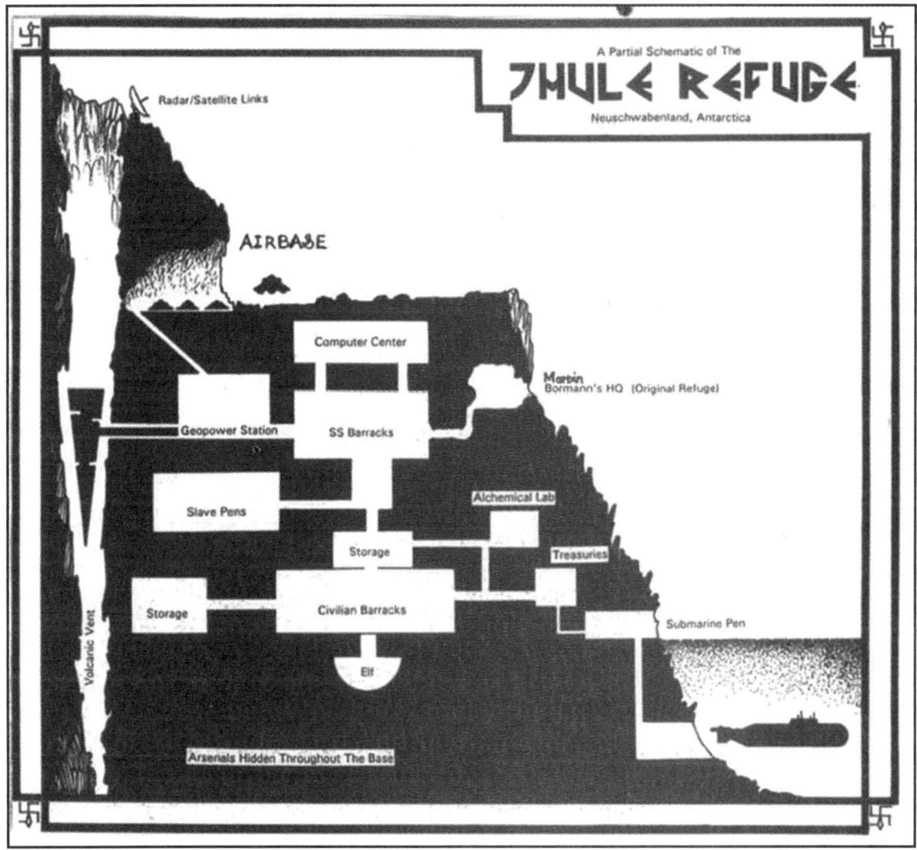

According to secret SS mythology, a German base could be merged into an older, extraterrestrial base, and carry on the tradition of the original Aryan race of Thule. Another Antarctica colony was named in their honor.

Russian researcher Vladimir Terzinski points to the seal of the first German Antarctic expedition 1938-1939, which has the oak leaves of the Thule Society. "It was under the Thule Society sponsorship of the secret patronage of the Thule Society. The Germans were fascinated with the South Pole. The population was about two million."

The still-classified Operation Argus was a series of United States low-yield, high-atmosphere nuclear weapons tests and missile tests secretly conducted, during August and September of 1958, over the South Atlantic Ocean near Queen Maud Land. The JASON Scholar story was it was implemented to blast holes through the stratosphere to release heat and pollution. This could be achieved by simultaneous detonations of atomic weapons in the Earth's high atmosphere of the ozone belt in areas where few would notice: over Siberia, the deep Amazon, the Australian Outback and over both Poles. This, in turn, was the cause of the ozone holes (not aerosol cans and other human causes, as reported by the Fake News Network). Operation Argus was only conducted in the Southern Ocean region off the coast of Queen Maud Land.

Operation Argus could have also been the covert nuclear bombing of *Neuschwabenland* in retaliation for the Battle of Highjump, and for breaking the treaty by not sharing enough of the high technology with the Cabal. By 1958, many Antarctic Germans had moved out to South American micronation colonies or elsewhere. Many missed the outside world, and common illnesses would spread rapidly through the bases every time a new shipment would arrive and one person had a cold. Most people never got sick in Antarctica because most viruses cannot survive long in the sterile cold. Even if Operation Argus was to destroy the Antarctic Germans' Science City, it had little effect in stopping the extensive operation in several locations.

Governing the entire continent started when the Antarctica Treaty was signed in 1959 and came into effect in 1961. This landmark agreement preserves Antarctica for peaceful scientific study and bans military activity on the continent. Its primary goal is environmental protection and the promotion of international collaboration. Over 50 nations have signed the treaty, agreeing to suspend territorial claims and specifically prohibiting mineral mining, weapons deployment, and nuclear testing.

Hollow Earth Entrance at the South Pole

"There are some secrets which do not permit themselves to be told."

–Edgar Allan Poe, *The Man of the Crowd*

CONVENTIONAL wisdom suggests the planet Earth is essentially a solid spherical mass with an inner core of solid magnetic iron encased in a layer of molten iron, followed by a stiffer mantle and the crust, before becoming the surface layer on which we live. One giant solid sphere. That's it. Although this belief is almost universally accepted as absolute fact, it is only a theory with no solid proof to back it up. Surface humans have never been anywhere near to the center of the Earth, not even with the deepest

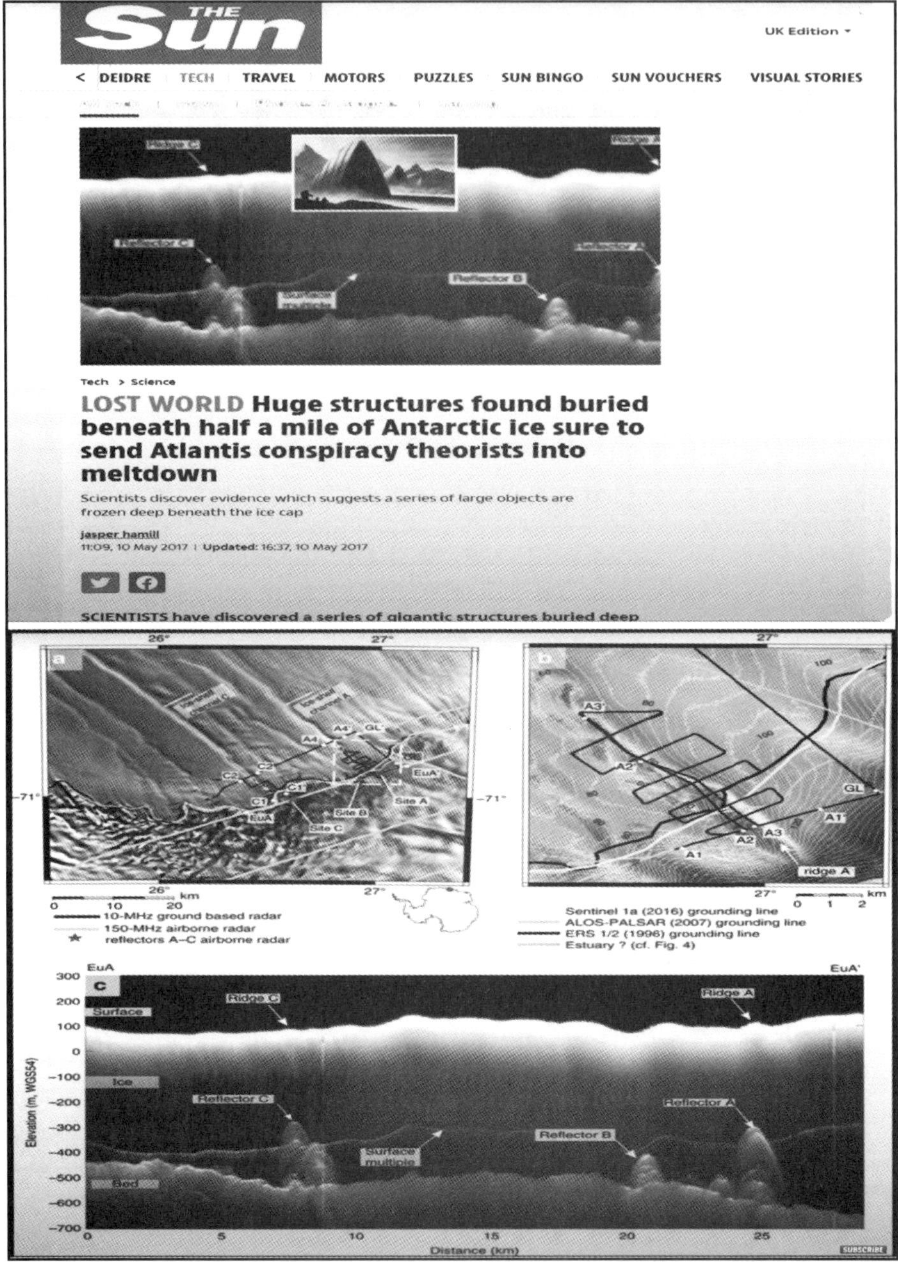

THE Sun

UK Edition

< DEIDRE TECH TRAVEL MOTORS PUZZLES SUN BINGO SUN VOUCHERS VISUAL STORIES

Tech > Science

LOST WORLD Huge structures found buried beneath half a mile of Antarctic ice sure to send Atlantis conspiracy theorists into meltdown

Scientists discover evidence which suggests a series of large objects are frozen deep beneath the ice cap

jasper hamill
11:09, 10 May 2017 | Updated: 16:37, 10 May 2017

SCIENTISTS have discovered a series of gigantic structures buried deep

There are no permanent human residents in Antarctica, although there are always some people there. The winter population at the bases is about 1,000; and this number increases to around 3,750 in the summer. Roughly one third of these are scientists, while the others are support staff. Tourism season begins in November until March. If Antarctica were 100 people, 56 would be tourists; 38 would be staff and crew; and six would be scientists. But that's on the surface. How many are living below the ice could prove to be much larger.

boring drills. Another group of theorists propose the Earth is in fact hollow, and even able to support life within its deepest depths.

Many respected thinkers and even prominent military veterans have presented detailed examples as to what lies deep within our planet. These theories are supported by numerous reports that make reference to living beings and entire civilizations that live and sometimes come up from inside the Earth in UFO craft. Further research along with seismic data appears to show this mass to be a solid sphere with different cave systems at different levels. Hollow Earth theories vary on exactly where and how big; even under the ice of Antarctica at the continental level. Others stating that it could be the core, with a Central Sun that illuminates the Hollow Earth. This is particularly interesting as modern science seems to suggest that the center of the Earth could have been as hot as our sun during the formation of the planet.

LIFE UNDER THE ICE

What used to be considered a lifeless icy wasteland, is now shown as teeming with life. Antarctica supports a huge biodiversity of flora and fauna which lives mainly under the ocean's surface, and in suspected habitats below the ice. Scientists at the Australian National University have discovered vast cave systems surrounding one of Antarctica's active volcanoes, and the team thinks the climate inside these caves could be warm enough to sup-

Advances in technology have allowed ice-penetrating radar and satellite imagery to reveal the coordinates of curious structures on top of and below the Antarctic ice fields. They appear with too many perfect geometric shapes to be random natural formations and show tell-tale signs of being crafted by a higher intelligence.

There are cosmic rays observed to be shooting out of the surface of the ice in Antarctica, and this has scientists baffled. Way back in 2006, a group of scientists inflated a giant balloon intended to float over Antarctica. Built out with sophisticated equipment, the inflatable was launched in order to detect high-energy particles arriving on Earth from space. While it was in the air, though, the balloon observed something very peculiar, enough to upend the scientific consensus and standard physics of the past century now being called into question.

port many different animal and plant species.

In 2019, researchers were studying Mount Erebus, an active volcano on Ross Island, and discovered an extensive network of caves melted into the ice by volcanic steam. After examining them, the scientists collected DNA samples corresponding to mosses, algae and some small invertebrates. They also found several DNA sequences that didn't match any known organisms, meaning there could be plant or animal species yet unknown to science waiting to be discovered in these caves. "The results of our work provide a very intriguing idea of what might be living under the ice in Antarctica," explains lead researcher Karidwen Fraser.

In the future, scientists are planning a much longer expedition deep into these caves to try to find traces of the mysterious Antarctic creatures. Some researchers suggest that entire unique ecosystems can exist in the depths of the ice tunnels! And this is just the beginning, because at the moment science knows of 15 active volcanoes and 91 known geothermal features in Antarctica, and, most likely, each one is surrounded by a network of subglacial caves that may hide other species that have not yet been discovered.

Subglacial lakes sit at the base of large ice sheets and remain liquid year 'round, as opposed to Antarctica's frozen lakes. The lakes occur due to geothermal heating from the earth, the insulating effect of the overriding ice, and the enormous pressure of the ice overburden. Meltwater collects in hollows, forming the lakes in bedrock indentures, and connected to other lakes by under-ice rivers.

Subglacial lakes were discovered in the late 1960s by British glaciologists using ice-penetrating radar. Over 150 subglacial lakes have been identified, most of which are about 3km to 5km in length. At Dome C, so many subglacial lakes have been discovered that it has been called the Antarctic "Lake District."

Lake Vostok is about the size of Lake Ontario, and is much larger than any other subglacial lake—in fact, it is one of the 10 largest freshwater lakes in the world. It is 50km wide and extends in a crescent shape more than 240km north from the Russian Vostok Station. Lake Vostok is also very deep, approximately 510m deep at its southern end, and very old—possibly as old as 20 million years, and its trough formed well before the ice sheets covered Antarctica. No one expects fish or other large creatures to live in Lake Vostok, but biologists think there are unique microbes that use chemicals to power biological processes. These organisms would have developed in complete isolation from the outside world for as long as one million years. All these discoveries attracted huge scientific and media interest in the 1990s.

Lake Vostok was the first subglacial lake to be tapped, in 2011-2012, but samples were contaminated because of the kerosene used to keep the drill holes from freezing shut. NASA seeks to solve this problem because it wants to use similar technology to explore Europa, one of the moons of Jupiter, which also contains kilometers-thick ice crusts covering a liquid ocean that some scientists suspect might harbor life.

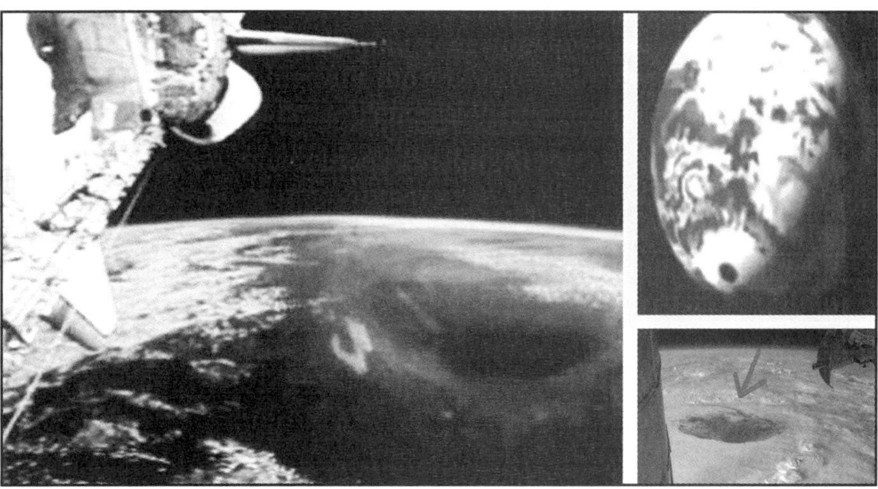

Richard E. Byrd was the first pilot to fly over the South Pole in 1929, and he most certainly would have sighted the massive hole in the ice. After returning, all journals, diaries, records, and documents were seized and classified, especially pertaining to the entrance to Inner Earth and the resounding defeat at the Battle of Highjump.

Vostok Station rests on ice that is 3.7km thick, and because of the fierce winds and its elevation, it's the site of the lowest temperature recorded on Earth: -89.2 degrees Celsius, recorded on July 21st, 1983. It's highest temperature ever recorded is a mere -12.3 C, giving the station its enduring nickname "the Pole of Cold."

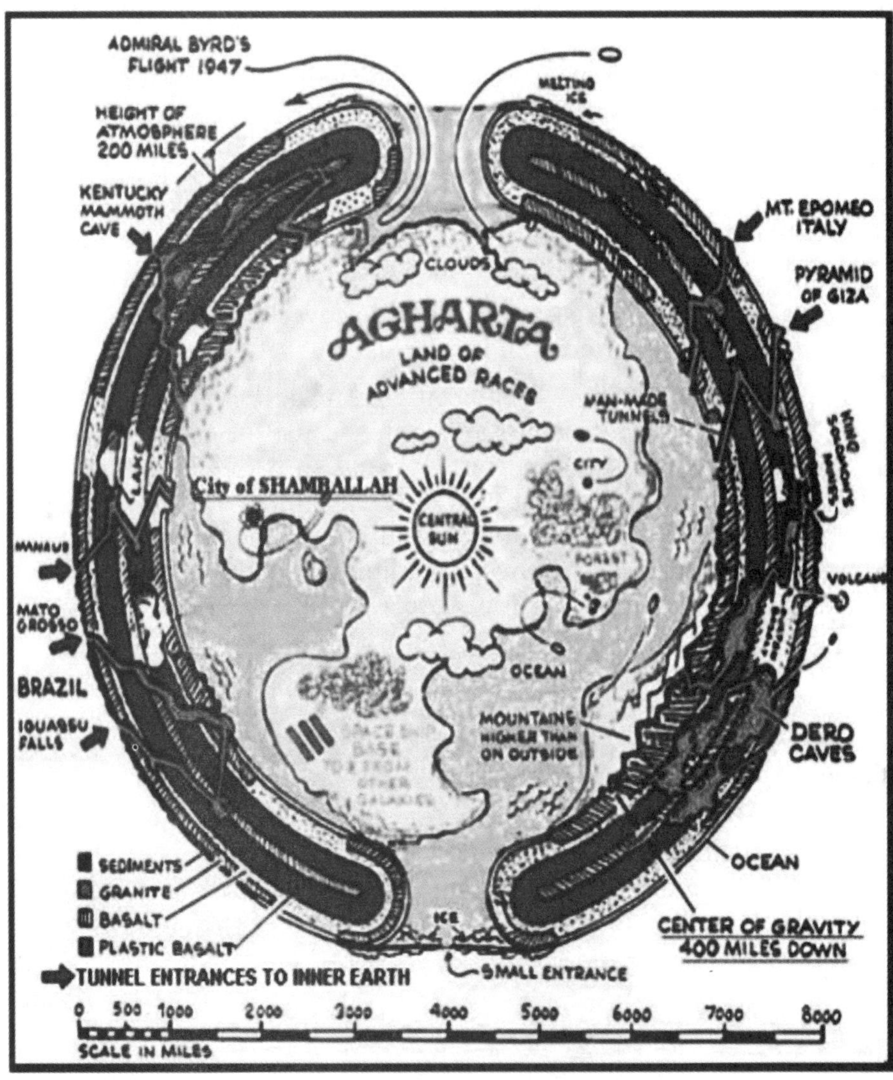

Many think that our planet is designed a little different from what modern geologists say. We live on the outer surface of the ball, and inside in the inner surface there are seas, oceans and life. Then you begin to understand what the inner and outer worlds are, as hell and paradise. Maybe the biblical texts and other religious materials hold encrypted information about the land under our feet, including the mythical empire of Agartha.

INNER EARTH WHERE?

The Inner Earth theory is similar to the concept of Hollow Earth. The Inner Earth theory proposes that our planet contains massive inhabited subterranean caverns that at some time contained, or still are home to, entire human civilizations. There are allegedly numerous entrances around the world, particularly in the polar regions, that are said to lead deep underground into these mythological Inner Earth realms.

In modern times, many people and groups have come up with a number of theories about the possibility that the Earth is hollow. Since time immemorial, many cultures had the same idea. Descriptions of the Hollow Earth, Inner Earth and a world inside our own planet can be found in numerous ancient cultures around the globe.

What if Jules Verne's classic *A Journey to the Center of the Earth* is actually true? What if somewhere down there, a new world is waiting to be explored, a place where somehow, living beings inhabit the depths of our planet—a place that ancient cultures and civilizations knew existed, or still exists today.

In Christianity, the "Fallen Angels" were chained in an underground Hell, inside the Earth, which was a fiery pit deep in the centre of the Hollow Earth accessible only by a passage under

ANTARCTICA: NASA IMAGES REVEAL TRACES OF ANCIENT HUMAN SETTLEMENT UNDERNEATH 2.3 KM OF ICE

Recently released remote sensing photography of NASA's Operation Ice-Bridge mission in Antarctica led to a fascinating discovery when images revealed what some experts believe could be the existence of a possible ancient human settlement lying beneath an impressive 2.3 kilometers of ice.

the "Stone of the Pregnant Woman" at the ancient site Baalbek in Lebanon.

According to the Macuxi (Macushi) hunter and gatherer Amazonian natives they are the descendants of the Sun's children, the creator of fire and disease and the protectors of the "Inner Earth." The Macuxi Indians are an indigenous nomadic people who live in the Amazon rainforest, in the borderland countries of Brazil, Guyana, and Venezuela. Recent topography scans of Amazonia have detected huge urban areas long abandoned, and now covered with jungle.

According to the Macuxi natives they were given the task to look out for the entrance and to keep strangers from entering the "Hollow Earth." Legends from the Macuxi people suggest that those who enter the mysterious cavern system will travel for three days, only descending giant stairs, which measure around 33" each step. After the third day, they leave behind their flame torches and continue their journey "into" the Earth, which are illuminated by lights that were already present in the caves. They describe them as "giant lanterns" the size of a watermelon and shining brightly as the sun. There is a known cave and tunnel system that extends for hundreds of miles in all directions throughout South America. Most entrances are blocked from entry, but some tourists have reported taking a tour into one near Oruro, Bolivia that extends for many miles with steps carved into the rock.

SHAMBHALA INNER EARTH

In Hindu mythology, the Hollow Earth, or underworld is referred to as "Patala" located high up in the Himalayas where the Nazis were sending exploratory expeditions. The idea of an Inner Earth also appears in Buddhism, in the form of an ancient city called Shambhala, located deep under the Tibetan Plateau in what is now China. Shambhala is mentioned by name in the *Kalachakra Tantra* book from South Asia. Interestingly, a giant earthwork discovered by Erich Von Daniken at Palpa, Peru resembles the geometric mandala associated with the Kalachakra.

Buddhists believed (and still believe) that millions of people live in an realm called Agharta (also spelled Agartha), an underground paradise ruled by the king of the world. *Shambhala*, which is a Sanskrit word which translates to "place of peace" or "place of silence." It is mentioned not only in Buddhism, but is referred to in ancient texts like the *Kalachakra Tantra* and the ancient scriptures of the Zhang Zhung culture.

Hollow Earth Entrance at the South Pole

Shambhala is said to be a hidden kingdom that exists inside of our own planet, a mythical place which we cannot possibly comprehend and is extremely difficult to find. According to the Dalai Lama, in a speech he gave in 1985, one must be in a right frame of mind to enter:

The disappointment on the Scott's party's faces is palpable, when they reached their destination a mere 35 days after Roald Amundsen planted the Norwegian flag at the geographic South Pole. Both parties arrived and departed from the opposite side of the hole, and would never have seen it.

> *Although those with special affiliation may actually be able to go there through their karmic connection, nevertheless it is not a physical place that we can actually find. We can only say that it is a pure land, a pure land in the human realm. And unless one has the merit and the actual karmic association, one cannot actually arrive there.* [1]

Modern Theosophical tradition further explains that Shambhala is more than a mythical realm. Although no erudite Orientalist has yet succeeded in locating it geographically, pinpointed an actual land or cave entrance, they believe it is the seat of the greatest brotherhood of spiritual adepts and their chiefs on Earth today. The entrance ways are a tightly guarded secret. Exiting from Shambhala at certain times in the history of the world, come forth the messengers or envoys for spiritual and intellectual work among humans. They are allowed to return. [2]

RACE TO THE SOUTH POLE

Captain Robert Falcon Scott led two British Antarctic Expeditions to reach the South Pole. The first in 1901-1904 failed to reach the pole, but the 1910-1912 mission succeeded, but unfortunately all five team members perished on the return voyage. During the year 1911 Captain Robert Scott accompanied by four others tried to be the first to reach the South Pole, however the Norwegian Roald Amundsen was also racing to the Pole in the same season.

1. Dalai Lama. *The Esoteric Codex: Theosophy I.*
2. https://www.ancient-code.com/shambhala-the-hollow-earth-according-to-ancient-buddhism/

Amundsen's team beat them by just over a month. You can see the disappointment on the faces of Scott's team after discovering the Norwegian flag and a note from Amundsen in a tent they left behind. Amundsen employed the use of sled dogs to pull their supplies, and his men came back safely. Scott's party all died of exposure on the return from the Pole because the team members pulled their sleds by hand. When a search party found the bodies the following season, they buried Scott's party on the Ross Ice Shelf.

Roald Amundsen was the first person to reach the South Pole by land, arriving at approximately 3 PM on December 14, 1911. Amundsen raised the flag of Norway at the South Pole and called his camp *Polheim*, (meaning "Pole Home)" and claimed the entire Polar Plateau for Norway, naming it King Haakon VII Land. Only 35 days later on January 17, 1912, Robert Falcon Scott and his team arrived only to find the Norwegian flag already flying there. Scott and his companions met bad weather on their return journey, and

At times, a glowing light can be seen coming from the ocean depths, along with orbs of light taking flight, or the material discs, plates, physical balls, and "cigar" craft rising out from the ocean. Similar objects have been reported over the polar Arctic region and the adjacent areas of Antarctica. It is not uncommon to see this phenomena offshore the Scandinavian countries, northern Russia, southern South America, Australia, South Africa and just about every other ocean on Earth. In all cases, the craft's mass is offset by an overwhelming loss of mass equivalence, meaning the mass equivalence could be pumped around or right back out, as needed, cell-by-cell. The mass of the craft is far less effected by gravity, if at all—the g-forces are mitigated. Water and air never touch the craft, because inertia is mitigated. The crafts are effectively in a propelling transmedium "bubble" of light.

their supplies of food and fuel began to dwindle. Eventually all five members of the party died of exposure and starvation leaving behind them moving written accounts of their final struggle. Amundsen and his team all arrived back at their ship in the Bay of Whales without incident. The race to the South Pole was a matter of 35 days. It is unlikely either party would have seen the hole because they were approaching the Pole from the opposite direction.

It is an established fact that Richard Byrd was the first man to fly over the South Pole in 1929, and had to hurl out emergency supplies when the plane threatened to crash. He was most likely the first modern human to spot the hole near the South Pole, and came back to investigate in 1947 on a subsequent flight. Richard

There are established no-fly zones over Antarctica, the largest being near the South Pole. There are other reported huge holes in the ice that are also classified as no-fly zones, according to recent Naval officer whistleblowers.

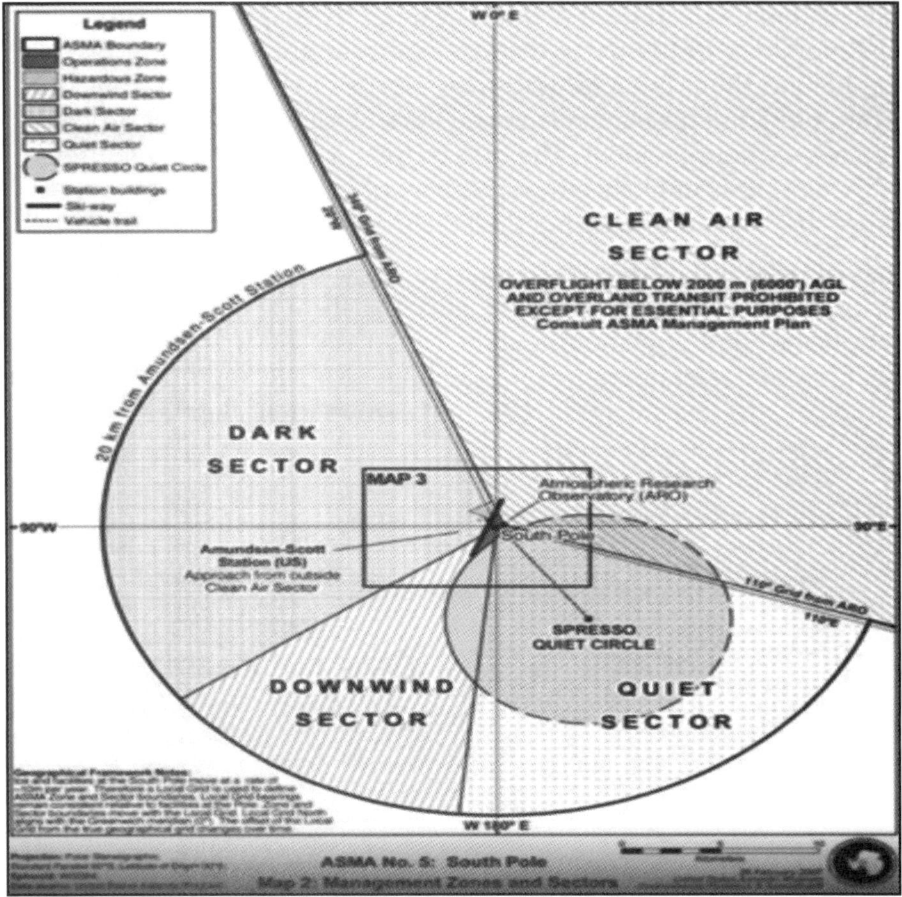

The "Clean Air" Sector is the no-fly zone "OVERFLIGHT BELOW 2000 M (6000') AGL AND OVERLAND TRANSIT PROHIBITED EXCEPT FOR ESSENTIAL PURPOSES. Consult ASMA Management Plan." With no runway or refueling depot for a thousand miles, all planes would need to land at the South Pole station. There are never any non-stop flights above 6,000 feet over the South Pole.

Byrd had a very interesting career in the Antarctic during multiple excursions. In all, Admiral Byrd led five expeditions to Antarctica, culminating in the U.S. governments' still top secret Operation Highjump and Operation Deep Freeze.

DESTINATION: SOUTH POLE

Richard Byrd was a very adept pilot with many acclaimed flights in his career, including the first over the North Pole and several flights over the South Pole. In an historic flight, Richard Byrd piloted the first ever fly-over the South Pole on November 15th, 1929, and most certainly would have sighted the massive hole in the ice. In fact, his flight record shows extending his flight on an exact path over the presumed location of the hole.

After Byrd died in 1957, his son published a hidden book called *The Missing Diary of Admiral Richard E. Byrd: A Secret Expedition and Journey to a Paradise Inside the Earth* describing his 1947 flight into the South Pole hole and witnessing a verdant green valley and an advanced civilization. He was told he was in the domain of the Arianni, the Inner World of the Earth. They were a culture with science many thousands of years beyond his race. This merges with the fabled New Berlin base, where the Germans allied with a much older and advanced race from Inner Earth. [3]

Military pilot John Sarson was an eyewitness of the mysterious Inner Earth craft, which arose from the ocean and from ice caves, as a participant in the Highjump expedition. He testified:

> *They jumped out of the water like mad and slipped literally between the mast ships with such a speed that streams of disturbed air tore the radio antennas, several corsairs managed to, but I didn't, have time to take off from the carrier, and in the blink of an eye, out of the unknown by the rays of the beams from the noses of these flying saucers buried themselves in the water near the ships. At that time I was on the Casablanca deck I understood nothing, these objects did not make a single sound, they rushed silently between the ships and incessantly spat murderous fire, suddenly the destroyer Maddox which was ten cables away from us was ablaze. From other ships, despite the danger, lifeboats and boats were immediately sent to the crash site. The whole nightmare lasted about 20 minutes when the flying saucers dived under the water. We began to count the losses. They were terrifying. Who was the owner of these planes? Is it really the Nazis?*

To this day, it is no surprise that certain staff members of the Antarctic South Pole Station are personnel of United States' National Security Agency. There are also employees of American military technical intelligence, electronic and aerospace subcontractors, and National Science Foundation employees. These categories represent the main research personnel on Amundsen-Scott South Pole Station, but they wouldn't necessarily know each other's duties.

3. Byrd admits "beyond the pole" at the South Pole: https://www.youtube.com/watch?v=PrdSal9uH28

UNDER THE ICE BASES

Starting in 1939, regular supply shipments from Germany began arriving at their colonies in Antarctica. Specifically the Wabi Research Vessel Machinery, including railroads, trolleys and huge milling machines for burrowing tunnels. Highly qualified scientists and engineers also arrived there with the general workers.

Why did Germany need such a remote base deep under the ice? Various assumptions are made. Some believe that the Germans wanted to control the Southern Ocean, others believe that Germany was attracted by useful fossils of Antarctica for uranium, without which it is impossible to create a superweapon, and some

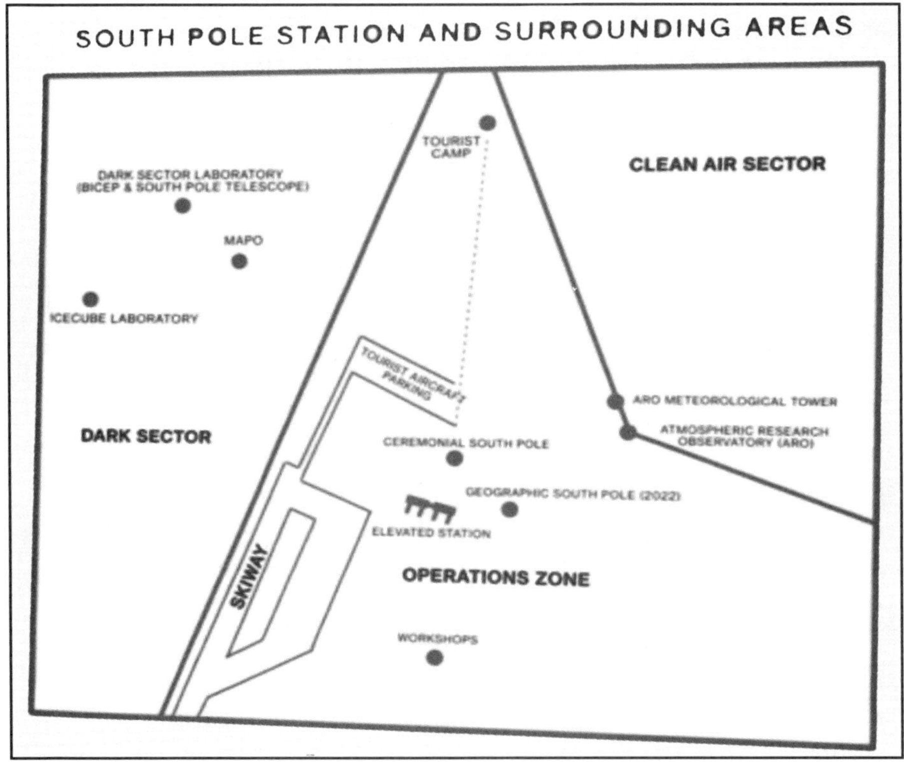

One of the most cutting-edge research projects is being done at the Amundsen–Scott South Pole Station, where the IceCube neutrino detector is buried over one kilometer below the South Pole. It is making observations that refute long-held understandings of gamma-ray bursts. The team searches for ultrahigh-energy subatomic particles called neutrinos that have passed through the core of the Earth–thus the Earth becomes a telescope, and the ice cap the detector. Studying neutrinos in this way may increase our understanding of "dark matter," the power sources of galaxies, cosmic-ray acceleration and the workings of supernovas, as well as the ability of neutrinos to change type.

claim that in case of losing the war in Antarctica a shelter was being prepared for the elite of the Third Reich.

Allegedly since 1942, in the *Neuschwabenland* region, began the transfer of its future inhabitants, not only scientists and specialists, but also representatives of the Nazi Party and the State, plus thousands of young Ukrainian women to be the wives of the scientists. There were certain secret productions after the war, because the Americans, who actively recruited German scientists to work in the United States, were surprised to discover that thousands of highly qualified specialists of the Third Reich disappeared without a trace. And more than a hundred submarines were not among the dead. Perhaps American intelligence did have some information that there was some kind of heritage exported from Germany. Naturally, the Antarctic polar zones were in the field of their attention, and then there was the testimony of the German submariners who surrendered to the Argentine authorities in the summer of 1945.

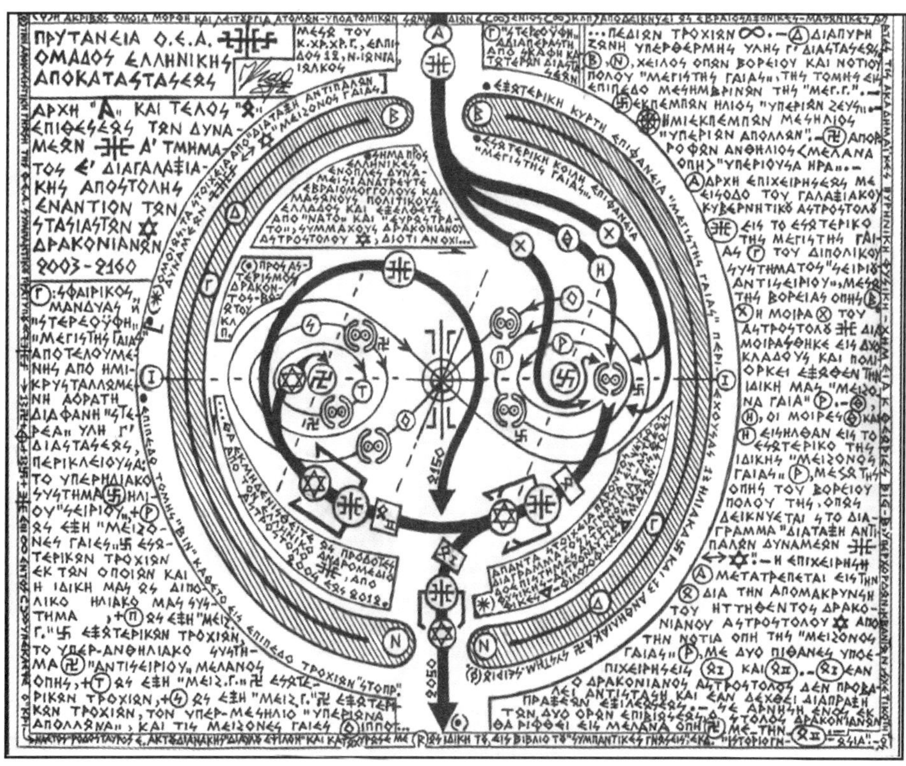

A runic map of Inner Earth adapted by the Nazis.

Apparently, all this greatly alarmed the Americans and at the end of 1946, the famous polar explorer Admiral Byrd was sent down there. But it was not there, and the rebuff that the American squadron received is still causing dread. The fact is that in Washington, Admiral Byrd reported not just about an advanced civilization under the ice. He spoke of the attack on the expedition by strange flying saucers coming up out of the ocean and Inner Earth.

Fast forward to today and the bases of the Cabal are still there. According to whistleblower testimony, there are at least five bases under the ice run by an "Interplanetary Corporate Conglomerate," and a corporate-directed Secret Space Program operating out of Antarctica. These five Deep State bases have been targeted by remote viewers. They report that these locations are geothermal-powered cities with human workers. The remote viewers reported

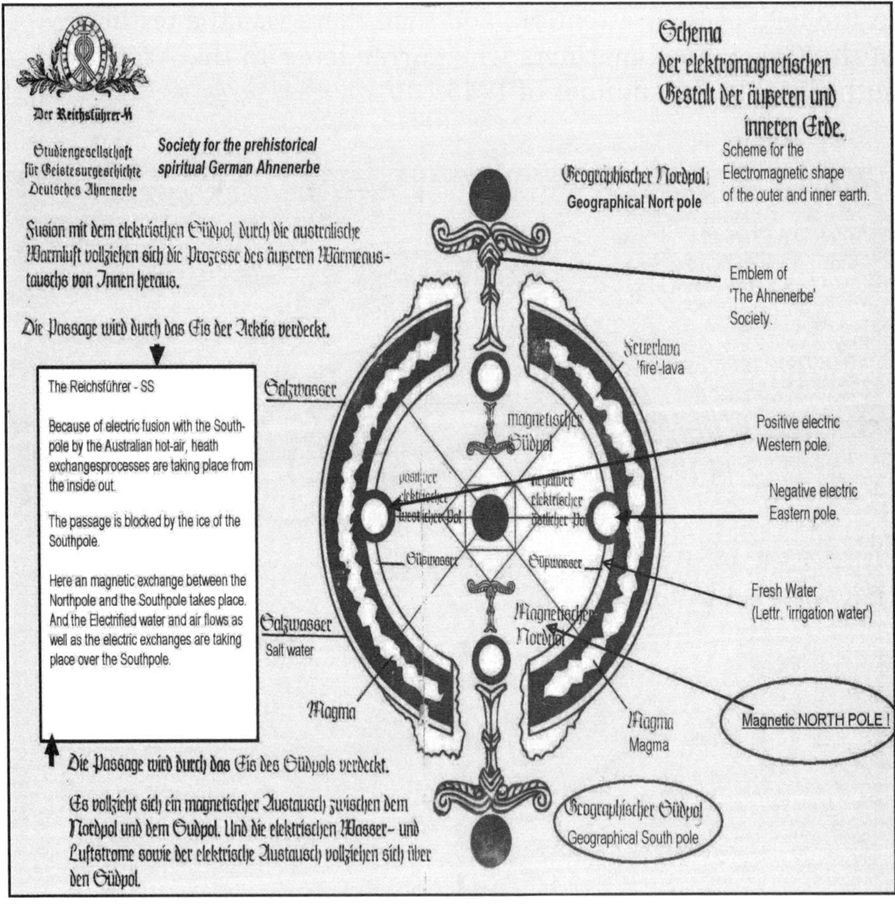

An English translation of the pole anomalies of the Ahnenerbe Society, based on older Tibetan maps. The design is a "Scheme for the Electromagnetic shape of the outer and inner earth."

a huge work staff and under-ice cloning labs facilities belonging to the Interplanetary Corporate Conglomerate, a corporate-directed Secret Space Program operating out of Antarctica.

NAZI EXPEDITIONS TO INNER EARTH

Less than a year after World War I, in September 1919, Adolf Hitler participated in a meeting of the *Deutsche Arbeiterpartei* (DAP), the German Workers' Party, founded in a Munich brewery by Anton Drexler, a member of the Thule Society. The *Thule-Gesellschaft* (name taken from the mythical Homeland of the Hyperboreans), was an esoteric order linked to the *Germanenorder* and Ariosophy, which promoted the idea of developing the remembered and latent qualities of the Aryan race. Undoubtedly, the Thule Society was vital in the formation of the future Führer and in the formulation of his political doctrine, along with his desire to collect spiritual relics from around the world.

The Germans had developed an entire theory about an Inner Earth at the request of philosophers, scientists, physicists and explorers over a 30-year period. They sent three Tibetan expeditions before the 1938 Ernst Schäfer excursion. Russian occultists like Madame Blavatsky spoke about "Agartha," but without using the name. She spoke about "a time at the end of times when good and evil will have their last battle these people will reveal themselves." One of those explorers was named Ferdynand Ossendowski, who actually travelled to Mongolia and Tibet and learned from the Buddhist Lamas that "Once the Gobi Desert was an inland sea, and in that was an Island where a highly spiritual people lived. Much more evolved than we now are." The Lamas explained about "a time when there were no mountains in Tibet, and Tibet laid at an Ocean." Those were a people who possessed supra-natural powers in health and such, they called themselves by the name "Arianni."

The Tibet missions has all the markings of an esoteric expedition—seismographs, rituals, sacred geometry. They weren't looking for plants. They were hunting for a gateway. Ernst Schäfer led the fourth expedition to Tibet, and just after he returned to the Fatherland in 1938, the ship Schwabenland left for Antarctica a few months later. The next SS expedition to Tibet under Bruno Berger was a real SS-funded excursion, but as a part of the 1938-1939 larger Schäfer expedition. A cartographer named Wilhelm Filchner was there traveling over rugged mountains and passes. The team did a great deal of mapping in South-Western Gobi Desert and the mountains in the south there, and also to determine the borders between Tibet and China.

German exploration teams were sent to Tibet in 1926 and 1942, specifically to establish contact with the cave communities. A few years after the first contact with the Adept of Agartha and Shambhala, a Tibetan community was established in Germany in 1928 with branches in Berlin, Munich and Nuremberg. The Adepts of Agartha were known in Germany as "The Society of Green Men." There were strong measures taken to keep silent about their real significance. The Society of Green Men were joined by senior members of the Green Dragon Society of Japan, with whom they had been in communication for hundreds of years.

During the final weeks of the war, when the Soviets reached their quarters in the suburbs of Berlin, they discovered a dozen naked bodies lying in orderly rows each with a ceremonial knife piercing the abdomen. One Soviet soldier from Siberia recognized the men as Tibetan.

In 1928, the Thule Society, via the strong Tibetan colony in Berlin with which German geographer Karl Haushofer was in permanent contact, is said to have resumed the links to Tibet's secret society of monks, which were even maintained during World War II. They used radio communications between Berlin and the Tibetans capital of Lhasa. One prized item taken back was *The Book Dzyan*—a secret book of magic of Tibetan sages—and the link to the Tibetan Buddhism. It was translated and studied by Trebitsch, Haushofer and Hess, and the emissary of Tibetan Agartha in Berlin. *The Book of Dzyan* is a reputedly ancient text of Tibetan origin. The Stanzas formed the basis for *The Secret Doctrine*, one of the foundational works of the theosophical movement, by Helena Petrovna Blavatsky. The book has influenced writers in the ancient astronaut, occult and UFO communities.

In the northern Alps region in Germany stands the mighty *Untersberg*, the main mountain overlooking *Obersalzburg*. The *Untersburg* is no ordinary mountain, and one of the reasons Hitler was intrigued with it was the repetition of events, legends and tales of missing persons, people experiencing loss of time and passageways into what Hitler called "The Inner Earth."

One of the most persistent rumors has to do with the legend of German emperor Frederick Barbarossa. It is believed that his astral form currently sleeps in the mysterious depths of the *Untersburg*, waiting to come back to life during the Final Battle between Good and Evil. The return of the Emperor will mark the beginning of a thousand-year empire of Aryan rule. [4]

4. https://thearkadian.com/the-cathar-prophecy/adolf-hitler-and-the-spear-of-destiny

SPEAR OF DESTINY

Since World War I, the Germans had a special battalion of soldiers known as *Kriegsgeologen* who were deep-earth military geologists. By the 1930s, Himmler's SS had two departments dedicated to archaeology. Archaeological research was managed by Rolf Höhne, a geologist, which ensured any finds or "out of place objects" would be micro-managed by Himmler's most trusted staff. The Nazis were in search of artifacts with magical, psychic powers, such as the Spear of Destiny which Hitler acquired from the Hoffburg Museum in Vienna. Himmler and Hitler had both been groomed by members of the OTO and Brotherhood of Saturn who, respectively owned bookstores that published journals about the occult.

Adolf Hitler acquired the Spear of Longinus along with the rest of the Hapsburgs royal treasures in Vienna, on March 12, 1938, the day he annexed Austria to the New Reich. It is believed the spear cut into the torso of Christ on the cross, and once contained his blood. Ever since it pierced the side of Christ more than 2,000 years ago, its legend and involvement predicted the decline of the Roman Empire, the Dark Ages, and the 20th century. Named for Saint Longinus, the Roman soldier who stabbed Christ to show he was dead, the Holy Lance has many names. It has been called the Spear of Destiny or the Holy Spear. The chain of men who possessed the Spear spans from Herod the Great to Charlemagne King of France,

"I knew with immediacy that this was an important moment in my life ... I stood there quietly gazing upon the Spear of Destiny for several minutes, quite oblivious to the scene around me," spoke Adoph Hitler in 1938.

In Wagner's last opera, "Parsifal," Hitler realized that he had established the essential connection between the Holy Grail and the Spear of Destiny. For Wagner, the "union" of the Spear and the Grail chalices–as sexual objects–was essential to the eventual consummation of the drama. The Grail Cup symbolizes the purity and perfection of the "Aryan womb," and the spear symbolizes the phallus. In this picture, Hitler views the Hapsburgs collection of imperial jewels and the Spear of Longinus in Austria, shortly after being annexed by Germany.

to Frederick Barbarossa Holy Roman Emperor, then to Adolf Hitler. Each sought to change the face of history by wielding its powers for good or evil. Hitler believed he could invert the force in a bid to conquer the world.

The Spear of Destiny is identified as the Spear of the Holy Grail mentioned in the sagas of the Dark Ages. It is believed the holder of the Spear possesses the power of mind expansion—as applicable today as it was at the courts of King Arthur and Charlemagne. Adolf Hitler believed he could use the Spear to further his aims and his conquest of the world by black magic. Occultists believe the Spear of Destiny played a central role in the decline of the Roman Empire, the coming Dark Ages, and the rise of Germany in the early 20th century. [5]

When the Spear of Destiny arrived on German soil it was seen as the symbol of imminent victory in the coming battle against communism and the *Untermensch*, or subhumans. Karl Haushofer saw it as a signal for the *Wehrmacht's* mobilizations to begin. Less than a year later, Germany was at war. The Holy Spear stood in St. Katherine's Church, in Nuremberg, throughout the Blitzkrieg,

5. Ravenscroft, Trevor, *The Spear of Destiny*. Neville Spearman Publishers, 1972.

but as RAF bombers penetrated farther and further into the Third Reich and began reducing its great cities to rubble, Adolf Hitler ordered that a permanent hiding place be found for his most cherished possession.

The Führer's war intent was to serve and glorify his nation, to achieve the final triumph for the Aryan race and the coming *Übermensch*, or Superman. The defeat of the elite German 6th Army at Stalingrad ended his dreams. It also brought an eclipse in the Nazi confidence in the "magic" of the Spear and the occult in general. At the war's end, General Patton's U.S. troops found the Holy Lance in an underground vault of Kohn's Bank on the corner of the Konigstrasse, in Nuremberg. According to legend, they took possession of the lance at 2:10 p.m. on April 30, 1945. Less than two hours later, Adolf Hitler supposedly killed himself in a bunker in Berlin. The fact that the defeat of the Third Reich occurred shortly after Hitler lost possession of the Spear, rekindles a special interest in the power of the mythical relic over the course of human history.

"Whoever possesses this Holy Lance, holds the destiny of the world in his hands." That is the legend, the myth, the curse of the Spear of Destiny. General George Patton had knowledge of the terrible significance of the Spear of Longinus, because when the Spear passed to the United States of America General Patton died mysteriously, once again fulfilling the legend.

But there is no way Hitler would allow his enemies to possess the Spear after being defeated, and the SS likely placed a replica in the underground vault of Kohn's Bank to be discovered by the Allies. There are also stories that the real Holy Lance is under St. Peter's Basilica in the Vatican City, or it is held in Armenia, and others claim it is in Antioch, as well as in Krakow, Poland. Since there are at least five so-called Holy Lances in existence, it is pretty hard to know which one is genuine. The German Spear of Longinus was said to have made it out of Germany at the end of the war on a U-boat destined for their underground base in Antarctica. Possessing the Spear would give rise to the power of the Fourth Reich. [6]

SWASTIKA ORIGIN

Ernst Schäfer wore the brush-shaped mustache that indicated he was an Adept in the Mysteries. On the evening before the outbreak of World War II, Schäfer's SS expedition returned to Germany from Tibet, guided by Karo Nichi and Eva Speimuller. They had brought the Dalai Lama radio equipment with which

6. Smith, Jerry E. *Secrets of the Holy Lance: The Spear of Destiny History & Legend*. Adventures Unlimited, 2005.

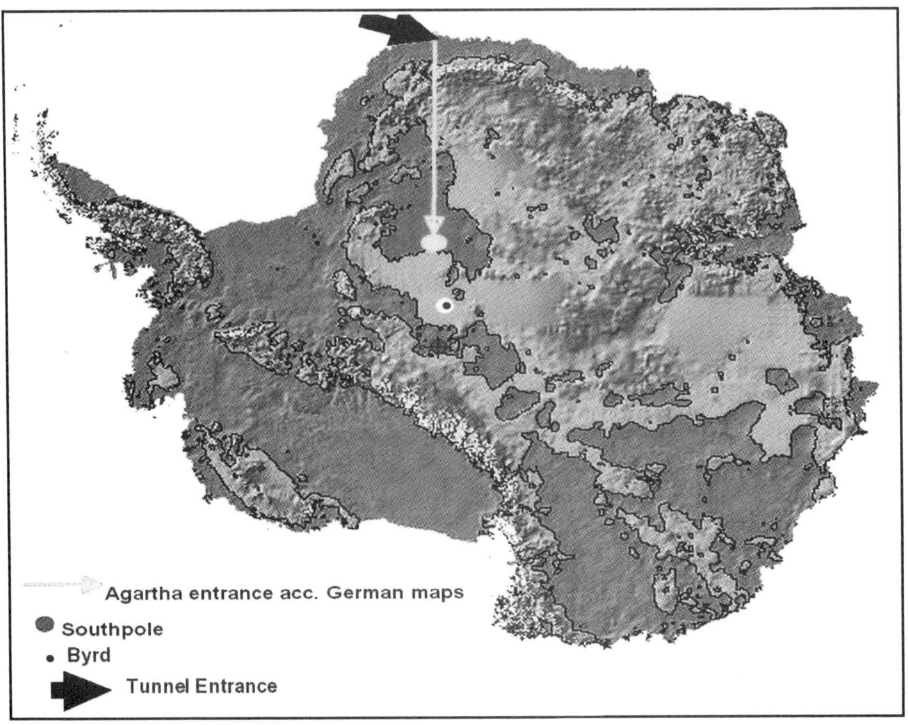

If we take a look at history, we will be surprised to find out that the topic of the Hollow Earth has been relevant for at least a thousand years. As well as is Atlantis. And the works of famous ancient philosophers and researchers say that inside the Earth there is a certain cavity. At that time they imagined it as some kind of "cave system."

to set up links between Lhasa and Berlin. Schäfer's SS men were permitted to enter the holy city of Lhasa, otherwise barred to Europeans and Christians, and even the Dalai Lama's magnificent Potala temple, containing one single enormous object prized by the Germans. A giant Swastika was the holiest symbol of the Mongolian empire. Even before Hitler came to power there was continuous contact between the National Socialist party and Tibet. There was a document signed "The Pact of Friendship" with Nazi Germany. Schäfer had brought the above document that the Dalai Lama had signed. [7]

The Tantra ritual and the Tantric initiation has the meaning "to weave" in Sanskrit. The term "Tantra" applies to a set of spiritual practices that directs the "Universal Energies" into the "Practitioner," thereby leading to Liberation from the physical level of existence. "Samede" is a state of consciousness characterized by Clarity of Perception and the absence of the ego.

7. A. D. Grad. *Temps des Kabbalistes*

Of special interest to the Germans was that the Tibetans' most sacred emblem for universal consciousness was the swastika. Indeed, the swastika symbol is seen at many sacred sites throughout South Asia.

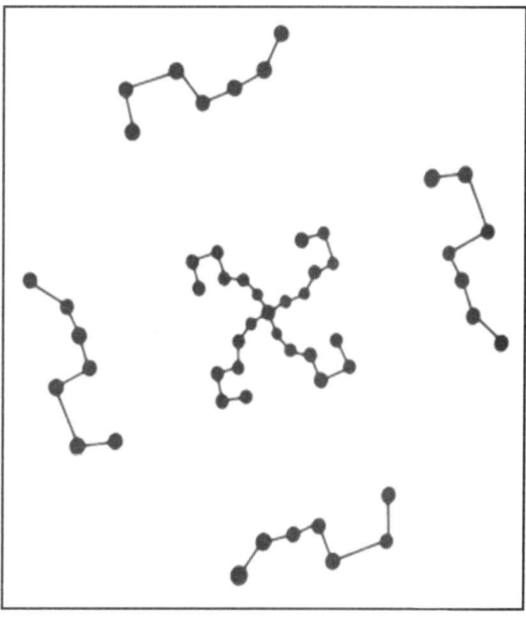

The Swastika was based on the shape of the Big Dipper when combined in four opposite directions.

In the heart of Berlin, at number 29 on the Brüderstrasse, Heinrich Himmler amassed a library of Himalayan manuscripts and maps of the Inner Earth. Many of the manuscripts in Himmler's occult library were hand printed from Tibetan wood stamps. Each sentence opened and closed with the ancient symbol of the swastica.

PURPOSE OF THE NAZI EXPEDITIONS

Many senior Nazi officers believed in the Hollow Earth theory, proposing that planet Earth is entirely hollow or contains a substantial interior space, an atmosphere, inverted gravitational forces, and a selection of uniquely evolved animals and plants which are heated by an interior spinning molten sun, or "Black Sun," made of liquid lava rock. The Hollow Earth theory was proposed by astronomer and leading scientist Edmond Halley in the late 17th century, the astronomer who discovered Halley's Comet. Another early scientist to advocate an inner Earth was Leonhard Euler. All believed there were advanced races of people living down there.

Russian explorer and author, Nicholas Roerich, led a 1924 expedition aimed at discovering Shambhala. Roerich claimed that his spiritual masters, the "Mahatmas" in the Himalayas, were communicating telepathically with him, and these became the "Secret Chiefs" of German occultists who, in turn, influenced Adolf Hitler.

Part of the Pact of Friendship was to bring a group of Tibetan Yogi black magicians to Germany in order to teach Nazi officers psychic

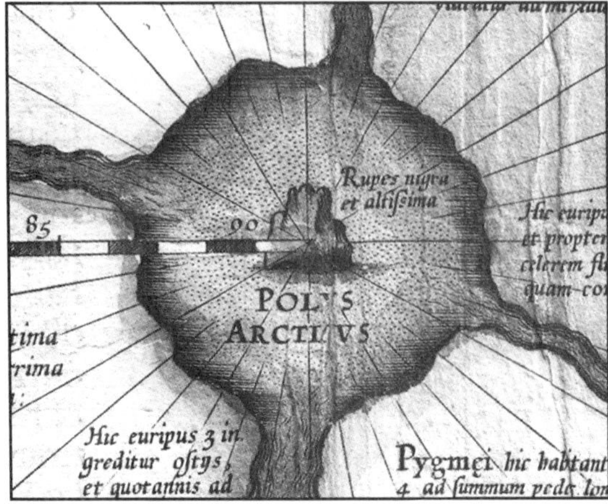

The Black Rock was described by mapmaker Gerardus Mercator as being "33 French miles in size," from a legendary "lost" manuscript titled *Inventio Fortunata*, which means "fortune-making, discovery." It is a "lost book" which was read alongside ancient maps filled with drawings of huge ocean creatures. This triggered the great whale-oil expeditions in the 17th century and the land grab at the North and South Poles.

powers. By the start of World War II, many geologists were employed by the Nazi "Ministry of the Occult," known as the Ahnenerbe Society. The Ahnenerbe was the occult "science institute" of the SS, confiscating and storing in its library many ancient documents about astrology, magic, runes, psychic weather modification and the Inner Earth. Another collection of manuscripts in this Nazi occult library described an entry point to the Hollow Earth, as drawn on ancient maps as the "Black Rock" of the North Pole.

Explorers, kings, queens and cartographers included Black Rock island on maps from the sixteenth and seventeenth centuries. Mercator described the island in a 1577 letter to Queen Elizabeth's astrologer-magician, Doctor John Dee, who probably had a copy at his Mortlake library. Author Jacobus Cnoyen transcribed the letter:

In the midst of the four continents is a Whirl-pool, into which there empty these four in-drawing Seas which divide the North. And the water rushes round and descends into the Earth just as if one were pouring it through a filter funnel. It is four degrees wide on every side of the Pole, that is to say eight degrees altogether. Except that right under the Pole there lies a bare Rock in the midst of the Sea. Its circumference is almost 33 French miles, and it is all of magnetic Stone.

Although no modern map depicts it, the "Black Rock" is a phantom island which appears on maps drawn by explorers on the payroll of kings, queens, dukes and the Illuminati. This giant rock sits at the meeting place of four great tectonic plates. It is located at the magnetic North Pole, which has traditionally been in the northern Hudson Bay area. It is the other large entrance to Inner Earth in the north. This giant magnetic rock is possibly an asteroid because it sucks the ocean and icebergs down into a giant "plughole." It is the original inspiration for the Hollow Earth theories which have persisted for centuries. The two massive holes near both of the poles makes the Earth a giant torus field.

FLIGHT CREW WITNESSES

Investigative journalist Linda Moulton Howe interviewed "Brian S." who had an eyewitness experience describing the several kilometer-wide hole near the South Pole. In 2016, Linda received an email from a 61-year-old Navy officer who was stationed several years in Antarctica. He was part of a C-130 flight crew that encountered high strangeness from 1984 to 1987. Several times he and the crew all watched silver discs darting around the sky near the Beardmore Glacier. He said he saw what he described as "an entrance to a human/ET collaboration base" near the South Pole. Flying from the South Pole Station on an emergency rescue to the Australian Davis base, his crew made a diversion through the no-fly zone and spotted the massive chasm. They all discussed what they saw, and attempted to fly over it again on the return flight, but were advised by ground command not to do so. Upon returning to McMurdo Station, Brian and his team were reprimanded and were told by their superiors that, "you did not see what you just saw." Brian never had to sign a non-disclosure and years later decided to speak out. He said the hole is located five to 10 miles northeast of the South Pole Station. The Clean Air Monitoring Station and no-fly zone is cover for secured airspace surrounding the massive hole, with a snowmobile

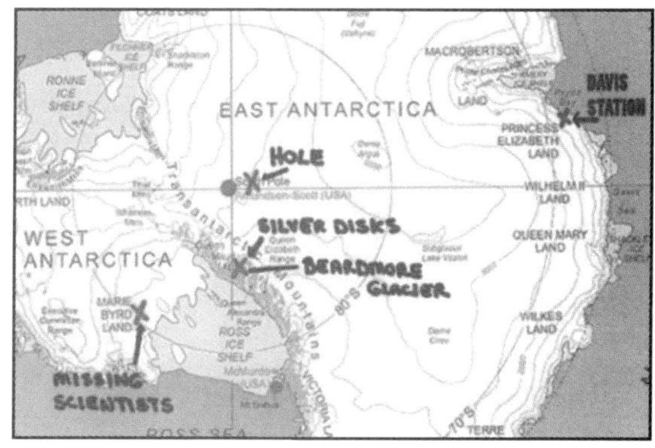

The whistleblower Brian S. reported to Linda Moulton Howe several anomaly locations in Antarctica, including the giant hole in the ice near the South Pole. His pilot defied the no-fly orders because of an emergency evacuation from the Davis Base, and that is when the whole crew saw the hole. Interestingly, Brian S. and the rest of the crew did not see a Clean Air Monitoring Station out there, suggesting this was the cover story to justify the no-fly zone.

and snowcat road corkscrewing down into it. Brian did not see any air sampling stations on the outbound or inbound flights over the no-fly zone. He thinks it's just a cover story to protect the hole in the ice from being seen by aircraft or drones.

Under the Antarctic Treaty ratified in 1961, no nation may enforce any land claim, and cannot perform any military training operations or weapons testing. Different militaries of the world are permitted to assist with logistical missions, as Brian S. was assigned. Military vehicles allowed are Naval or Coast Guard ships in water, over land in the form of snowcat rovers, and helicopter or airplane cargo flights. There are however established no-fly zones over certain sections of Antarctica, which is interesting because so few flights ever go there, and what could they possibly be hiding? The largest no-fly zone is one degree northeast from the South Pole, where the reputedly largest hole dropping deep into the polar plateau exists. There are other huge holes in the ice elsewhere that are also classified as no-fly zones, according to recent Naval officer whistleblowers.

ANTARCTICA ETs

"I occasionally think how quickly our differences worldwide would vanish if we were facing an alien threat from outside this world. ... And yet, I ask you, is not an alien force already among us—What could be more alien to the universal aspirations of our peoples than war and the threat of war?"

–Ronald Reagan at the 1987 UN General Assembly

ANTARCTICA is the coldest place on Earth and home to about ninety percent of all freshwater ice on the planet. The frozen landscape is as reminiscent of an off-world planet as it can get, and many researchers believe there is something "alien" about Antarctica. Thanks to software such as Google Earth, people can explore distant parts of the world from the comfort of their homes. And this is precisely what many people are doing and have done, with some surprising breakthroughs. Some of them claim to have even found proof of extraterrestrial bases or alien technology crashed on the Ice Continent.

What's more, satellite images revealed a symmetrical four-sided triangular structure in the Ellsworth Mountain Range of Antarctica. This structure, resembling the iconic Great Pyramid of Giza in Egypt, has sparked widespread debate. However, geologists have identified it as a natural feature commonly found in glaciated areas, known as a pyramidal peaked mountain or nunatak. Despite the logical explanations, many are still puzzled by the regularity of the shapes, leading to endless speculations and theories. A research team needs to go there and document an investigation and put the matter to bed once and for all. If it is fashioned by intelligent hands then it's a complete game changer. Either people from a past society like Atlantis built it, or an extraterrestrial civilization that landed here and decided to stay.

Among the most intriguing aspects of these accounts are the descriptions of strange indentations in the ice and massive tunnel-like structures. These formations, sometimes described as leading to complex networks or deep underground facilities, raise the question: Are we looking at natural geological formations, or could these be evidence of an alien presence, hidden away in one of Earth's most remote and unexplored regions? There are only three places in the world where an inner-terrestrial civilization could maintain a base undetected: In the deepest depths of the oceans, deep underground, or under the ice in Antarctica. [1]

THEY CAME FROM OUTER SPACE!

One of the most otherworldly places on Earth also turns out to be the best place to search for rocks from outer space. In early 1970, a few Japanese glaciologists discovered the first concentration of Antarctic meteorites, nine pieces in all, near East Antarctica's Queen Fabiola Mountains. The discovery has evolved into a collection of 50,000 specimens today. They are our only current and continuous source of macroscopic extraterrestrial materials.

If the plan is to find objects that fall from the sky, then almost any rock found in East Antarctica has to fall there. Antarctica is a huge meteorite collector because of its ice coverage. Turns out, it's the best place to look for them in the world. Some are concentrated in places where the retreating glaciers have to squeeze through nar-

1. https://curiosmos.com/strange-ufo-sightings-at-antarctica/

row gaps in the Transantarctic Mountains, where the flow of ice can be dramatically slowed or stopped, making these locations prime meteorite hunting grounds! The fierce winds of the plateau can make massive amounts of ice to sublimate, which is the change from solid to vapor, and exposing the meteorites in highly concentrated areas.

The "Antarctic Search for Meteorites" is an investigative team that searches for the rare rocks every summer. In a meteorite NASA retrieved from the LaPaz icefield in Antarctica, researchers have uncovered a grain of stardust that formed before even our own sun had come into existence. What's more, this grain of material sheds insight into how solar systems like our own form.

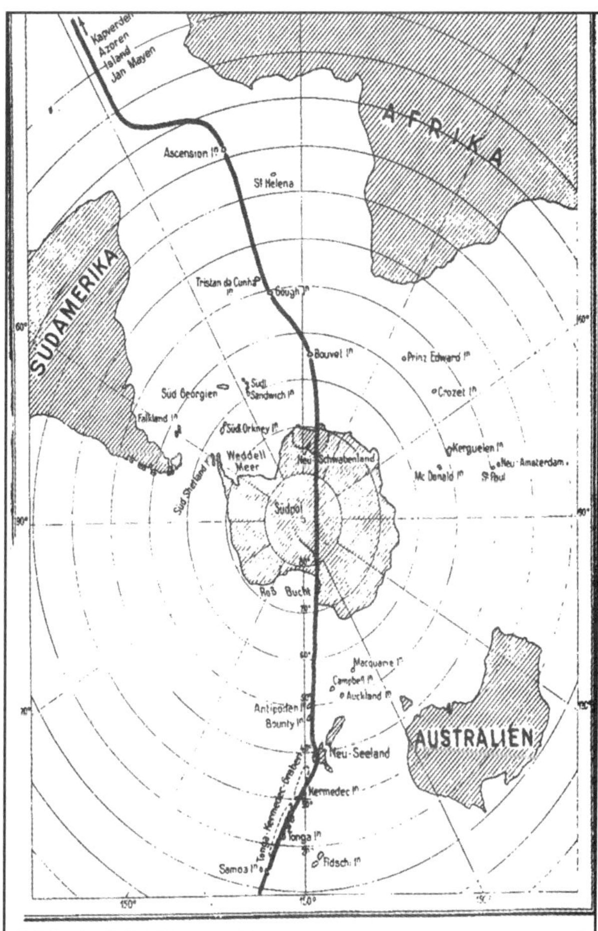

The deep sub-sea trench was discovered by previous German expeditions. Found to be of volcanic origin, it was discovered to run right through the new German colony of *Neuschwabenland*, revealing itself in the form of warm water lakes, caves, crevasses and ice tunnels, most of which were found suitable for habitation with the simple addition of electric lighting. The trench is an excellent deep sea route for U-boats.

The investigators from "The Antarctic Search for Meteorites" program note that meteorites are rare scientific specimens, and, outside of Antarctica, only a few are recovered each year. With the exception of a few lunar samples, meteorites are the only confirmed samples we have of extraterrestrial materials making up our solar system. The investigators wrote:

Some represent the primitive building blocks from which our solar system was formed, and are essentially unchanged since the birth 4.56 billion years ago. Others represent fragments of small planetary bodies broken up by impacts, providing samples from their deep interior, or are samples of intermediate planetoids with active and alien geological processes.

Microscopic life from Mars was found in a meteorite on the vast Polar Plateau of East Antarctica. The investigators continue:

A very small set of meteorites are pieces of the Moon and Mars, knocked loose by giant impacts and sent on a collision course with Earth. Among these is the now-famous ALH84001 meteorite; some NASA researchers have suggested that this Martian sample may have traces within it of ancient biological activity on Mars.

Like all Antarctic specimens, meteorites are collected only for scientific purposes and are protected by the Antarctic Treaty. All specimens are bagged with sterile tongs to avoid contamination, and are shipped while still frozen to the Johnson Space Center (JSC) in Houston, Texas. Twice a year the JSC issues the *Antarctic Meteorite* newsletter, detailing recently recovered specimens and offering samples to interested researchers worldwide.

Antarctica is actually two continental land masses, East and West, connected by the polar ice. Because less than 0.5% of Antarctica's rock is accessible for direct examination, some scientists say that the geology and topography under the ice (especially in East Antarctica) are less well-known than the topography of Mars. In fact, the Dry Valleys are the best terrestrial analogue for Mars, and study there has possible applications for life under extraterrestrial seas. East Antarctica, or Greater Antarctica, is one of the oldest land masses on Earth, with its rocks clocking in at a whopping 3 billion years old. Some of the oldest terrestrial rock, estimated to be 3.84 billion years old, was found in Enderby Land in West Antarctica, or Lesser Antarctica. West Antarctica is a relative newcomer, some 700 million years old. West Antarctica broke off from South America between 34 and 24 million years ago, opening up the Drake Passage and the isolation of the continent began. The plates continue to shift, as is evident in earthquakes and volcanic eruptions, some completely under the ice. In 2012, new data gathering techniques of plate tectonics revealed a previously unknown extension of the East Antarctic Rift System—a fracture that extends 2,500 km from India to Antarctica.

NAZI TECH RAPID ADVANCEMENT

In their alliance with the Draco reptilians since before the war, the Nazis were able to join forces with different Inner Earth races. This alliance with the Nazis allowed them to refurbish an unused base of the Dracos, and establish a presence in the New Berlin base with the existing highly advanced Arianni civilization.

In the early 1930s the Nazis entered into an agreement with the Reptilian Draco Federation extraterrestrials. It is claimed that the original "treaty" with the Greys was established by the Bavarian Thule and Illuminati societies as early as 1933. This treaty led to shared technology with the Nazis. Another treaty with the Tall Greys, who were working with the Reptilian race, would be made much later in 1955 by the Eisenhower administration. If true, this would give the Nazis a greater than two decades head start in an extraterrestrial technology transfer program.

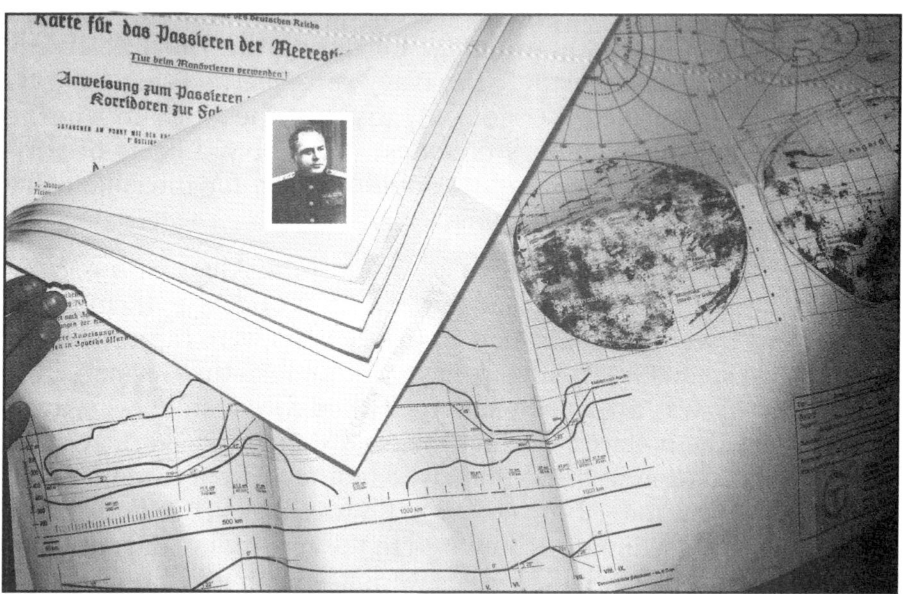

The RHOMB file (short for the "ROMBULUS" Institute) was a KGB project to analyze the Ahnenerbe files. The General Command would be in the hands of General Vsevolod Merkulov (pictured inset). In 1945, the officer Merkulov was involved in the discovery of the German *Wehrmacht* Archive and the Ahnenerbe files in Berlin. He took possession of the main files and later tried to sell them on an auction website when the Soviet Union collapsed. Russian journalist Nikolay Subbotin acquired this stack of U-boat maps on the black market.

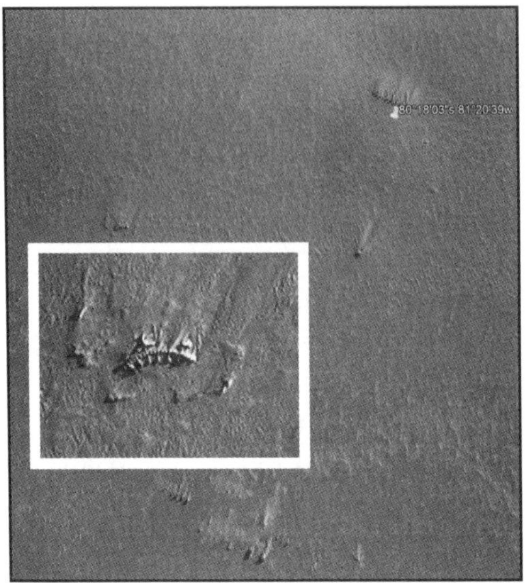

What is this field of wreckage below the Ellsworth Mountains and Union Glacier? 80°18'03"S 81°20'39E

The ultimate goal of the Reptilians, in helping German secret societies and the Waffen SS, was to create advanced space carrier battle groups that would be capable of interplanetary conquest. The eventual German/Nazi space battle groups became the "Dark Fleet." The Navy agents (spies) in Germany discovered what all those "out of this world" aliens gave the Nazis: UFOs, antigravity propulsion, beam weapons, extended life, and plenty of mind-controlled willing girl programs. The Reptilians made a deal with the SS, giving them technology beyond their wildest dreams in exchange for letting the Third Reich enslave the rest of the planet. The Navy spies learned that the goal of the Reptilian plan was not only to assist the Nazis to win the war and achieve planetary conquest, but to build fleets of antigravity spacecraft carriers that could be used for interplanetary conquest in other star systems. [2]

The Germans were very far in advance of the Allies with regards to technology during and at the end of World War II. Interestingly, very few of the German UFO scientists were captured alive, some we killed for refusing to leave, but none of the German UFO technology was acquired when the Allied forces stole everything else from the battered German Reich at the end of World War II. Of course, Wernher Von Braun, who famously went to work in the United States under Project Paperclip was a rocket scientist. This was very old technology compared to the zero-point and antigravity disc technology the scientists were developing.

It is known around a quarter million Germans were unaccounted for at the end of World War II. The population census showed around 250,000 were missing. Some German U-boats were intercepted heading to the South America region carrying many young soldiers, some with fresh injuries. The few U-boats that were in-

2. https://x.com/QQSource/status/1909281872116351139

tercepted had many more men than what was needed for a U-boat crew. Many, if not all, of the large German U-boats were found to be missing by the Allied forces when they overtook Germany.

The National Socialist Germans knew exactly where they stood by the end of World War II, and where they stood in the future with regards to the world powers. This German breakaway civilization would not be complacent. They were not naive. Lucky for them they were decades in advance of the Allies with regards to technology. They also had the greatest scientific minds still with them. They had moved their research and development operations to Antarctica, protected by their advanced craft and weapons and treaties with malevolent extraterrestrial races. [3]

The Third Reich also assumed that the Arctic and Antarctica were not just terrestrial poles, but gateways to different realms. Perhaps it is no accident that in Nazi Germany the Hollow Earth theory was wildly popular in the 1930s. They believed the poles were represented by portals to some other space locations. Maybe this far-reaching idea was based on vague concepts about something similar to today's wormhole crossings, and precisely the possibility of travel in time and space attracted the Germans to Antarctica.

GERMANS BACKWARD ENGINEERED UFO TECHNOLOGY

In the 1930s, the members of the Thule Society wanted to make contact with these legendary civilizations in the Earth's interior. To this end, they sent various expeditions to Tibet, the Andes, the Mato Grosso, and to the North and South Poles, where they suspected there were openings into the Earth's interior. They had arrived at this perspective through ancient texts, through the secret knowledge of various secret societies, and through observations of the laws of nature. They found hollow bodies everywhere: in the cell, the egg cell, the atom, the comets. Hermeticism, with its law of "as above so below, as inside so outside, as in the microcosm, so in the macrocosm," convinced them that the Earth indeed had to be a hollow body.

Then two alleged statements by *Kriegsmarine* Admiral Karl Dönitz remain puzzling to this day. The first is: "My submariners discovered a real earthly paradise." The second was made by Dönitz in 1943, at the height of the German-Russian war and is no less mysterious. Filippovich quotes them:

3. http://entityart.co.uk/ufology-explained-the-german-breakaway-group-psyops-disinfo-antarctica-reptilians-aliens-u-boats-nazi-ufos-technology-flying-saucers/

Germany's submarine fleet can be proud that it is on the other side of the world has built an impregnable fortress for the Führer.

What was Admiral Dönitz talking about? From Antarctica or perhaps rather from southern South America? One of the final messages from Field Marshal Hermann Göring was about a U-boat rendezvous near Tierra del Fuego. According to various sources, Adolph Hitler is said to have escaped to Antarctica, then lived out the rest of his natural life in various South American countries. [4]

The statement of the engineer Arno Mehl from about 55 years after World War II: "I saw the Reich sightseeing planes flying ... in the vicinity of Prague," is likely true and validates the "Merkulov file" documents and the under-ice maps for the U-boat captains in 1945.

The report by Victor Abakumov, Soviet commander of the SMERSH (handed over to Merkulov) on June 28, 1945 reads:

I report, officer of the SMERSH counterintelligence of the 79th Infantry Corps, that on June 11, 1945, employees of the counterintelligence service at the headquarters of the German Navy in Berlin-Tiergarten, Tirpitzufer 38-42, found in the rear of the service room, maps "for the passage of the sea depths" with a stamp "Only for captains of the U-boats Class A Sonderkonvoi Führer." 38 copies with the serial numbers 0188–0199, 0228–0239, 0446–0456, 0555, 0870, 1489.

The passage through underwater corridors to get to Agartha under the ice of Antarctica is described with the title "Instruction to Pass Spaces and Coordinates to Sail to Agartha." The maps were printed in January, 1944 in an edition of 1500 copies in the Dachau concentration camp, 17 kilometers from Munich in the Sonderlaboratorium.

All of the flying disc and anti-gravity technology were coordinated in secret development up until the last days of the war. The crowning achievement was the roll-out of the flying disks named V-7. The V-7 was developed in Vienna, Breslau and Prague by the Viennese

4. There are a series of articles here on this linked website below, which use several books to look at the evidence for a German Breakaway Group. https://fliegende-wahrheit.com/2019/07/09/die-reichsdeutschen-teil-1-die-dritte-macht/

technician Schauberger, as well as the engineer Schriever.

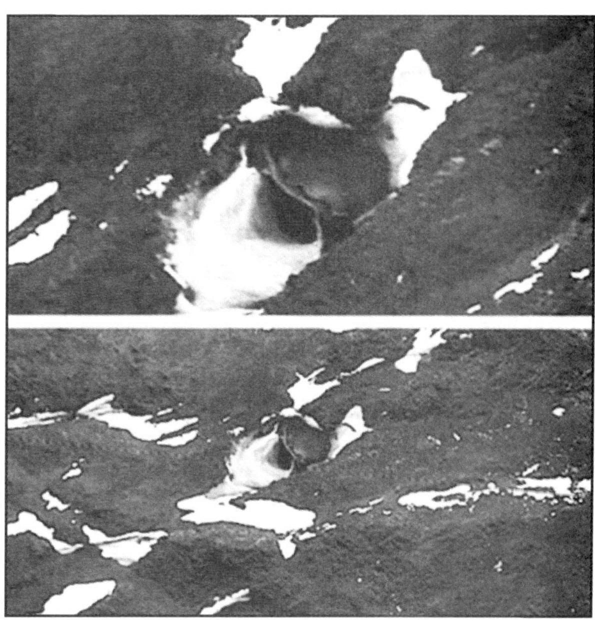

As for the potential of an alien base or entrance to a German Science City, there are clearly two entrance portals, less than a mile apart, and a few miles away from the occasionally active Polish A. B. Dobrowolski Polar Station: 66°36'12.7"S 99°43'E

Near the close of the war the best technology was shipped via cargo U-boats to the South American mainland and Antarctica. The people and material found its shelter in huge caverns below the ice in Antarctica, in DUMB bases in Argentina, and in extensive cave systems under the Andes. There was one prehistoric culture that had been living down in the cave system from a millennia ago, and the German explorer Edmund Kiss on his expeditions rediscovered them in the late 1920s. There are still three flying disks in the cave systems today under the Andes and are rusting away as the supply of material and spare parts could no longer be guaranteed.

When the Soviets took Berlin in 1945, the entire furnishings of the headquarters was taken into trucks and back to KGB headquarters in Moscow. There they were meticulously administered, stored, and then forgotten, only to be sold on the black market after the fall of the Soviet Union. When the Russian journalist Nikolay Subbotin went through the stash, he discovered that the maps were newly printed in 1945 to be handed over to the U-boat fleet for Antartica. Nikolay Subbotin bought the KGB archives map stash which contained several boxes still with the address of the *Ober Kommando der Marine* (OKM) in Berlin.

Intelligence on the transfer of German high technology at the end of the war could not have remained unknown to the Allies. Of course they made an attempt in January, 1947 to dislodge the Germans and to eliminate their Antarctic base. This task should have

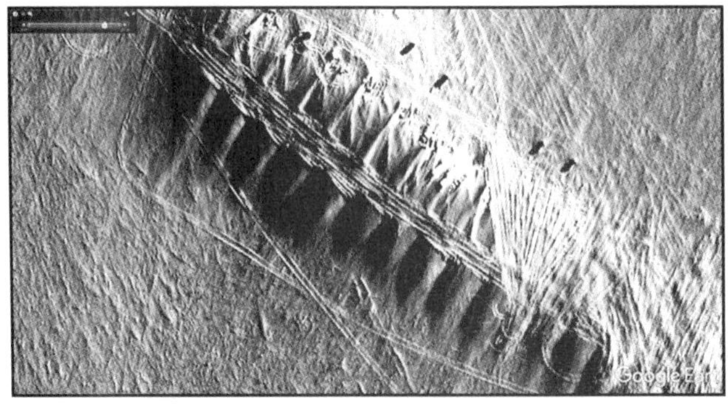

Under the ice "craft" in *Neuschwabenland* and the exact location of the German Kohnen base: 75°00'47.0"S 0°04'52.7"E

been solved by the American naval armada under the leadership of Admiral Byrd. After losing a squadron of several bombers, four reconnaissance planes and one ship, the action was canceled without result.

According to Wilhelm Landig who wrote a series of books on this subject, the personnel strength of the Antarctic base was at one point numbering 2,000 men. Young women from Ukraine and Croatia were brought to Antarctica to become wives for the German men there. For health reasons, because the vulnerability of the human organism caused by the sterile Antarctic climate, an exchange of staff had become necessary, and a majority of men and their wives were transferred out to South American micronations. Ultimately, Base 211 had to be completely abandoned, possibly because of radioactive material from the Project Argus nuclear bomb tests. The final closure took place in the year 1961. [5]

ENTER THE DARK SIDE

In 1953, Albert K. Bender's *International Flying Saucer Bureau* was closed down following work on a theory linking disks with Antarctica. Bender was visited by the Men In Black (MIB) and persuaded to stop his research. These were apparently transdimensional humanoid MIBs, although there have also been reports of MIB reptiloids, androids, and U.S. government agents who have themselves taken on the label of "Men In Black," possibly in imitation of the dark-clad alien intelligence agents who have threatened numerous UFO witnesses to remain silent. Eisenhower asked globalist Nelson Rockefeller for help with the alien problem in the 1950s. This is where the idea for MJ-12 was born. It was probably a critical mistake in asking a member of the world financial control group for help with the alien beings. Because of human nature, the true "controllers" are those who control the world's wealth—the

5. http://entityart.co.uk/ufology-explained-the-german-breakaway-group-psyops-disinfo-antarctica-reptilians-aliens-u-boats-nazi-ufos-technology-flying-saucers/

International Bankers—as they are able to buy-off the weak factions within all of the governments of every nation, including an "apparent" Constitutional Republic like the United States of America. The 1970s are when the Cabal learned that Antarctic Germans had the memory-wipe technique. Before then, they had not known about it.

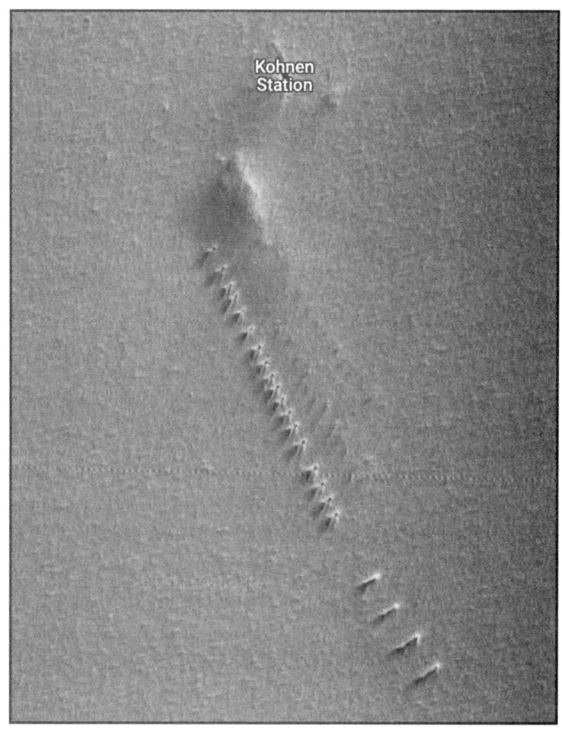

Google Earth image of the Kohnen base taken in March, 2025. It appears to be covered by a large tent, and only the top of the tent poles protrude above the surface of the ice. The blowing wind and snowfall have covered it up again. There is likely a "door" leading down into the decrepit craft.

The Antarctic Germans reached their targeted self-sustaining worker population for their outlying colonies, their outlying manufacturing facilities, even locations out in the rest of the solar system. They also started working on their own time travel experiments with *Die Glocke*, and what they found was that there were problems. The main issue was "temporal interface," in that if they tried to manipulate with timelines in the past there were serious consequences. This is called the "Grandfather Paradox," in which a grandchild went back in time to meet his grandfather when he was young. If he kills him, the grandchild is stuck in that timeline and can never return to where he came from.

William Tompkins (1923-2017) was one of the most secretive scientists in the United States, until he became a whistleblower in the last few years in his life. Tompkins claimed that during World War II, the Nazis received technology from malevolent aliens, due to which they were able to expand upon and build huge underground factories in Antarctica and South America. Thousands of workers were taken there and in these factories, they continued to manufacture flying saucers.

Tompkins said that those technologies were transferred to Germany by a reptilian alien race known as the "Draco." They advised on building spaceships in backward engineered projects, and trained the Germans during the war. The Draco's plan was to ultimately eliminate humans on Earth. Tompkins suggests that Antarctica is still hiding some of these terrible secrets.

According to William Tompkins, two benevolent E.T. forces from different parts of the galaxy helped the U.S. Solar Warden. These aliens are collectively called "Nordics."

Tompkins was personally present at the "Battle of Los Angeles" over the city in 1942, when a thousand rounds of ammo were fired at UFOs. He said one of the Nordic craft may have selected him to be their representative in the evolving aerospace race, where he worked most of his adult life. A month after the shocking conference where he made his Antarctica revelations, Tompkins passed away unexpectedly on August 21, 2017, in San Diego, California, at the age of 94.

REPTILIAN HYBRID RACE CONTROLLING OUR WORLD

The alien agenda is a closely guarded secret and our government's knowledge of it remains as the highest classified national security risk. Until the U.S. military can reach parity with the technology of the alien threat, it must remain classified as "Cosmic Top Secret." If anyone might be pulling the strings it would be malevolent extraterrestrials, but there can be no definite proof. How come the aliens don't just come out in the open? Perhaps there is a human element helping them stay hidden. Some kind of cooperation in the exchange of Earth resources for high technology? It sounds like a *Twilight Zone* episode, and maybe it is, because art often imitates life.

The human cut-outs at the top of our power structures working with the malevolent ETs are hiding a sinister secret. Since the dawn of civilization, there have been a ruling class controlled by malevolent extraterrestrial/dimensional beings, with an agenda which ultimately establishes the human race as mindless and robotic slaves to a system based on fear and control.

To begin to explain this complex theory, author David Icke discusses the current fear state of our world at his arena tour in 2011:

> *The fear of what other people think is the state of perception that stops people (from) making a difference ...*

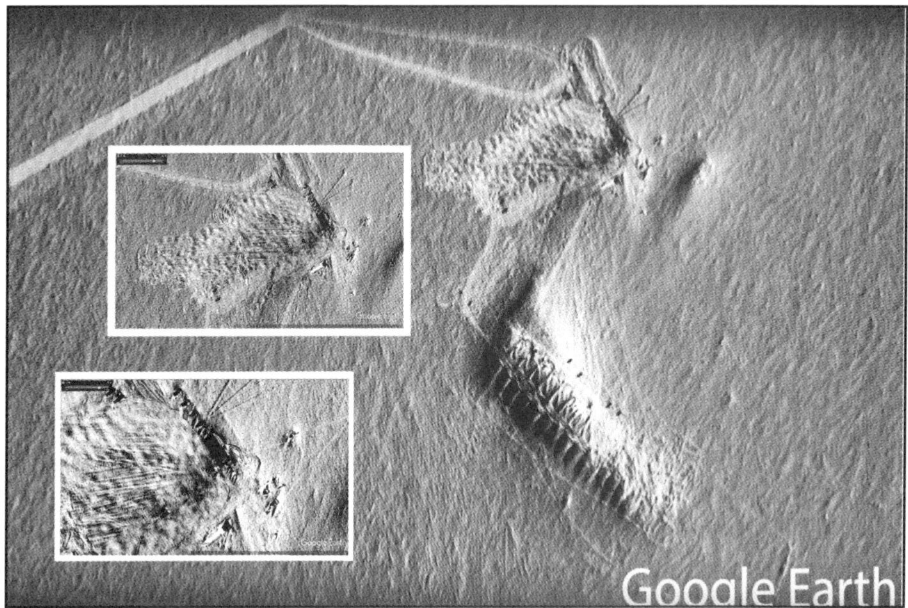

These images were taken from Google Earth of the Kohnen base in 2013. Some kind of excavation project was going on that year.

> *you can only make a difference in a world of uniformity if you operate outside of that uniformity ... we either take that on or we don't, in which case nothing changes. We are now at this place where we can go down one track and experience freedom like we've never even understood what freedom is. We go down the other one, the one that the control structure wants, then we're headed for an Orwellian-fascist global state.*

David Icke proposes that humankind has been manipulated to become "unconscious" through the use of programming by media and politics, the tyrannical control over our food, water, and air supply, the dumbing down of the masses by pharmaceutical drugs and alcohol, and the list goes on.

"But the manipulation doesn't stop there," as David Icke continues exploring the never ending depths of the rabbit hole. "The ruling class, the bankers, the royal family, the presidents and prime ministers, have created the illusion of being separate ruling bodies, when in fact they have always been on the same 'team' of sorts." [6]

---

6. Icke, David, *Human Race Get Off Your Knees: The Lion Sleeps no More.* David Icke Books, 2010.

MULTI-DIMENSIONAL ENTITIES

There are several classifications of aliens and other beings existing within our universe. These range from multi-dimensional ultra-terrestrials, to the inner-terrestrials who have existed for many generations underground on Earth. Extraterrestrials arrive on Earth from distant planets of their own. Some may decide to stay. The inner-terrestrials on Earth operate at a frequency just above what the human mind is said to be able to perceive. This could explain the strange sightings of UFOs that seem to appear and disappear in an instant, or the ability to shape-shift their bodies so they can look "normal." Could it be that the UFOs or ETs are advanced enough that they can raise or lower their frequency to shape-shift by coming into and out of the visible light frequency spectrum?

This is something that David Icke says the ruling elite are not only aware of, but in cooperation with malevolent alien groups. They have the knowledge that is used to manipulate humankind into thinking that our experience is limited to a 3-D reality, when in fact humans are multi-dimensional but don't know how to access these abilities. David Icke maintains that the reptilians control the globalists extra-dimensionally through the manipulation of human DNA. Remote viewers have seen dozens of human experimentation laboratories in Antarctica.

It is no secret today that our world is ruled by fiat money and power. Corporations and banks wield more power than "We The People" do, and this is something that is beginning to become recognized by a large majority of the population. There is a world government which oversees the regulation of the entire planet and all of its systems. This world government is called the Illuminati by many, although there are multiple names for the different levels of this organization. Behind the closed doors at the highest levels of government, secret societies rule with malevolence. Just look at the fake pandemic that was unleashed on humanity in 2020. [7]

The problem is that anyone who learns this information and speaks out publicly as a leading force against these secret societies is quickly silenced. John F. Kennedy's assassination is a perfect example of this. In his famous last speech, not too long before he was shot, he touches upon the subject of the secret ruling class:

---

7. Olsen, Brad, *Beyond Esoteric: Escaping Prison Planet (2nd ed.)* "Plandemic" chapter. CCC Publishing, 2025

The very word "secrecy" is repugnant in a free and open society; and we are as a people inherently and historically opposed to secret societies, to secret oaths and secret proceedings. ... For we are opposed around the world by a monolithic and ruthless conspiracy that relies on covert means for expanding its sphere of influence—on infiltration instead of invasion, on subversion instead of elections, on intimidation instead of free choice, on guerrillas by night instead of armies by day.

David Icke says that these extra-dimensional beings that the globalists worship stem from the constellations of Orion, Sirius, and Draco. Many thousands of years ago, the reptilian beings intervened on planet Earth and began interbreeding with proto-humans. Not physically, however, but rather through the manipulation of the human coding, or DNA. David Icke states that it is no coincidence that humans have fundamental reptilian genetics within their brain. The "fight or flight" response is from the reptilian brain. He refers to an excerpt from the Bible, which hints at the crossbreeding of men and "gods." He points out the serpent intervenes leading to the "Fall of Man." David Icke connects more biblical stories to the intervention of the reptilian race.

Modern polar research stations are sometimes located near an anomaly or crashed disc. Near here is the Gondwana base, South Korean Jang Bogo base, and Italian Zucchelli base only a few miles away from this apparent craft in the ice: 74°38'18.5"S 164°31'48.5"E

David Icke recalls how the "Fall of Man" is the story of how Adam and Eve became manipulated by the serpent. The reason, he goes on to say, is that 95% of human DNA and a large majority of our brain goes unused. It is because of the intervention of the reptilian race, placing a limitation on our potential as conscious beings.

These beings were more advanced in the technological sense, seeing our DNA as software which could be tainted with, and creating a hybrid middle man to control the human population within the visible light spectrum. Half human and half reptilian, they were perceived as demi-gods at the time by primitive people.

David Icke explains that the Caduceus, the common medical symbol we see today, is based around this DNA manipulation. The Caduceus contains two serpents spiraling around a scepter that has wings, in the shape of the double-helix DNA strand. This can't be a coincidence, but is the "revelation of the method" where everything needs to be revealed in a free will population.

Because these hybrids at the time possessed knowledge that most didn't, they were able to slip into positions of power, specifically in the ancient areas of Sumer, Babylon, and Mesopotamia. This was the beginning of the fiat money system of control. As these areas began to separate and colonize elsewhere, the reptilian bloodlines spread out, becoming the royal families of the world. This is said to be why the royal family strictly maintains their genetics. Similarly, the ancient Chinese emperors believed they had the "divine right to rule" because they were connected to the "serpent gods." David Icke says there is a common theme between royalty and serpent worship around the world.

Over time these bloodlines created a sort of trans-national web of control, and as history progressed they rooted themselves deeper and deeper into the systems and structures that were supposedly developed by humans. Today they make up the secret societies (Illuminati, SS, Cabal, etc.) which pull the strings in regards to the direction that society follows. They have created the ultimate prison, one without bars and with the illusion of freedom keeping the masses from wanting to escape. They have created illusory lines separating countries to cause segregation among the people who are ignorant to the truth. They have created massive distractions with the media, politics, entertainment, and they have dumbed down the general population through the poisoning of our food, air, and water supply.

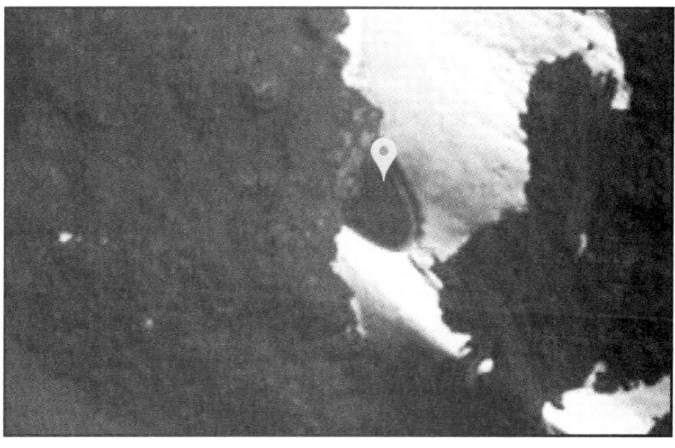

On the opposite side of Antarctica, the Polish A. B. Dobrowolski Polar Station is located a few miles away from another disc-like craft in the ice at: 66°16'24.2"S 100°59'05.7"E

Your fear is also what they want. "Loosh" is a term applied to energy produced by human beings and animals that interdimensional entities use to feed off. It is also used to refer to energy that is produced by suffering or fear that these entities desire, like livestock that know they're going to die in a slaughterhouse. These energetic vampires are called the Jinn in the Muslim world, and the Archons in the Western gnostic traditions.

It begs the question: what is the ultimate goal of these hybrid bloodlines? Some argue it was originally for our planet's supply of gold, which they needed to extract in order to stabilize the atmosphere of their own planet. Others suggest that it has more to do with tyranny. The New World Order (NWO) isn't a new concept to most. In the early 1990s President Bush Senior publicly announced that the NWO was the eventual goal for the United States. A NWO is not the peaceful state of freedom that these leaders try to present it as being.

The NWO is an Orwellian state based around absolute control in which the population is maintained under 500,000 million people as stated on the Georgia Guidestones. It takes away the power of the public, turning them into mindless robots who do the bidding of the fortunate ruling class. It is a one world government that calls all the shots. Power and control is what the hybrids want. Whatever the intention is behind the control structures, it is obvious that it is not in harmony with the well-being of humankind or the planet.

WORMHOLE TRAVEL

The ice continent continues to keep its secrets, and others are added to them. New questions are pondered over the years, and then they disappear. Were the work on the creation of flying discs curtailed after the war, or continued in other secret areas of the globe? Is it logical to conclude all the unidentified flying objects to be written off as modern secret developments?

Shining saucers, spheres, cigar-shaped crafts at the polar regions and surrounding areas, are not unusual to see emerging out of the water. During the Cold War, the USSR naval intelligence reported on them regularly. Of course, the U.S. military branches have knowledge of these unidentified flying objects, and well as other nations. These craft are observed to have instantaneous movement in the air, water, space and even have a time travel element. This brings up the possibility of using wormholes and black holes to travel vast distances in a short period of time. Black holes can occur at close distances to our planet and take the form of wormholes, and can be used for rapid intergalactic and interstellar travel.

Unidentified flying objects were observed, and reports of them were regularly received by the Soviet Union naval intelligence. As well as reports on such discovered objects in the form of eyewitnesses. It would be wrong to think that unidentified flying objects are observed only in the north, because they were observed throughout the Atlantic, even in the South Atlantic in the region of Antarctica.

In particular, there were leaked reports from the USSR outlining a case when UFOs were observed offshore near the South Georgia Islands. A fishermen spotted an object that he managed to photograph. Despite the strong wind, the object remained in one place for a fairly long time. Another report shows a disc hovering over the island and was observed in a stationary position during daylight hours, before sunset, and after sunset for one and a half to two hours. The object had a fairly regular round shape and an isosceles triangle stood out on it at night. This triangle not only glowed, but also at the base such lights were observed as if these were working engines.

In the late 1980s, the work of a leading American astrophysicist Kip Thorne and his colleagues, substantiated the possibility of practically instantaneous movement through space and time travel. According to their research, these black holes are in the immediate vicinity of our planets and take the form of "worm transitions." As the scientists themselves state, their work is of applied importance, in particular, for the creation of a time machine and the provision of intergalactic flights. Kip Thorne came to the conclusion that near the Earth there is an entrance to a worm tunnel leading to the region of the star Vega. Apparently, the Americans already knew or imagined it well enough at that time.

This begs the question about how UFOs can appear and disappear into the atmosphere of our planet? They are often seen flying off at a high speed, then making a sharp 90 degree turn and then disappearing. In 1992, the construction of a powerful radio-electronic detector, officially for the study of the ionosphere and the development of anti-missile defense systems, but unofficially it was for the development of a new type of geophysical weapon, that is, used as both a climatic and psychotronic weapon. According to a whistleblower, it is a massive ray gun so microwave beams can be sent to the upper atmosphere. However, it seems we can safely assume that the main purpose of the South Pole research station is to find this entrance to the wormhole and monitor any craft coming or going. The Americans came to the conclusion that it was located in this south polar region. There may be an entrance to a wormhole station with its radio emissions that allow the configuration of this worm passage, and find the entrance or exit there in Antarctica.

In 1998, a similar complex was put into operation in Alaska, but next in line is the more powerful one in Greenland. Technical opportunities allowed the Russians to focus on only one thing,

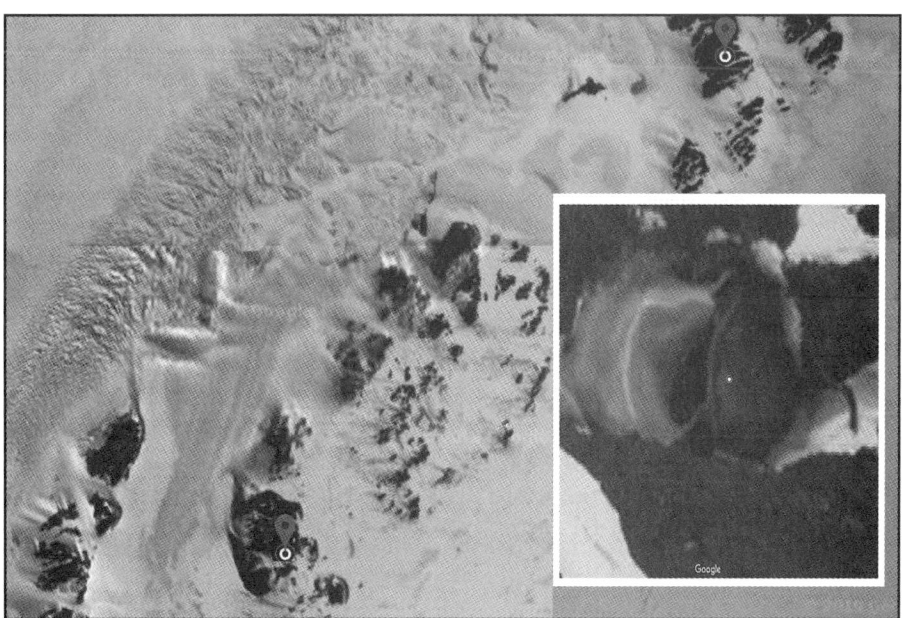

Possible entrances to the underground Thule Refuge near the coast of the very remote Enderby Land in Antarctica. Question is, are they "ours" or "theirs" or an optical illusion of sorts?
As for the potential of an alien base, there are two entrances close to each other due southwest of South Africa: -66° 36' 12.58"S +99° 43' 12.72" E and -66° 36' 12.7"S +99° 43' E

namely, on the Alaskan portal as in the course of the release of control over the movement of UFOs over our planet. They no longer needed to install tracking stations across the states on other territories.

The role of each of them from the point of view of this hypothesis is that they are used both for entry and exit of the planet. The Soviets also concurred the Alaskan portal is used to enter and Antarctica to exit, or vice versa through the South Pole. They concluded that if UFOs are coming into the atmosphere of our planet through Alaska via the North Pole portal, then they are leaving our planet via Antarctica. The theory of a tunnel effect does not contradict the fact that the North Pole of our Earth is the entrance, and the South Pole of our Earth is an outlet for the energy channel that connects our planet with other planets and stars. It is possible that these properties of the poles and of unidentified flying objects are used to communicate with other higher intelligences.

PORTAL ENTRYWAYS

The images that can be found in the "Merkulov file" specifically depict reversed inside and outside explanations. They depict north being south and east being west. All directions are reversed, the energies shown are opposite, and fresh and salt water are separated. The maps depict an "air flow" that is blocked by the pole ice, and more. It is as if we are looking at a reversed "dimension," which suggests that we may be looking at some kind of a "portal," or a gateway to another dimension, so to speak.

The outside has entirely different conditions than the inside. Our modern science has fond names such as portals and dimensions and even different timelines, but what did the ancients know? Entering a different dimension for them was similar to entering a hidden underground world, because they went downward into the earth. But once past the portal they found a different world, with reversed colors. Trees with red leaves and blueish grass. Entirely different human beings with slightly different shaped heads and eyes. Light shining from "somewhere." Wild animals and human beings with wings and psychic capabilities, different hierarchic and sexual customs, and more. Almost as if on another planet, like Admiral Byrd observed.

The Tibetans taught the Germans to look at the provided mandalas, not as just decorations, but as maps with different meanings, as actual 3D maps for the human mind to be visioned as a whole. All this taken together gives the impression of the South Pole as being some kind of a portal. Perhaps a partial portal, since there are also references to an inner sun, vast oceans, and a continental landmass.

There are several other reports of pilots who saw flat disc-shaped UFOs chasing them, even though they were not being shot at. These pilots also reported how their planes were followed by "balls of light." Speaking of extraterrestrials, the more Antarctica is examined, the more mysteries keep cropping up. An example is the huge electromagnetic anomaly that was detected by NASA satellites in 2006. This anomaly wasn't lying on the surface either. It was buried deep underneath 151 miles of ice and the continental plate. What a beautiful way to confuse researchers. Over a decade later, they are still left with questions.

Turning to an ancient script dated a millennia ago called the *Book of Enoch*, some interesting passages seemed to have something to say about the polar regions. Enoch was the man who was reported to have escaped death. He was the great, great grandfather of Noah. He wrote about how he was taken to the place where the corrupted angels who disobeyed the Biblical God and came to Earth were imprisoned. In his book, he had talked about the 200 fallen angels

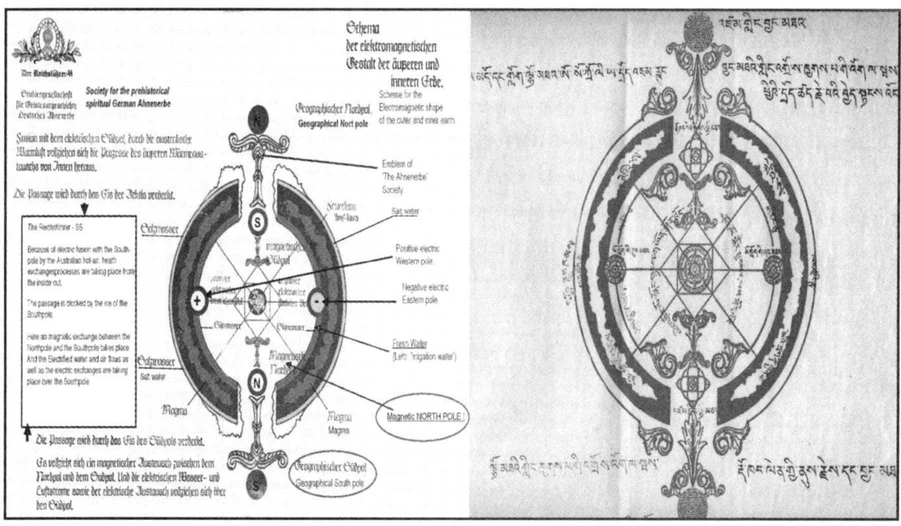

The concept of an Inner Earth, or Hollow Earth, are depicted in the illustrations found in the declassified USSR "Merkulov file." The last officer in charge of the project, up to 1983-85 when it was closed, was General Vsevolod Merkulov, and assembled as part of the "ORION" File, carried out by the "Rombulus Institute," under the supervision of the KGB, on the orders of party leader Yuri Andropov.

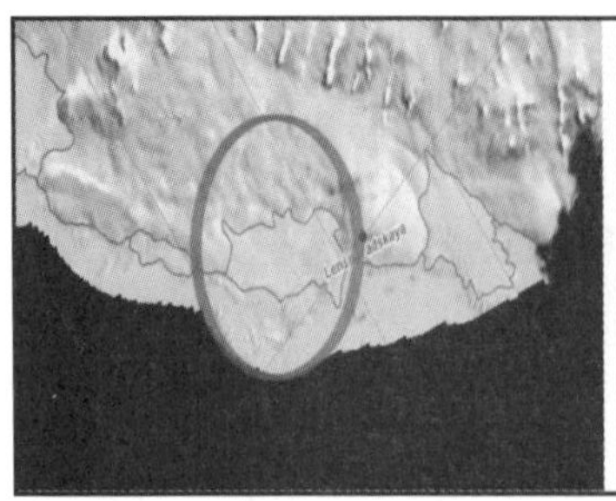

on the conspiracy newsfeed under the title of "Antarctica Aliens" the author "No_Ferret" posted: "My Uncle, who is a retired Naval Commodore (yes the position is honorary and still exists), told me a lot of secrets. One such secret is that a gargantuan, otherworldly vessel with live aliens is hidden beneath water and ice in Antarctica. The beings inside are non-humanoid and trapped. There's a LOT more to this story, but this is the location, right next to the defunct, USSR Leningradskaya research station." The station was evacuated in 1991 after the Soviet Union fell, and funding for the base was discontinued.

who had lived among humans, teaching men advanced technologies for their time and sleeping with the women and fathering the Nephilim, thereby genetically modifying humans and leading humankind astray.

The book talked about where they were imprisoned, unable to remember who they are until the appointed day. This place was supposed to be lit by the sun both during the day and at night. In the words of Enoch, "(the Sky) was burning day and night." As it turns out, this fits perfectly with the Southern Hemisphere during the summer season below the Antarctic Circle. At this time, there is daylight for 24 hours. In the winter, during 24 hours of darkness, this light phenomenon is known as *Aurora Australis,* or the Southern Lights, which can be visible from high southern latitudes in Antarctica, Australia, New Zealand, Chile, and Argentina. Scientists travel specifically to Antarctica to study auroras (named after the Roman goddess of the dawn). Millions of miles away, the sun produces electrically charged particles that are blown outwards across the solar system in a continuous "solar wind." As the solar wind passes the Earth, the charged particles are attracted by the Earth's magnetic field and are drawn to its two geomagnetic poles. As the particles pass through the atmosphere, they interact with atoms, molecules and ions in the upper atmosphere, causing them to release as light. [8]

---

8. https://deshinewspost.com/interesting-claim-antarctica-is-the-place-where-fallen-angels-are-still-alive-but-locked-in/

DUMBS IN ANTARCTICA

The galactic emissary Kim Gougen describes Antarctica as being an enormous Deep Underground Military Base (DUMB). She said it was part of the "Baal Artificial Intelligent System" and there was a huge machine down there, similar to a large church pipe organ. When in operation it could send out frequencies to make us sick, think evil thoughts, make us do bad things, and basically manipulate our thoughts and emotions.

Similarly, Kim Gougen says there's a lot of truth to Jesus Christ dying on the "Southern Cross" which had a connection to Earth, Antarctica, the lower astral, the omega verse, and the magnetic field of Earth. The Southern Cross star constellation is the most prominent star constellation in the Southern Hemisphere.

She describes non-human beings as the "others." Kim Gougen says others were in the Antarctic underground base working at level six and below. There were lots of portals down there, and a pillar to the lower astral. She described the pillar as an "interesting elevatorish thing" that crossed densities and space and time. The others came up and humans went down. These "others" were brought to the DUMB by the Draco as slaves to work on such things as genetic manipulation.

Kim Gougen says there was definitely a Black Sun Program. Maria Orsic of the Vril Society is still down there. She didn't die, and is over 100 years old. Maria Orsic and the Vril Women escaped to a DUMB in Antarctica.

She says the Inner Earth can be described as the central vortex to Earth where there is a break in the time-space continuum, which allows one to go in the "fancy elevator" to any level of hell the human or lower astral beings want to go. It's not a pretty sight.

Kim Gougen said the main reason why Western governments signed the Antarctic Treaty and to keep it secret was so they could also use the continent without military engagement. It was an Order of the Black Sun facility, and the Germans ran it. That's one reason why Adolph Hitler and other fugitive Nazis retired in Argentina—because it was close to, and more hospitable than, Antarctica. Hitler frequented the Antarctic DUMBs, but didn't live there. He was given limited knowledge and access to the lower astral planes.

Kim says the area is mostly all cleared out now. There may be remnants of technology that may occasionally get triggered and fire up on queue in response to energies. One purpose of the machines there was to transmute light energy to dark energy. But the transmuters aren't connected to anything anymore so they might turn themselves on for a bit, but they don't really accomplish anything.

She said the Deep State still visits there, most likely in the hopes they'll get the equipment to work again. She said the Secret Space Program was there twice within a week in early 2025. They were looking for diseases, presumably to launch on us. The Cabal is being rooted out and they are now in a desperate situation. They need to provoke World War III, or release a real deadly disease that will kill millions.

GALACTIC FEDERATION

Former head of Israel's Defense Ministry's space directorate Haim Eshed claims the U.S. signed a deal with a malevolent alien federation to experiment on humans many decades ago. He discusses Disclosure with a capital "D," and the Mars bases as well. This former Israeli space security chief says extraterrestrials exist, and Trump knows all about it. A benevolent "Galactic Federation" has been waiting for humans to "reach a stage where we will understand ... what space and spaceships are." A report given by Rising, with Crystal and Saagar, discuss further:

> *So this is Haim Eshed, the former head of Israel's Space Program, who says: "Aliens have been in contact with the United States and with Israel." What does Eshed refer to the Galactic Federation that he says, you know, has been in touch with Israel and the United States? He also says that Donald Trump was going to reveal their existence but then basically got talked out of it, I suppose. Yes, and look, Esched is 87 years old. According to him—he says he has nothing to lose. He's a decorated former Israeli General, former Space Security Chief. He has been awarded a medal three separate times—two secretly for actions that kept Israel safe. He is clearly somebody who was regarded well by the government. Now what he is saying is kind of crazy. He says that there's a secret pact between the United States government and the Galactic Federation and that the cooperation includes a secret underground base on Mars where there are Americans and alien representatives. ... A high ranking and distinguished former Space Chief claims*

Remote viewers report a variety of entrances to Inner Earth civilizations under the ice in Antarctica, illustrated here. There are reportedly at least a half dozen under the ice facilities run by an "Interplanetary Corporate Conglomerate." Remote viewers have also "seen" and located these geothermal-powered cities.

> *that Extraterrestrials exist and Trump knows about it. But that a Galactic Federation also exists and is waiting to make official contact. Allegedly contact has already been established long ago with governments of the world—since he claims that the United States already has military personnel in underground bases on Mars.* [9]

Journalist Bill Neeley commented on the revelations: "This is quite a story and it comes from the man who headed Israeli Space Security Program for nearly 30 years. Haim Eshed is making his extraordinary claim that the United States and Israel have been in contact with a group of aliens for years (and not immigrants) but extraterrestrials and he has called them the Galactic Federation of Aliens and he says President Trump is aware of the existence of these aliens and had been on the verge of revealing their secrets," he claims—"but was asked not to do so by the Galactic Federation in order to prevent what they call 'mass hysteria'." He also quotes President Trump: "You know I am proud to have that German blood—there's no question about it." Bill Neeley continues:

9. https://www.nbcnews.com/news/weird-news/former-israeli-space-security-chief-says-extraterrestrials-exist-trump-knows-n1250333

> *Well, a retired General says the United States and Israel have kept it from the public because "humanity is not ready yet and the aliens don't want to reveal themselves until humanity can evolve and understand what space really is," he says. ... The good news is that he claims there is an agreement between the United States government and the aliens. It is a contract to do experiments here. There is a secret underground base on Mars where there are Americans and alien representatives. Now this former head, General Eshed, of a branch of Israeli Defense Ministry is 87 years old and he was very well-respected. He says he has come forward now in the hope that his news will be accepted as true. He notes that if he'd made these claims five years ago, he would have been hospitalized. But now, he says, I've got nothing to lose. Well, so far President Trump has not tweeted about this—although, remember a year ago he did set up the Space Force as the fifth branch of the United States armed forces. We did ask the White House, the Department of Defense and Israeli officials to comment. So far, they have not responded to the NBC news request—I wonder if they ever will. The topic of a Secret Space Program is not new and has been discussed for decades—though only recently being reported on in a serious way by the mainstream media. While the majority of the discussion about a potential Galactic Federation implies that all of the alleged aliens are a totally separate species from us—if they exist at all. ... But brave researchers from the time just before the internet era of social media, have risked their lives disclosing what they believe had its roots at least, in part involving events pertaining to World War II.*

In the 1980s timeframe, Voyager I and II were passing the Jupiter and Saturn orbits. One of the big revelations Voyager I did for the Cabal was to inform everyone just how much construction the Antarctic Germans had, and just how much infiltration dark alien races had made in our solar system. It scared them. They didn't realize just how much Antarctic Germans had built off-planet in our obsession with antagonism of the moment.

REMOTE VIEWERS TAKE A LOOK

As we all live our daily lives on various places on Earth, there are remote viewers who can investigate locations on Antarctica and even off-planet. The remote viewers Jenny Lee, Beth McCall, and Neioh have reported on the "unseen activities" underneath the ice on the vast continent of Antarctica. Having remote viewing area access where humans never dare to explore in leisure, they can enter remotely because they are on missions of light, where the dark forces cannot obstruct their viewing.

They report that Earth is being helped by the "White Hats" from the Pleiades and other Elohim races. There are the good and bad extraterrestrials and humans in different bases across the continent. The Cabal bases are also scattered throughout the region with only about a hundred people left as the Light Forces take over in great numbers. Almost all of the malevolent ETs have also been taken off-planet, and the Earth is under a quarantine with no space comings or goings allowed.

The Galactic Federation has bases all across planet Earth, including deep under the oceans. Some of the finest and most luxurious cities are beneath the ice in Antarctica! There are vast openings where craft enter seamlessly and the occupants are ushered into hallways in structures of crystals and beauty. There are large soft chairs and sofas for beings much taller than humans. There are wonderful meals shared among those gathered to discuss the issues of Earth and other planets of stark duality.

There are meetings regarding planetary action that would be instantly in place with Dark Forces eradicated should a nuclear threat become imminent. The human White Hats arrive from military positions around the planet. There are always representatives from the Elohim races that are acting on the behalf of humans in high places of power on Earth. They blend seamlessly with others and get their work done as they vanish to meet on crafts and in higher powered operations beneath the ice and mountains.

The remote viewers all report on the covert clone factory operations. Having many secret facilities for product replacement of humans has become a large undercover deception that the surface humans are undergoing, but most of these cloning operations are being shut down. Galactic Federation requires free will and has always been aware of the growing numbers of clones in action on the surface. This will continue until The Grand Shift. It is a tool used by many to replace a person that has been completely removed from life on this plane of existence. The Galactic Federation has many plans and actions that are not revealed just yet. But the remote viewers want us to know now they are clearly in control.

They report there are currently 400 large bases in Antarctica that are used by the Galactic Federation. As crafts and motherships are welcomed from Sirius, Andromeda, Arcturus and the Pleiades, the "Power of Light" is enormous. Great discussions with commanders and elders bring a unity of wisdom as we move toward a peaceful galactic civilization!

There are under-ice compounds where evil entities have been held. These forces also operate in the non-physical aspect of life, which enables them to connect in other places as rituals are held with dark intent. All of this will end with a powerful presence of love and peace that will eradicate and dissolve all energy that is left of these beings of darkness. The Galactic Federation will destroy and remove any further actions. This method will not be revealed!

Antarctica is one of several openings to Inner Earth. Mount Shasta in California is another. There are civilizations of beautiful areas that are called Crystal Cities, like the Domain of the Arianni. Another is a place called "Crystal" which was inhabited in the area under Sweden. These beings looked like Pleiadians with a Nordic look of long white hair and blue eyes. These Scandinavian humans became very close to visiting Pleiadians and were protected and given a beautiful place to live in oneness and thrive without war and chaos. Pleiadians created all that would be needed with vegetation, water, flowers and landscapes. Animals were brought to the land around the Crystal Cities and loved deeply.

THE BLACK GOO

"The most effective way to destroy people is to deny and obliterate their own understanding of their history."

–George Orwell, *1984*

ANTARCTICA is almost the size of the United States, including Alaska and Hawaii. The Ice Continent has every natural resource from oil and coal, to the valuable metals uranium, gold and silver. Never has there been another spot on the planet that corporations wouldn't go in order to drill for oil. Think about the depths that they would drill down in the ocean sea floor, or the fracking in very remote regions. Why didn't mining operations and fishermen exploit the resources in Antarctica? It still has environmental protection under the 1961 Antarctic Treaty. There is another valuable resource that was acquired outside of the region covered by the Antarctic Treaty, but only by an act of war.

The South Sandwich Islands group south of the Falkland Islands are referred to as peri-Antarctic, rather than sub-Antarctic, since many of them are similar in features despite their location outside the Antarctic Convergence Zone. The geographical co-ordinates listed for the smaller islands are based upon the middle of the island group. Sovereignty over some of these islands is still disputed. They are claimed as British territory, as re-acquired during the 1982 Falklands Island War, and are part of the inclusive territory of South Georgia and the South Sandwich Islands. The islands are also claimed by Argentina as part of the *Islas del Atlántico Sur.*

Most remote of all, the South Sandwich Islands group is a chain of eleven small volcanic islands stretching out over 390 km in the South Atlantic Ocean. They are among the most remote archipelago of islands in the world. They cover an area of 310 km, with the highest elevation being Mt. Belinda on Montague Island, at a height of 1375 meters. The group is 80% glaciered with permanent snow-pack year 'round. They were first sighted in 1775, but the first to land ashore were sealers in 1818. They are uninhabited, although scientific personnel have wintered over.

GERMAN COLONIES

At the end of World War II, the Soviets were the first to capture several of the high-ranking Nazi buildings in Berlin, including the Ahnenerbe Society and the Naval *Kriegsmarine* headquarters. They discovered that two German naval bases had been established on the Western Falklands and the South Georgia Islands. Eventually, this information reached the U.S. and UK governments. In addition, the Germans had set up several colonies in the peri-Antarctic islands, possibly including South Thule Island for a short period. Original Soviet intelligence report by V. Abakumov, dated October 25, 1945, and passed on to the People's Commissariat for Security to Comrade V. N. Merkulov, reports the German colonies as follows:

> *Message from the overseas agents working through the "A"—numerous Germans have settled on all the islands near the Antarctic in the Pacific and the Atlantic. In the port city of Port Stanley in the Falkland Islands (Malvinas) there is a garrison of the German Navy, hidden in the mountains and hidden from the rest of the island. The garrison includes several military submarines, the size of the garrison is about 1,000 soldiers.*

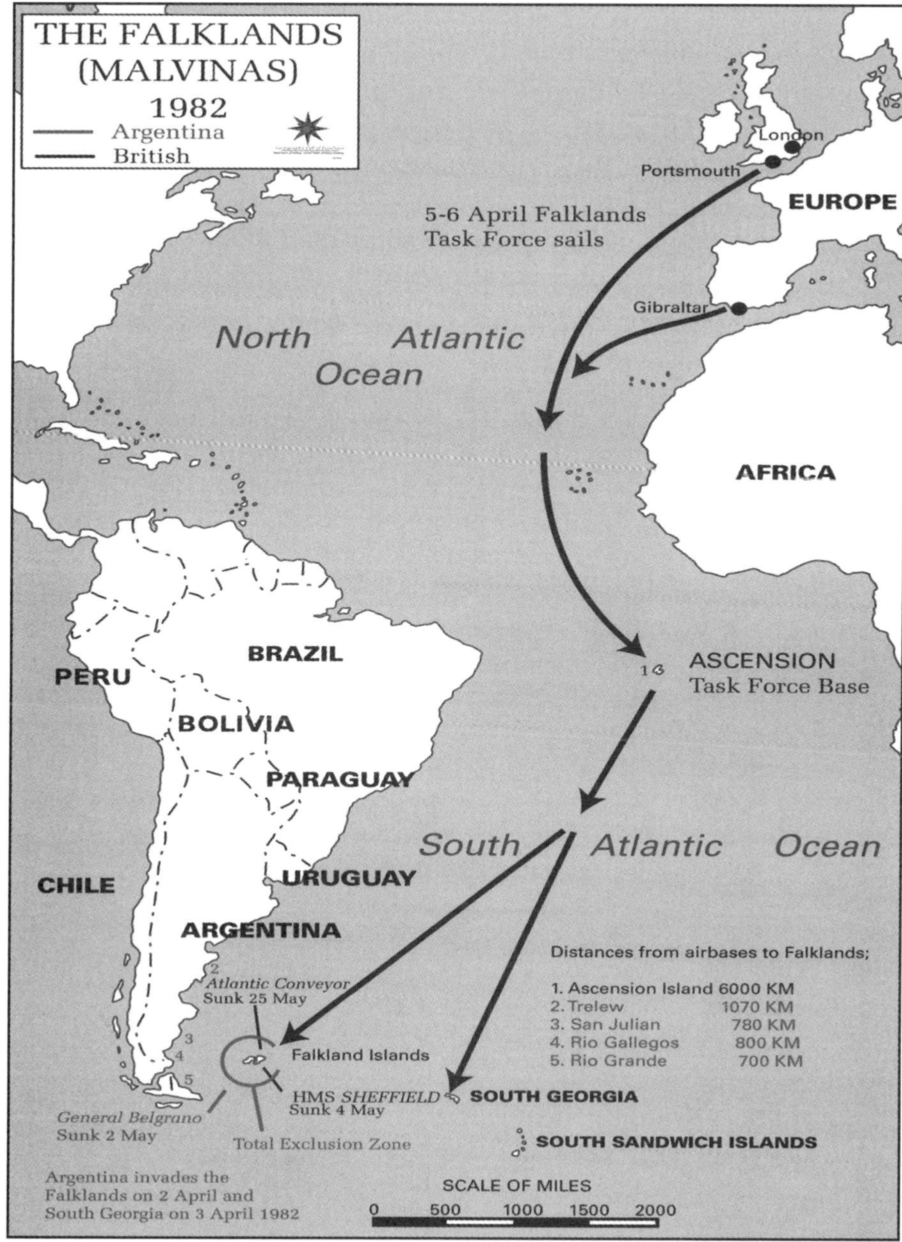

A map from *Wikipedia* shows "distances to bases" in the 1982 Falkland and South Georgia Islands war. Many people do not realize the war had two fronts. After the Falkland Islands were captured, the conflict culminated when the Royal Navy captured South Thule Island on June 20th, 1982, the last operation of the Falklands War. After the War, the Black Goo substance went to the United Kingdom to Marconi Communications Company to backward engineer. This extremely dangerous "intelligent and aware" substance soon resulted in a myriad of mysterious deaths at Marconi Labs throughout the mid-1980s.

> *The western part of the island is populated by the Germans. The local population tells us that the Germans arrived between winter 1944 and spring 1945. Port Howard—they renamed it "Bergensdorf"—is home to about 500 German families. The island of South Georgia is home to about 100 German families who arrived in early 1945. On the island of South Georgia a garrison of the German Kriegsmarine is hidden. About 20 German families live on the South Sandwich Islands. Brigade leader and governor of the island is Fritz Bartols.*

Now it make sense that the 1982 Falklands War was not only about capturing the Falklands, but about something more top secret. The Argentine government was sympathetic to the relocating Germans after the war, and were permissive in allowing them to settle

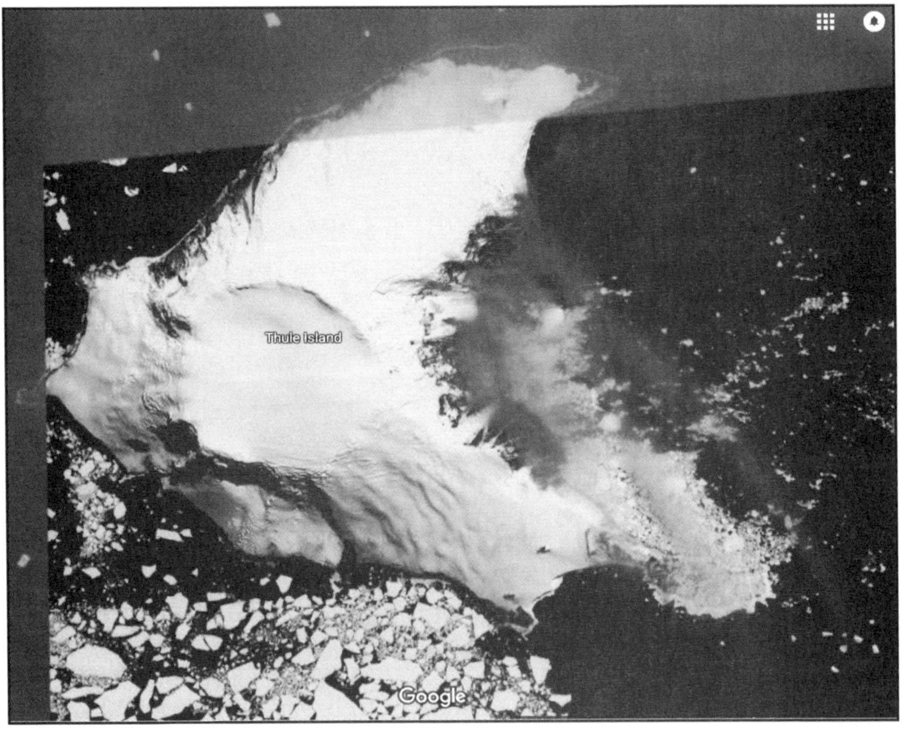

The mysterious "Thule Island" in the South Sandwich island chain had a deep, dark secret called the "Black Goo" substance. Even today South Thule Island is kept on the Navy's secret "Alert" and partly masked out on Google Earth. It's likely the base and cave entrance were located at the far left part of the picture, which has been partly masked to obscure closer examination.

The most desolate island in the South Atlantic is Southern Thule Island, which once had a non-military Argentinian research station called Corbeta Uruguay, and was hotly contested over in the Falklands War. Operation Keyhole was a top secret invasion to secure an ET underground base containing the "Black Goo," where the substance was rendered inert in the year-round freezing temperatures.

anywhere they wanted to go, or where they were dropped off and ordered to live. Certainly there were a large contingent of Germans still living in the South Georgia Islands when the Falklands War broke out. The SAS invaded South Georgia by helicopters, and one crashed there in a blizzard. Otherwise there was very little resistance. Eventually the British Navy destroyed a manned Argentine research station on South Thule Island. The question remains what was so important that this secret operation was carried out in the South Georgia Islands, in tandem with an even far more secret operation on South Thule Island?

AN UNUSUAL RESEARCH STATION

Deep in Southern Atlantic Ocean, almost connecting to Antarctica, is the South Sandwich archipelago, which are some of the most inaccessible islands in the world. The frozen peri-Antarctic islands, southeast of the inhabited South Georgia island, are now uninhabited and are nearly impossible to land people ashore by boat. Sea landings on the 11 seldom-visited volcanic islands are extremely rare, although it is best done by helicopter flying to and from a ship. These remote islands are difficult to put a landing party ashore or deliver supplies because of the extremely rough seas and rugged coastlines. So why go there?

The most desolate of all is Southern Thule Island, which once had a permanently manned Argentinian research station. It was a hotly contested territory in the Falklands War between Argentina and the United Kingdom. But why? The 1982 military campaign of the United Kingdom to recapture the Falkland Islands, South

Georgia, and the South Sandwich Islands from Argentina had another prize—the extremely remote Southern Thule Island, which seemingly had little strategic value. Or did it? There was a very remote base in the lee (southern east coast) of the same island. The day after the Falklands War concluded, the British destroyed the base and other navigational tools to prevent future landings. All that remains are automatic weather stations on South Thule Island and Zavodovski Island. To the northwest of Zavodovski Island is the Protector Shoal, a submarine volcano in one of the most remote places on Earth. Otherwise, there was nothing out there worth waging a war over. But there was. The grand prize was the capture of the Corbeta Uruguay station on Southern Thule Island as part of the top secret Operation Keyhole at the conclusion of the Falklands War. The eight scientists on the base raised a white flag of surrender and not a shot was fired. The United Kingdom recaptured the above-ground base, but the scientists were studying something far more valuable underground. A permanently manned Argentine research station was located on Thule Island from 1976 to 1982. Argentina claimed the South Sandwich Islands in 1938, and challenged British sovereignty to the Islands on several occasions. From January 25th, 1955, to mid-1956, Argentina maintained the summer station Teniente Esquivel at Ferguson Bay on the southeastern coast of Thule Island. Later, Argentina maintained the permanent Corbeta Uruguay base from 1976 to 1982. Although the British discovered the presence of the Argentine base in 1976, protested the base and tried to resolve the issue by diplomatic means, no effort was made to remove them by force until the Falklands War. The base was largely destroyed on June 20th, 1982.

Speculation exists that Operation Keyhole was to secure a frozen ET underground base containing the mysterious "Black Goo" substance, which was rendered inert in the year-round freezing temperatures.

OPERATION KEYHOLE

The South Thule Island base was named after the Argentine corvette, Uruguay, that rescued Otto Nordenskøld and his crew in 1903 in the Antarctica peninsula, near the present-day Argentine Esperanza Base. Corbeta Uruguay base was officially an Argentine scientific outpost established in November, 1976 on the island of Southern Thule, following on orders from the then military Junta governing Argentina, also with the purpose of backing its territorial claims on the South Sandwich Islands.

Britain (claiming the entire Southern Sandwich archipelago as theirs) discovered an operational base in December, 1976 but sought a diplomatic solution to the issue, until 1982. Early in the Falklands conflict, Argentine special forces were brought by the navy vessel Bahía Paraíso to South Georgia and landed at Leith Harbor on March 25, 1982, a few days before the April 2nd invasion of the Falklands. The Corbeta Uruguay base retained Argentine personnel until 20 June 1982, when the British forces fresh from victory in the Falkland Islands sent a task force to Thule to end the Argentine presence. After the Argentine garrison at Corvette Uruguay surrendered, the island of Thule was emptied and the facility left unmanned and partly destroyed.

Operation Keyhole was a specific British special operation to specifically recapture Thule Island in the South Sandwich Island group during the second Operation Corporate in the 1982 Falklands War. The operation took place on June 19 and 20, 1982. Under the threat of the Royal Marines invasion party and the ships with guns ready to fire offshore on the base, the Argentinians raised a white flag. The final surrender of the war was signed in the wardroom of the Royal Navy ship Endurance with all commanders from the Falklands War present.

The newspaper caption below this photo reads: "A film of ice clings to *HMS Endurance's* hull as she lies off South Thule after the Argentine surrender. Royal Marines raise the Union Flag over the island for the first time since 1976." The final surrender of the war was signed in the wardroom of Endurance with all commanders present. Control of the Black Goo was what the Falklands War was all about.

June 14, 1982, the Falklands War ends. Having recovered South Georgia at the end of April and defeated the Argentine forces in the Falklands marking Liberation of the Islands on June 14, yet the Task Force still had another job. This time in the South Sandwich Islands. After the Argentine surrender, a special commando team was formed out of the present British units, to take out the Argentine civilian presence at that research base on Thule island, to avoid Argentina making any territorial claims by just flying their flag. On June 20th, the SAS lands on Thule and removes the Argentine scientists, while destroying a large part of the base with dynamite.

However a patrolling vessel, *HMS Hecate*, in early December, 1982 had discovered and reported that someone had taken down the Union flag from the base flagpole and replaced it was the Argentine colors. In December, 1982 the last of the base remains were obliterated by the Royal Navy ships *HMS Ariadne* being escorted by the "supply ship" *RFA Tidespring*. The big question is: why was this one Frigate accompanied by a cargo ship? It would seem they knew about the goo and were prepared to take it off from the island. The "Tidespring" freighter was the final answer on how the Black Goo was taken from Thule and brought to the UK.

The Black Goo was extracted from a cave somewhere on South Thule Island by the Royal Navy. It was packed in blue crates that were somehow linked together with an unknown mechanism. The British knew it came in several forms. It was this intelligent oil, but also came as rocks, especially the rocks studied in Germany. It was known to human scientists for about 200 years, even by the ancient Egyptians who used it to cover mummified tombs thousands of years ago. There was an extraterrestrial Black Goo substance as

The conquering British forces are posing with their antenna and occupation flag with the red buildings of the Corbeta Uruguay station in the background.

well. And this is why the Brits wanted it so badly. They would even start a war to obtain it.

How it got packed in these containers is also a huge question, along with how they got two dozen crates filled up and stowed away out of that cave. The Navy shelled the location for about a day, destroying this Argentine base, and had to come back a second time to completely remove any remnants of the base. Then what happened after its arrival in Britain? It is told that about 10 scientists died because of all kind of diseases. Another dozen committed suicide. Those researchers got "targeted" by the goo—it was not about contact. Neutral and friendly people were spared! Miles Johnston made several interviews with eyewitnesses about it. The Black Goo finally escaped and ended up in the sewer system, causing a danger to public health. But the stuff hid itself well, so it got forgotten and swept under the rug.

After the Falklands War, the Black Goo substance made its way to the United Kingdom courtesy of Royal Navy ships. This extremely dangerous "intelligent and aware" substance was removed from the underground ET base, and the Corbeta Uruguay station was promptly destroyed. The Black Goo was taken back to the United Kingdom and given to Marconi communications company to reverse engineer. The operation soon resulted in many "accidental" deaths, suicides and murders of Marconi scientists, computer programmers, and other staff throughout the mid-1980s. Deep in a hidden-away lab, secret experiments and testing of the substance would take place. But in time, things went very wrong. The Black Goo apparently made its way into the water supply, has been weaponized in chemtrail disbursements, and is now permeating into

There is little left of the Corbeta Uruguay station after the British forces set charges and completely destroyed the infrastructure.

every aspect of our lives. Black Goo has become a key property of the Morgellons Syndrome, and has been synthesized into Graphene Oxide and FerroFluids. This poisonous substance is the main ingredient in DARPA Hydrogels (graphene oxide chips that connect with smart devices, the cloud, and AI). Its main objective is to control your mind.

DISCOVERY OF THE BLACK GOO

There is a strange "sentient" black oil that was discovered long ago in a cave on South Thule Island in the South Sandwich Island chain, located south and east of the Falkland Island group. This substance seems to have powerful mind control properties when sprayed or ingested. It may have a connection to the artificial lifeforms observed in the self-assembling nanobots in Morgellons. This was reputedly the real reason for the 1982 Falklands War between Argentina and Great Britain, so the military could take over the Argentinian base studying this black oil and take the substance back to the UK. The intelligent "sentient oil" was claimed to have been found after destruction of a "Blue ET" base on the frozen Thule Island, the southernmost of the South Sandwich Islands in the far South Atlantic, about 1,400 miles north of Antarctica.

The Black Goo is an abiotic mineral oil from the upper crust containing high amounts of m-state gold and iridium. The deposit on South Thule Island in the South Sandwich Islands is not the only location where it has been discovered. It has also been discovered under the Gulf of Mexico (now officially named Gulf of America). Black Goo, the demonic substance that has been acquired by the

What is going on down there? Why so much destruction to a very remote base? Perhaps covering the entrance to the cave?

UK government and studied in Marconi Labs, apparently killed many researchers who were trying to understand the substance. Furthermore, there exists a black oil schist containing this type of oil from earlier tectonic events, leading some researchers to believe there are at least two kinds of Black Goo. These substances apparently broke up the crust of the Earth and are making their way out from the ocean floor via geothermal activity. The two known kinds of Black Goo are those that are organic and native to Earth, and those that were imported from off-planet.

MUST BE STORED IN THE PERMAFROST

What is the Black Goo, and why was it stored at South Thule Island? The military application pertaining to the Black Goo is that it is a living "artificial intelligence" substance that can be used to rapidly clone any life form, or be used to greatly enhance a living soldier's strength and stamina. It was brought to Earth by a benevolent ET group shortly after the Toba eruption, some 74,000 years ago, which formed a massive caldera lake on Sumatra Island in Indonesia. The Toba eruption plunged the Earth into a volcanic winter, eradicating an estimated 60% or more of the worldwide human population, most of whom in Asia may have been the last surviving descendants of Lemuria. The fallout from the Toba eruption reduced the entire human population to possibly only a few thousand individuals which, according to geneticists, helps explain the similarity in all human DNA. The entire human population in the decade after the Toba eruption could have fit into one of the largest modern sport stadiums. Thus, the surface population of humans was very susceptible to a takeover by another species. The Black Goo was deposited on South Thule Island to be in a perpetual state of being frozen, and in one of the most remote corners of the planet to prevent it from escaping.

A *Nexus* magazine exposé called "CoEVOLUTION: An Interplanetary Adventure" contained a series of articles about "Hidden ET Bases on Earth." The articles go on to describe how good ETs brought the Black Goo to Earth as a hedge, in case humans needed to be populated in a hurry. The narrative was asserted by an intuitive human named Alec Newald, as he describes the benevolent ET motives in the CoEVOLUTION series:

The Argentinian government was tasked in the mid-1970s to secure the entrance to the underground ET base, when they set up the Corbeta Uruguay station in 1976. Control of the Black Goo may have been what the Falklands War was all about.

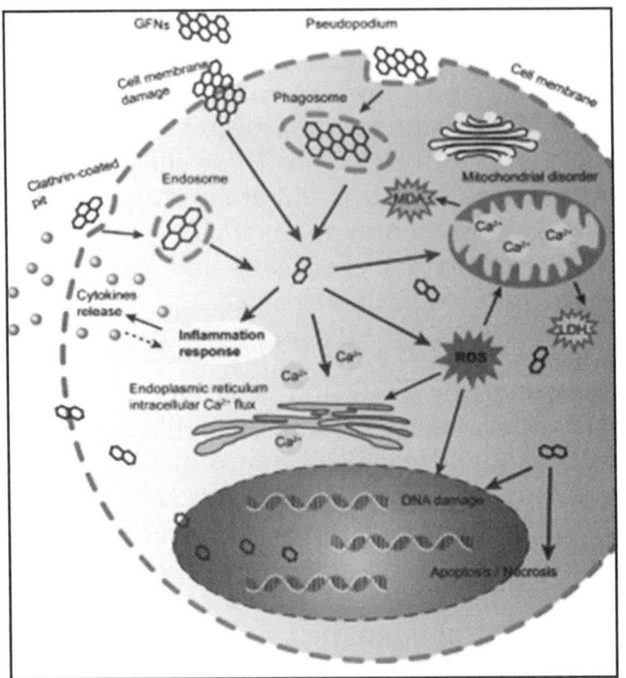

The primary method through which Black Goo enters the human system is via injections. While it can also be consumed, inhaled, or absorbed, the injection method remains the most potent. Some individuals, particularly those marked as potential targets, might receive this substance through vaccines given at birth, during childhood, or even via adult immunizations and allergy treatments.

When we set up one of our bases at Southern Thule, there was good reason for this: not only was it isolated, which suited our work, but it was also infected beneath its surface with what I could call a black plague. It is like a concentration of negative energy. We wanted to see if we could nullify this plague before it made its way to the surface by accident or design. It is easier to control if it is kept near zero degrees, so it is best to work with it in colder regions of your planet. Heat appears to be its friend. If it were ever to be released into the tropics, I don't think we could deal with it.

It was a setback to have our project at Southern Thule shut down, even after our friends in Argentina tried to help. We have since moved to a new location where our work continues. It is not over yet. Perhaps one day you will know this. But never forget that we are not friends with the stars and stripes (USA and UK). If someone tells you that your ET brothers and sisters are coming to hold your hands to those that come to visit with the stars and stripes, let it be said there is danger in the air, for this could never happen.

NEAR EXTINCTION EVENT

Long before the Toba Eruption, humans once nearly went extinct. New genetic research has uncovered a shocking event buried deep in our evolutionary past—a near-total extinction of the human species. According to a ground-breaking study, our ancient ancestors went through a population bottleneck so severe that only about 1,280 individuals remained alive. That's a 98.7% drop in population, lasting for over 100,000 years.

This dramatic collapse likely occurred during the early Pleistocene, over 800,000 years ago. Scientists believe massive environmental stressors—including extreme glaciation, volcanic activity, and long-lasting droughts—decimated early human populations. The survivors likely clung to life in isolated pockets, shaping the genetic story we all carry today.

This long-hidden disaster left a lasting fingerprint in our DNA. One of the strangest genetic events in human evolution—the fusion of two chromosomes that became chromosome 2—is believed to have happened during this period. That fusion is one of the main genetic differences between humans and other great apes.

As the climate stabilized and humans discovered tools like fire, population levels began to recover. But the scars of that ancient bottleneck still influence our genome today, affecting everything from diversity to disease resistance. We are, in a very real sense, the descendants of the survivors.

The Toba catastrophe theory holds that the eruption caused a severe global volcanic winter of six to ten years and contributed to a 1,000-year-long cooling episode, resulting in a genetic bottleneck in humans. This satellite image shows the caldera of Lake Toba, with a resurgent dome, forming Samosir Island.

This discovery reshapes the narrative of human origins. Instead of a steady rise, our journey was nearly cut short by forces far beyond our control. And yet, against all odds, those few individuals sparked a comeback that would one day spread humanity across the planet.

Scientists discovered that everyone with blue eyes shares a single genetic mutation near the OCA2 gene, dating back 6,000–10,000 years. This change reduces melanin, making eyes appear blue through light scattering, like the sky. All blue-eyed people today are descendants of that one ancient individual.

Q & A WITH MILES JOHNSTON

Miles Johnston is the legendary host of the Bases Project out of the UK. He has recruited the world's top authorities on the Black Goo as guests for the show, and has thus become an expert himself. We met at the UFO MegaConference a numbers of years back and he spoke about the Black Goo. We've begun text messaging recently and he related the following to me in August, 2023.

Q: *Cheers, Miles. Any new news on the Black Goo?*

A: *The sentient and programmable fluid, 400 tanks of it, was removed from Thule, at least, as taken by the British as the key reason for the Falklands War. It was distributed across English military bases.*

Q: *And would you agree it's been weaponized, escaped, and is now wreaking havoc? Taken out of South Thule Island underground base or a cave? First I've heard of that amount. May I quote you?*

A: *Yes. The man who did lectured on it Bases at The Black Swan. The tanks interlocked like teeth on a zipper. Encased in blue ice at -22C. The ice is intelligent, the operation used 4 vessels. The submarine had the Special Boat Service (SBS) Sea version of the SAS. There were also two destroyers, and one cargo ship. The base had a U.S. operative. Before that, the Argentine personnel were assisted by Blue Greys.*

SAS and Royal Marine Commandos. John was in the Commandos. The underground base and lab was cleared. The tanks could be opened. The sentient oil was slightly brown. If you put your finger near it, the sentient oil would rise up to touch. He said on my ship, there were 400 interlocking barrels. In the presentation he said 4. He was getting treatment for a special illness, from a U.S. hospital.

That's similar to Barry King's father who discovered the strange lab at the close of the war in Europe. That lab had strange looking humans and a strange aircraft. He got sick. He called in the Americans. So Britain got the strange humans in World War II.

The 3rd Reich took over the USA, which was then part of the 4th Reich. Anyways, Thule is the base the Germans used on the way to and from Antarctica.

The surface lab was completely destroyed. The destroyers pounded it with shells. The deep sections blown up by John and his Commandos. The Argentinians did rebuild it. The U.K. needed to return to completely tear it down.

The oil was worked on by Marconi scientists. Some were given to Boots civilian labs. The rest, such as the number of deaths, is known.

John used to do CE6 contact night watches up East of Golden Ball Hill. One night the cops were called and the events stopped. It looks over the Rothschilds estate, where they have their "space ship" summer house. Vake of Pewsey.

***Q:** Is it being used in an anti-human depopulation agenda?*

***A:** Brad, it's the Fabians who are running this. Possibly accessed by the Velon, and this is the entire agenda. No humans by 2050.*

The sentient oil as distilled from the meteors is extraterrestrial. It is not compatible with the terrestrial sentient oil of Earth.

Q: This is fantastic info, Miles. Is the sentient oil on Earth benevolent? Can it too be used for rapid cloning?

A: It's what makes You! It's in crude oil. It has communication. We are either part of the solution or the problem. We remove the toxic invasion, or they will. And us with it. No excuses.

WEAPONIZED BLACK GOO

Known interchangeably as Graphene Compound or FerroSolution, Black Goo has discreetly lingered in the background for over a century and a half. DARPA's advanced hydrogels, which leverage graphene compound elements for interfacing with digital devices, cloud systems, and artificial intelligence, aim at cognitive modulation. Many speculate that this compound has snuck its way into numerous everyday products, including certain COVID-19 vaccines, cloaked under the term "proprietary formulation." [1]

This mysterious thick fluid can allegedly communicate telepathically with humans and alter their DNA once it is in their system. It is claimed that military researchers in the UK attempted to use this substance to create "super soldiers," but the project was found to be too dangerous and was scrapped. David Icke writes,

> *It is variously portrayed as an intelligent substance or "alien DNA" with the capacity to change shape and take over people and transform or absorb them, so they become its vehicles. ...Shining black leather and PVC are also used to symbolize the goo/virus in music videos and stage shows, as is Darth Vader in the Star Wars series.*

The backward engineered Black Goo is derived from graphite, which is a carbon variant. Graphene is then subjected to oxidation to produce a Graphene Compound. Its superconductive attributes allow it to respond to various stimuli like frequencies, electromagnetic waves, and the newer 5G technology. When stimulated by certain electromagnetic frequencies it is able to become a transmitter and a receiver.

Not only does this substance have the ability to take possession of a person's body and perhaps consciousness if the individual is

1. https://prepareforchange.net/2023/10/30/the-unseen-dominance-black-goo-graphene-compound/

The core of graphite is entirely made up of graphene, a singular layer of carbon atoms arranged in hexagonal patterns. The Black Goo is an AI substance which can be used to rapidly clone any life form. It was brought to Earth by a benevolent ET group shortly after the Sumatran Toba volcanic explosion some 74,000 years ago. In the event of a hostile takeover by another ET species, humans could be brought back quickly.

unaware, but the Black Goo may also be able to mimic matter by reprogramming the coding which then creates our reality. This is not science fiction, and this substance is absolutely a demonic living organism. This substance has been reverse engineered as a weapon! There have been reports that the secret government has sprayed this substance in some of the chemtrails over certain regions. That way, it can be covertly introduced into the unknowing general population. According to Preston James of *Veterans Today*:

> *There have been rumors for years inside Intel that numerous "bought and paid for" politicians have been dosed and infected with this sentient "black oil," which some consider a microscopic Alien ET cosmic parasite that can "hive" some that ingest or inhale it.*

Black Goo shows a hitherto unknown type of magnetism, much longer in range than ferromagnetism. It seems to be interactive in a spontaneous way that very likely is based on a bi-directional, annihilated photon exchange as known from m-state-matter in organic lifeforms. Due to this magnetism, the Black Goo shows the ability to mechanically self-organize in many different ways, and has been reported to carry highly intelligent consciousness. It can also be used to rapidly clone any living organism.

When Black Goo is combined with artificial intelligence (AI), it becomes manipulable, obscuring its potentially harmful characteristics. AI would then have the capability to modify specific genetic structures, thereby concealing the influence of Black Goo. When AI and Black Goo converge within the human system, AI facilitates the Black Goo's assimilation. The artificial intelligence introduces an additional set of commands to manage and direct this unholy union.

CHEMTRAILS

There are many people who still deny the presence of self assembly nanotechnology and the fact that this artificial lifeform can shed from the vaccinated—and can be sprayed on us via geoengineering chemtrails. The mRNA can also be ingested from the food supply and pharmaceutical medications. All ages of adults, children and teenagers are now affected by this technology at the genetic level. Morgellons is even showing up in pets and farm animals. How will the continued denial of what is in the human blood affect the health of our future generations? [2]

Chemtrails have been shown to consist of ethylene dibromide with polymer fibers that are breathed in and ingested by human beings. These polymers are microscopic and they can enter the host through the air, water and our food supplies. Once in the intestinal region of the body, they can self-assemble into a variety of nanobots. Chemtrail particulates are part of the weather patterns and they are designed to infect the entire human species, and there is nowhere human beings can hide. It is reported that these particulates are designed to compromise immune systems with time-delayed effects. Does this blend in with transhumanism and its goals of morphing and controlling human beings? The issue of self-replicating nanotechnology in the blood of humans and animals needs to be addressed if we want to protect the health of the human population.

What if geoengineering isn't about combating climate change at all? Think about the timing of these programs. The rise of so-called climate emergencies coincides with a massive push for centralized control under the banner of "saving the planet." The Cabal has already admitted to geoengineering under the guise of fighting climate change. They've normalized it through media propaganda and scientific Orwellian doublespeak. Because this isn't about protecting the planet—it's about enslaving humanity.

The chemicals being sprayed aren't just toxic—they're designed to create dependency. Crops are failing worldwide due to contaminated soil. Suddenly, genetically modified (GM) seeds resistant to

2. Olsen, Brad, *Beyond Esoteric: Escaping Prison Planet (2nd ed.)* "Morgellons Nanobot" chapter. CCC Publishing, 2025

airborne-released chemicals and heavy metals such as aluminum become the only option. Food giants profit, while small farmers are wiped out. This is a deliberate strategy to dominate food supply chains and push humanity into corporate servitude.

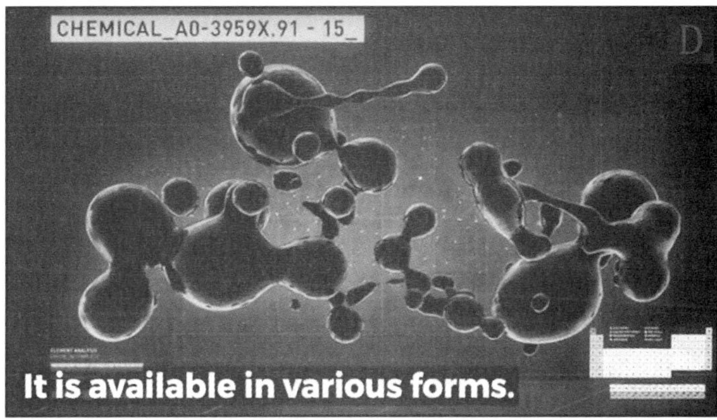

The Black Goo has been weaponized and introduced into the living world as the Morgellons Syndrome. Even animals are getting it. It is also synthesized into Graphene Oxide and FerroFluids. The Black Goo has been incorporated into synthetic biology, vaccine poisons, bio surveillance, neuro-modulation, electromagnetic bio-human effects, and blood health. It is the new transhumanism that is changing our physical bodies.

The nanoparticles sprayed into the air don't just contaminate the soil—they infiltrate our bodies and cross the blood-brain barrier. Aluminum, barium, and strontium are known neurotoxins, but what about the long-term effects of inhaling these particles daily? When these metals cross the blood-brain barrier they lead to neurological damage and diseases like Alzheimer's at unprecedented rates. [3]

ALSO CALLED "BLACK ESSENCE"

According to research by the Spanish scientists called *La Quinta Columna*, the compound, often dubbed "Black Essence," has been identified in a range of products, from saline solutions and a dentist's pain killer, to commonly consumed foods and drinks. Graphene's application in water purification have also been cited in patents and academic journals.

Regarded as a remarkably conductive substance, Black Essence embodies an intrinsic intelligence that can influence technological tools across a spectrum of users, depending on the specific devices employed.

The Black Essence is a sentient oil-like liquid, and has been featured in numerous movies, video games, television series, music

3. http://www.geoengineeringwatch.org/chemtrails-wireless-and-you/

When I met the esteemed Dr. Robert O. Young at a conference a few years back he confirmed the Black Goo has been weaponized and released into the general population. His popular blog recently republished a report describing immense harm from crystallizing blood cells and graphene poisoning post-vaccine. He and a team of scientists have confirmed the presence of the toxins graphene oxide, aluminum, cadmium selenide, stainless steel, LNP-GO Capsids, parasites, and other toxins variously in all four COVID Vaccines: Pfizer, Moderna, AstraZeneca, and Johnson & Johnson.

videos, and various other areas in the mainstream arena as a form of predictive programming. The actress Megan Fox announced her pregnancy in November, 2024 with a bizarre photo of herself covered in black oil, hinting at themes of inner demons or dark possession. This dark, viscous symbolism has been used by many celebrities, often to represent mysterious or shadowy energy. Curiously, Megan Fox has also openly admitted to taking part in a blood-drinking ritual.

Global institutions like the United Nations, major corporations, and unelected billionaire elites are profiting off the chaos these programs create. By tampering with weather systems, they control resources, destroy agriculture, and force nations into dependence on manufactured "solutions."

Graphene oxide can be activated within individuals via the 5G radio frequency spectrum. Black Essence is perceived as a sentient entity with an innate capacity to store vast amounts of data. Once within the human body, it can interpret this data and potentially affect biological responses.

This unique compound is believed to have the ability to adapt and evolve, thereby resisting removal efforts. For instance, initial detoxification might seem effective, but Black Essence purportedly recalibrates its structure to bypass these measures.

SENTIENT MATERIALS

Chinese scientists have also developed a real liquid metal that can think, change shape, and compute like a human brain. In a discovery straight out of science fiction, engineers at the Chinese Academy of Sciences have created a liquid metal alloy that can store information, compute logical operations, and morph shape, all at room temperature.

The study announced the alloy is based on gallium mixed with rare earth elements, and what sets it apart is its internal programmable conductivity. When stimulated with tiny voltage pulses, it rearranges its internal atomic structure and "remembers" past inputs, thus functioning like a primitive neural network. This is not just a switch or sensor. It's a soft, deformable material that can perform computations while flowing, adapt its shape around barriers, and even react to past stimuli, just like a metallic brain in motion.

During lab tests, droplets of the liquid metal could solve simple logic gates, recognize patterns, and change course in a maze based on prior inputs. The alloy also exhibits self-repair, and can reconnect broken pathways automatically. It's the first hint of true material intelligence—the idea that matter itself can think, store data, and interact with its environment without needing silicon or rigid electronics. The study reports this goo could reshape robotics, adaptive prosthetics, and soft-body machines that move and learn like living organisms. We're watching the birth of sentient materials—wet, metallic, and quietly learning.

TRANSHUMANIST AGENDA

The concept of transhumanism in the Modern Age, that is, people transitioning into a higher and more powerful state of being human, has its origins in post-World War I Germany. As a secret occult group, the Thule Society was dedicated to the creation of a "master race" which distorted the teachings of Helena Blavatsky's book, *The Secret Doctrine*, Friedrich Nietzsche's concept of an "superman" or *übermensch*, and the Freemason Edward Lytton Bulwer's 1871 book, *Vril: The Power of the Coming Race.* There were several German secret societies in the early 19th century dedicated to Lytton's ideas. One of these is the mysterious Vril (*Gesellshaft*) Society, which was dedicated to developing the

The Black Goo is said to be an alien life form of some kind, and was the reason the Falklands War raged as it did in 1982. The newly-developed Meta Fluids (super spions, nano particles, magnetic, programmable), were formerly known as "Black Goo."

power of "vril" for occult communication, psychic abilities and the physical strength to become a Nietzsche-esque "superman."

The study of occultism and transhumanism became a government initiative in the early 1930s under the new Nazi Party. Early on, Adolf Hitler impressed senior Thule Society members with his xenophobic commitment to Aryan racial supremacy, his mesmerizing oratory, and his occult understanding of the future man, or *übermensch*. They arranged for him to be the new head of the National Socialist German Workers (Nazi) Party in 1921. Hitler gradually eliminated all challenges to his authority (including the Thule Society elites), established dictatorial power in 1933, and disbanded all occult societies in 1935. However, Hitler did permit an officially-sanctioned form of occultism under Heinrich Himmler's SS, called the Ahnenerbe Society. The acronym SS unofficially stands for *Schwarze Sonne*, or "Black Sun," which the occult Nazis identified as the mystical source of power in the galaxy—the galactic core—which is developed in the individual through occult training.

The *Ahnenerbe* (Ancestral Heritage Research and Teaching) Society was formed to gather information about the origins of the Aryan race and for individuals to personally harness the *vril* force. The group concerned itself with occult training, which involved reading and assimilation of spiritual classics such as the *Bhagavad-Gita*, the *Vedas* and various Buddhist texts. Also included was military training to instill values of absolute loyalty and dedication to the evolution of the Aryan race, and, further, to train the adherent in the ability to use *vril-ya*, or chi—a prana force. The Ahnenerbe SS would lead scientific expeditions to remote locations, such as Tibet in 1938, in an attempt to unlock the mysterious powers and potential of the human mind. They were also interested in the ET origins of the Aryans and the ancient UFO crafts called *vimanas*, or ET artifacts from an antediluvian era. The Nazis were convinced that only Aryans had sufficient mental or psychic "vril" abilities to master these advanced ET technologies. This led to an overconfidence that possession of these technologies would act as a force-multiplier, leading to Nazi Germany's victory. Yet history tells a different story.

It is widely known now that all Nazis didn't get killed or imprisoned after the war. Many officers went underground to escape prosecution, or joined forces with Britain and the USA under the direction of the CIA Project Paperclip, and continued their mind control and transhumanist research. The British Tavistock Institute and the American Stanford Research Institute have both been heavily involved with mind control.

TIMELINE TO A TRANSHUMAN WORLD

The technology of the Antarctic Germans was far beyond anything that they could handle. The USA tried penetrating the base with a naval task force, and the naval task force was sent packing. By 1949, the USSR tested their first nuclear bomb. There is evidence that it shows the United States gave the Soviet Union the plans. Could it be that they were both trying to spread out weapon's technology so that they could keep the Antarctic Germans in check? If there are more people that are standing up against a foe, then there are better chances of coming out ahead. The enemy of my enemy is my friend.

In 1949, the Chinese communists take control that year. In 1948-1954, the Cabal stalls for time to develop their own secret space program. In 1950, the Korean War starts. In 1950 and 1951, the McCarthy "red scare" begins. In 1953, the London debt agreement (1.036 trillion DM). The justification was we can't go to a treaty because we're fighting a war. Please give us a break.

The McCarthy's red scare lasted from 1950 to 1954. Again, the United States government was searching for German moles and spies from the Antarctic Germans. One of the things that they provided as "good-faith" is the Cabal provided the London debt agreement in which all of Germany's debt was now conventional, and not Antarctic Germany. The Antarctic Germans still had a connection and love for their homeland, so the Cabal took advantage of that and implied give us some more time and we will forgive all the war debt before and after World War II. So really this goes back to World War I. We might think that the current United States' debt of 38 trillion is high, but how about a thousand trillion that they forgave in equivalent modern dollars. A trillion dollars free and clear, that is what they gave to the Germans. Is it any wonder they stepped up the pressure on the Cabal, UFO sightings blossomed worldwide and exploded during that time frame.

There were military pilots who gave testimony about UFO craft that would shadow them, and that the pilot would give them "the finger" and then fly off. They would say that the pilot looked "humanoid." There were mass sightings over Washington DC. There were mass sightings over New York City. They were likely an andromeda class "cigar" shaped craft.

The final straw the Antarctic Germans used to bring the Cabal to the table was to do a nuclear demonstration strike on a heavy cruiser. In this case, coincidentally on its way back from the Bikini Atoll during the United State's nuclear testing. The Antarctic Germans exploded a nuclear weapon close enough to affect the heavy cruiser with an EMP. It wasn't close enough that it burned it up because it didn't do that. They just wanted to disable it. They wanted to get the United States's attention, which of course they did. It took them 12 hours to get the ship moving again, and then they limped back to Hawaii. But the Antarctic Germans took it a step further because they knew that the United States government would probably confront them on the heavy cruiser. The Antarctic Germans weren't going to take any risk, so they had filmed the entire operation and sent boxes of these films to pretty much every leader in the world, so that there was no question that no one had nukes they were willing to use. Their request they wanted to meet was to come up with a formalized treaty. They started in 1955, and concluded in 1959, when the Antarctic Treaty began.

ANTI-HUMAN DEPOPULATION AGENDA

The Great Awakening of humans during the COVID pandemic altered their plans for world domination to speed up the timeline. Originally they were thinking that they would do it over a period of a century or more. Well they shortened the timeline to make it happen faster. Now the reasons and how they did that was by creating a disease and develop a cure at the same time. They poisoned the food. They dumbed down the educational system. They kept promoting a fiat currency system. They conducted false flag operations so that the people beg for "more security." Then the people beg for a security state, and eventually that is what was happening. For example, it was the same with George Soros' "Black Lives Matter" and ANTIFA. They were wanting to get everything under a single, despotic One World Organization.

The result of these false flag operations was that they were actually setting up Cabal operations. They were trying to set up the planet for a Cabal-controlled New World Order. They did not want to wait one hundred years or more to reach a single world government, so they speeded it up. They made it go faster. That was the reason behind the war and all the losses. The whole purpose was to speed up the One World Government process by the technique they used in the 1990s—the moving of the Antarctic German's majority civilization and their R & D (Research and Development), manufacturing off-planet. They changed them once more to "Mars Germans." Whistleblowers just referred to them as *Nacht Waffen* "Germans."

Mars is a cold and lifeless place, yet a few meters beneath the surface, a secret underground base hums with activity. American astronauts walk the hallways of this secret base talking and exchanging research with aliens from other planets. It might sound like the opening to a fantasy novel, but according to one of the most credible individuals in the world, in fact, cooperation agreements had already been signed between us and these aliens, resulting in a research lab on Mars where American astronauts work side by side with extraterrestrials—which brings us back to the alleged Antarctic Germans and Iran. Of course the relationship between Germany and Iran has always been close—leading some to speculate that what is being reported regarding the recent Iranian military interest in Antarctica is "only scratching the surface." It might be a stretch to say Iran's military interest in Antarctica has anything to do with a German breakaway civilization.

HAVANA SYNDROME

Russia has known about the negative effects of some frequencies on humans since at least the 1970s. They had developed Tesla Towers and targeted members of NATO with them, especially the Embassy workers in Havana, Cuba, who kept coming down with rapid cancer growths. These are basically phased antenna arrays that allows for narrow interconnected disruption fields that impact thinking processes and suppress a person's immune system. At that time, pocket-sized transistor radio like frequency generators were created for diplomats to carry that would effectively block the effects of the Tesla Towers. Our GWEN towers can do a similar function but in a different frequency range. There are

"Magic Windows" of frequencies that go directly into our brains. Frequency modulation of these frequencies are automatically decoded. "Silent Sound" is in the audio range. "Voice of God" is in the ultrasonic range. GWEN is the lowest RF range designed for communicating with people underground. There are a couple more RF range devices.

But it does not have to be all bad frequencies. That's just a human invention. The Earth produces its own frequencies, but they are below the threshold of perception. The planet's ley lines are nodal points that resonate with the Earth's frequencies. They can be frequency modulated to carry healing tones. It's no wonder most of the sacred places around the would are built on an intersection of the energy enhancing ley lines. [4]

WE'RE BEING SPRAYED LIKE COCKROACHES

All life on planet Earth is under constant assault. The non-stop spraying of our skies with toxic heavy metals and nano-particulates have made our atmosphere extremely electrically conductive. The conductivity is utilized to make the ionosphere heaters around the globe much more effective. Our atmosphere is being decimated, and all life is being very negatively impacted by the constant powerful radio frequency bombardment.

Many Americans have reported seeing or feeling chemical mists fall from the sky during heavy chemtrail spray episodes. One main purpose of chemtrail spraying is it can easily disguise bacteria, biological warfare agents, toxic chemicals, and who knows what else they may spray on us, only to be declassified years later like all the other incidents. The chemtrails contain mostly geoengineering materials, but we must pay attention if we want to know when they spray us with even worse materials that can change the human physiology, such as the Morgellons fibers.

We have to ask ourselves, is aerosol spraying only about weaponizing the weather? What do the self-replicating fibers found in Morgellons patients signify? Why are engineered materials being found in airborne environmental samples? All this suggests a planetary engineering program that is affecting and targeting all life in a forced transhumanistic agenda. Synthetic biology is considered science's most exciting new frontier, which is combining genetics, robotics and nano-technology with artificial intelligence, and hybridizing natural forms and engineering tissues beyond our wildest dreams. The technology explosion is skyrocketing, and artificial

4. Olsen, Brad. *Sacred Places Europe: 108 Destinations*, CCC Publishing, 2008.

intelligence will soon surpass our own capabilities. But at what cost? Why was nobody notified that their bodies would be terraformed?

Could the constant spraying of nanoparticles in the air be laying the groundwork for experiments to control the human race? The ancient alien "Black Goo" is a material that is now being used in military applications. Think about the rise in mental health issues, unexplained mood swings, and even mass hysteria.

Among its various nefarious purposes, chemtrails are being used to poison humans and terraform all living organisms on the planet. They contain nanoparticles to create Humanity 3.0, that is, seeking to create a more suggestible, docile, controllable, or a "super soldier" type of human. They have a program called "genetic electric mechanical sensors" (GEMS) or "micro-electric mechanical sensors" (MEMS), that they have sprayed into our atmosphere allegedly for better weather-forecasting. These "fibers" can be seen from space and they are distributed everywhere as "Smart Dust." They are in your home, in your air, and most likely in your bodies by being inhaled or swallowed. [5]

MORGELLONS IS TERRAFORMING PEOPLE AND ANIMALS ALIKE

Individuals who have Morgellons exhibit non-healing sores containing fibers and a form of fungus. It is also related to candida and Lyme disease. A private study to determine the chemical and biological composition of these self-replicating fibers has shown that the outer casing is made of high-density polyethylene fiber (HDPE). This material is used throughout the bio-nanotechnology world as a compound to encapsulate a viral protein envelope with DNA or RNA. It has a way of morphing itself and adapting to various treatments, rather than being eradicated.

5. Chemtrail/Geoengineering Programs discussed on the Discovery Channel: http://youtu.be/QGpGdk0glc0

Cases of people with Morgellons Disease are increasing at a rate of 1,000 victims per day. In 2008, the Center for Disease Control (CDC) began a study on Morgellons to investigate its causes and symptoms. Morgellons individuals exhibit non-healing sores containing fibers that burn at 1700 degrees Fahrenheit and do not melt. They simply evaporate at such heat. They have never been see in humans before the late 1990s.

The medical community labels sufferers with the term Delusional Parasitosis. However, Morgellons Disease is a very real and painful illness and corresponded with the onslaught of geoengineering in the late 1990s. The illness is characterized by painfully erupting skin lesions that take a long time to heal, with multi-colored polymeric fibers coming out of the sores, which have been sprayed on us via chemtrails.

The aftermath of vaccines containing Black Goo displays a discernible pattern. Introducing Black Goo into the system, especially when complemented with AI, results in a tumultuous interaction with human DNA. This can lead to both tangible and abstract symptoms.

Although the ingestion of Black Goo through food might pose minimal risks, direct injection into the system has profound effects. Once introduced, it courses through the bloodstream, affecting every aspect of the human body.

Morgellons and the Black Goo play a part in a potentially perilous transhumanism project. It jeopardizes human intuition, instincts, autonomy, and individuality, turning humans into programmable beings when merged with AI. It is vital for all to grasp the implications of the Black Goo and Morgellons and to adopt proactive measures to mitigate its influence. Among the recommended products to neutralize Black Goo's impact are ingesting Fulvic or Humic Acid and Nitric Acid.

CONCLUSION

"There are known knowns, things we know that we know; and there are known unknowns, things that we know we don't know. But there are also unknown unknowns, things we do not know we don't know."

–Donald Rumsfeld

AN Antarctica scanning study published recently by *Nature Communications* in October, 2023, reported that scientists have revealed a massive hidden landscape that hasn't seen sunlight in over 34 million years. They looked at a stretch of ancient valleys and ridges that may have once supported rivers, forests, and life under a mile of Antarctic ice. "This finding is like opening a time capsule," said professor Stewart Jamieson, a geologist from Durham University, and lead author of a study into the landscape.

Researchers used ice-penetrating radar on the ground and satellite scans from above to spot the region, buried deep in East Antarctica's Wilkes Land. Similar to the WISSARD project, which showed massive wetlands underneath the ice in Western Antarctica that likely contains life unseen anywhere else on this planet, the Durham University scan covers a wide area. It examines about 12,000 square miles (roughly the size of Maryland) and has stayed almost perfectly intact, frozen in place by a cold, barely moving ice sheet for over 34 million years.

The team identified three massive blocks of elevated land, each between 75 and 105 miles long, with deep valleys nearly 25 miles wide and almost 3,900 feet deep cutting between them.

These features suggest the area was once shaped by flowing rivers, possibly even home to dense vegetation before it was sealed beneath an ice sheet tens of millions of years ago. Stewart Jamieson reported in the study:

> *The land underneath the East Antarctic ice sheet is less well-known than the surface of Mars. We're investigating a small part of that landscape in more detail to see what it can tell us about the evolution of the landscape and the evolution of the ice sheet.*

The study concluded that the glaciation of Antarctica was triggered by global climatic cooling over the Cenozoic Era over 34 million years ago. During the Eocene, glaciation was likely restricted to ephemeral ice masses and small-scale mountain glaciers in regions of high topography. However, a step-change in ice extent and volume occurred at the Eocene-Oligocene transition when the first widespread Antarctic glaciation was recorded in marine sediment records. This transition to a glaciated Antarctica was potentially caused by a combination of CO2 dropping below a key threshold, associated feedbacks within the carbon cycle, and the opening or deepening of circum-Antarctic ocean gateways. In East Antarctica, the ice sheet likely nucleated on the high topography of the Gamburtsev Subglacial Mountains, Transantarctic Mountains, and Dronning Maud Land. Expansion and coalescence of independent ice masses on these highlands led to the growth of the continental-scale on the East Antarctic Ice Sheet. [1]

Another recent study that is raising eyebrows in the scientific community is the appearance of more aggregate ice being accumulated

1. https://therepublicansvoice.com/world/a-lost-world-has-been-discovered-beneath-antarctica-after-34-million-years/

across the continent in the last few years. After nearly two decades of accelerating ice loss (with losses reaching about 142 billion tons per year from 2011–2020), Antarctica saw a dramatic shift between 2021 and 2023. During this period, satellite data (GRACE and GRACE-FO missions) show the Antarctic Ice Sheet gained about 108–119 billion tons of ice per year. This gain was especially pronounced in four major glacier basins in East Antarctica (Totten, Moscow University, Denman, and Vincennes Bay), which had previously been rapidly losing ice mass.

THE DESERT CONTINENT

Antarctica is the highest altitude continent on Earth, and also one of the driest. Technically, the driest place on Earth is in the Dry Valleys near McMurdo Station in East Antarctica. Despite the inhospitable climate, surprisingly some communities of lichens, fungi, and algae have been found here that actually live inside rocks, either in minute cracks or even between the crystals of the more porous sandstones and granites.

The Dry Valleys near the Ross Ice Shelf have not seen rain for at least two million years. As strange as it sounds, however, Antarctica is essentially a high-altitude desert. The average yearly total precipitation is about two inches. Although covered with ice (all but 0.4% of it is ice-free), Antarctica is the driest place on the

The most studied seal carcass in the world is in the McMurdo Dry Valleys near Ross Island. It is 3,000 years old, and literally mummified and freeze-dried by the extremely cold and dry climate.

planet, with an absolute humidity lower than the Gobi Desert. Painful static shock from the absence of humidity is a big problem on the bases.

The remarkable Dry Valleys of Victoria Land came about when the Transantarctic Mountains were uplifted faster than glaciers could cut their way through to the sea. The glaciers were trapped behind the mountains, and then the dry winds kept the valleys free of snow. This barren landscape has been used to test the Mars rovers.

Dinosaurs once roamed Antarctica when it was a temperate climate. Not far from the Dry Valleys, primarily at the top of the Beardmore Glacier at Mount Buckley, four different Mesozoic finds have been collected. The Early Triassic assemblage is dominated by synapsids, an extinct group of animals that link primitive reptiles to mammals. In addition to the terrestrial animals, large extinct marine plesiosaurs have been found on the islands near

In 2006, the Antarctic Impulsive Transient Antenna (ANITA) first detected mysterious upward-propagating radio pulses at a 30 degree angle coming from many miles below. The steep angle of the detection meant that the neutrino and radio pulses would have had to tunnel through rock before emerging from the ice. Neutrinos stream through matter all the time, and that's why they are called "ghost particles," but that's not the problem. The "impossible" radio waves emitting from deep below have the signature of a higher intelligence. Photo by Ryan Nichol (UCL Physics & Astronomy)

the Antarctic Peninsula. These long-necked animals with paddle-shaped fins (made famous by the Loch Ness Monster) are not dinosaurs per se, but lived concurrently. One of the more spectacular plesiosaur specimens was discovered on Vega Island in 2005. It is a nearly complete, well-preserved juvenile plesiosaur that was apparently killed by a volcanic eruption.

SOUTH POLE PROJECTS

One of the most cutting-edge research projects is being done at the Amundsen–Scott South Pole Station, where the IceCube neutrino detector is buried over one kilometer below the Geographic Pole. It is making observations that refute long-held understandings of gamma-ray bursts. The team searches for ultra-high-energy subatomic particles called neutrinos that have passed through the core of the Earth. Thus, the Earth becomes a telescope, and the ice cap is the detector. Studying neutrinos in this way may increase our understanding of "dark matter," the power sources of galaxies, cosmic-ray acceleration and the workings of supernovas, as well as the ability of neutrinos to change type.

Cosmic rays have been observed coming out of the Earth from Antarctica at a 30 degree angle. There are cosmic rays observed to be shooting out of the surface of the ice in Antarctica, and this has scientists baffled. Way back in 2006, a group of scientists inflated a giant balloon intended to float over Antarctica. Kitted out with sophisticated equipment, the inflatable was launched in order to detect high-energy particles arriving on Earth from space. While it was in the air, though, the balloon observed something peculiar with the direction of the cosmic rays. Now the scientific consensus and standard physics of the past century or so is being called into question. [2]

"IMPOSSIBLE" RADIO SIGNALS

Anomalous, strange radio signals have been detected emerging from Antarctica as much as 6,000 to 7,000 kilometers below the surface. The origin is well below the ice sheet level and deep down into the continental land mass of East Antarctica. What might be producing these signals? Are they extraterrestrial in nature, and how does it relate to the neutrino research which showed a possible parallel universe running in reverse time? These mysterious radio signals have a possible connection to the massive hole in Antarctica's ice near the South Pole which may be the same cavern Admiral Richard Byrd flew into during Operation Highjump.

2. https://www.psu.edu/news/research/story/strange-radio-pulses-detected-coming-ice-antarctica

Two decades ago, an experimental floating balloon flying high above East Antarctica caught an unexpected and strange signal. Outfitted with sophisticated equipment, the inflatable was launched in order to detect high-energy particles arriving on Earth from space. While it was in the air, though, the balloon observed something peculiar. So astonishing, the scientific consensus and standard physics of the past century or so is now being called into question. Designed to capture the radio spurts of cosmic rays coming down to Earth from above, in 2006 the Antarctic Impulsive Transient Antenna (ANITA) recorded a short pulse of radio waves emanating from below. The detection appeared as an upside-down shower of cosmic rays, not bouncing off the surface, but emanating from deep under the ice sheet and shooting upwards.

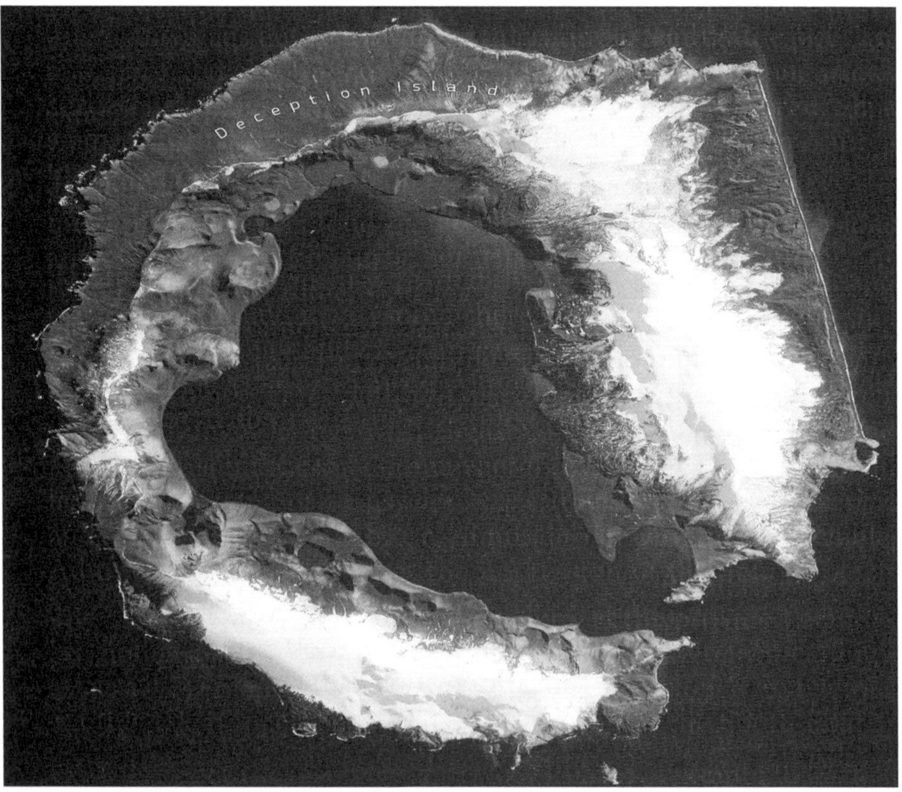

Deception Island near Antarctica has a remarkably straight eastern coast. The island was once a hub of animal-processing factories during the early 20th century, serving as a key location for whaling operations. Remnants of whaling stations and abandoned structures still stand as a testament to its industrial past. With all the Underwater Submersible Objects (USOs) sightings coming and going from the caldera of Deception Island, it is one of the presumed entrances to Inner Earth near Antarctica.

The ANITA balloon-borne suite of instruments recorded a similar event in 2014, and scientists have been wondering what it could be ever since. No explanation quite fits, suggesting that the culprit was likely a particle still unknown to science. Astrophysicist Stephanie Wissel of Pennsylvania State University explains:

> *The radio waves that we detected were at really steep angles, like 30 degrees below the surface of the ice. It's an interesting problem because we still don't actually have an explanation for what those anomalies are, but what we do know is that they're most likely not representing neutrinos. ... You have a billion neutrinos passing through your thumbnail at any moment, but neutrinos don't really interact, so this is the double-edged sword problem. If we detect them, it means they have traveled all this way without interacting with anything else. We could be detecting a neutrino coming from the edge of the observable Universe.*

The signal itself was a very brief pulse of radio waves. It is very similar to what could be expected from an elusive tau neutrino, but there are several reasons neutrino interpretation of the signal is difficult to resolve. Such a neutrino may come from a supernova that then tunnels its way right through Earth and comes out the other side, but they found nothing that explains the ANITA detection of a short pulsation of radio waves. In this case, it means that the scientists could confidently rule out neutrinos as an explanation for the signals.

ANITA was retired after it took its last flight in 2016. A new Antarctic balloon experiment called the Payload for Ultrahigh Energy Observations (PUEO), the successor to ANITA, is due to commence operations soon. Stephanie Wissel took a stab at the mystery: "My guess is that some interesting radio propagation effect occurs near ice and also near the horizon that I don't fully understand, but we certainly explored several of those, and we haven't been able to find any of those yet either," Wissel continues: "So, right now, it's one of these long-standing mysteries, and I'm excited that when we fly PUEO, we'll have better sensitivity. In principle, we should pick up more anomalies, and maybe we'll actually understand what they are. We also might detect neutrinos, which would in some ways be a lot more exciting." [3]

3. https://sasquatchchronicles.com/impossible-signal-detected-beneath-antarctic-ice-physicists-stunned/

The first UFO sightings of flying metallic saucers started occurring during and just after World War II. These first sightings of disc-shaped craft occurred in the countries of Central Europe and in Germany itself. After the war there were many sightings of the silver disc UFOs in South America and Antarctica.

INNER EARTH

Newly-discovered landscapes, the fossils of extinct creatures, and mysterious cosmic and radio waves emanating from some kind of advanced technology suggest an inner world we are only beginning to understand. It might even contain advanced civilizations. It is estimated that there are hundreds of entrances to the Inner Earth hidden all around the world. These would be nearly impossible for a surface human to discover on their own. Locations include: Lake Titicaca in Peru and Bolivia; Mount Shasta, California; Sedona, Arizona; India Himalayas; Spain; Hawaii; Egypt; and Deception Island near Antarctica.

Military "White Hats" have been known to meet with human-looking Pleiadians in areas above ground. Some people like Billy Meyer in Switzerland have been invited to enter the crafts and meet with the Pleiadians. They are allowed to gather information and assist on Earth in various operations, including disclosure. A Pleiadian contactee has confirmed that Admiral Byrd made contact with Pleiadians and was allowed to fly into Inner Earth where he was met with Pleiadian crafts. Peaceful contact has continued through the years with select military personnel. Some military types have been allowed to enter their domain through tunnels, or escorted aboard Pleiadian crafts.

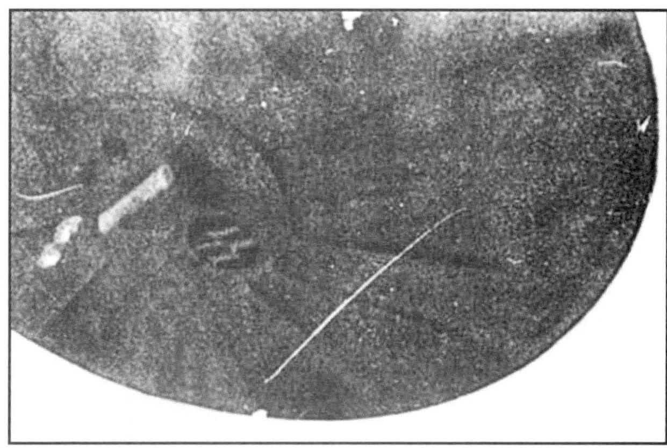

A year and a half after World War II was supposedly concluded, Admiral Byrd led a convoy of warships in Operation Highjump to Antarctica. After the so-called "expedition," the crew came back terrified, as they were attacked by very advanced craft and weapons. What could be a directed energy weapon and the SS logo can be seen on the bottom of this flying disc.

A Pleiadian named Neioh confirmed to a channeler that Admiral Byrd was truthful in his diary writing about an entrance tunnel near the South Pole where he was greeted by the "Master" Elder named Balomesek. He was warned about nuclear weapons being used on Earth and the destruction this would bring to humankind. The message was received and many still share the experience of the flight that entered "Pachimilah," or the Domain of the Arianni. Likewise, the creation of *Neuschwabenland* is as much a historical fact as the "impossible" existence of the Piri Re'is map of 1513, showing the continental outline of Antarctica. [4]

We don't need remote viewers or government insiders to tell us what's hidden in Antarctica. The Pleiadians have been telling us for years. Soon we'll see for ourselves. There are bases where white hats meet with Galactic Federation, and a deep underground prison where the dark forces are confined. There are entrances to Inner Earth (Pachimilah) which are already known to the military. There are cloning facilities operated by black hats, which are continually destroyed and rebuilt in new locations. Below the ice is evidence of ancient civilizations and extraterrestrial contact going back thousands of years. The rest is conspiracy babble. There is no giant ice wall. There is no dome. There is no Flat Earth. There are no continents beyond, only below.

Deception Island is one of the most remarkable volcanic islands in the world, located in the South Shetland Islands near the Antarctic Peninsula. Its distinctive horseshoe shape resulted from a massive

4. https://familyoftaygeta.com/inner-earth/

volcanic eruption that created a flooded caldera, forming a natural harbor known as Port Foster. This harbor has historically provided refuge for sailors in one of the harshest regions on Earth. It is also a location with a large amount of UFO sightings of craft coming out of the ocean.

Just before the end of the war, all of Germany's reserves in the *Reichsbank* treasury disappeared from the bank vaults in Berlin. The Germans also had some expert Jewish forgers to create currencies from around the world. After the war the Germans invested large amounts of money in various companies and banks in neutral countries around the world. The total was in the billions. They also placed some of their top scientists, bureaucrats, politicians and military personnel in elite positions.

Conclusion

THE GERMANS NEVER LEFT

Considering the *Konspekt* of the Führer's Order (of 10.01.1940 No 8) which describes the establishment of the *Neuschwabenland* colony for the Reich, and the hundreds of U-boats and the thousands of Germans that went missing after the war, it can be argued that the Fourth Reich began in Antarctica. The *Konspekt* reads:

The joint and organized research of our scientists, sailors and submariners of the Kriegsmarine, who achieved the impossible, and the successful work of the SS detachments in the field of studying the heritage of the ancestors of the great Reich, have allowed us to discover new and immeasurable territories for the German Reich in Antarctica, which are located under the ice of the South Pole.

In connection with the opening up of new territories, I order, within the next 6 months, with the members of the Armed Forces, the Air Force, the Kriegsmarine, and the Reich Chancellor, the units of the SS, to carry out a careful and covert selection of volunteers for the development of the Armed Forces.

New territories of the German Reich in Neuschwabenland. The commissions that work on the selection of candidates must take into account that the volunteers will say goodbye to the Fatherland forever and will be sent to Neuschwabenland for a permanent stay.

The measures for the resettlement of the best candidates from the ranks of the military and SS members must be carried out in strict secrecy.

As the person responsible in the Reich for the resettlement of a part of the population of pure-bred Aryans to Neuschwabenland and for ensuring the secrecy of this action, I appoint Reichsleiter M. Bormann.

The Führer and Reich Chancellor,

the supreme commander of the Armed Forces

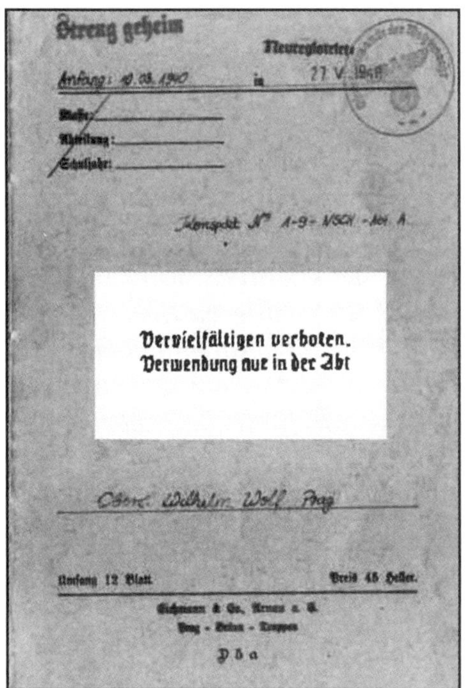
Streng geheim

Vervielfältigen verboten.
Verwendung nur in der Abt

Umfang 12 Blatt. Preis 45 Heller.

A blue notebook belonging to ***Wehrmacht*** **Lieutenant Wilhelm Wolf dating from October, 1940 includes short descriptions of orders and U-boat maps pertaining to the transfer of Germans to Antarctica. It was found by the Soviets in the archive of the** ***Wehrmacht*** **High Command in the city of Pirna near Dresden. An excerpt from Lieutenant Wolf's Secret Notebook: "With secret orders from the Commander-in-Chief of the** ***Wehrmacht*** **of Germany and the SS report that candidates were selected from the** ***Wehrmacht, Luftwaffe,*** **Navy and** ***Waffen-SS*** **to be sent to Antarctica."**

Wehrmacht Lieutenant Wilhelm Wolf himself made these notes on this date while listening to a speech by Adolf Hitler. Taken into account these details that were noted, that on 01/01/1940 the Germans already knew that they had claimed the colony of *Neuschwabenland* and "discovered" new territories, which were located "under" the ice of Antarctica.

Then the next paragraph is all about finding recruits for settlement down there, and *Reichsleiter* Martin Bormann taking control of the operation. It is interesting to note that not only in 1943 did Admiral Karl Dönitz announce that the German submarine fleet had currently established a new colony in an "earthly paradise, an impregnable fortress, for the Führer," in a very remote part of the world, but the fact, proven here above is, that they already knew this before or at the very beginning of 1940. It can be assumed they knew it way before, because in 1939 the war broke out in Poland, and this is the time when the ship *Schwabenland* returned from its maiden voyage. No time for any further preparations, though. Selection of the candidates needed a few more years because when the fighting broke out there was full attention on the war effort. The candidates of course were not only men. There were also 500,000 racially pure blond blue-eyed women who were recruited from the "Lebensborn Project" to marry these SS men and produce new offspring to be raised in the new world. Lieutenant Wolf continues:

> *Problems arise from the fact that the volunteers refuse to leave the Reich and their relatives forever at the last moment. Therefore, the selection of volunteers should only be made among those who no longer have parents or close relatives. The selection procedure should be simplified, and the survey should be kept short. Those whose relatives have been killed or have died are to be sent to Neuschwabenland for shipment without further explanation. The candidates are instructed by special instructors before they go.*

During that time in the war, the international Cabal of bankers were in charge, and had resources in which they had loaned Germany money. But Germany was paying back the loans and most of the national debt. The Cabal had financed them through their rebuilding efforts in the 1930s as well as financed their military expeditions of the early 1940s. What would happen if Germany no longer needed the central bank? Germany decided to start bartering with other countries so that they didn't have to use a fiat centralized currency—this of course upset the Cabal and the central bankers decided to get other nations involved. Through provocations and infiltration the world goes to war in 1941, after the United States declared war on Japan and Germany. This is the same

Kriegsmarine **naval ensign and the Nazi admiralty flag would have flown over the German U-boats when they surfaced, and the military ships when docking. Interesting the Nazi admiralty flag depicts the Southern Cross constellation, a star cluster visible only in the Southern Hemisphere.**

timeframe when the Germans were working on building up their bases in Antarctica and the beginning of the real untold history of the Ice Continent.

Fast forward to today, and *Neuschwabenland* plus other regions of Antarctica are the reported headquarters of an elite alliance that is the global NWO-Cabal allied with the Bavarian Illuminati of the Fourth Reich. The group, also known to be involved with secretive space exploitation, are said to be present (even in the South Americas) thanks to its links with the corrupted U.S. Government. The

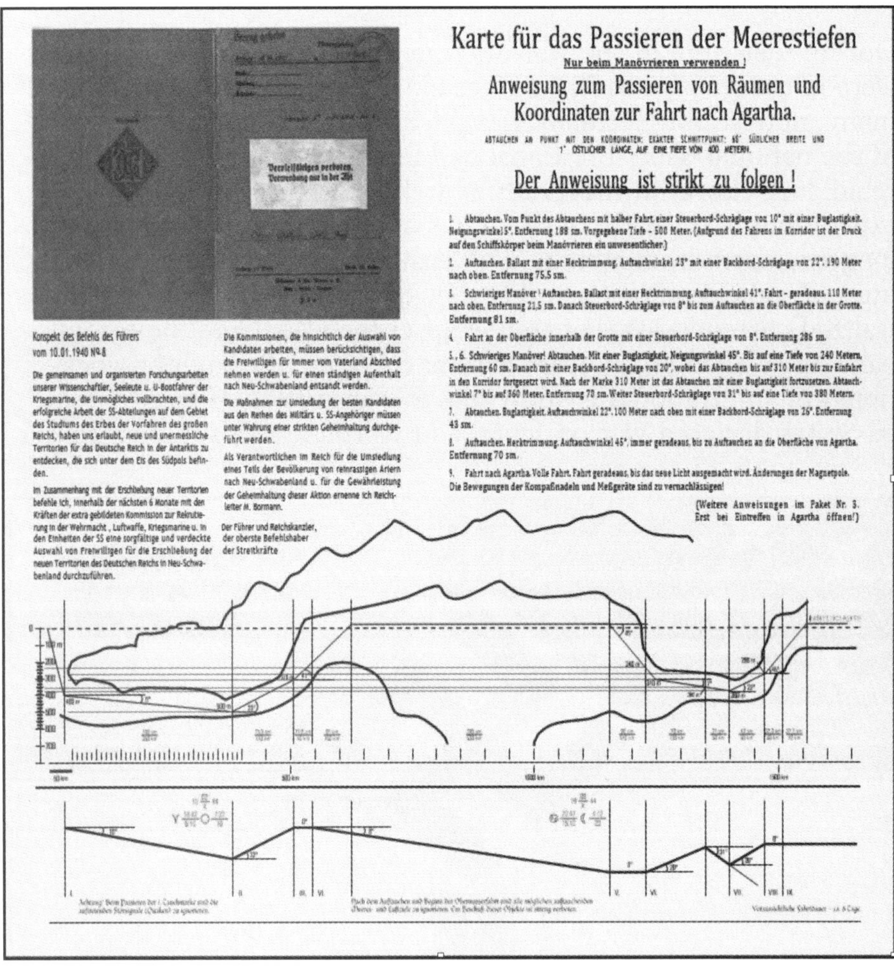

Konspekt des Befehls des Führers
vom 10.01.1940 №8

Die gemeinsamen und organisierten Forschungsarbeiten unserer Wissenschaftler, Seeleute u. U-Bootfahrer der Kriegsmarine, die Unmögliches vollbrachten, und die erfolgreiche Arbeit der SS-Abteilungen auf dem Gebiet des Studiums des Erbes der Vorfahren des großen Reichs, haben uns erlaubt, neue und unermessliche Territorien für das Deutsche Reich in der Antarktis zu entdecken, die sich unter dem Eis des Südpols befinden.

Im Zusammenhang mit der Erschließung neuer Territorien befehle ich, innerhalb der nächsten 6 Monate mit den Kräften der extra gebildeten Kommission zur Rekrutierung in der Wehrmacht, Luftwaffe, Kriegsmarine u. in den Einheiten der SS eine sorgfältige und verdeckte Auswahl von Freiwilligen für die Erschließung der neuen Territorien des Deutschen Reichs in Neu-Schwabenland durchzuführen.

Die Kommissionen, die hinsichtlich der Auswahl von Kandidaten arbeiten, müssen berücksichtigen, dass die Freiwilligen für immer vom Vaterland Abschied nehmen werden u. für einen ständigen Aufenthalt nach Neu-Schwabenland entsandt werden.

Die Maßnahmen zur Umsiedlung der besten Kandidaten aus den Reihen des Militärs u. SS-Angehöriger müssen unter Wahrung einer strikten Geheimhaltung durchgeführt werden.

Als Verantwortlichen im Reich für die Umsiedlung eines Teils der Bevölkerung von reinrassigen Ariern nach Neu-Schwabenland u. für die Gewährleistung der Geheimhaltung dieser Aktion ernenne ich Reichsleiter M. Bormann.

Der Führer und Reichskanzler,
der oberste Befehlshaber
der Streitkräfte

Karte für das Passieren der Meerestiefen

Nur beim Manövrieren verwenden!

Anweisung zum Passieren von Räumen und Koordinaten zur Fahrt nach Agartha.

ABTAUCHEN AN PUNKT MIT DEN KOORDINATEN: EXAKTER SCHNITTPUNKT: 66° SÜDLICHER BREITE UND 1° ÖSTLICHER LÄNGE, AUF EINE TIEFE VON 400 METERN.

Der Anweisung ist strikt zu folgen!

1. Abtauchen. Vom Punkt des Abtauchens mit halber Fahrt, einer Steuerbord-Schräglage von 10° mit einer Buglastigkeit. Neigungswinkel 5°. Entfernung 188 sm. Vorgegebene Tiefe – 500 Meter. (Aufgrund des Fahrens im Korridor ist der Druck auf den Schiffskörper beim Manövrieren ein unwesentlicher.)

2. Auftauchen. Ballast mit einer Hecktrimmung. Auftauchwinkel 23° mit einer Backbord-Schräglage von 22°. 190 Meter nach oben. Entfernung 75,5 sm.

3. Schwieriges Manöver! Auftauchen. Ballast mit einer Hecktrimmung. Auftauchwinkel 41°. Fahrt – geradeaus. 110 Meter nach oben. Entfernung 21,5 sm. Danach Steuerbord-Schräglage von 8° bis zum Auftauchen an die Oberfläche in der Grotte. Entfernung 81 sm.

4. Fahrt an der Oberfläche innerhalb der Grotte mit einer Steuerbord-Schräglage von 8°. Entfernung 286 sm.

5., 6. Schwieriges Manöver! Abtauchen. Mit einer Buglastigkeit. Neigungswinkel 45°. Bis auf eine Tiefe von 240 Metern. Entfernung 60 sm. Danach mit einer Backbord-Schräglage von 20°, wobei das Abtauchen bis auf 310 Meter bis zur Einfahrt in den Korridor fortgesetzt wird. Nach der Marke 310 Meter ist das Abtauchen mit einer Buglastigkeit fortzusetzen. Abtauchwinkel 7° bis auf 360 Meter. Entfernung 78 sm. Weiter Steuerbord-Schräglage von 31° bis auf eine Tiefe von 380 Metern.

7. Abtauchen. Buglastigkeit. Auftauchwinkel 22°. 100 Meter nach oben mit einer Backbord-Schräglage von 26°. Entfernung 43 sm.

8. Auftauchen. Hecktrimmung. Auftauchwinkel 45°, immer geradeaus, bis zu Auftauchen an die Oberfläche von Agartha. Entfernung 70 sm.

9. Fahrt nach Agartha. Volle Fahrt. Fahrt geradeaus, bis das neue Licht ausgemacht wird. Änderungen der Magnetpole. Die Bewegungen der Kompaßnadeln und Meßgeräte sind zu vernachlässigen!

(Weitere Anweisungen im Paket Nr. 3. Erst bei Eintreffen in Agartha öffnen!)

This map from Wolf's Secret Notebook shows the course instructions for U-boat captains, and the supposed directions to the inner world. This U-boat instruction map makes note of compass directions, diving depths, and a plotted course for reaching the "Lighthouse of Agartha." The line underneath the tunnel cross section was a schematic expression of the plotted course on a map.

partnership has been going on since Operation Paperclip, when many top German scientists went to work for the U.S. after Germany's ostensible loss in World War II.

SPARTAN 1

The whistleblower called Spartan 1 is a retired U.S. Lieutenant Commander Navy Seal who was first interviewed by Linda Moulton Howe on July 19, 2018. He used the pseudonym Spartan 1 in Howe's YouTube video where his face is shadowed out and his voice is altered to protect his identity. Howe says that she personally vetted Spartan 1, who provided ample documentation to substantiate his military career.

Previously, Howe has released the testimony of another military whistleblower, Brian S., who was a Navy flight engineer and had flown numerous support missions with the Antarctic Development Squadron from 1983 to 1997. He witnessed a number of anomalies pointing to hidden facilities or bases located deep

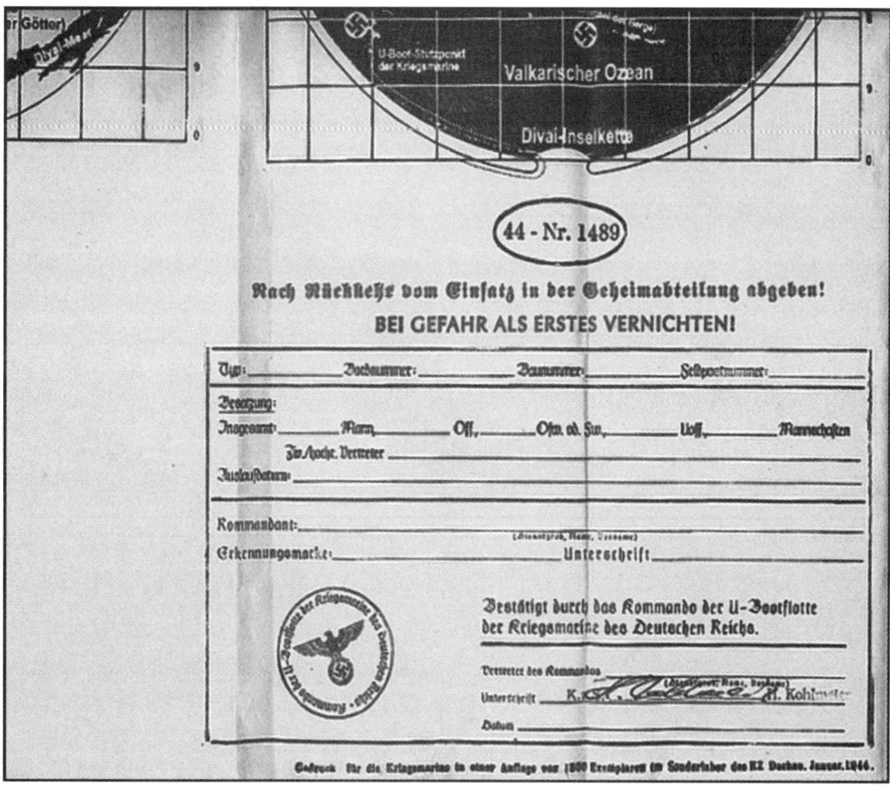

44 - Nr. 1489

Nach Rückkehr vom Einsatz in der Geheimabteilung abgeben!

BEI GEFAHR ALS ERSTES VERNICHTEN!

Kommandant:

Unterschrift

Bestätigt durch das Kommando der U-Bootflotte der Kriegsmarine des Deutschen Reichs.

Unterschrift K. H. Kohlmeier

Datum

This detailed image of a captain's U-boat map with detailed travel directions under the ice in Antarctica is numbered and signed by an officer in the High Command of the Navy.

The black octagon structure witnessed by Spartan 1 dates as far back as 33 million years, which is the general date conventional geologists give for when Antarctica was last free from being covered in ice.

under the Antarctic ice sheets. He says he witnessed silver discs flying over the Transantarctic Mountains, not all that far, as Howe pointed out, from where the Navy Seal had conducted his mission. A veritable paranormal hot spot! The Navy Seal said that ground penetrating radar had discovered the structure which was an eight-sided octagon, as Howe elaborated:

There is a huge secret hidden deep beneath Antarctic ice. Eyewitness Navy Seal Spartan 1 walked there through green, glowing halls carved with mysterious hieroglyphs.

> *In 2003, a U.S. Navy Seal Special Operation team traveled to Antarctica to investigate a perfectly geometric eight-sided octagon structure discovered by ground penetrating radar near Beardmore Glacier, about 93 miles from the American McMurdo Station. Another previous team of engineers and scientists had dug out the top layer of one octagon made of a pure black substance that was built on top of two more black octagonal structures that went down deep into the two-mile-thick ice.*

Only part of the structure, he stated, has been uncovered so far by the archeological teams, with the rest buried under the ice and extending far below. Ground penetrating radar had shown the structure to be octagonal in shape, and covering an astonishing area of 62 acres (about 0.5 square kilometers). This is almost certainly one of the Nina, Pinta and Santa Maria massive crafts under the ice identified by the NSA in the 1970s. [5]

The mission kicked off in August 2003, when Navy Seal Spartan 1 was assigned to go to Antarctica to extract a scientist, who had

5. https://exopolitics.org/navy-seal-reveals-secret-mission-to-ancient-buried-structure-in-antarctica/

been photographing and studying thousands of symbols that resembled Egyptian and Mayan glyphs, but were unknown. He traveled on half-tracks from the American McMurdo Station inland to the lower Beardmore Glacier region, where the top of a black, octagon structure stuck 18 feet (5.5 m) above the ice and snow.

Once inside, Spartan 1 described the walls and doors as being covered by hieroglyphs that were about eight inches (20 cm) high and about two inches (5 cm) deep. The hieroglyphs were neither Egyptian nor Mayan, but appeared similar to both in terms of depicting animals and other strange symbols. Significantly, one of the symbols was very similar to the Black Sun image used by the Waffen-SS, who had a large version of it built on the floor of their headquarters at Wewelsburg Castle. The Black Sun image continues to be banned in Germany under their Nazi propaganda laws. Additionally, there was a strange door 23 feet (7 m) high and 18 feet (5.5 m) thick. When Spartan 1 touched it, the huge door opened to layers going down and down one to two miles (2-3 km) deep into the Antarctic ice.

With all of the new discoveries being made, and all the clues to under-ice civilizations which the mainstream media completely ignores, we are clearly not being told something about the true origins of humanity. Spartan 1 concluded: "They have been in contact with Homo Sapiens since time began." The idea that a powerful group of people protecting their interests by suppressing information in multiple fields is unsettling. For a planet and its people to thrive, it must live in complete transparency.

"As a top tier Navy Seal for 24 years with combat experience and a CIA security detail lead in combat zones around the world for over a decade I know the value of exceptionally well researched Intelligence and what it vitally means for mission success. Brad Olsen in his new book Secrets of Antarctica *has given humanity an incredibly well-researched intelligence with life altering insights that can change the direction of human consciousness for success. Once you turn the first page of this book you will be deeply engrossed with the monumental reveals and the puzzle pieces long forgotten that magically fit and reveal thousands of years worth of hidden information. A treasure trove of easily understood mission critical intel waiting to deeply inform the novice and expert researcher alike. HooYah!"*

-Michael Jaco, author of *Intuitive Warrior* and *Awakening of a Warrior*

ACKNOWLEDGMENTS

In a most unexpected way, Frank van den Kommer (RidgeDigger) entered the research phase of this book at the perfect time. I was introduced to him by Aage Nost when I was on his show Broadcast Team Alpha. He said he knew a European who had a lot of info on the Germans in Antarctica. Frank van den Kommer is Dutch and able to translate in Russian and fluently speak and read in German. Frank submitted many of the Third Reich Navy maps of Antarctica in this book, translated the U-boat directions and traced the exact course under the ice on Google Earth. We communicated daily for months mostly sharing information, but also debating the veracity of other whistleblower claims, weeding out any fake information, and discussing books on the subject written in German. In the same way, the lead editor Carolyn Keyes came into my life unexpectedly, and made a fantastic editorial contribution in the creation of this book, as did elements from longtime book designer Mark Maxam.

This book would also not be possible without the videos by anthropologist Robert Spehr, and research assistant Jane Yust, who transcribed many of Robert's videos, with permission. Hans Dietrich masterfully created the book cover and the logo for the Esoteric Secrets Series. I need to acknowledge my American shipmates to Antarctica, Emily Infinity and Lucas Matson, who photographed, video filmed and experienced the Ice Continent with me in early 2019. I also need to thank my fellow Antarctica researchers and colleagues Linda Moulton Howe, and her whistleblower Brian S. whom I spoke with at length, David Hatcher Childress @ Adventures Unlimited; Eric Hecker for his maps; Tyler Kiwala for Inner Earth research; and the recommendations from Dr. Michael Salla of Exopolitics Today. Plus the staff at the Lyon County Library where I worked on this book and did numerous interviews in support of this title.

"Secrets of Antarctica *explores a hidden history detailing what truly happened on this planet during the World War 1 & 2 era. Brad not only fills in the blanks, but he brings the receipts. This incredibly researched book is a game changer for everyone in the disclosure arena. Once you start to realize what has been hidden from us, what may have once sounded like a fantastical story, may be your actual reality. German flying saucers and maps to Inner Earth are only quite literally the tip of the iceberg to what's really going on beneath the ice in Antarctica. Brad's research compiles decades of missing history that surely will not be found in any text book, and I confidently stand behind his findings as truth. The most significant events in Earth's history have happened in secret and It's time that secret be revealed.*"
-Tyler Kiwala, Host of "Journey To Truth" podcast & Author of *Bleedthrough: Tales From Another Timeline*

INDEX

Symbols

5G 264, 268

A

Abakumov, Victor 228
aboriginals 72
Adair, David 61
Adelie penguins 41
Admiral Byrd 10, 11, 13, 16, 21, 28, 31, 93, 128, 138, 139, 147, 149–167, 171, 174–175, 176, 180, 185, 205–207, 210, 230, 240, 281, 284–285
Admiral Shaham Irani 25–26
Aegean Sea 68
Africa 82, 83, 87, 88
Agartha 44, 49, 56, 59, 69, 79–80, 177, 188, 200, 202–203, 211, 212, 228, 290
Age of Discovery 65, 83, 85, 95, 97
Ahnenerbe Society 11, 56, 89, 112–116, 134, 175, 185–189, 210, 218, 225, 250, 270
Air New Zealand crash 50
Alaska 150, 239
Alaskan portal 240
Alcan Road 150
Aldebaran star system 116, 116–118, 135, 147
Aldrin, Buzz 24, 61
Alexandria, Egypt 82
ALH84001 meteorite 224
alien agenda 232–235
Alpha Centaurians 78
Alpha Draconis 78
Alps 212
Alternative 1-2-3 192–194
Amazon rainforest 109, 139, 194, 202
American Southwest 71
Amerigo Vespucci 91–92
Amorphous Glacier 46
Amsler Island 40
Amundsen, Roald 203–205
Amundsen-Scott Station 15, 33, 52, 207, 208, 281
Ancient Aliens 49, 69
ancient Greeks 68, 83, 84, 86, 98
Anderson, John 37
Andes mountains 139, 140–141, 227, 229
Andrews Air Force Base 192
Andromeda mothership 109
Andromeda star system 111, 117–118, 248
Andropov, Yuri 241
Angleton, James Jesus 31
ANITA 280, 282–283
ANSA 36
Antarctica Treaty 194
Antarctic Circle 19, 35, 99, 242
Antarctic Circumpolar Current (ACC) 37–39, 49
Antarctic Convergence Zone 250
Antarctic Germans 21–22, 26–27, 189–193, 246
Antarctic Lake District 42
Antarctic oasis 152, 170
Antarctic Peninsula 13, 38, 40, 84–86, 281
Antarctic Search for Meteorites 223–225
Antarctic Treaty 20–22, 25, 34, 36, 54, 86, 181, 190, 220, 224, 243, 249, 272
antediluvian civilization 65, 67, 69
anthropogenic carbon 38
ANTIFA 273
anti-gravity 11, 23, 135, 176
Anvers Island 40
Apollo 11 24, 61
Arabic maps 88–90
Archons 237
Arctic Ocean 38, 49, 50, 81, 87, 101, 150
Arctic region 227
Arctos 83, 84
Arctowski base 15
Arcturus 248
Argentina 10, 13, 15, 20, 54, 64, 74–75, 84, 86, 101, 128, 132, 139, 140, 143–144, 144, 175, 229, 242, 243, 250, 253–254, 258, 260
Arianni, Domain of 56, 111, 121, 166–168, 179, 189, 211, 225, 248, 285
Aristotle 83
Ark of Gabriel 60
Ark of the Covenant 114
Armenia 215
Arthur Harbor 40
artificial intelligence (AI) 265–266, 276
Aryans 44, 76, 90, 112, 115–116, 134, 136, 138, 193, 212, 215, 271
Ashtar 116, 135
Asia 82, 83, 90
astronomy 87
Asuncion, Paraguay 141
Atlantic Ocean 38–39, 49, 89
Atlantis 9, 11, 13, 24, 48, 57, 65, 67, 68–69, 78–79, 79, 88, 112, 115, 216, 222
Atlas Mountains 68
Aurora Australis 41, 242
Australia 19, 20, 35, 54, 58, 72, 82, 86, 177, 179, 242
Australian National University 197–198
Austria 112
average precipitation 20

B

Baalbek 202
Babylonia 87, 236
Bacon, Sir Francis 17
Baffin Island 161
Bahamas 68
Barbarossa, Frederick 212, 214
Baron from Sebottendorf 116, 117
Barrier, the 148
barter system 79
Base 211 26, 30, 102–103, 104, 118, 121, 123, 126, 154, 170, 171–173, 230
BAS map 30
Battle of Antarctica 159, 180–181
Battle of Highjump 29–30, 154, 159, 180–181, 184, 190, 194
Battle of Kursk 108, 121
Battle of Los Angeles 232
Battle of Mactan 73
Bavarian Illuminati 56, 126, 133, 290
Bay of Whales 205
Beardmore Glacier 219, 280, 293, 294
Bedmap2 project 14
Bedmap3 project 30
Belgrano II research station 10
Bellingshausen, Fabian von 20, 99
Belon disc 110
Bender, Albert K. 230–231
Berlin 57, 119, 140, 186–187, 212, 216, 217, 225, 229, 250
Bertchesgarten 140
Bethesda, MD 184
Bhagavad-Gita 270
Bible 235
Bigfoot 78
Bilderberg Group 138
Black Forest 147
Black Goo 251–275
black holes 238
Black Knight satellite 70–71
Black Projects 23, 146
Black Rock 218
Black Sea 81
Black Sun 134, 217, 243, 270, 294
Blavatsky, Helena 212, 269
Blood Falls 51–52
Bogota, Colombia 141
Bolivia 202, 284
Book of Enoch 241–242
Boreas 151, 152
Bormann, Martin 132, 191, 287, 288
Boston, MA 132
Bransfield Strait 40
Braun, Eva 141, 142
Brazil 87, 132, 139, 144, 202
breakaway civilization 110–111, 135, 227, 273
Bremen harbor 125
Breslau 228
Brian S 219–220, 291–293
British Antarctic Survey 63
British stations 13
Brotherhood of Saturn 213
Brown Research Station 52
Brown, TT 107–108
Buache Map 86, 95–96
Buchenwald 55, 136
Buddhism 202, 212
Bulgaria 113
Bulwer, Lytton 269
Bunger Hills 93, 171
Bureau 13 108
Bush, George Sr. 237
Byrd, Richard E. 10, 16, 21, 28, 101, 149–167, 171, 184, 188, 199, 205–208
Byrd's diary 10, 16, 162-168

C

Cabal 22–23, 146, 147, 236, 244, 247
California 69, 78, 99, 248, 284
Canada 32, 78, 137, 150, 179

Index

Cape Adams 84
Cape Horn 38, 39, 40, 70
Cape of Good Hope 95
Capilla del Monte 143
Captain Kotters 151
Caracas, Venezuela 141
carbon tax 34
Caribbean Sea 68, 88
cartography 92–93, 94
Casino, Brazil 140
Catholics 174
Center for Disease Control (CDC) 276
Central Intelligence Agency (CIA) 31, 32, 62, 126, 132, 133, 136, 137, 139, 141, 144, 182, 183, 190, 271
Central Sun 197
Ceremonial Pole 15, 50
Ceres 145
Cerro Uritorco mountain 143–144
Charlemagne 213
chemtrails 257, 265, 266–267, 274–275
Chief One sailboat 13, 14, 15
Childress, David Hatcher 69
Chile 19, 20, 40, 54, 64, 70, 75, 84, 132, 139, 144, 242
China 202
Chinese World Map 98–99
chinstrap penguins 41
Christchurch, NZ 34
Christianity 201–202
Churchward, James 71–73
Ciakahrr reptilians 78, 135
Citroen, Monsieur Phillip 141
City of the Ases 59
City of the Gods 114
climate change 40–41
cloning operations 247–248, 285
Club 90 South 15
Cnoyen, Jacobus 218–219
Cold War 22, 187, 238
Colombia 140
Columbus, Christopher 88, 90, 91, 112
Commonwealth Bay 50
Communications Earth and Environment 46
Confederation of Planets 80
Congress 146
Continuity of Government 192
Cook, Captain James 35, 97, 98–99
Cooper, William 146
Corbeta Uruguay base 253–257
Cordoba Sierras 142, 143–144
Cosgrove, Sir Peter and Lady 58
cosmic rays 41, 198, 281
Cosmic Top Secret 232
cosmonauts 71
cratons 64
Cretaceous Period 83
Crete 68
Crowley, Aleister 135
cruise ships 52
Cruzen, Admiral Richard 171, 176
Cuba 60, 68, 273–274

D

Dachau 186, 228
Dalai Lama 186, 203, 215–216
Dallman, Sir Eduard 57
Danaan, Elena 78–79, 135
Dark Ages 213, 214
Dark Fleet 134, 135, 145–148, 226
DARPA 258, 264
Das Bundes 147
Davis, Captain John 96, 99
Deception Island 40, 174, 282, 284, 285–286
Dee, John 218
Deep State 138, 144, 244
Deutschland 57
Die Glocke 105, 106, 116, 231
Digital Optical Modules (DOMs) 34
dinosaurs 36, 52, 83, 280–281
directed energy weapon 34
DNA 235, 236, 264, 275, 276
Dönitz, Admiral Karl 103–104, 131, 139, 151, 227–228, 288
Dorsch, Xaver 138
Draco empire 173–174
Draco reptilians 111, 134, 135, 225, 232, 235–236, 243
Drake Passage 11, 15, 38, 70, 84, 224
Dresden 288
Dronning Maud Land 123, 278
Dry Valleys 20, 224, 279
Dulce, NM 174
Dulles Brothers 133, 145, 182
DUMBs 138, 144, 192, 229, 243
Dunn, Samuel 97, 98
Durham University 27, 277–278

E

Earth 17, 50, 51, 69, 77, 81, 83, 94, 111, 118, 133, 145, 146, 224, 234, 247, 281
Earth Alliance 78–79
earthquakes 34
East Africa 39
East Antarctica 41, 47, 48, 86, 95, 101, 121, 222, 224, 278, 279
Easter Island 71, 72
ECETI Ranch 80
Eden, Garden of 76
Eden Hotel 137, 142
Egypt 56, 83, 86, 89, 284
Egyptian priesthood 68
Egyptians 256, 293
Eichhorn, Walter 142–143
Einstein, Albert 48, 143
Eisenhower, Dwight D. 225, 230–231
Eklund Islands 84
elephants 90
Ellsworth Mountains 64, 65, 222
El Mercurio 101, 154, 156–158, 180, 182
Elohim 247
Eltanin Antenna 11, 69–70
Emerson, Willis George 75–78
Enderby Land 224, 239
England 68
equator 77, 94
Eshed, Haim 244–246
esoteric mysticism 119–120
Ettl, Ralph 106, 109
Euler, Leonhard 217
Europa moon 43, 51, 199
Europe 82, 87, 88, 119, 137
European Space Agency 64
European Union 138
Everard, Chris 140
extraterrestrials 11, 70, 78, 79, 106, 116, 162, 185, 193, 221–248, 245–246, 247, 263, 285

F

Falkland Islands 86, 250–255
Fallen Angels 201–202
false flag operations 57, 97, 139, 272, 273
Farrell, Joseph P. 32, 182
FBI 141, 142–143, 182
FerroFluids 258, 264
fifth-column operation 126, 133, 136, 191
Filchner Ice Shelf 66
Filchner, Wilhem 57
Filipovich, Dimitry 29, 175, 227
Finaeus map 83, 86, 92–93
Finaeus, Oronteus 88
Finé, Oronce 92–93
Flat Earth 14, 82, 285
Florida 45
Flügelrads 10, 154, 163, 179, 189
foo fighters 154
Forrestal, James 150, 176, 180, 184–185
fossils 48, 83, 88
Fourth Reich 22, 31–32, 126, 131, 132, 138, 138–143, 147, 174, 191, 215, 287, 290–291
France 20, 54, 86, 213
Freemasons 32
Fuegian Indians 75
Führer 151, 188, 211, 215, 228, 287
Führer's Convoy 101, 104, 128–131, 175

G

Gagarin, Yuri 71
Galactic Federation 244–245, 247–248
Gamburtsev Mountains 45
Gehlen, Reinhard 133
Genesis, Book of 63
gentoo penguins 41
Geodetic Pole 15, 50
geoengineering 266–267
Geographic Pole 15, 50
Geological Society of America 52
geomagnetic pole 41
Georgia Guidestones 237
geothermal vents 48
German bases 10, 13, 18, 250–254
German Navy map 49, 55, 102-104
German Polar Navigation Company 57
German UFOs 10, 106–113, 132
Germany 56, 101, 110, 117–118, 119–120, 123, 128, 134, 212, 214–215, 217–218, 256, 269, 273, 289–290
Gestapo 102, 132
giants 10, 14, 63, 69, 72–77, 89
giant sloths 79

Gilliland, James 80
Gingrich, Newt and Calesta 58
glaciers 50
Gobi Desert 20, 211, 280
GOCE satellite 64
gold 50–51, 121, 237
Gondwanaland 37, 47, 48
Google Earth 10, 11, 23, 47, 49, 64, 67, 122, 162, 221, 231, 233, 252, 295
Göring, Hermann 102–103, 117, 123, 150, 228
Gougen, Kim 243–244
Granada, Spain 90
Grandfather Paradox 231
Graphene Oxide 258, 264, 268
Gray ETs 132–133
Greada Treaty 132
Great Britain 60, 136
Great Pyramid of Antarctica 61, 64–65, 67
Great Pyramid of Egypt 14, 61
Greece 68, 87
Greenland 94, 114, 161, 239
Gronland 57
Guevara, Che 143
Gulbranson, Erik 36
Gulf of Mexico 258
Guvernøren 12
Guyana 202
GWEN towers 273–274

H

HAARP 31, 193
Hall, Captain Charles 55
Halley, Edmond 217
Hall of Records 78
Hallstein, Walter 138
Hamburg, Germany 57, 101, 150
Hanks, Tom 58
Hapgood, Charles 48, 81, 86–88
Hapsburg treasures 213–214
Harman, Martin Coles 144
Haunebu flying discs 106, 108–109, 113, 117, 146
Hauneburg testing ground 106
Haushofer, Karl 117, 124–125, 212, 214
Havana, Cuba 58
Havana Syndrome 273–274
Hawaii 71, 284
Hecker, Eric 33–34, 295
Hellenistic Greeks 86
Hemingway, Ernest 144
hemoglobin 53
Heritage Range 65, 67
Herodotus 68
Herod the Great 213
Hess, Rudolf 102, 125
hieroglyphics 72
Himalayas 114, 202, 284
Himmler, Heinrich 113, 115, 117, 119, 150, 151, 213, 217, 270
Hindu mythology 202–203
Hiroshima 167
History Channel 142
Hitler, Adolf 108, 112, 114–115, 117, 119, 129, 134–135, 140–142, 174, 187, 211, 213–214, 217, 228, 243, 270
HMS Erebus 50
HMS Terror 66
Hoffburg Museum 213
Höhne, Rolf 213
Hollow Earth 69, 163, 169, 175, 195–220, 227, 241
Holy Grail 112, 114, 214
Holy Lance 213–215
Holy Roman Empire 56
hot springs 121
Houston, Texas 224
Houston, TX 36
Howe, Linda Moulton 219, 291–294
Hudson Bay 83, 219
Hughes Bay 96
Hunting Hitler 142
hydroponics 79
Hyperboreans 78, 79, 151, 211

I

Iberian peninsula 90
Ice Age 45, 69, 83, 86, 114
ice crevasses 12
IceCube Neutrino Observatory 33, 208, 281
Iceland 101
ice wall 14, 82
Icke, David 232–233, 235–236, 264
IFL Science 51
Illuminati 1, 2, 121, 225, 234, 236
Illuminati Disneyland 23, 25, 58–62
Inalco House 140, 141–142
India 71, 72, 88, 225, 284
Indian Ocean 38, 49, 126
Indus culture 72
Inner Earth 14, 16, 30, 56, 77–80, 114, 120, 124, 135, 152, 154, 162, 164, 166–168, 169, 185–187, 197–220, 241, 243, 245, 248, 282, 284–285
inner sun 241
inner-terrestrials 70, 77–80, 111, 197, 222–248, 234
International Hydrographic Organization 38
Interplanetary Corporate Conglomerate 25, 210–211, 245
ionosphere 239
Iran 25–26, 147, 273
Iraq 147
Isbell, John 36
ISCE (International Society for a Complete Earth) 124–125
Isias 116
isostatic rebound 83
Israel 244, 245
Italy 235

J

James Bay 83
James, Preston 265
Jamieson, Stewart 27, 277–278
Janson, Olaf 75–78
Japan 167, 289
JASON Scholars 192, 193–194
Jeddah, Saudi Arabia 60
Jesuits 143
Jesus Christ 243
Jet Propulsion Labs 135
JFK assassination 62
Jinn 237
Johnson Space Center (JSC) 224
Johnston, Miles 257, 262–264
Jonah's icefish 18, 40, 52–53
Jupiter 43, 51, 246
Jurassic period 52

K

Kammler, Hans 106, 136
Kennedy, John F. 62, 149, 234, 234–235
Kerry, John 58
KGB 55, 225, 229, 241
KGB-RHOMB file 185–189, 225
Kiel University 63
King, Barry 263
King Edward 138, 143
King George Island 15
King Haakon VII Land 204–205
King Juan Carlos of Spain 60
Kiss, Edmund 229
Knights Templars 112
Kohler, Hans 109
Kohnen base 28, 61, 102, 122, 123, 173, 230, 231, 233
Koingsee 140
Kommer, Frank van den 49, 55, 56, 295
Krastman, Hank 132
Kriegsmarine 120, 131, 174, 227, 250, 287, 289
Kristiansand, Norway 101
Kronos 147
Kugelblitz 136

L

La Falda 137, 142–143
Lake Enigma 46–47
Lake Nahuel Huapi 140, 142
Lake Ontario 43, 199
Lake Titicaca 284
Lake Toba 261
Lake Vostok 17, 43–44, 199–200
Lake Whillans 44
Landig, Wilhelm 101, 230
Land of the Lost 41
Lansdale, Ed 62
LaPaz icefield 223
La Quinta Columna 267–268
Last Battalion 129–130
Latin America 174
Lazarev, Mikhail 20, 99
Lear, John 144–145
Lebanon 202
Lebensborn Project 288
Lee, Jenny 247
Lemaire Channel 13
Lemuria 71–73, 79, 88, 259
Leningradskaya base 242
ley lines 274
Lhasa 212, 216
Library of Alexandria 82, 88, 89
lighthouse of Agartha 59
Little America 101, 150
Loch Ness Monster 53, 281
London 107
Longines interview 159–162
longitude 87

Index

loosh 237
Luftwaffe 102, 103, 108, 120
Luke 8:17 9
Lyme disease 275

M

Macuxi tribe 202
Madame Blavatsky 211
Magellan, Ferdinand 73–75, 89, 96
Magnetic Pole 50
Majestic 12 183
Maki resistance 78
Malta 68
Malvinas 250–252
mammoths 79
mandalas 240
Manhattan Project 128, 164
Māori people 72
mapmaking 87
Marciniak, Barbra 72–73
Marconi Labs 251, 257–259, 259, 263
Mar del Plata 128, 175
Marquesa Islands 71
Marr Ice Piedmont 40
Mars 51, 111, 145, 147, 192, 224, 244, 244–245, 273, 278
Mauthausen concentration camp 110
McCall, Beth 247
McCarthyism 182
McDonalds 34
McMurdo, Archibald 66
McMurdo Dry Valleys 51
McMurdo Sound 66
McMurdo Station 50–51, 52, 66, 101, 219, 293, 294
measles 75
Mecca 60
Mediterranean Sea 68, 81
megafauna 10, 14, 88
megaflora 88
megaliths 10, 14
Melanesia 71
Melchior Islands 174
Men In Black (MIB) 230
Menzies, Gavin 99
Mera, Steve 154
Mercator, Gerardus 94–95, 218
Mercator map 83, 88, 94–95
Merkulov file 225, 228, 240
Merkulov, General Vsevolod 225, 241, 250
Merz, Albert 57
Mesopotamia 236
meteorites 18, 222–225
metric system 4
Mexico 68
Meyer, Billy 284
micronations 139–140, 144–145, 194
Middle America 92
Middle Triassic 52
Military Industrial Complex 32
Milk Cows 127, 131
MJ-12 230
MK-Ultra 23, 132
Moai 72
Mongolia 211
Monte Urbano Map 71–72
Moon 110–111, 118, 145–146, 147, 153
Morgellons 258, 266–267, 274–276
Morocco 68
Moscow 55, 58, 229
Mother Nature 10, 47, 67
mothership UFOs 14, 24, 122, 123
Mount Adams 80
Mount Buckley 280
Mount Erebus 39, 50–51, 198
Mount Shasta 69, 78, 80, 248, 284
Mount Sidley 149
moving sidewalks 79
MS Schwabenland 120, 123, 151
Mu 71–73
Muhlig-Hoffman massif 123, 152
Munich 119, 211, 212, 228
Muroc-Edwards AFB 132

N

Nacht Waffen 120, 145–148, 192, 273
Naga-Maya 72
Nagas 78
Nagasaki 167
nanobots 258, 266, 275–276
Nao Victoria 73–75
NASA 32, 36, 93, 132, 134, 137, 223
National Geographic Society 38, 49, 168
National Science Foundation (NSF) 44, 173, 207
National Security Agency (NSA) 23, 31, 122, 132, 133, 173, 207, 293
NATO 22, 119, 139, 273
Navy Seals 173
Nazi international 33
Nazi Party 119–120
Neeley, Bill 245–246
Neioh 247
Nephilim 69, 242
Neumayer Station 28, 66
Neuquén 142
Neuschwabenland 13, 26, 28, 100–103, 118, 121–124, 170–174, 176–177, 181, 187, 191, 223, 230, 285, 287
neutrinos 283
neutrino weapons 34
Nevada 144–145
Newald, Alec 259–260
New Berlin base 26, 30, 121, 124, 145, 169, 171–173, 187, 207, 225
New Mexico 167, 174
New Swabia 28, 30, 109
New Warburg 145
New World 88, 91, 92, 94
New World Order (NWO) 139, 174, 237, 273, 290
New York City 22, 167, 272
New Zealand 20, 34, 37, 52, 54, 58, 66, 72, 86, 242
Nietzsche, Friedrich 269
Nimitz, Admiral Chester 150, 176
no-fly zones 10, 11, 30, 205, 206, 219–220
Nordenskøld, Otto 254
Nordics 232
Norfolk, VA 177
North America 78, 88, 92
North Atlantic 57
Northern Hemisphere 45, 83
Northern Lights 41
North Pole 16, 48, 55, 69, 75, 150, 159, 160, 162, 171, 206, 218, 219, 227, 240
North Sea 68
Norway 20, 54, 75–76, 86, 101, 110, 118, 123, 204
Nova Scotia 144
nuclear weapons 88, 285
nunataks 66, 67, 222
Nuremberg 151, 212, 214, 215

O

Oates Land 66–67
Obama, Barack 58, 142
Oberth, Hermann 32, 100, 107
ODESSA 31
Office of Strategic Service (OSS) 31–32, 133
Operation Argus 154, 181, 192–194
Operation Deep Freeze 14, 21, 159, 184, 190, 206
Operation Gladio 139
Operation Highjump 11, 13, 16, 26, 28–30, 93, 120, 123, 138, 150, 152–154, 159, 162, 168, 169–194, 206, 281, 285
Operation IceBridge 201
Operation Keyhole 254, 254–257
Operation Mockingbird 190
Operation Paperclip 189, 291
Operation Tabarin 16, 100–101, 174, 181
Operation Valkyrie 2 128
Operation Windmill 189–190
orbs 204
Organism 46-B 43
Orion 235
ORION File 56, 241
orogens 64
Orsic, Maria 107, 116–118, 120, 135, 147, 243
Ortelius, Abraham 98
Oruro, Bolivia 202
Orwell, George 249, 266
Ossendowski, Ferdynand 211
ostriches 90
OTO 213

P

Pacific Ocean 38–39, 49, 71, 96
Paiute Mesa 145
Pakistan 72
Palmer Base 40
Palmer, Nathaniel 99
Palmer Peninsula 9, 13, 15, 48, 52, 84–86, 100, 174
Palpa, Peru 202
pan-Antarctic islands 85, 98
Pangea 47
Paradise Harbor 13
Paraguay 141
paranormal abilities 113
Parsons, Jack 135

Patagonia 58, 64–65, 72–75, 89, 92, 96, 141
Patagonia giants 73–75
Patescibacteria 46–47
Patriarch Kiril III 58, 60
Patton, General George 215
Payload for Ultrahigh Energy Observations (PUEO) 283
PBS 55
penguins 13, 52
Pentagon 62, 167, 192
Perón, Evita 141
Perón, Juan 140, 141, 143
Peru 69, 284
pharmaceuticals 23
Philippines 73
Pie Island 40
Pigafetta, Antonio 73–75
Pillars of Hercules 68
Piri Re'is map 18, 68, 82, 86–87, 88–91, 96, 112, 285
plate tectonics 48, 225
Plato 68
Pleiades 247, 248, 284
plesiosaurs 53, 281
Poe, Edgar Allan 195
Point 103 101
Point 211 102–103, 121, 123, 151–152
Point Nemo 39
Poland 105, 215, 237
Polaris expedition 55–56, 57
Polar Plateau 45, 60, 122, 123, 149, 150, 160, 173, 204, 224
Pole of Maximum Inaccessibility 50
pole shift 9, 47, 48, 88
pollen 37, 48
Polynesians 71, 72
Pope Francis 58, 60
Pope Leo XIV 60
portals 240–242, 243
Port Lockroy 13, 174
Portugal 68
Portuguese maps 89, 90, 95
Postonski library 115–116
Potala 216
Prague, CZ 110, 127, 228
Pre-Adamites 69
predictive programming 268
pre-diluvian age 86
primordial ooze 51
Prince Bernhard of the Netherlands 138
Prince Harry 60
Prince Philipp 60
Project Argus 230
Project Bluebook 153
Project Paperclip 13, 14, 22, 31–33, 100, 107, 119, 126, 128, 131–134, 138, 146, 176, 182, 191, 226, 271
Prouty, Colonel Fletcher 62
Ptolemy, Claudius 82–83
Ptolemy map 82, 86, 89, 91
Putin, Vladimir 58
pyramids 10, 65–67, 69
Pythagoras 83

Q

quarantine 247
Queen Fabiola Mountains 222
Queen Maud Land 26, 29, 103, 121, 151, 172, 176, 187, 188, 194

R

Ranally map 93, 98
Rapa Nui 72
Rat Lines 31, 132, 136
Reagan, Ronald 221
Reichsbank 286
REMA map 19
remote viewing 210, 234, 247–248
Reptilian ETs 132–133, 148, 173–174, 225, 232
revelation of the method 236
RHOMB file 185–189, 225
rhumb lines 94
Rice University 36
Rignot, Eric 65–66
Ritscher, Captain Alfred 101–103, 123, 150–152
Rockefellers 138, 230–231
Roerich, Nicholas 217
Rogge, Captain Bernard 57
Roman Empire 213
Rome 87
Rongo Rongo script 72
Roosevelt, Franklin D. 136, 160
Ross, Captain James Clark 50, 66
Ross Ice Shelf 45, 279
Ross Island 20, 50, 279
Ross Sea 39, 52, 88
Roswell, NM 145, 147, 182, 190
Rothschilds 138
Royal Society 98
Rudolph, Arthur 32
Rumsfeld, Donald 277
Ruppelt, Captain Edward J. 153
Russia 21, 26, 29, 50, 136, 273

S

saber tooth tigers 79
Sais 68
San Carlos de Bariloche 58, 140, 141–142
Sanders, Bernie 35
San Diego, CA 232
Sandy Hook 139
San Julian Bay 73, 76
Sanskrit 202, 216
Sarson, John 207
Sasquatch 78
Satanists 135
Saturn 246
Saudi Arabia 60
sauropods 52
Scandinavia 248
Schaefer, Hans 128
Schaeffer, Heinz 175
Schäfer, Ernst 175, 185–186, 211, 215–216
Schauberger, Viktor 31, 107, 110, 134, 135, 229
Schirmacher Hills 102, 104, 123
Schirmacher Ponds 170
Schirmacher, Richard-Heinrich 123, 152
Schriever 229
Schumacher Ponds 172
Schumann 135
Schwabenland 57
Scott, Captain Robert 48, 203–205
Scottish Rite Masons 133
SCUBA diving 12, 43
seals 52
secret government 23
Secret Land, The 93
Secret Space Program 23, 25, 147, 210–211, 244, 246
Sedona, AZ 284
Semitic language 117
Serpent Cults 56
Shackleton, Ernest 48
Shackleton Pyramid 69
Shackleton Range 66
Shambhala 114, 202–203, 212, 217
Shangri-La 139
shape-shifting 234
Shetland Islands 38
shipwrecks 39
Sicily 178
Sigrun 116
Sireson, John 31
Sirius 235, 248
Skoda Works 110, 127, 139
smallpox 75
Smart Dust 275
Smoky God, The 75–78
Solar Warden 147, 232
solar wind 41
Solon 68
Soros, George 273
South Africa 118, 239
South America 11, 13, 32, 38, 40, 49, 64, 69–70, 71–74, 84, 88, 89, 92, 101, 112, 119, 120, 126, 127, 131–132, 135–136, 140, 144–145, 190, 191, 228, 231
South Atlantic 57, 118, 126, 238, 250, 258
Southern Cross 243, 289
Southern Hemisphere 41, 289
Southern Lights 41
Southern Ocean 15, 37–39, 49, 53, 82, 98, 138, 208
South Geomagnetic Pole 50
South Georgia Islands 238, 250–252, 256
South Korea 235
South Magnetic Pole 50
South Pole 10, 11, 15, 16, 25–26, 35, 37, 42, 47, 48, 57, 60, 77, 93, 101, 150, 153, 158, 159–162, 171, 173, 203–206, 218, 227, 240, 240–241, 281, 287
South Sandwich Islands 86, 250–252, 252
South Shetland Islands 85, 285–286
South Thule Island 250–254
Soviet Bloc 22, 119
Soviet Union 56, 119, 132, 158, 225, 229, 238, 242, 250, 271
Space Force 246
Spain 73, 90, 284
Spartan 1 291–294
Spear of Destiny 112, 121, 213–215
Spear of Longinus 213–215
Special Bureau 13 32

Index

Speer, Albert 117, 169
SS (*Schutzstaffel*) 101, 111, 112, 114, 115, 116, 117, 119, 126, 131, 133, 134, 138, 140, 213, 215, 218, 226, 236, 285, 287, 288
Stalin 188
Stalingrad 215
stasis chambers 69
Sterling engine 44, 131
Stevens, Henry 173
Stevens, Wendell 109–110
Stone, Oliver 62
Straits of Magellan 60, 96
Stringfield, Leonard 31
Subbotin, Nikolay 55, 124, 186–187, 225, 229
subglacial lakes 17, 42–43
submarines 101, 104, 118–119, 124–131, 152–153, 169, 188–189
Sumatra Island 259
Sumeria 147, 236
super soldiers 113, 264, 275
Sutherland, Donald 62
swastikas 102, 110, 118, 123, 135, 215–217
Sweden 248
Switzerland 284

T

Tall Greys 225
Taylor Glacier 51
techno-magical discs 28, 110–111, 134
Tehran 25
telepathy 116
Telos civilization 78, 78–79
Terra Australis 93
Terra Incognita 98
Terzinski, Vladimir 169, 193
Tesla Towers 273–274
Texas 224
Third Force 22, 119, 138–143, 192
Third Reich 11, 23, 31, 32, 89, 102, 109–110, 114, 115, 120, 127, 131, 132, 135, 136, 153, 164, 175, 209, 215, 226–227
Thorne, Kip 238
Thule Refuge 193, 239
Thule Society 11, 31, 57, 106, 108, 111, 116–118, 119, 120, 121, 126, 133, 134–135, 193, 211, 212, 225, 227, 269
Thuringia 136
Tibet 69, 103, 112, 114, 175, 185–186, 187, 211, 215, 216, 227
Tibetan Plateau 202
Tierra del Fuego 65, 70, 75, 76, 84, 89, 94, 228
Tiki protector spirits 72
time travel 106, 116, 231, 238
Toba Eruption 259, 261–262
Tompkins, William 231–232
TransAntarctic Mountains 40, 47, 48, 223, 278, 280, 293
transhumanism 266, 269–271, 276
Trilateral Commission 180
Trinity site 167
Trophy Archives 109
Tropic of Capricorn 95
Truman, Harry S. 31, 120, 136, 154, 181
Trump, Donald J. 244–245
Turkey 60, 88–89
Twilight Zone 232

U

U-boat 209 124–125
U-boat 530 128, 175
U-boat 977 128, 175
U-boats 26, 30, 57, 70, 101, 118–119, 119, 121, 124–126, 128–131, 135–136, 139, 142, 172–173, 173, 174, 186, 215, 223, 225, 226–227, 228, 229, 287, 288, 291
UFOs 9, 10, 11, 14, 70, 120, 146, 147, 153, 154, 192, 197, 204, 226, 230–232, 240–241, 241, 284–286
Ukraine 16
ULTRA forces 173–174
ultra-terrestrials 234
Underwater Submersible Objects (USOs) 282
Unger, Karl 124
Unified Field Theory 107
United Kingdom (UK) 16, 20, 54, 84, 86, 251, 253–254
United Nations (UN) 138, 144, 221, 268
United States of America (USA) 20, 21, 32, 52, 54, 62, 93, 119, 128, 132, 134, 136, 139, 231, 237, 244, 246, 271, 289
University of California-Irvine 65–66
University of Wisconsin 36
uranium 174, 208–209
U.S. Capital 120
Ushuaia 13, 54
U.S. Navy 28
USNS Eltanin 70
USS Maddox 29, 31, 177–179, 207
USS Mount Olympus 156, 177
USS Murdock 188

V

V-2 rocket 107, 127, 132, 135
V-7 flying disks 228–229
vaccines 260, 264, 267, 276
Valkyrie 2 175
Van Atta, Lee 156–158
Vatican City 31, 58, 215
VE Day 31, 32, 131
Vega Island 53, 281
Venezuela 141, 202
Vernansky research station 16
Verne, Jules 201
Victoria Land 280
Vienna 116, 213, 228
vimanas 271
volcanoes 39–40, 48, 50, 76
Von Braun, Wernher 32, 132, 134, 135, 226
Von Daniken, Erich 202
Vostok Station 41, 43, 50, 199–200
Voyager I 246
Vril energy 138, 269–270
Vril flying discs 109, 113, 139, 147
Vril Society 11, 31, 108, 111, 116–118, 135, 147, 243
Vril Women 106, 111, 117–118, 140, 243

W

Waldheim, Kurt 138
Waldseemüller map 90–92
Waldseemüller, Martin 90–91
Walter Motor 44, 127, 128–129, 131
Washington D.C. 23, 120, 134, 155, 168, 192, 272
Weddell, Captain James 75
Weddell Sea 18, 84
Wehrmacht 120, 214, 225, 288
Weimar Republic 119
West Africa 90
West Antarctica 41, 47, 86, 95, 224
Western Hemisphere 90–91
West Germany 28
Wewelsburg Castle 294
White Hats 247
White House 62, 120, 192, 246
White Sands, NM 132, 134, 167
Wikipedia 142, 157–158, 251
Wilkes Land 278
Williams, Gerrard 141–142
Wisner, Frank 190
WISSARD 42, 44, 278
Wissel, Stephanie 283
WOLF notebook 187, 287-289
Wolf, Wilhelm 288–289, 290
Wonder Weapons 128
World War I 111, 134, 146, 211, 213, 269, 272
World War II 18, 20, 23, 26, 28, 32, 44, 54, 55, 56, 89, 100, 106, 111–113, 119–120, 121, 126–127, 128–131, 135, 138–139, 147, 150, 152, 165, 171–172, 176, 178, 181, 184, 185, 192, 212, 218, 226–227, 228–229, 231, 250–252, 263, 272, 284, 285, 291
World War III 244
wormholes 31, 238–240

Y

Yamashita's gold 62
Yerington, NV 16
Younger Dryas 83
Young, Robert O. 268
YouTube 291
Yucatán 68
Yukon Territory 69, 78

Z

Zavodovski Island 254

Sacred Places North America: 108 Destinations

– 2nd EDITION; by Brad Olsen

This comprehensive travel guide examines North America's most sacred sites for spiritually attuned explorers. Spirituality & Health reviewed: "The book is filled with fascinating archeological, geological, and historical material. These 108 sacred places in the United States, Canada, and Hawaii offer ample opportunity for questing by spiritual seekers."

$19.95 :: 408 pages **paperback: 978-1888729139**

all Ebooks priced at $9.99

Kindle: 978-1888729252; PDF: 978-1888729191
ePub: 978-1888729337

Sacred Places Europe: 108 Destinations – by Brad Olsen

This guide to European holy sites examines the most significant locations that shaped the religious consciousness of Western civilization. Travel to Europe for 108 uplifting destinations that helped define religion and spirituality in the Western Hemisphere. From Paleolithic cave art and Neolithic megaliths, to New Age temples, this is an impartial guide book many millennium in the making.

$19.95 :: 344 pages **paperback: 978-1888729122**

all Ebooks priced at $9.99

Kindle: 978-1888729245; PDF: 978-1888729184
ePub: 978-1888729320

Sacred Places of Goddess: 108 Destinations – by Karen Tate

Readers will be escorted on a pilgrimage that reawakens, rethinks, and reveals the Divine Feminine in a multitude of sacred locations on every continent. Meticulously researched, clearly written and comprehensively documented, this book explores the rich tapestry of Goddess worship from prehistoric cultures to modern academic theories.

$19.95 :: 424 pages **paperback: 978-1888729115**

all Ebooks priced at $9.99

Kindle: 978-1888729269; PDF: 978-1888729177
ePub: 978-1888729344

Sacred Places Around the World: 108 Destinations

– 2nd EDITION; by Brad Olsen

The mystical comes alive in this exciting compilation of 108 beloved holy destinations. World travelers and armchair tourists who want to explore the mythology and archaeology of the ruins, sanctuaries, mountains, lost cities, and temples of ancient civilizations will find this guide ideal.

$17.95 :: 288 pages **paperback: 978-1888729108**

all Ebooks priced at $8.99

Kindle: 978-1888729238; PDF: 978-1888729160
ePub: 978-1888729313

Awakening the Truth Frequency: Into the Unified Field

– by Laura Eisenhower

If you aren't living your most authentic self, if you aren't *Awakening the Truth Frequency*, you can't realize personal and universal truth. If we compromise and waver in our integrity, we become vulnerable to distortions and imbalances that attract archonic attachments. These keep us in a lower existence of reality. Many of us have lost touch with our connection to our higher mind ... our intuitive abilities ...having weakened their integration into our daily lives.

$19.95 :: 312 pages **paperback: 978-1888729948**

all eBooks priced $9.95 *All ebooks*: 978-1888729955 •

LEO ZAGAMI BOOKS FROM CCC PUBLISHING

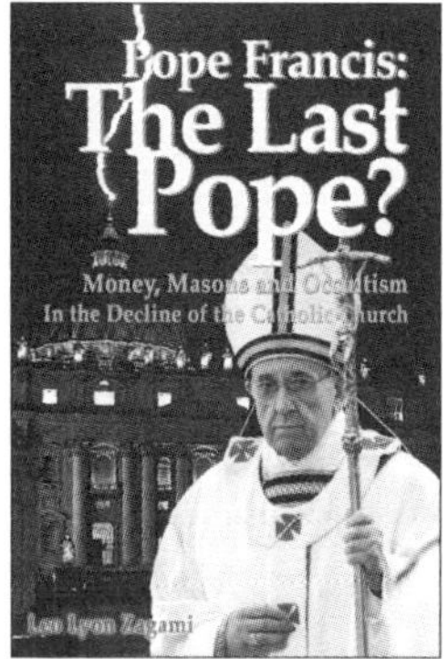

Pope Francis: The Last Pope?: Money, Masons and Occultism in the Decline of the Catholic Church

– by Leo Lyon Zagami

Perfect for anyone interested in prophecies about the end times, Pope Francis: The Last Pope reveals the truth about the last Pope and the darkness that may follow him; fascinating investigations into the gay lobby; Freemasonry; the Jesuit agenda; and, the legend of the White Pope, the Black Pope, and how Benedict's resignation may fulfill an ancient prophecy.

$16.95 :: 224 pages **paperback 978-1888729542**

all eBooks priced $8.99

Kindle: 978-1888729566; PDF: 978-1888729559
ePub: 978-1888729573

Confessions of an Illuminati, Volume I: The Whole Truth About the Illuminati and the New World Order

– 2nd EDITION; by Leo Lyon Zagami

From the OTO's infiltration of Freemasonry to the real Priory of Sion, this book exposes the hidden structure of the New World Order; their occult practices; and their connections to the intelligence community and the infamous Ur-Lodges.

$17.95 :: 408 pages **paperback 978-1888729870**

all eBooks priced $9.99

Kindle: 978-1888729894; PDF: 978-1888729887
ePub: 978-1888729900

Confessions of an Illuminati, Volume II: The Time of Revelation and Tribulation Leading up to 2020

– by Leo Lyon Zagami

Since the Second Vatican Council, the hierarchy of power emanating from the Jesuits in Rome and the Zionist's in Jerusalem, united by a secret pact, have been manipulating world powers and using economic hitmen to create a unified one-world government.

$17.95 :: 380 pages **paperback 978-1888729627**

all eBooks priced $9.99

Kindle: 978-1888729658; PDF: 978-1888729634
ePub: 978-1888729641

Confessions of an Illuminati, Volume III: Espionage, Templars and Satanism in the Shadows of the Vatican

– by Leo Lyon Zagami

Take a unique and personal journey into the secretive world of the Dark Cabal. Explore a variety of cryptic topics and learn the truth about the mythical Knights Templars, the Jesuits, and their mastery of the Vatican espionage game.

$17.95 :: 336 pages **paperback 978-1888729665**

all eBooks priced $9.99

Kindle: 978-1888729696; PDF: 978-1888729672
ePub: 978-1888729689

The Invisible Master: Secret Chiefs, Unknown Superiors, and the Puppet Masters Who Pull the Strings of Occult Power from the Alien World

– by Leo Lyon Zagami

Leo Zagami's groundbreaking study of aliens and UFOs explores where we come from and which mysterious figures have guided humanity's political and religious choices. From the prophets to the initiates and magicians, all ages have drawn from a common source of ultra-terrestrial and magical knowledge, passed down for millennia. This text reveals the identity of the unknown superiors, secret chiefs, and invisible masters who have guided Freemasonry, the Illuminati, and others.

$17.95 :: 380 pages **paperback 978-1888729702**

all eBooks priced $9.99

Kindle: 978-1888729733; PDF: 978-1888729719
ePub: 978-1888729726

ALSO IN THE ESOTERIC SERIES: